Music Theory in Late Medieval Avignon

The manuscript Seville, Biblioteca Colombina y Capitular 5-2-25, a composite of dozens of theoretical treatises, is one of the primary witnesses to late medieval music theory. Its numerous copies of significant texts have been the focus of substantial scholarly attention to date, but the shorter, unattributed, or fragmentary works have not yet received the same scrutiny. In this monograph, Cook demonstrates that a small group of such works, linked to the otherwise unknown Magister Johannes Pipudi, is in fact much more noteworthy than previous scholarship has observed. The not one but two copies of *De arte cantus* are in fact one of the earliest known sources for the *Libellus cantus mensurabilis*, purportedly by Jean des Murs and the most widely copied music theory treatise of its day, while *Regulae contrapunctus*, *Nota quod novem sunt species contrapunctus*, and a concluding set of notes in Catalan are early witnesses to the popular *Ars contrapuncti* treatises also attributed to des Murs. Disclosing newly discovered biographical information, it is revealed that Pipudi is most likely one Johannes Pipardi, familiar to Cardinal Jean de Blauzac, Vicar-General of Avignon. Cook provides the first biographical assessment for him and shows that late fourteenth-century Avignon was a plausible chronological and geographical milieu for the Seville treatises, hinting provocatively at a possible route of transmission for the *Libellus* from Paris to Italy. The monograph concludes with new transcriptions and the first English translations of the treatises.

Karen M. Cook is Associate Professor of Music History at the University of Hartford. She specializes in late medieval music theory and notation, focusing on developments in rhythmic duration. She also maintains a primary interest in musical medievalism in contemporary media, particularly in video games.

Royal Musical Association Monographs

Series Editor: Simon P. Keefe

This series was originally supported by funds made available to the Royal Musical Association from the estate of Thurston Dart, former King Edward Professor of Music at the University of London. The editorial board is the Publications Committee of the Association.

No. 33: The Cyclic Mass: Anglo-Continental Exchange in the Fifteenth Century
James Cook

No. 34: The Pre-History of The Midsummer Marriage Narratives and Speculations
Narratives and Speculations
Roger Savage

No. 35: Felice Giardini and Professional Music Culture in Mid-Eighteenth-Century London
Cheryll Duncan

No. 36: Disinformation in Mass Media
Gluck, Piccinni and the Journal de Paris
Beverly Jerold

No. 37: Music Theory in Late Medieval Avignon
Magister Johannes Pipardi
Karen M. Cook

For more information about this series, please visit: www.routledge.com/music/series/RMA

Music Theory in Late Medieval Avignon
Magister Johannes Pipardi

Karen M. Cook

LONDON AND NEW YORK

First published 2021
by Routledge
2 Park Square, Milton Park, Abingdon, Oxon OX14 4RN

and by Routledge
605 Third Avenue, New York, NY 10158

Routledge is an imprint of the Taylor & Francis Group, an informa business

© 2021 Karen M. Cook

The right of Karen M. Cook to be identified as author of this work
has been asserted by her in accordance with sections 77 and 78 of the
Copyright, Designs and Patents Act 1988.

All rights reserved. No part of this book may be reprinted or
reproduced or utilised in any form or by any electronic, mechanical,
or other means, now known or hereafter invented, including
photocopying and recording, or in any information storage or
retrieval system, without permission in writing from the publishers.

Trademark notice: Product or corporate names may be trademarks
or registered trademarks, and are used only for identification and
explanation without intent to infringe.

British Library Cataloguing-in-Publication Data
A catalogue record for this book is available from the British Library

Library of Congress Cataloging-in-Publication Data
A catalog record has been requested for this book

ISBN: 978-0-367-69128-8 (hbk)
ISBN: 978-0-367-69130-1 (pbk)
ISBN: 978-0-367-69129-5 (ebk)

Typeset in Times New Roman
by codeMantra

Contents

List of figures	vii
List of tables	ix
Manuscript Sigla and Abbreviations	xi
Acknowledgments	xiii

Prologue   1

1 The Seville Manuscript   5

2 The Practical Art of Measured Song   18
2.1 The Libellus cantus mensurabilis *18*
2.2 De arte cantus *26*

3 The Rules of Counterpoint   39
3.1 The Ars contrapuncti secundum
     Johannem de Muris *39*
3.2 Regulae contrapunctus *43*
3.3 Nota quod novem sunt species
     contrapunctus videlicet ... *48*
3.4 The Catalan notes 51

4 Introducing Johannes Pipardi   57
4.1 "In arte musice peritus" *60*
4.2 The case of Alma polis religio/Axe poli cum artica *65*
4.3 In the household of Jean de Blauzac 67
4.4 Johannes Pipardi: A conjectural biography 71
4.5 Sev revisited 76

vi *Contents*

Epilogue   87

Appendices
    Appendix 1: A preliminary list of members of
                Jean de Blauzac's household   89
    Appendix 2: Texts and translations   91
        Appendix 2a: De arte cantus 94
        Appendix 2b: Regulae contrapunctus 124
        Appendix 2c: Catalan notes 136
        Appendix 2d: Nota quod novem sunt
                species contrapunctus videlicet ... 140

Works cited   145
Index   153

Figures

1	Biblioteca Capitular Colombina, sign. 5-2-25, f. 99r, © Cabildo Catedral de Sevilla	11
2	Biblioteca Capitular Colombina, sign. 5-2-25, f. 101v, © Cabildo Catedral de Sevilla	12
3	The backward-C grapheme; Biblioteca Capitular Colombina, sign. 5-2-25, f. 104r, © Cabildo Catedral de Sevilla	35
4	Statement of attribution to magister Johannes Pipudi; Biblioteca Capitular Colombina, sign. 5-2-25, f. 105r, © Cabildo Catedral de Sevilla	57
5	Watermark on bifolio 103–104; Biblioteca Capitular Colombina, sign. 5-2-25, f. 104r, © Cabildo Catedral de Sevilla	78
6	Watermark on bifolio 100–107; Biblioteca Capitular Colombina, sign. 5-2-25, f. 107r, © Cabildo Catedral de Sevilla	79
7	Briquet, watermark 3527	80
8	Briquet, watermark 3542	81
9	BITECA watermark 067017	82
10	BITECA watermark 067002	83
11	Watermark on f. 120v; Biblioteca Capitular Colombina, sign. 5-2-25, f. 120v, © Cabildo Catedral de Sevilla	85

All images from Seville 5-2-25 are reprinted here with kind permission of the Biblioteca Capitular y Colombina: *BCC, sign. 5-2-25, f. 99r, 101v, 104r, 105r, 107r y 120v © Cabildo Catedral de Sevilla.*

Tables

1	Codicological Layout of Seville 5-2-25	2
2	The Four Sev Treatises and Their Concordances	16
3	Organization of the Contents of the *Libellus*, Berkeley 3, and *De arte cantus*	23
4	Rules of Imperfection in the *Libellus*, Berkeley 3, and *De arte cantus*	29
5	Works in Which ᴐ Indicates Imperfect Tempus and Minor Prolation	36
6	Datable Attributions to Material Concordant with the Three Pipudi Treatises	56

Manuscript Sigla and Abbreviations

Apt	Apt, Cathédrale Sainte-Anne, Trésor 16bis	F-APT 16 bis
Bergamo MAB 21	Bergamo, Civica Biblioteca "Angelo Mai," MS Σ.IV.37	I-Bge 37
Berkeley	Berkeley, University of California, Bancroft Library MS 744 (*olim* Phillipps 4450)	US-Bem MS 744
Brussels 4144	Brussels, Bibliothèque royale, II 4144	B-Br II 4144
Cambridge 410 II	Cambridge, Corpus Christi College, 410 II	GB-Ccc 410 II
Catania D.39	Catania, Biblioteche Riunite Civica e Antonio Ursino Recupero, D.39	I-CATc D 39
Chantilly	Chantilly, Bibliothèque du Musée Condé, 564	F-CH 564
Chicago 54.1	Chicago, The Newberry Library, MS 54.1	US-Cn MS 54.1
Durham C.I.20	Durham, Cathedral Library, C.I.20	GB-DRc C.I.20
Florence 1119	Florence, Biblioteca Medicea Laurenziana, Ashburnham 1119	I-Fl Ashburnham 1119
Florence Plut.29.48	Florence, Biblioteca Medicea Laurenziana, Plut.XXIX.48	I-Fl Plut. XXIX 48
Gent 70 (71)	Gent, Universiteitsbibliotheek, 70 (71)	B-Gu 70 (71)
Ivrea	Ivrea, Biblioteca Capitolare 115	I-Ivc 115
London 4909	London, British Library, Add. 4909	GB-Lbl Add. 4909
London 23220	London, British Library, Add. 23220	GB-Lbl Add. 23220
Mod A	Modena, Biblioteca Estense e Universitaria α.M.5.25	I-MO α.M.5.25
Pad A	Oxford, Bodleian Library, MS. Canon. Pat. Lat. 229	GB-Ob 229
Panciatichi	Florence, Biblioteca Nazionale Centrale, MS Panciatichiano 26	I-Fn 26

xii   *Manuscript Sigla and Abbreviations*

Pit	Paris, Bibliothèque nationale de France, Département des Manuscrits, Italien 568	F-Pn 568
Rome B.83	Rome, Biblioteca Vallicelliana, B.83	I-Rv B.83
Rome 1146	Rome, Biblioteca Apostolica Vaticana, Reg.lat 1146	I-Rvat Reg.lat 1146
Rome 5321	Rome, Biblioteca Apostolica Vaticana, Reg. lat.5321	I-Rvat Lat. 5321
Sev	Seville, Biblioteca Capitular y Colombina, 5-2-25	E-Sc 5-2-25
Siena	Siena, Biblioteca Comunale, L.V.30	I-Sc L V 30
Squarc	Florence, Biblioteca Medicea-Laurenziana, MS Mediceo Palatino 87	I-Fl 87
Trém	Paris, Bibliothèque Nationale de France, MS fonds nouv. acq. fr. 23190 (Trémoïlle)	F-Trem F-Pn naf 23190
Wash J6	Washington (DC), Library of Congress, Music Division, ML 171.J6 Case	US-Wc ML 171 J6 Case
DIAMM	Digital Image Archive of Medieval Music https://www.diamm.ac.uk/	
RISM	Répertoire International des Sources Musicales, var. eds. and vols.	
TML	Thesaurus Musicarum Latinarum http://www.chmtl.indiana.edu/tml/	

Acknowledgments

This project started a number of years ago as an off-shoot of my dissertation. I was intrigued then by the second copy of *De arte cantus* in the Seville manuscript, but had not spent much time with the other treatises in the two fascicles I discuss here. Linking these various treatises to works attributed to Jean des Murs is not unexpected, given their popularity, but I had not imagined then just how similar they would reveal themselves to be to the Berkeley manuscript. Nor did I ever imagine that I might find Johannes Pipudi, or as we can now call him, Pipardi. Working on this project has led me down rabbit holes of ecclesiastical and university history, through a century of papal records, and into the depths of fourteenth-century theoretical developments. I owe sincere thanks, first and foremost, to those that most frequently helped me obtain research materials: Laura Williams and Nicholas Smolenski at Duke University and Christine Bird and Tracey Rudnick at the University of Hartford. There have been numerous times when I have called upon the assistance of others, and I am grateful for their generosity of time, resources, and insights. In particular, I extend my deepest gratitude to Isaac and Samantha Arten, C. Matthew Balensuela, Margaret Bent, Bonnie Blackburn, Thomas Brothers, Giuliano Di Bacco, Santiago Galán, Barbara Haggh-Huglo, Jan Herlinger, Andrew Hicks, Leofranc Holford-Strevens, Paula Higgins, Karl Kügle, John Nádas, Alejandro Enrique Planchart[†], Joelle Rollo-Koster, Pamela Starr, Anne Stone, Jason Stoessel, Ryan Taycher, Andrew Tomasello, and "the Hs," and I offer my humblest apologies to anyone inadvertently left out. I am particularly indebted to David Catalunya, who generously shared materials with me and played an equal if not larger role in transcribing and translating the Catalan notes. I also thank Maria del Carmen Gómez for her foundational work on these treatises, and Kerry McCarthy for her incisive proofreading; any errors that remain belong to myself alone. I gratefully

xiv   *Acknowledgments*

acknowledge the Biblioteca Capitular y Colombina for granting permission to reprint images from the manuscript Seville 5-2-25. This work was supported by a professional development grant from the American Council of Learned Societies and by faculty development funds from the University of Hartford. Lastly, my ideas on Pipardi's biography were shaped in part by John Andrew Bailey's keen insights, shared with equal measures of humor and precision over a coffee or Negroni in the Amherst Early Music Festival faculty lounge. I dedicate this work to *Magister Johannes*, in loving memory.

Prologue

> "... magister Johannes Pipudi, canon of Saint-Didier in Avignon, arranged these rules ..."

Just who was *magister* Johannes Pipudi? To date, the only scholar to focus specifically on this otherwise unknown theorist, and the treatises associated with him in the manuscript Seville, Biblioteca Capitular y Colombina, 5-2-25, is Maria del Carmen Gómez. She provided the first brief but detailed study of the three works in the eleventh fascicle of the Seville manuscript (Table 1). She noted, as did several prominent scholars before her, that the first of the three treatises, *De arte cantus*, was a revision of the *Libellus cantus mensurabilis*, often attributed to Jean des Murs. She also observed that the second treatise, the *Regulae contrapunctus* that contains the above attribution to Pipudi, was very similar to the treatises that comprise the *Ars contrapuncti*, also credited to Jean des Murs. Lastly, she reviewed the third set of notes, intriguingly copied in a mix of Latin and Catalan, and concluded that they, likely along with the two preceding works, were class notes made by a student of Pipudi.

Despite their strong links to Jean des Murs, subsequent studies of works attributed to him have largely passed over Gómez's foundational work on these treatises. In Chapter 1 I explore the history of scholarly work on the Seville manuscript (hereafter Sev), questioning whether the poor condition of this particular fascicle has kept it from being more closely examined. I also call attention to a second copy of the first treatise, *De arte cantus*, surprisingly found just a few folios later in Sev. Perhaps unbeknownst to Gómez and only briefly mentioned in other scholarship, this copy is invaluable for restoring the text lost in the damaged first copy, and calls us to revisit Gómez's work and the eleventh fascicle in its entirety. To that end, appendices at the end of

Table 1 Codicological Layout of Seville 5-2-25

Codicological Unit	Gathering	Folios	Contents
I	1–3	1–22	Assorted Latin and Italian works
II	4–5	23–39	Assorted Latin works
III	6–7	40–59	Assorted Latin works; assorted musical works
IV	8	60–69	Assorted Latin works
V	9	70–77	*Libellus cantus mensurabilis* (hereafter *Libellus*); Marchetto, *Lucidarium* (excerpt)
VI	10	78–83	Assorted Latin works; anonymous Kyrie
VII	11	84–85	*Tractatus figurarum*
VIII	12	86–87, 90–91	*Libellus; Tractatus figurarum* (exc)
IX	13	88–89	*Libellus* (exc)
X	14	92–97	Assorted Latin works

Codicological Unit	Gathering	Folios	Contents		
XI	15	99–108	99r–104v	*De arte cantus*	Copyist A
			104v–107	*Regulae contrapunctus*	
			107v–108v	Catalan notes	
XII	16	110–136	110r–v	*Nota quod novem sunt species contrapunctus videlicet …*	Copyist B
			111–114	*De arte cantus*	
			114–116	*Tractatus figurarum*	
			116	*Nota quod quando quidem cantus cantatur in prolacione minoris perfecti …*	
			116–117v	Petrus Capuanus de Amalfia, *Compendium artis motectorum Marchecti*	
			117v–119v	*Ad evidenciam tam mensuralis quam inmensurabilis musice …*	
			120–123v	blank	
			124–128	Marchetto, *Lucidarium* (exc.)	
			128v–130	*Sexquialtera, emiola, dyapente…*	
		[130v–136v		blank]	
XIII	17	137–138	One Latin work; one musical work		

The four units shaded in gray are believed by Giuliano Di Bacco to have originated together; each of the other units originated independently. This study focuses on the four bold-print treatises found in the bordered units XI and XII.[1]

1 This table is derived largely from Giuliano Di Bacco's provisional reconstruction of Sev in "Original and Borrowed, Authorship and Authority. Remarks on the Circulation of Philipoctus de Caserta's Theoretical Legacy," in *A Late Medieval Songbook and Its Context: New Perspectives on the Chantilly Codex (Bibliothèque Du Château de Chantilly, Ms. 564)*, eds. Anne Stone and Yolanda Plumley, Epitome Musical (Turnhout: Brepols, 2009), 329–364, at 354–355; see also RISM B III 5, 110–120.

4 *Prologue*

this volume contain new transcriptions and the first English translations of *De arte cantus*, *Regulae contrapunctus*, the Catalan notes, and *Nota quod novem sunt species contrapunctus videlicet ...* (hereafter *Nota quod novem*), an additional short work found adjacent to the second copy of *De arte cantus*.

In Chapter 2, I discuss the relationships between the two copies of *De arte cantus* and their connections to the *Libellus cantus mensurabilis*. Following recent research into the variants, revisions, and patterns of transmission for the *Libellus* by Christian Berktold, Giuliano Di Bacco, Lawrence Earp, Daniel Seth Katz, and Christian Meyer, all cited below, I point to the inclusion of certain passages, specific elements of mensural theory, and other manuscript evidence in *De arte cantus* as indicative of probable chronological and geographical milieus for this work. This treatise, in turn, sheds more light on the *Libellus* tradition as a whole.

In similar fashion, I build on the work of Di Bacco, Ryan Taycher, and others in Chapter 3 to re-examine the expansion of the theories in the *Ars contrapuncti* collective as documented in *Regulae contrapunctus* and *Nota quod novem*. Lastly, I reassess the concluding work copied in a mix of Latin and Catalan, thought to be evidence of classroom pedagogy, exposing this work's unexplored connections to other aspects of the *Ars contrapuncti* complex while still allowing for the possibility that it, and in fact the whole collection of treatises, might indeed point to a teaching tradition participated in by magister Johannes Pipudi—or, as I will discuss in Chapter 4, Johannes Pipardi.

1 The Seville Manuscript

In 1927, Higini Anglès published an overview of extant medieval music manuscripts in his native Spain.[1] Included in his list was a composite manuscript that he described as containing around thirty fourteenth- and fifteenth-century theoretical treatises in various stages of completion, most if not all of which were Italian in origin. These treatises were collected during the sixteenth-century travels of Hernando Colón (1488–1539), son of Cristóbal Colón. A well-known scholar, Colón accumulated a massive library housed in Seville, which would eventually include his famous father's collections after his death in 1506.

Colón's desire was to have his library maintained and expanded in perpetuity, but its ownership was contested after his own death in 1539. After years of dispute, the library, along with Colón's detailed catalog of its contents, was finally donated in 1552 to the Cathedral of Seville. Despite the library's vast reduction in size—the donated materials were well under half of Colón's original collection—these theoretical treatises were among those preserved in the new Biblioteca Colombina. While Colón's catalog contained intricate details about the contents, provenance, and purchasing price of each of his library's items, the treatises comprising this manuscript unfortunately do not appear to have been documented.[2] They were only bound

---

1 Higini Anglès, "Die Mehrstimmige Musik in Spanien vor dem 15. Jahrhundert," in *Beethoven-Zentenarfeier vom 26. bis 31. März 1927*, ed. Michael Hainisch (Vienna: Universal-Edition, 1927), 158–163. Seville 5-2-25 had been described previously in 1877 by Juan Facundo Riaño under its old cataloguing number: Z, 135, 32, wherein he listed only nine of the theoretical works and none of the musical compositions in the manuscript; see Riaño, *Critical & Bibliographical Notes on Early Spanish Music* (London: B. Quaritch, 1887), 67.

2 Anglès stated that these treatises were of an accord with Colón's item 1139 in his *Regestrum*. However, F. Alberto Gallo cites Dragan Plamenac as observing that that number refers to a printed book, not a collection of handwritten documents.

6 *The Seville Manuscript*

together in their present form by librarian Juan de Loiasa in the later seventeenth century. Today the composite manuscript, consisting of 138 parchment and paper folios and still bound in de Loiasa's original parchment covers, bears the shelf mark 5-2-25.[3]

Since Anglès's initial publication, the significance of the manuscript as a primary witness to late medieval music and theory has been widely recognized. In a later publication highlighting the musical sources preserved in the Biblioteca Colombina, Anglès referred to it again as a "precious collection of musical theory of the Middle Ages."[4] He also clarified his original assessment of the manuscript's contents: it now comprised approximately thirty-one treatises, many fragmentary, some of which originated as early as the thirteenth century. Anglès isolated three brief contiguous works on folios 99–108v as being of particular interest: a treatise he calls *De arte cantus*, a treatise containing some rules of counterpoint, and a shorter, less formal work written in a mix of Latin and Catalan in the same hand as the previous two works.[5] The first two treatises, he noted, were authored by the otherwise unknown theorist "Johannes Pipudi, *canonicus Sancti Desiderii Avionensis* [sic]."

Several decades later, F. Alberto Gallo revisited Anglès's work on Sev, narrowing the dates of the manuscript's contents once more to the mid-fourteenth and fifteenth centuries, and expanding the list of

---

F. Alberto Gallo, "Alcune Fonti Poco Note di Musica Teorica e Pratica," in *L'Ars Nova Italiana del Trecento: Convegni di Studio 1961–67* (Certaldo: Centro di studi sull'Ars nova italiana del Trecento, 1961–1968), 49–76; Dragan Plamenac, "'Excerpta Colombiniana': Items of Musical Interest in Fernando Colón's 'Regestrum'," in *Miscelánea en Homenaje a Monseñor Higinio Anglés*, Vol. II (Barcelona: Consejo Superior de Investigaciones Científicas, 1958–1961), 663–688. Archer M. Huntington's facsimile reprint of the *Regestrum* (1905) is digitally available at https://archive.org/details/CatalogueOfTheLibraryOfFerdinandCo. For more on Hernando Colón's library, see Edward Wilson-Lee, *The Catalogue of Shipwrecked Books: Christopher Columbus, His Son, and the Quest to Build the World's Greatest Library* (New York: Scribner, 2019). Recently, Colón's lost library catalog, the *Libro de los Epítomes*, was rediscovered in Copenhagen; hopefully, the forthcoming transcription and translation of the catalog by Wilson-Lee and José María Pérez Fernández (Yale University Press, expected 2021) will reveal new details about the works comprising the Seville manuscript discussed here.

3 The folios have been numbered 1–138 in a later hand, possibly that of de Loaisa; however, other foliation, perhaps original, does remain visible in some places. Also see the information on the manuscript on the Digital Image Archive of Medieval Music (DIAMM): https://www.diamm.ac.uk/sources/70/#/

4 Anglès, "La música conservada en la Biblioteca Colombina y en la Catedral de Sevilla," *Anuario musical* 2 (1947): 3–39 at p. 8.

5 Ibid.

The Seville Manuscript 7

treatises from thirty-one to forty-seven.[6] In an accompanying index, he also identified nine musical works, some of which are fragmentary as well. Gallo divided the treatises into three broad categories. The first and largest of these deals primarily with *musica plana*, and several treatises in this category draw on the *Lucidarium* by Marchetto of Padua or the *Introductio musice* by Johannes de Garlandia.[7] The second group, again largely anonymous, treats the basics of organum, discantus, and contrapunctus. The last group considers mensural music and includes the treatise *Omni desideranti notitiam*, three different versions of the *Tractatus figurarum*, and no fewer than six different witnesses to the treatise commonly known as the *Libellus cantus mensurabilis*, often attributed to Jean des Murs.[8] Among them, Gallo included Pipudi's *De arte cantus*, which he labeled in his inventory by its incipit as item XXXV: "*[P]ro introducione cognicionis habende de valloribus notularum.*"

Gallo's revised approach to Sev laid the groundwork for many later studies focused on the larger or attributed works. Giuliano Di Bacco's investigation of the *Tractatus figurarum*, for example, led him to provisionally revise the manuscript's inventory, and he identifies thirteen distinct units based on codicological and paleographical evidence (see Table 1).[9] Michael Scott Cuthbert clarified this inventory even further in a study of the musical compositions interspersed throughout the manuscript.[10] The smaller, fragmentary, anonymous theoretical

---

6 Gallo, "Alcune Fonti ..."
7 Jan W. Herlinger, *The Lucidarium of Marchetto of Padua* (Chicago, IL: University of Chicago Press, 1985); Nigel Gwee, "De plana musica and Introductio musice: A Critical Edition and Translation, with Commentary, of Two Treatises Attributed to Johannes de Garlandia" (PhD diss., Louisiana State University, Baton Rouge, 1996).
8 The *Libellus cantus mensurabilis* is also known as the *Ars practica mensurabilis cantus secundum Johannem de Muris*. For more information on the choice of title for this treatise, see Daniel S. Katz, "The Earliest Sources for the Libellus cantus mensurabilis secundum Johannem de Muris" (PhD diss., Duke University, 1989). See also F. Alberto Gallo, *La Teoria della notazione in Italia dalla fine del XIII all'inizio del XV secolo* (Bologna: Tamari, 1966), 79 fn. 151.
9 Giuliano Di Bacco, "Original and Borrowed ...," 354–355.
10 Michael Scott Cuthbert, "Palimpsests, Sketches, and Extracts: The Organization and Compositions of Seville 5-2-25," in *L'Ars Nova Italiana del Trecento VII. Dolce e Nuove Note: Atti del quinto convegno internazionale in ricordo di Federico Ghisi (1901–1975), Certaldo, 17–18 Dicembre 2005*, ed. Agostino Ziino (Lucca: Libreria musicale italiana, 2009), 57–78.

8 *The Seville Manuscript*

works that comprise the bulk of Sev, however, have received much less attention.[11]

Anglès and Gallo both singled out the fascicle comprising folios 99–108v as significant.[12] Because of the segment in Catalan, Gallo even

---

11 One exception to this generality was made by Di Bacco, who pointed out that both the *Regule contrapuncti* attributed to Philippotus de Caserta and an anonymous treatise on counterpoint found on folios 110r–v are derived from *Cum notum sit*, the second part of the *Ars contrapuncti* conglomerate often attributed to Jean des Murs. See Di Bacco, *De Muris e Gli Altri: Sulla Tradizione di un Trattato Trecentesco di Contrappunto* (Lucca: Libreria musicale italiana, 2001); also Nigel Wilkins, "Some Notes on Philipoctus de Caserta (c.1360?–c.1435)," *Nottingham Mediaeval Studies* 8 (1964): 82–99 and Ryan Taycher, "*De Fundamento Discanti*: Structure and Elaboration in Fourteenth-Century Diminished Counterpoint" (PhD diss., Indiana University, 2019). For more on these works, see Chapter 3.

12 "… and I note the unknown master by the name of Johannes Pipudi, *canonicus Sancti Desiderii Avinionensis*, who presents us here with two interesting treatises on medieval music. These treatises are followed by another anonymous one, written in Catalan and Latin and copied by a Catalan hand in the 15th century." (… i dono nota del mestre desconegut, de nom *Johannes Pipudi, canonicus Sancti Desiderii Avinionensis* qui se'ns presenta aquí amb dos tractats interessantissims sobre música medieval. Aquests tractats van seguits d'altre d'anònim, escrit en català i en llatí i copiat per mà catalana en el s. xv.) Higini Anglès, "La música a veus anterior al segle XV dins l'Espanya," *Revista Musical Catalana* 24 (1927): 138–144, at 140.

"In the case of the Spanish musical history of this collection the following little works are especially interesting: *(a)* Fols. 99–104v: 'De arte cantus' of the unknown Johannes Pipudi, canonicus Sancti Desiderii Avionensis. [sic] *(b)* Fols. 104v–107: 'Secuntur regule contrapenctus [sic] per supra dictum magistrum facte sive ordinate.' *(c)* Fols. 107v–108v: An incomplete Latin-Catalan treatise by an anonymous author, copied by the same scribe who copied the two previous works and who began 'Quando tres minime pro semibreve.'" (Para el caso de la historia musical española interesan especialmente de esta colección los opúscolos siguientes … "De arte cantus" del desconocido Johannes Pipudi … Tratado latino-catalán incompleto de autor anónimo, copiado por el mismo amanuense que copió los dos anteriores y empieza "Quando …") Anglès, "La música conservada …," 8.

"They are all anonymous compilations, except … no. 36 reports at the end several rules attributed to Magister Johannes Pipudi, canonicus Sancti Desiderii avinionensis. The remaining material relates to the notation of mensurable music and, except for nos. 37 and 43, which are only short notes, includes all major works. The well-known Libellus of Johannes de Muris is reported three times … Furthermore, no. 30 is an abbreviation of the first section, while nos. 35 and 40, substantially overlapping, constitute a revision of the entire work." (Sono tutte compilazioni anonime, tranne … il n. XXXVI riporta nella parte finale alcune regole attribuite al *Magister Johannes Pipudi canonicus Sancti Desiderii avinionensis*. Il restante materiale riguarda la notazione della *musica mensurabilis* e, a parte i nn. XXXVII e XLII che sono solo brevi appunti, comprende tutte opere importanti. Il noto *Libellus* di Giovanni de Muris è riportato tre volte … Inoltre il n. XXX è una *abbreviatio* della parte iniziale, mentre i nn. XXXV e XL, sostanzialmente

The Seville Manuscript   9

speculated that it might have originated in Colón's native Spain, rather than in Italy as the rest of the treatises.[13] Neither, however, followed up further on their interest in this fascicle. Nor did any other scholar until Maria del Carmen Gómez, who in a 1976 article focused exclusively on the fascicle's three treatises.[14] As Anglès before her, Gómez noted that all three were written in the same hand; I will refer to this person as Copyist A. She clarified Anglès's report on their authorship, though, observing that while no author is named in the first treatise, the incipit to the second treatise clearly states that the two were written, or perhaps more appropriately created, by the same person: "*Secuntur regule contrapunctus per supradictum magistrum facte sive ordinate ut sequitur.*" On folio 105, that person is named as magister Johannes Pipudi, "*canonicus Sancti Desiderii Avinionensis*"—a canon at the church of Saint-Didier in Avignon. Since the third treatise repeatedly cites "*lo maestre*" and appears to be notes on elements of mensural theory, Gómez proposed that the three treatises were copied by a Catalan student of Pipudi in Avignon, not in Spain as Gallo suggested.[15]

Gómez's account of the first treatise, which after Anglès she calls *De arte cantus*, briefly elucidates its relationship to the *Libellus cantus mensurabilis*.[16] With the exception of the rhythmic modes, *De arte cantus* contains all of the elements of music theory found in the *Libellus*. Additionally, it includes newer theoretical concepts, such as note values smaller than the minim and expanded types of mode and color.

The second treatise is a set of rules of counterpoint that Gómez titles *Regulae contrapunctus* after its incipit.[17] She notes that it has a number of similarities with two of the three treatises thought to comprise what Edmond de Coussemaker called the *Ars contrapuncti secundum*

---

 coincidenti, costituiscono una rielaborazione dell'intera opera.) Gallo, "Alcune Fonti ...," 60–61.

13 "A parte il fascicolo comprendente i fogli tra il 98 e il 109 che contiene un trattato in lingua castigliana e sembra quindi sicuramente di origine spagnola, gli altri fascicoli si possono ritenere scritte in ambiente italiano tra la metà del secolo XIV e l'inizio del secolo XV." Gallo, "Alcune Fonti ...," 59.

14 Maria del Carmen Gómez, "*De arte cantus* de Johannes Pipudi, sus *Regulae contrapunctus* y los Apuntes de teoria de un estudiante catalán del siglo XIV," *Anuario musical* 31/32 (1976/1977): 37–49. Gómez also publishes under the name Maricarmen Gómez Muntané.

15 Ibid., 37.

16 The treatise ends on folio 104v with the phrase "*et per hoc fit finis (abreviacionem) de arte cantus.*"

17 The treatise appears to read "regule," not "Regulae," yet I will retain Gómez's spelling here for the sake of consistency with existing literature and to eliminate some potential confusion with other similarly named treatises.

10 *The Seville Manuscript*

Johannem de Muris.[18] Much like the relationship between *De arte cantus* and the *Libellus*, that between *Regulae contrapunctus* and the two *Ars contrapuncti* treatises is not exact. Rather, Gómez shows that concepts stated in the *Ars contrapuncti* works have here been reordered, reworded, and expanded; for example, there are now nine consonances instead of seven. The treatise includes four extensive tables of consonances built on the degrees of the different hexachords.

The documentation of the teachings of *"lo maestre"* closes the fascicle. This section begins with a brief description of prolation, tempus, and mode in Latin. Copyist A then switches to Catalan, first to lay out the types of consonances built on certain hexachordal degrees, as in the previous tables, then to demonstrate the consonances used in counterpoint.[19]

Gómez concludes her study with a semi-diplomatic transcription of the three treatises, including the musical examples and tables. Due to the condition of several folios, however, large swaths of text are missing from *De arte cantus*. Folio 99–99v is ripped diagonally and the lower third of the page is now missing (Figure 1). Other folios suffer markedly in places from ink bleedthrough and corrosion (Figure 2). Complicating matters further is that in *De arte cantus* in particular, and to a lesser degree in the other two treatises, Copyist A's handwriting is not always clear. In certain places the Latin is substandard, and while the copyist seems to have caught some errors in the moment and corrected them immediately, others went unnoticed. All of these factors make a confident transcription challenging. As such, Gómez's

---

18 The three constituent treatises are *Quilibet affectans*, *Cum notum sit*, and *De diminutione contrapuncti*; these works often appeared in some combination with each other in late medieval manuscripts and frequently carried an attribution to Jean des Murs. The first two, usually dated to the 1340s or 1350s, were both well known and frequently expanded upon in later treatises, and are those with similarities to *Regulae contrapunctus*. See Giuliano Di Bacco, *De Muris e Gli Altri*; Ulrich Michels, *Die Musiktraktate des Johannes de Muris* (Wiesbaden: F. Steiner, 1970); Klaus-Jürgen Sachs, *Der Contrapunctus im 14. und 15. Jahrhundert: Untersuchungen zum Terminus, zur Lehre und zu den Quellen* (Wiesbaden: Franz Steiner Verlag, 1974); Ryan Taycher, *"De Fundamento Discanti."*

19 RISM and Di Bacco treat these notes as three separate items, as follows:

107v	Prop. Mens. Quando	The opening section on mensural notation
107v-108r	"Primo en gamaut ha tres consonantes ..."	Hexachordal degrees
108r-v	"Item diu lo mestre nosaltres ..."	Consonances in counterpoint

The Seville Manuscript 11

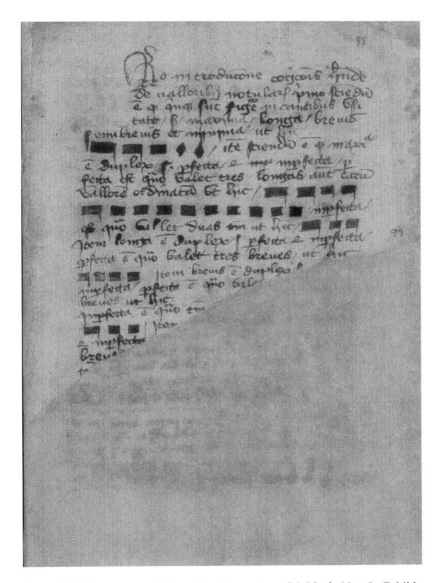

Figure 1 Biblioteca Capitular Colombina, sign. 5-2-25, f. 99r, © Cabildo Catedral de Sevilla.

12 The Seville Manuscript

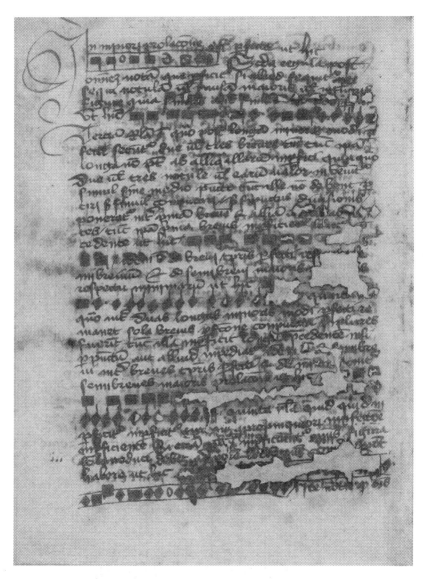

Figure 2 Biblioteca Capitular Colombina, sign. 5-2-25, f. 101v, © Cabildo Catedral de Sevilla.

The Seville Manuscript   13

transcription contains corrections, ellipses denoting missing text, and footnotes describing passages as illegible.

Perhaps because of the poor quality of the *De arte cantus* text, or because the supposed relationships between these treatises and their parent works marked them as outliers to a mainstream tradition, few scholars subsequently focused any critical attention toward the treatises in this fascicle.[20] *De arte cantus*, however, proved relevant to my dissertation research due to its description and depiction of note values smaller than the minim.[21] In reviewing Gómez's transcription, I discovered that it does not match what Copyist A documented on folios 99–104v. Sections of the Sev text are missing, while different material is included elsewhere. Examining Sev more closely, I realized that another treatise copied in a neater, smaller hand just a few scant few folios later was in fact a second copy of *De arte cantus*, an observation that F. Alberto Gallo had mentioned fleetingly in 1968.[22] So similar are the two texts, in content if not in page layout or paleography, that Gómez appears to have transcribed parts of both copies.

Since the first copy of *De arte cantus* is heavily flawed due to the partially destroyed first folio, the corroded text, and Copyist A's occasionally faulty Latin, it goes without saying that a new concordance is invaluable. The second copy not only restores the text lost due to damage, but also provides additional text that was never included in the first version—for example, the well-known description of Guillaume de Machaut allowing the imperfection of a perfect breve in

---

20 Neither the treatises nor Gómez's article is cited in the later studies of the Sev manuscript mentioned previously. Nor, despite Gómez's connections of *De arte cantus* to the *Libellus cantus mensurabilis* and *Regulae contrapunctus* to the collective known as the *Ars contrapuncti secundum Johannem de Muris*, is either of these treatises included in recent scholarship on either the *Libellus* or the works of Jean des Murs. See Oliver B. Ellsworth, *The Berkeley Manuscript: University of California Music Library, Ms. 744 (Olim Phillipps 4450)*, Greek and Latin Music Theory 2 (Lincoln: University of Nebraska Press, 1984); Katz, "The Earliest Sources"; Christian Berktold, *Ars Practica Mensurabilis Cantus Secundum Iohannem de Muris: Die Recensio Maior des Sogenannten "Libellus Practice Cantus Mensurabilis"* (München: Verlag der Bayerischen Akadamie der Wissenschaften, 1999); Christian Meyer, *Écrits Sur La Musique* (Paris: CNRS Éd., 2000); Di Bacco, *De Muris e Gli Altri*.

21 Cook, "Theoretical Treatments of the Semiminim in a Changing Notational World, c.1315–c.1440" (PhD diss., Duke University, 2012).

22 Gallo notes that this treatise is substantially similar to his item 35, which is the first copy of *De arte cantus*, but does not go into greater detail about the contents of either. I independently connected these two copies of *De arte cantus* in my dissertation; Gallo's observation was unknown 4, 13 fn 20, 18 fn 1, 18 fn 2, 20, 20 fns 7–10, 21, 21 fn 16, 22 fn 20, 26 fn 22, 30 fn 29, 31 fn 32, 34, 38, 86, 132 to me at the time. Gallo, "Alcune Fonti ....," 60–61.

14   *The Seville Manuscript*

minor prolation by a single minim, or of an imperfect breve in major prolation by two minims, a phenomenon known in mensural theory as *mutatio qualitatis*.[23] In addition to such textual differences, the two copies also offer variants in mensural notation, especially with regard to note values smaller than the minim.[24] The array of notational options preserved in the second copy suggests new connections to other theoretical literature and sources of notated music, which in turn deepens the understanding of the contexts for *De arte cantus* taken as a whole.

Like the first copy of *De arte cantus*, the second copy is embedded within a fascicle comprising several other works, all of which appear to have been copied by the same hand; I will refer to this person as Copyist B. Significantly, one of these works is also a version of the *Ars contrapuncti* complex; the short treatise *Nota quod novem sunt species contrapunctus videlicet ...* (hereafter *Nota quod novem*) begins the fascicle, followed immediately by the second copy of *De arte cantus*. The other items are tables, charts, musical examples, and shorter works, akin to the previous fascicle, but also longer, better-known treatises: one of the many copies of the *Tractatus figurarum*, the *Compendium artis motectorum Marchecti* by Petrus de Amalfia, and an excerpt of the *Lucidarium* by Marchetto of Padua (see Table 1).

This fascicle is thus a good bit longer than the previous one, at twenty-seven folios as compared to the twelve of the former. Overall, it is also in better shape; whereas the first folio of the first copy of *De arte cantus* is torn in half and many of the subsequent pages are damaged, this fascicle has survived intact and with no signs of bleedthrough or corrosion.

The hands of the two copyists are quite distinct, which impacts their respective arrangements of material on the page.[25] Both copyists employ a type of rounded cursive and make copious use of abbreviations. But Copyist A leaves wider margins at the sides, and a smaller one at the bottom, with larger words and some space between each line of text. Certain capital letters at the beginnings of sections are lightly decorated, and ascenders at the tops of pages can be rather exaggerated. Musical examples are, for the most part, given quite a

---

23 This phenomenon is described at length by Lawrence Earp, who lists this second copy of *De arte cantus*—or, rather, one of its folios—as an anonymous source for the Machaut statement. Earp, *Guillaume de Machaut: A Guide to Research*, Garland Composer Resource Manuals, v. 36 (New York: Garland, 1995).

24 On this see Cook, "Theoretical Treatments."

25 Neither hand, to the best of my ability to ascertain, is found elsewhere in Sev.

The Seville Manuscript   15

bit of room, especially those that occur on the large, free-form staves included throughout. The examples of ligatures, for example, take up over a page in space. The three works are copied back to back, and although Copyist A left some blank space between *De arte cantus* and *Regulae contrapunctus*, no title or decorated initial sets apart this second work.

Copyist B, however, leaves very small margins on the sides and a larger one at the bottom. Words are smaller, and lines of text not only contain many more words than in the first copy but also have less vertical space between themselves. Musical examples are worked into the same vertical space as is the text, as much as possible. The same section on ligatures that took up an entire page in the first copy takes up barely a third of one here; interestingly, the copyist alternates between full-black and void ligatures, but with no mensural significance. The only exception to this layout of musical examples is the depiction of rests, which, as in the first copy, are placed on a staff. No initials are decorated, although at the tops of some pages, ascenders drift gracefully upward. Copyist B left no space between works; with the exception of the four blank folios in the middle of the fascicle, all of the treatises are copied contiguously, in most cases without much more than a small dash to separate the incipit of a work from the end of the previous one. The overall impression is that the second fascicle is much more crowded, but simultaneously often neater.

Scholarly knowledge to date surrounding the person named magister Johannes Pipudi and the works connected to him in Sev can thus be summarized as follows. The first treatise in the eleventh fascicle comprising folios 99v–104v, *De arte cantus*, is a version of the well-known and widely copied *Libellus cantus mensurabilis*, often attributed to Jean des Murs. The second treatise in that fascicle, *Regulae contrapunctus*, is related to the *Ars contrapuncti* complex, also regularly attributed to Jean des Murs. Here, these treatises are indeed linked to the same author, but it is not Jean des Murs; rather, the ascription at the end of the second treatise points to a magister Johannes Pipudi, canon at the church of Saint-Didier in Avignon (Table 2). The person who copied these two works and provided the ascription to Pipudi did so in occasionally awkward but serviceable Latin, then shifted between Latin and Catalan for the third and final "treatise," a collection of notes about the teachings of *"lo maestre"*—presumably Pipudi, the magister to whom the first two treatises appear to be attributed. Gómez and others speculated that the copyist, whom I call Copyist A, might have been a student of his at some institution in Avignon. Because of the absence of the rhythmic modes, the generally accepted mid-century

16 The Seville Manuscript

Table 2 The Four Sev Treatises and Their Concordances

Sev—Unit XI, Copyist A	Sev—Unit XII, Copyist B	Primary Concordances	
	Nota quod novem (late 14th/early 15th century?)	Quilibet affectans/Cum notum sit (c.1340–1350?)	Regule contrapuncti (late 14th/early 15th century?)
		attrib. Jean des Murs	attrib. Philipoctus de Caserta
			Regula contrapunctus (late 14th century/early 15th century?)
			attrib. Philipoctus de Caserta
De arte cantus 1 (late 14th/early 15th century?)	De arte cantus 2 (late 14th/early 15th century?)	Libellus cantus mensurabilis (c.1340?)	Berkeley 2/3 (1375)
			Catania D.39 (1453–1473)
		attrib. Jean des Murs	attrib. Goscalcus of France
Regulae contrapunctus (late 14th century?)		Quilibet affectans/Cum notum sit (c.1340–1350?)	Berkeley 2 (1375)
104v: "Next, the rules of counterpoint, made or arranged by the <u>aforementioned magister</u>, as follows."		attrib. Jean des Murs	
105: "Likewise, <u>magister Johannes Pipudi</u>, canon of Saint-Didier in Avignon, arranged these rules ..."			
Catalan notes (late 14th century?)			
108: "Likewise, <u>the master says</u> that we have seven species of counterpoint…"			

This table also shows Copyist A's attribution to Johannes Pipudi in *Regulae contrapunctus* and the contextual connections to *De arte cantus* and the concluding notes. Attributions for the concordant sources are given for reference.

The Seville Manuscript 17

dates of the predecessor treatises (the *Libellus* and the *Ars contrapuncti* complex), and the newer mensural concepts added into *De arte cantus*, Gómez believed all three of the Sev treatises to date from the second half, and probably the last third, of the fourteenth century.

This fascicle has certainly brought its share of as yet unanswered questions to the table. But much new information has come to light in the forty years since Gómez's study that drastically reshapes the roles that *De arte cantus*, *Regulae contrapunctus*, and Johannes Pipudi played within the history of mensural theory. With the rediscovery of the second copy of *De arte cantus* alongside yet another witness to the *Ars contrapuncti* complex just a few folios away in Sev, the idea that any of these treatises were class notes per se is called into question. The new text and note shapes available in the second copy of *De arte cantus*, moreover, illuminate the connections between this treatise, the *Libellus*, and other related works, bringing into focus probable chronologies and provenances that affect our understanding of the works that were copied alongside them. Placing a revised assessment of *De arte cantus* alongside a fresh study of the *Regulae contrapunctus* witness to the *Ars contrapuncti* complex and the notes in Catalan, as well as newly discovered biographical information about Johannes Pipudi, reshapes our current perspective on the contexts of mensural theory in the late fourteenth century.

2 The Practical Art of Measured Song

2.1 The *Libellus cantus mensurabilis*

The *Libellus cantus mensurabilis* was one of the most widely copied and most influential music theory treatises of the late medieval period, yet its origins and authorship remain speculative.[1] Of the around fifty manuscript sources for the *Libellus*, most carry the subtitle "*secundum Johannem de Muris.*" The choice of the word "*secundum*"—"according to"—has cast doubt on des Murs's authorship of the popular treatise; both Coussemaker and Johannes Wolf described it as anonymous, whereas numerous later scholars have at least allowed the possibility of, if not argued in favor of, des Murs as the author.[2] The fact that most of the manuscript sources for the *Libellus* are Italian and date to the fifteenth century keeps the treatise at arm's length from des Murs, who

---

1 The *Libellus* was first published by Edmond de Coussemaker in the third volume of his series *Scriptorum de musica medii aevi*. Daniel Seth Katz makes the point that the *Libellus* appears to be the third most widely copied music theory treatise of the manuscript era, the other two being Boethius's *De institutione musice* and Guido's *Micrologus*; see Katz, 8–9. Katz and Berktold also note that the title *Libellus cantus mensurabilis* is not given in the text itself; one source does mention a "*Libellus practice cantus mensurabilis secundum Johannem de Muris*," though, and two other sources contain similar phrasing. The treatise is also known as the *Ars practica cantus mensurabilis secundum Johannem de Muris*, a title more closely related to the incipit found in many copies: "*Quilibet in arte practica mensurabilis cantus … compilata secundum magistrum Iohannem de Muris.*" See Katz, "The Earliest Sources," 23–24; Berktold, *Ars practica cantus mensurabilis*, IX fn. 1.
2 Coussemaker, *Scriptorum de Musica Medii Aevi*, vol. 3 (Hildesheim: G. Olms, 1963); Johannes Wolf, *Geschichte Der Mensural-Notation von 1250–1460* (Leipzig: Breitkopf & Härtel, 1904). See works by Heinrich Besseler, Oliver Ellsworth, F. Alberto Gallo, Daniel S. Katz, Christian Meyer, and Christian Berktold; Lawrence Gushee, C. Matthew Balensuela, and Jeffrey Dean, "Muris, Johannes de," in *Oxford Music Online: Grove Music Online*, 2001, https://doi.org/10.1093/gmo/9781561592630.article.14237

The Practical Art of Measured Song 19

disappears from the historical record in 1345. So too does its expansion upon the mensural theories contained in des Murs's more securely attributed musical works, the *Notitia artis musicae* and *Compendium musicae practicae*, as well as its emphasis on more practical concerns.

Despite a lack of consensus on Jean des Murs's role in the *Libellus*, the dating for the treatise has hinged on des Murs and his other works. Heinrich Besseler first proposed that the *Libellus* dates from c.1340 to 1350, which subsequent scholarship gradually reduced to c.1340—a date created, and later upheld, out of the need to have a sufficiently long enough gap between the *Notitia* and *Compendium* (traditionally dated to c.1320) and the *Libellus* to allow for the theoretical developments the latter describes.[3] The same idea is put forth in the Grove biography for des Murs, which states that

> whether or not we assume Muris's direct authorship, the *Libellus cantus mensurabilis* must be a considerably later work. In contrast to the [*Notitia* and *Compendium*], it gives a complete, if highly condensed, exposition of the developed mensural practice of the mid-14th century.[4]

However, recent work by Karen Desmond and Anna Zayaruznaya have called into question the traditionally accepted dates not just for des Murs's earlier treatises, but also the *Speculum musicae* of Jacobus, and indeed of the entire *ars nova*. Based on careful examination of des Murs's treatises, musical and otherwise, Jacobus's *Speculum*, other *ars nova* works, and contemporaneous philosophical ideas, Desmond suggests that the *Conclusiones* attached to des Murs's *Notitia* and possibly the *Compendium* could be pushed into the later 1320s, and the *Speculum* into the 1330s.[5] Zayaruznaya has taken such redating even further, proposing that book 7 of the *Speculum* could have been written as late as the 1350s.[6]

---

3 Heinrich Besseler, "Johannes de Muris," in *Die Musik in Geschichte Und Gegenwart* (New York: Bärenreiter Kassel, 1958); see also Michels, *Die Musiktraktate des Johannes de Muris*; Katz, 13 fn. 23.

4 Gushee, Balensuela, and Dean, "Muris, Johannes de." See also Sarah Fuller, who describes the *Libellus* as containing a "mature, 'classic' fourteenth-century mensuration system" stemming from the earlier des Murs sources. Fuller, "A Phantom Treatise of the Fourteenth Century? The *Ars Nova*," *The Journal of Musicology* 4, no. 1 (December 1, 1985): 23–50, at 37.

5 Desmond, *Music and the* Moderni, *1300–1350: The* Ars Nova *in Theory and Practice* (Cambridge: Cambridge University Press, 2018).

6 Zayaruznaya, "Old, New, and Newer Still in Book 7 of the *Speculum Musice*," *Journal of the American Musicological Society* 73, no. 1 (April 1, 2020): 95–148.

20 *The Practical Art of Measured Song*

Regardless of whether des Murs authored or played any sort of pedagogical role in the creation of the *Libellus*, shifting his earlier works, and those of his contemporaries, years or even decades further into the fourteenth century impacts whether the *Libellus* can still be thought to encapsulate "the developed mensural practice" c.1340. Instead, if the mensural theory found in the *Libellus* is still at some remove from those foundational texts, it might have been written or compiled later than we have thought. I will return to the questions of dating and authorship in later chapters.

As Christian Berktold systematically lays out, the textual tradition of the *Libellus cantus mensurabilis* is not at all homogeneous, nor is there a single parent text.[7] Looking carefully at textual variants, he sorts the extant versions into several separate traditions. His largest group, which he calls the *Recensio maior*, circulated in central and southern Europe, particularly in Northern Italy; this collection can be further subdivided into groups A and B.[8] The smaller group of six *Recensio minor* sources, on the other hand, was transmitted in the northwest of continental Europe, largely France and England, and exhibits its own textual alternatives.[9]

In fact, Berktold describes these six sources as rather disparate, although they all maintain similarities with the third treatise of the Berkeley manuscript (hereafter Berkeley 3).[10] While according to Oliver Ellsworth, this gloss must postdate the *Libellus* proper for its use of the past tense and its expansion upon some material found in other versions, it is actually the earliest dated witness to the *Libellus* currently known.[11] The explicit of Berkeley 3 states that it was "compiled in Paris in the year from the birth of the Lord one thousand three hundred seventy-five, the twelfth day of the month of January."[12] A concordant version in the much later manuscript Catania D.39 contains

---

7 "Die zahlreichen, weit verstreut liegenden Manuskripte, die nach unserer heutigen Kenntnis zur Überlieferung des sogenannten „Libellus practice cantus mensurabilis" beitragen, können keineswegs als ein homogenes Korpus von Quellen betrachtet werden, das nur einen einzigen Text von unzweideutiger Identität mitteilt." Berktold, *Ars practica mensurabilis cantus*, IX.

8 Berktold identifies twenty-one main sources for his *Recensio* A, and five for his *Recensio* B.

9 Unfortunately, the *Recensio minor* remains without a critical edition, and most of the versions of the *Libellus*, including those that Berktold places in his *recensio variae*, have yet to be transcribed individually.

10 Berktold, *Ars practica cantus mensurabilis ...*, X–XI.

11 See Ellsworth, *The Berkeley Manuscript*, 4–7. After Berkeley, the next securely datable source for the *Libellus* is Chicago 54.1, dated to 1391.

12 "... compilati Parisius anno a nativitate Domini millesimo trecesimo septuagesimo quinto, die duodecima mensis Ianuarii." Trans. Ellsworth, *The Berkeley*

The Practical Art of Measured Song   21

a similarly dated explicit but adds "*per Eximium Doctorem Goscalcum francigenam*"—"by the Excellent Doctor Goscalcus of France."[13]

The number of extant sources of the *Libellus*, which date well into the eighteenth century, attests to its longstanding influence. Beginning in the later fourteenth century, theorists also used the *Libellus* as a blueprint for their own efforts, at times revising it heavily, at others condensing it, or updating it by adding new theories or practices. Prosdocimo de Beldemandis wrote his extensive commentary, the *Expositiones tractatus pratice cantus mensurabilis Johannis de Muris*, in 1404; Ugolino of Orvieto followed suit a few decades later with his own commentary, book 3 of the *Declaratio musicae disciplinae*; and Franchino Gafori cites the *Libellus* heavily in his *Extractus parvus musicae*.[14] The anonymous late fourteenth-century *Ars cantus mensurabilis mensurata per modos iuris* borrows considerably from the *Libellus*.[15] And as previously mentioned, Berkeley 3, considered to be a gloss of the *Libellus*, is in fact its earliest datable witness.

De arte cantus should be viewed within this broader context of the *Libellus* and its subsequent reputation. Both Gallo and Gómez attest that it is a version of the *Libellus*, although it is not counted as such in later inventories of *Libellus* sources. Neither copy of the treatise is listed in Daniel Seth Katz's 1989 dissertation, or in Ulrich Michel's extensive survey of works by Jean des Murs, or in Christian Berktold's or Christian Meyer's detailed studies and critical editions of the *Libellus*.[16] In fact, Katz singles out the six versions of the *Libellus* that Gallo identified in Sev as examples of the blurred lines between sources, expansions, or glosses on the one hand and new works based on the

---

Manuscript, 182–183. Unless otherwise stated, all other translations in this article are the work of the author.

13 Ibid., 13ff, 182. The manuscript appears to read "Gostaltus," but in modern scholarship the name is generally given as "Goscalcus."

14 F. Alberto Gallo, ed., *Prosdocimi de Beldemandis opera: Expositiones tractatus practice cantus mensurabilis magistri Johannis de Muris*, Antiquae musicae Italicae scriptores 3 (Bologna: Università degli Studi di Bologna, Istituto di Studi Musicali e Teatrali, 1966); Albert Seay, ed., *Ugolino of Orvieto: Declaratio Musicae Disciplinae*, vol. 1–3, Corpus Scriptorum de Musica 7 ([Rome]: American Institute of Musicology, 1959); Clement A. Miller, "Early Gaffuriana: New Answers to Old Questions," *The Musical Quarterly* 56, no. 3 (1970): 367–388. Seay dates Ugolino's treatise to between 1430 and 1442, Earp to 1430–1435. Earp, *Guillaume de Machaut: A Guide to Research*, 69.

15 C. Matthew Balensuela, ed., *Ars Cantus Mensurabilis Mensurata per Modos Iuris = The Art of Mensurable Song Measured by the Modes of Law*, Greek and Latin Music Theory 10 (Lincoln: University of Nebraska Press, 1994).

16 Berktold, *Ars Practica Mensurabilis ...*, Katz, "The Earliest Sources ...," Meyer, *Jean des Murs: Écrits Sur La Musique*, Michels, *Die Musiktraktate des Johannes de Muris*.

22 *The Practical Art of Measured Song*

Libellus on the other. In his inventory, Gallo separated the three main witnesses identified in Répertoire International des Sources Musicales (RISM) as *Libellus* excerpts from three others as here: "Sevilla, Biblioteca Capitular Colombina, 5 2 25, ff. 70r–76r e 86r–86v e 88r–88v (e 88v–89r e 99r–104v e 111r–114r)."[17] Katz asks:

> how should we regard the three treatises or fragments in *E-Sco* [Sev] that Gallo included parenthetically in his list of *Libellus* sources ... and which every other list, including that given in the present work, has omitted? Although they contain some passages that obviously do not belong to Muris' text (e.g., descriptions of note forms not yet in use in the mid-fourteenth century), other passages seem to come directly out of the *Libellus*, and yet others are problematic, containing what appear to be statements from the *Libellus*, but varying just enough so that although the presence of the *Libellus* is undeniable, one still hesitates to consider that these passages are indeed Muris'.[18]

The first of Gallo's parenthetical fragments, 88v–89r, has since been combined with the fragment immediately before it on 88r–88v, and the collective is listed as a *Libellus* source in RISM and by Giuliano Di Bacco.[19] This leaves the other two parenthetical treatises, which just so happen to be the two copies of *De arte cantus*. Katz implies that they have been omitted from inventories of *Libellus* witnesses, including his own, due to the liberties they have taken with the text, amending certain statements and adding new information. Yet while Katz counts Berkeley 3 as both gloss of and earliest source for the *Libellus*, an act that opens the door for commentaries to count as source texts, he seems not to have noticed that *De arte cantus* takes strikingly similar liberties. The general contents of the treatises can readily be compared side by side (Table 3).[20]

---

17 Gallo, *La Teoria della notazione*, 79 fn. 151.

18 Katz, "The Earliest Sources," 11 fn. 18.

19 Di Bacco, "Original and Borrowed," 354.

20 As Katz, Balensuela, and others have pointed out, both scholars and sources disagree as to the division of topics in the *Libellus*; in this table and elsewhere, I follow the organization of the Berkeley treatise as found in Ellsworth, and *Recensio A* of the *Libellus* as edited by Berktold and Meyer.

The Practical Art of Measured Song   23

Table 3 Organization of the Contents of the *Libellus*, Berkeley 3, and *De arte cantus*

Libellus (Recensio A)	Berkeley 3	De arte cantus 1	De arte cantus 2
Implicit: *Quilibet in arte practica mensurabilis cantus erudiri mediocriter affectans ea scribat diligenter, que sequuntur summarie compilata* **secundum magistrum Iohannem de Muris**	Implicit: *Quilibet* **igitur** *in arte practica mensurabilis cantus erudiri mediocriter affectans,* **post hec que superius dicta sunt**, *ea scribat diligenter que sequuntur summarie compilata*	Implicit: **Pro introductione cogniciones habende de valloribus notularum**	Implicit: **Pro introductione cogniciones habende de valoribus notularum**
1. Parts of Prolation Mx, L, B, S, M [Maxima, Longa, Breve, Semibreve, Minim]	1. Parts of Prolation Mx, L, B, S, M ***Berkeley 2:*** ***Addite Fusas Semiminime [Sm] Semibreves caudatas***	1. Parts of Prolation Mx, L, B, S, M **Additas Fusas Seminas Semibreves caudatas**	1. Parts of Prolation Mx, L, B, S, M **Additas Fusas [↓↓] Semibreves caudatas**
2. Mode, Tempus, and Prolation Perfect and imperfect modus: L-B Perfect and imperfect tempus: B-S Perfect/major and imperfect/minor prolation: S-M	2. Mode, Tempus, and Prolation **Major perfect and imperfect modus: Mx-L** **Minor** perfect and imperfect modus: L-B Perfect and imperfect tempus: B-S Perfect/major and imperfect/minor prolation: S-M	2. Mode, Tempus, and Prolation **Major perfect and imperfect modus: Mx-L** **Minor** perfect and imperfect modus: L-B Perfect and imperfect tempus: B-S Perfect/major and imperfect/minor prolation: S-M	2. Mode, Tempus, and Prolation **Major perfect and imperfect modus: Mx-L** **Minor** perfect and imperfect modus: L-B Perfect and imperfect tempus: B-S Perfect/major and imperfect/minor prolation: S-M
3. Imperfection **A parte ante/post** **Imperfection by partes propinquae/ remotae/remotiores** **7** Rules of imperfection	3. Imperfection A parte ante/post **Imperfection by partes propinquae/ remotae/remotiores/ remotissimae** **6** Rules of imperfection	3. Imperfection A parte ante/ post	3. Imperfection A parte ante/ post

(Continued)

24 The Practical Art of Measured Song

Libellus (Recensio A)	Berkeley 3	De arte cantus 1	De arte cantus 2
Machaut and *mutatio qualitatis*	Machaut and *mutatio qualitatis*		Machaut and *mutatio qualitatis*
		5 Rules of imperfection **[4.] Sincopa (abbrev.)**	**5** Rules of imperfection **[4.] Sincopa (abbrev.)**
4. Alteration Three rules	4. Alteration Three rules	5. Alteration (**Two rules**)	5. Alteration (**Two rules**)
5. Puncti punctus perfectionis	5. Puncti punctus perfectionis (**additionis, augmentationis**)	6. Puncti punctus perfectionis	6. Puncti punctus perfectionis
punctus divisionis	punctus divisionis	punctus divisionis	punctus divisionis
		7. Ligatures Ascending and descending	7. Ligatures Ascending and descending
		8. Rests Mx, L, B, S, M	8. Rests Mx, L, B, S, M
6. Distinguishing Mode, Tempus, and Prolation **Quadrangle (present)** Circle and semicircle, three or two dots	6. Distinguishing Mode, Tempus, and Prolation **Quadrangle (past)** Circle and semicircle, three or two dots Ciphers		9. Distinguishing Mode, Tempus, and Prolation
	Rests Puncti Written instructions and canons	Rests Puncti Black and red notes	Rests Puncti Black and red notes
Black, red, **void** notes	Black, red, **void** notes	Written instructions and canons Circle and **backward** semicircle, three or two dots Ciphers	Written instructions and canons Circle and semicircle, three or two dots Ciphers
Brief mention of coloration, canons, rests, and signs			

The Practical Art of Measured Song   25

Libellus (Recensio A)	Berkeley 3	De arte cantus 1	De arte cantus 2
7. Rhythmic modes (present)	**Rhythmic modes (past)**		
8. Ligatures Ascending and descending **8 Rules**	7. Ligatures Ascending and descending **7 Rules**		
8. Sincopa	8. Sincopa		
9. Rests Mx, L, B, S, M, **Sm**	9. Rests Mx, L, B, S, M, Sm		
10. Diminution **4 Notes**	10. Diminution **4 Rules**	10. Diminution **(4 notes)**	10. Diminution **(4 notes)**
11. Color and Talea	11. Color and Talea	11. Color and Talea **largo modo** **corto modo**	11. Color and Talea **largo modo** **stricto modo**
Explicit: *Et predicta **quamvis rudia** sufficient in arte practica mensurabilis cantus anhelantibus introduci*	Explicit: *Et **hec predicta quamquam reduci** sufficient in artem mensurabilis cantus practicam **mediocriter** anhelantibus introduci, **et per hec sit finis huius libri, compilati Parisius anno a nativitate Domini millesimo trecesimo septuagesimo quinto, die duodecima mensis Ianuarii***	Explicit: ***Et per hoc sit finit abreviacionem de arte cantus***	Explicit: ***Et per hoc sit finis de arte cantus.***

The differences between the sources are emphasized in bold print

26   *The Practical Art of Measured Song*

2.2 *De arte cantus*

As mentioned in the previous chapter, several scholars such as F. Alberto Gallo and especially Maria del Carmen Gómez took note of the copy of *De arte cantus* on folios 99–104v for its close connections to the *Libellus*. As Gómez explained, the only chapter of the *Libellus* not copied at least in part into *De arte cantus* is that on the older rhythmic modes, which briefly summarizes them as presented by Johannes de Garlandia and revised by Franco of Cologne.[21] While some later theorists expanded the traditional six modes to nine, Franco combined Garlandia's modes 1 and 5, reducing the total number of modes to five. The *Libellus* concludes its brief report on the rhythmic modes with a statement reflecting this possibility: "Yet some say that there are only five modes, and they put the fifth with the first and the sixth in place of the fifth."[22] As the modes became less relevant in an era focused on developing more precise mensural notation, even treatises thought to gloss the *Libellus* began to excise this information. Thus, while Berkeley 3 discusses the rhythmic modes in the past tense, neither *De arte cantus* nor *Ars cantus mensurabilis mensurata per modos iuris* retains this material.[23]

A number of other concepts or references in the *Libellus* and Berkeley 3 are also missing in *De arte cantus*. As with the outdated rhythmic modes, *De arte cantus* does not discuss the older quadrangular mensuration signs that contained either three or two dashes to indicate perfect or imperfect mode. Both Berkeley 3 and the *Libellus* describe black, red, and void notes as means by which to distinguish perfect from imperfect, but *De arte cantus* only includes black and red notes, with no mention of void notation. All three treatises contain a section on the *punctus* in which the dots of perfection and division are defined, but whereas Berkeley 3 informs the reader "some needlessly call [the *punctus perfectionis*] a *punctus additionis*, others a *punctus augmentationis*," neither the *Libellus* nor *De arte cantus* includes this tangent.[24] Nor does *De arte cantus* retain the subsequent indication that notes or

---

21 See Erich Reimer, *Johannes de Garlandia: De Mensurabili Musica* (Wiesbaden: F. Steiner, 1972).

22 "*Dicunt tamen aliqui solum esse quinque modos, et illi ponunt quintum cum primo et sextum loco quinti.*" This statement is also found in Berkeley 3 as well; Berktold, *Ars practica cantus mensurabilis...*, 56; Ellsworth, *The Berkeley Manuscript*, 172–173. See also Anna Maria Busse Berger, "The Evolution of Rhythmic Notation," in *The Cambridge History of Western Music Theory*, ed. Thomas Christensen (Cambridge: Cambridge University Press, 2002), 628–56.

23 Balensuela, *Ars cantus mensurabilis*, 48–49.

24 Ellsworth, *The Berkeley Manuscript*, 167, fn 5.

The Practical Art of Measured Song   27

perfections can be separated from one another through the use of a *virgula*, or small stroke; however, several of the musical examples inserted into the first copy include just such a stroke in lieu of a punctus. Lastly, in the chapter on rests, *De arte cantus* does not mention that for the semiminim, which is described in both the *Libellus* and the Berkeley 3.

In other places, *De arte cantus* has condensed or rearranged the information found in the *Libellus* and Berkeley 3. Whereas the chapters on ligatures, *sincopa* or syncopation, and rests occur successively after the chapter on the rhythmic modes in the *Libellus* and Berkeley 3, *De arte cantus* relocates the two chapters on ligatures and rests to follow the chapter on puncti. The chapter on rests is fairly similar in all sources, although as mentioned above *De arte cantus* does not include the semiminim rest. The chapter on ligatures is even more abridged. After defining ascending and descending ligatures, *De arte cantus* leaves out the rules laid out in the *Libellus* and Berkeley 3 to distinguish ligated note values and instead describes perfection and propriety. The reader is left to determine the differences between shapes, stems, and directions using the long series of subsequent examples.[25] The chapter on *sincopa* is likewise relocated, tucked in at the end of the rules of imperfection in Chapter 3 after being drastically shortened to a single sentence: "Likewise, note that all reduction of notes to each other is called *sincopa*." And in the brief section on using ciphers to indicate tempus and prolation, *De arte cantus* has condensed the definitions as given in Berkeley 3 to such an extent that what remains is rather garbled.

Other chapters are also altered. For example, in the third section on imperfection, all four treatises offer a set of rules, but while the *Libellus* gives seven rules and a final series of explanations, *De arte cantus* only has five (Table 4). *De arte cantus* combines the information in the *Libellus*'s Rules 5 and 6; as does Berkeley 3, it relocates the portion of the final addendum that discusses division into three parts to an introductory statement, and it leaves out Rule 7.[26] This might be due to redundancy, as Rule 7's idea that two similar note values found

---

25 As shown in Appendix 2.1, each copy of *De arte cantus* provides these examples in a slightly different order.

26 Rule 6 in Berkeley 3 is one of the more intriguing portions of this treatise, since it cites the tenor of an otherwise unknown work called *Flos virginum*. Oliver Ellsworth reported that "it is tempting to suggest the motet" *Apta carol/Flos virginum*, a popular motet copied in Chantilly, Mod A, Ivrea, Durham C.I.20, and Trém and cited in the *Tractatus figurarum*, often copied adjacent to verions of the *Libellus*, but noted that its tenor does not contain the rhythmic gesture noted here. Ellsworth, *The Berkeley Manuscript*, 159 fn 2.

28　The Practical Art of Measured Song

together form a perfection is largely covered already by Rule 3. Perhaps similarly, the remainder of the last addendum, which treats imperfection with respect to the whole or to its parts, is a summary of material already explained throughout this section. The *Libellus* and Berkeley 3 precede the rules with an extra section defining the different types of remote imperfection, defining *a parte ante* and *a parte post* as well as the *partes propinquae, remotae, remotiores,* and *remotissimae*; *De arte cantus* does not, and in fact seems to quibble with the language used to describe imperfection with respect to parts. Berkeley 3 states:

> And it must be noted here that to imperfect the maxima with respect to the parts or a part is not to imperfect the maxima itself, but only the part or parts. As is shown from the aforesaid, to imperfect is to subtract a third part from the value of that which is imperfected in this manner; it follows that a third part of the value of some part of the maxima itself is not a third part of the value of the whole maxima. Therefore, the maxima can be perfect with respect to the whole (that is, its body); its parts may sometimes be imperfect and conversely.[27]

De arte cantus critiques the way unnamed others discuss the same phenomenon:

> [I]t first must be known that the perfect maxima, in its whole and in all of its parts, can be imperfected by a long or by its value, following by a part after or preceding by a part before, and this with respect to the whole of its body ... Likewise, it can be imperfected by a breve, **as some say**, with respect to one of its longs. **Certainly, this is very improperly stated, because then a long is imperfected, and not the maxima itself**. Likewise, [it can be imperfected] by two breves with respect to two of its longs, according to the aforementioned reasoning, and this by a part after or a part before ... (emphasis added)

Throughout this chapter, *De arte cantus* explains the various ways that each perfect note value might be imperfected, whether with respect to its whole or its parts. Remote imperfection therefore appears to be both accepted and prescribed, and the criticism leveled at some unknown party is directed at the description of the maxima itself being

---

27 Ellsworth, *The Berkeley Manuscript*, 155.

The Practical Art of Measured Song   29

Table 4 Rules of Imperfection in the *Libellus*, Berkeley 3, and *De arte cantus*

Libellus/Berkeley 3	*De arte cantus*
	Note briefly: anything divisible into three can be imperfected, and as many times as a thing can be divided by three, so often can it be imperfected
1 *Similis ante similem* in major mode/tempus/prolation	1 *Similis ante similem* in major mode/tempus/prolation
2 If a note is imperfect, it must be followed by a greater or smaller note value or rest (*similis ante similem*)	2 If a note is imperfect, it must be followed by a greater or smaller note value or rest (*similis ante similem*)
3 Two or three note values following a larger note value do not imperfect that note value unless there is a punctus of division	3 Two or three note values following a larger note value do not imperfect that note value unless there is a punctus of division
4 A single note value following a larger note value imperfects that note value unless separated by a punctus	4 A single note value following a larger note value imperfects that note value unless separated by a punctus
5 A single note should be understood as occupying its nearest possible mensural place	5 A single note value should be understood as occupying its nearest possible mensural place; any imperfected note value is imperfected by the nearest note value *[Berkeley 3 also condenses Rules 5 & 6]*
6 Any imperfected note value is imperfected by the nearest note value	
7 Two similar note values found together should be calculated together and not separately	
Furthermore: a note is imperfected with respect to the whole, or with respect to its parts; anything divisible into three can be imperfected, and as many times as a thing can be divided by three, so often can it be imperfected	

30   *The Practical Art of Measured Song*

imperfected by a remote note value.[28] In fact, this "improper" statement might have motivated the lengthy catalog of all acceptable ways of imperfecting perfect note values, as well as the revision and relocation of the final addendum.

The *Libellus* and Berkeley 3 conclude this section with a brief mention of Guillaume de Machaut. The *Recensio A* version reads:

> And note that some singers, such as Guillaume de Machaut and several others, imperfect a perfect breve of minor prolation by one single minim, and an imperfect breve of major prolation by two minims together, following or preceding, as here. And they call this *mutari qualitatem* ("to change the quality"); in fact, they treat the perfect breve of minor prolation as though it were an imperfect breve of major prolation, and conversely the imperfect breve of major prolation as though it were a perfect breve of minor prolation.[29]

Machaut is mentioned here within the context of the phenomenon known as *mutatio qualitatis*: changing the quality of a breve to allow it to be imperfected in a way that should not otherwise be able to occur. As the preceding section has carefully explained, imperfection can only happen by a third of a perfect note value, or by a third of one of a note value's perfect constituent parts. Imperfecting a perfect breve of minor prolation would remove a semibreve, not a minim; imperfecting (the semibreve of) an imperfect breve of major prolation would remove only one minim, not two. In order to create a wider range of rhythmic possibilities, then, Machaut and the other unnamed singers momentarily treat one type of breve as though it were the other.[30] This reference is therefore to a mensural convention that surpassed earlier *ars nova* theory as expressed in des Murs's *Notitia*, as it requires both

---

28 In this respect, *De arte cantus* is similar to the anonymous *Ars cantus mensurabilis mensurata per modos iuris*, which also describes the myriad ways a perfect maxima might be imperfected; see Balensuela, *Ars cantus mensurabilis mensurata per modos iuris*, 163–173.

29 Berktold, *Ars practica cantus mensurabilis...*, 25–26.

30 This notational and compositional device as it is found in Machaut's works has been discussed extensively by both Lawrence Earp and Carla Vivarelli. Earp points out that the ballade *De petit po* contains an example of the first kind of *mutatio qualitatis*; the rondeau *Rose, liz, printemps, verdure* contains an example of the second. See Earp, *Guillaume de Machaut: A Guide to Research*, 67, and Vivarelli, "La 'Mutatio Qualitatis' Nella Teoria e Nella Prassi 'Subtilior': Una Regola Disattesa?," *Studi Musicali* 38, no. 2 (2009): 273–308.

The Practical Art of Measured Song 31

a fully fledged system of major and minor prolation and the development of remote imperfection. While this section is not found in the first copy of *De arte cantus*, the second copy includes it in full, albeit without the notated examples found in many copies of the *Libellus*.[31]

As it did with the rules of imperfection, *De arte cantus* provides an alternate reading of the rules of alteration. The three rules as given in the *Libellus* and Berkeley 3 are as follows:

1. No note value can be altered before an identical or smaller note value.
2. Every note value that can be altered can be altered before the next larger note or rest, but no other.
3. Whenever two identical note values are found together in between or preceding two larger note values in such a way as to form a perfection, the second note value is altered.[32]

De arte cantus, however, does not call any of these precepts "rules." It also does not include a version of Rule 1, perhaps because the stipulation in Rule 2 that note values can only be altered before the next larger note value renders the first rule unnecessary. All sources continue into a further discussion of alteration, but *De arte cantus* does not clarify, as the others do, that an altered note can be imperfected *a parte ante*, nor does it include either the definitions of *recta* and *altera* note values found in the other sources or the statement unique to Berkeley 3 that describes alteration of black notes before red ones and vice versa.

Similarly, the rules of diminution included in Berkeley 3 are not called rules in *De arte cantus*, but neither are they called rules in either major *Recensio* of the *Libellus*. The information contained therein is very similar across all four treatises, with two small exceptions. All begin with a statement that diminution occurs in the tenors of motets,

---

31 Other contemporaneous treatises drawing on the *Libellus*, but also incorporating the newest in notational advancements, include a discussion of *mutatio qualitatis*. For example, the *Ars cantus mensurabilis mensurata per modos iuris* cites "magister Johannes de Muris," who declared that Machaut (there named Guilielmus de Mastodio) changed the quality of the breve in order to imperfect it in various ways. The author cites the rondeau "Rose sans per," found in Ivrea and Panciatichi 26, which itself cites Machaut's "Rose, liz, printemps, verdure." One small change, though, is that the reference to *mutatio qualitatis* is done within the section on red and void notation, not within the chapter on imperfection as in the *Libellus*. See Balensuela, 231–235.

32 Paraphrased from Berktold, *Ars practica cantus mensurabilis...*, 36–41. and Ellsworth, *The Berkeley Manuscript*, 165–167.

32   *The Practical Art of Measured Song*

then all four lay out the ways in which diminution occurs. At the conclusion of the chapter, both Berkeley 3 and *De arte cantus* reiterate that examples can be found in motet tenors. However, most of *Recensio A* and one source in the *Recensio B* of the *Libellus* only state that examples are found in motets, and all other sources for the *Recensio maior* leave out this statement. A negligible difference, perhaps, but the *Recensio B* alone declares that in diminution, a minim is replaced by a semiminim, a note value never otherwise defined in the *Libellus*-Berkeley 3 tradition and which, along with the minim, would not have occurred in motet tenors.[33]

De arte cantus and the Berkeley manuscript both diverge from the *Libellus* in fascinatingly similar ways. Some are matters of word choice; Daniel Seth Katz, for example, observes that instead of the word "*nota,*" both the Berkeley and Catania treatises frequently use "*notula,*" as do both copies of *De arte cantus.*[34] Others are more complex, expanding on theories in the *Libellus* in like fashion or even in identical language.

Oliver Ellsworth notes that Berkeley 3 appears to be the earliest surviving source to describe the expansion of the modus system upward to include the relationship between maxima and long. That relationship is called major modus, while minor modus refers to the relationship between long and breve, and either modus can be perfect or imperfect.[35] The same relationships are described in very similar fashion in *De arte cantus.* Likewise, both Berkeley 3 and *De arte cantus* add a short clause to the end of the section on alteration, stating that *reductio,* or note values belonging to the same perfection that have been displaced through syncopation, does not affect alteration according to the given rules.[36] In the chapter on distinguishing mode, tempus, and prolation, both Berkeley 3 and *De arte cantus* expand on the *Libellus* to include ciphers, rests, puncti, and written instructions or canons. While Berkeley 3 also introduces ciphers in the past tense, it describes them in the present tense, as does *De arte cantus.* However, in the same section, Berkeley 3 describes the older quadrangular mensuration

---

33 Although she does not mention the *Recensio B* inclusion of the semiminim in diminution, Ruth DeFord states that "the motet tenors [Muris] has in mind never include notes shorter than semibreves." See DeFord, "On Diminution and Proportion in Fifteenth-Century Music Theory," *Journal of the American Musicological Society* 58, no. 1 (Spring 2005): 1–67 at 11 fn. 28.
34 Katz, "The Earliest Sources," 215–216.
35 Ellsworth, *The Berkeley Manuscript,* 6.
36 See Ellsworth, *The Berkeley Manuscript,* 167 fn. 3.

The Practical Art of Measured Song   33

signs in the past tense, and immediately thereafter describes the rhythmic modes in the same way, both of which *De arte cantus* eliminates.

Most intriguing are the new note values given at the [beginning of *De arte cantus*. The author includes four note values outside the traditional five parts of prolation, all of which are proportional, meaning that they occur in groups in order to replace groups of other traditional note values. The *fusa*, also known as the *dragma*, is a double-stemmed semibreve figure (♦), two of which replace three minims.[37] Two downward-stemmed semibreves, here called *semibreves caudatas* (♦), replace three semibreves in major prolation. The other two note values are smaller than the minim: two *seminas* (likely a misspelling of semiminimas) replace one minim, while four *additas* replace three minims.[38] The only other work known to include the same four notes values, in the same order, and using nearly identical terminology, is Berkeley 2, found in the Berkeley manuscript, Catania D.39, and London 23220. The semiminim, fusa, and semibreves caudatas were listed in numerous other sources throughout the fourteenth and early fifteenth centuries, but *De arte cantus* and Berkeley 2 are the only two treatises to use the term additas or *additae* for the note values that act in sesquitertia proportion to minims.[39] Three other treatises include such note values: the *Compendium totius artis motetorum*, a central European source in which these notes are called *minimae additae*, and the later fourteenth-century *Tractatus figurarum* and *Ars cantus mensurabilis mensurata per modos iuris*, in both of which they are called

---

37 *De arte cantus* 1 reads "fusatis," whereas *De arte cantus* 2 reads "fusas."

38 *De arte cantus* 1 contains the term "seminas," whereas *De arte cantus* 2 does not name these note values.

39 "Tagged" or stemmed semibreves have recently been thoroughly discussed in Karen Desmond, *Music and the* Moderni, esp. 136ff. However, the types described in *De arte cantus* have a particular mensural relationship with semibreves in major prolation, which is not found in any other source except for Berkeley 2. The downward-stemmed semibreve is given other mensural durations in the *Compendiolum artis veteris ac novae* by Coussemaker's Anonymous III, for example. The fusa or dragma can be seen in treatises as early as the 1351 *Quatuor principalia*, the *Compendium totius artis motetorum* c.1350, the *Compendiolum artis veteris ac novae*, also c.1350, and Jacobus's *Speculum musice*, which Anna Zayaruznaya has recently suggested might also date as late as the 1350s. See Zayaruznaya, "Old, New, and Newer Still"; Luminita Florea Aluas, "The *Quatuor Principalia Musicae:* A Critical Edition and Translation, with Introduction and Commentary" (PhD diss., Indiana University, 1996); Gilbert Reaney, André Gilles, and Jean Maillard, eds., *Philippi Di Vitriaco: Ars Nova*, Corpus Scriptorum de Musica 8 ([Rome]: American Institute of Musicology, 1964). For a detailed history of the semiminim, see Cook, "Theoretical Treatments ..."; Zayaruznaya, "Old, New, and Newer Still."

34 *The Practical Art of Measured Song*

imperfect minims.[40] The use of the term additas and the similarities in the descriptions of all four note values mark *De arte cantus* as a unique concordance to the second half of Berkeley 2, as well as Berkeley 3.

Lastly, *De arte cantus* contains several small but telling changes to the *Libellus* and Berkeley 3. The first type of variation is brief, perhaps a short sentence or two added to introduce or summarize a given topic. For example, just before the aforementioned section on newer mensural note values, Copyist B includes a quick digest of alteration and imperfection; in version 1, this section is largely lost due to the torn folio. A maxima cannot be altered, and a minim cannot be imperfected, as they mark the outer boundaries of mensural duration. But all note values in between, namely, the long, the breve, and the semibreve, can be altered or imperfected according to the ensuing rules. The subsequent section on mensurations begins with an introductory statement not found in the other treatises, declaring that all song comprises mode, tempus, and prolation. And *De arte cantus* introduces the chapter on distinguishing such mensurations first by describing again that anything able to be calculated by three is perfect, unless such a grouping is created through an impediment of some sort.

In the same chapter, all four sources mention the use of the circle and the semicircle to indicate tempus, with either two or three dots in the center to indicate prolation. While in all versions of the Recensio A and Recensio B as documented by Berktold, and in Berkeley 3, the semicircle given is the typical C-shaped grapheme, the first copy of *De arte cantus* depicts a backward semicircle (Figure 3).

Jason Stoessel and Anna Maria Busse Berger both provide a thorough analysis of this mensuration sign, demonstrating that although uncommon, the backward semicircle was present in both theory and notational practice.[41] Busse Berger observes that in notated music, and occasionally in theory, it typically indicates a sesquitertia proportion at the minim level. Stoessel notes that it also indicates imperfect tempus in the *Summa* of Johannes Hanboys (c.1375) and in Johannes

---

40 See Balensuela, esp. 246–251; Philip Evan Schreur, *Tractatus Figurarum = Treatise on Noteshapes*, Greek and Latin Music Theory 6 (Lincoln: University of Nebraska Press, 1989), 84–85; Johannes Wolf, "Ein Anonymer Musiktraktat Aus Der Ersten Zeit Der 'Ars Nova,'" *Kirchenmusikalisches Jahrbuch* 21 (1908): 34–38.

41 Stoessel, "The Interpretation of Unusual Mensuration Signs in the Notation of the 'Ars Subtilior,'" in *A Late Medieval Songbook and Its Context: New Perspectives on the Chantilly Codex (Bibliothèque Du Château de Chantilly, Ms. 564)*, eds. Yolanda Plumley and Anne Stone (Turnhout: Brepols Publishers, 2010), 179–182, 185–187; Busse Berger, "The Origin and Early History of Proportion Signs," *Journal of the American Musicological Society* 41, no. 3 (Autumn 1988): 403–433.

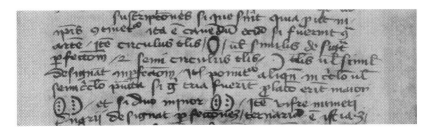

Figure 3 The backward-C grapheme; Biblioteca Capitular Colombina, sign. 5-2-25, f. 104r, © Cabildo Catedral de Sevilla.

Ciconia's *De proportionibus* (1411). However, only Hanboys permits ↄ to represent both major and minor prolation, depending on whether it has a single punctus or no punctus at all.[42] For Ciconia, ↄ can only indicate imperfect tempus and minor prolation, as can the more common c and the cipher $\frac{2}{2}$.[43] Stoessel identifies several works in which ↄ works in such fashion, either on its own or in combination with another cipher, sign, or coloration (Table 5).

The sign ↄ as it is presented in *De arte cantus* is thus a bit of an anomaly; its closest relative appears to be the version in the *Summa*, which can indicate imperfect tempus and major or minor prolation depending on the presence or absence of a single punctus. Stoessel observes that the shift from using multiple puncti to using one or no puncti to indicate type of prolation was under way by c.1375, and by c.1400 most sources preferred the latter, while Busse Berger more generally suggests that the use of one or no puncti was in practice in the fifteenth century.[44] Provided that the backward-C grapheme was copied intentionally, the first copy of *De arte cantus* is thus a witness to this transitional period, retaining the almost-antiquated multiple puncti to indicate prolation while simultaneously utilizing ↄ in an uncommon and short-lived fashion otherwise only proposed by Hanboys and Ciconia.

---

42 Peter Lefferts, *Robertus de Handlo: Regule/The Rules and Johannes Hanboys: The Summa*, Greek and Latin Music Theory 7 (Lincoln: University of Nebraska Press, 1991), 266–267.
43 Oliver B. Ellsworth, ed., *Johannes Ciconia: Nova Musica and De Proportionibus*, Greek and Latin Music Theory 9 (Lincoln: U of Nebraska Press, 1993), 442–443.
44 Stoessel, "Unusual Mensuration Signs," 181; Busse Berger, "The Evolution of Rhythmic Notation," 636–637.

36 *The Practical Art of Measured Song*

Table 5 Works in Which ꝺ Indicates Imperfect Tempus and Minor Prolation

Title	Composer	Manuscript	Date	Provenance
"Sus une fontayne"	Johannes Ciconia	Pad A	Late 14th/ early 15th century	Padua
"Je ne puis avoir plaisir"	Anonymous	Chantilly	Late 14th century	Florence
		Panciatichi	Late 14th/ early 15th century	Florence?
Inclite flos	Matheus de Sancto Johanne	Chantilly	Late 14th century	Florence
Sub Arturo plebs/Fons citharizancium/In omnem terram	Johannes Alanus	Chantilly	After 1395	Florence
Gloria	Gherardello da Firenze	Pit	1406–1408	Florence or Lucca
"Era Venus al termin del suo giorno"	Paolo Tenorista	Pit	1406–1408	Florence or Lucca
"Donna se per te moro"	Andrea da Firenze	Squarc	c.1410–1415	Florence

The second interesting variant occurs in the very last section of the treatise, which discusses color and talea. Both Berkeley 3 and the *Libellus* state that color is when the same or similar note values repeat many times; however, "some singers" differentiate between color and talea, the former being when the same pitches are repeated, regardless of rhythm, and the latter when the same rhythms are repeated, regardless of pitch. These two definitions of color are further clarified in *De arte cantus*. Here, the more generic definition of color (which the first copy of *De arte cantus* refers to as "*largo modo*") is where the same pitches or the same rhythms repeat many times. If the same pitches are repeated but they have different rhythms, the first copy of *De arte cantus* refers to this as "*corto modo*," the second copy "*stricto modo*." No distinction is made here between color proper and what "some

The Practical Art of Measured Song   37

singers" do; rather, it seems that *De arte cantus* preserves the views of those who already distinguish between color and talea.[45]

In preliminary summation, it appears that *De arte cantus* is not only another reworking of the *Libellus*, but one in the same vein as Berkeley 3. Oliver Ellsworth identified only the later Catania D.39 as a concordance for Berkeley 3.[46] But the author or copyists of *De arte cantus* were clearly familiar with the theoretical concepts found in both Berkeley 2 and Berkeley 3, as they took the liberty not only to excise some of the older notational phenomena transmitted in Berkeley 3 but to update it with newer material, such as the backward semicircle and the different definitions of color, and the four newer note values in Berkeley 2.

It is difficult to say with certainty whether the author or copyists had direct access to the Berkeley manuscript versions of these treatises, to Catania, or to another exemplar or exemplars now lost to time. However, there is at least one place in the copies of *De arte cantus* that connects to Catania alone.[47] In the section on imperfection, *De arte cantus* walks the reader through all of the various ways in which a maxima can be imperfected, finally ending with the summary that the maxima, which should at its greatest duration be worth 81 minims, can be imperfected to the point where it is worth only 16. This statement does not appear in the Berkeley version, but it does in Catania.[48] The third Berkeley treatise can now be said to have three concordances: Catania D.39 and the two copies of *De arte cantus* found in Sev.

Such new connections are as problematic as they are exciting. The Seville manuscript is generally assumed to be of Italian provenance, collected piecemeal by Hernando Colón; the fascicle containing the

---

45 For more on color and talea in both theory and practice, see Anna Zayaruznaya, *Upper-Voice Structures and Compositional Process in the Ars Nova Motet* (New York: Routledge, 2018), esp. 34–35.

46 See Ellsworth, *The Berkeley Manuscript*, 13ff. The five treatises in the manuscript have a different array of concordances, as follows:
Berkeley 1: Catania D.39, Bergamo Σ.4.37, London 23220
Berkeley 2: Catania D.39, Rome 1146, Cambridge 410, London 23220 (now also Sev)
Berkeley 3: Catania D.39 (now also Sev)
Berkeley 4: Gent 70 (71)
Berkeley 5: Catania D.39

47 Some of the musical examples appear to be closer to Catania as well, such as the identical inclusion of two minims in the beginning section on the parts of prolation.

48 Ellsworth, *The Berkeley Manuscript*, 156 inc. critical notes.

38   *The Practical Art of Measured Song*

first copy of *De arte cantus* has also been thought to have Iberian origins, given its Catalan contents. Yet the textual tradition of the *Libellus* that circulated in Italy, according to Christian Berktold, is the *Recensio maior*. Berkeley's witness to the *Libellus*, on the other hand, is much more akin to the *Recensio minor*, which circulated in England and the northwest of France. *De arte cantus* thus becomes a bit of a proverbial thorn in the side, for even if it had originated in Avignon, it would be the *Recensio minor* witness copied the furthest afield, and the closest geographically to the *Recensio maior* tradition. In the next chapters, I will explore some possibilities for how the earlier northwestern Parisian tradition might have found its way south to Avignon.

3 The Rules of Counterpoint

3.1 The *Ars contrapuncti secundum Johannem de Muris*

As with the *Libellus*, the *Ars contrapuncti secundum Johannem de Muris* was given its name by Edmond de Coussemaker, once again in the third volume of his series *Scriptorum de musica medii aevi*.[1] While the *Libellus* is more or less one "treatise" despite its varying textual traditions and often fragmentary transmission history, the *Ars contrapuncti* is actually a collection of three related treatises, now known by their incipits: *Quilibet affectans*, *Cum notum sit*, and *De diminutione contrapuncti*. The only one of the three to circulate independently of the others is the first, *Quilibet affectans*; it appears by itself in four of the fourteen sources for the works.[2] In all but two of the remaining ten sources, the three works are copied contiguously.

Once again, Jean des Murs is named the author in several sources, although many modern scholars dispute this attribution; in no small part this is because his known works do not discuss counterpoint, but also because, again like the *Libellus*, the bulk of the sources are from fifteenth-century Italy.[3] Giuliano Di Bacco, however, states that *Quilibet affectans* is "probably the only work on counterpoint written by De Muris, between 1340 and 1350," and suggests that *Cum notum sit* and *De diminutione contrapuncti* might have originated in Italy as a result

---

1 Coussemaker was aware that the work was a composite, and also expressed doubts about the authorship of Jean des Murs, calling the treatise anonymous. See Coussemaker 3, xix; also see the discussion in Oliver B. Ellsworth, "The Berkeley Manuscript (Olim Phillipps 4450): A Compendium of Fourteenth-Century Music Theory" (PhD diss., University of Michigan at Ann Arbor, 1969), 74–75.

2 Taycher, Table 0.2, "*De Fundamento Discanti*," 19.

3 See Gushee, Balensuela, and Dean, "Muris, Johannes de."

40   *The Rules of Counterpoint*

of the influx of popular French-Murisian theory, perhaps including *Quilibet affectans.*[4]

Quilibet affectans begins with an exhortation to learn counterpoint through the principles laid out in this treatise, which were compiled by Jean des Murs. It permits six consonances within the octave, namely, the unison, the minor and major third, the fifth, the sixth, and the octave itself, all of which are also called by their Greek names (*semiditone, ditone, diapente, diapente-cum-tono,* and *diapason*). There is no need to discuss intervals greater than the octave because they simply replicate these smaller intervals. Several specific intervallic progressions are prescribed, first from perfect intervals and then from imperfect. All song should begin and end on a perfect consonance, and such a consonance can only be approached through stepwise motion. Moreover, there can be no parallel perfect intervals, but two to four consecutive parallel imperfect intervals are acceptable, and contrary contrapuntal motion is preferred.

Cum notum sit includes much of the same material, although it eliminates some things and updates others. It too begins with a kind of exhortation to learn counterpoint, defined here as note-against-note polyphony, although such study is encouraged in order to produce more skilled and pleasing discant. There are now seven consonances: the minor and major thirds in *Quilibet affectans* are conflated, while the tenth and the twelfth are added. No specific intervallic progressions are given, but the treatise does outline some general rules for two-part counterpoint. Again, all songs should begin and end on a perfect interval. An imperfect consonance should follow a perfect one, but one kind of perfect interval can move to another one if necessary. No parallel perfect intervals are permissible, but two or three parallel imperfect intervals are, as long as they are then followed by a perfect consonance. New here are the explicit mandates that the discant should not repeat a note lest it sound too much like the tenor, and that the penultimate interval be imperfect. The concluding recommendation for contrary motion is left out.

De diminutione contrapuncti, on the other hand, is a systematic itemization of all of the ways a breve in each of the four prolations might be subdivided over a sustained tenor. In other words, while the preceding two treatises deal with pitch, this last work considers the basics of rhythm and mensuration.

---

4 Di Bacco, *De Muris e Gli Altri,* 357ff. Taycher suggests the 1340s and 1350s for all three treatises: "*De Fundamento Discanti,*" 17ff.

The Rules of Counterpoint   41

Regardless of which combination of the three treatises comprise each extant version of the *Ars contrapuncti* conglomerate, they are often found in the proximity of, if not contiguous with, the *Libellus cantus mensurabilis*.[5] Of the fourteen sources, only Brussels 4144 does not contain some form of the *Libellus*; interestingly enough, it is the earliest source for the *Quilibet affectans*, and otherwise only contains works by Marchetto of Padua.[6] Two sources have the *Libellus* and some part of the *Ars contrapuncti* copied contiguously, while an additional four copy the *Tractatus figurarum* in between. Five more contain both works but at a greater distance from one another. The last two copy the *Ars contrapuncti* alongside a work associated with Jean des Murs: in Wash J6, the *Quilibet affectans* immediately follows Petrus de Sancto Dionysio's gloss on the *Notitia*, whereas Florence Plut.29.48 has the entirety of the *Ars contrapuncti* subsequent to *Ars cantus mensurabilis mensurata per modos iuris*, Anonymous V's reworking of the *Libellus*.

As C. Matthew Balensuela observes, the author of this treatise indicates in the Prohemium that a work on counterpoint beginning "*Cum notum*" should accompany it, although no extant manuscript source contains one. But since Florence Plut.29.48 includes *Cum notum sit* as part of the subsequent *Ars contrapuncti*, Balensuela leaves open the possibility that that was in fact the work that was intended to be included.[7] He dates the *Ars cantus mensurabilis mensurata per modos iuris* to the last quarter of the fourteenth century, noting that it had to have been written after the motet *Rex Karole/Leticie pacis/Virgo prius*, composed in 1375–1376.[8]

To such reworkings others must be added. One such is the Berkeley manuscript. The opening section of Berkeley 2 is an adaptation of *Quilibet affectans*, with additional ties to *Cum notum sit*. Berkeley 2 agrees

---

5 Di Bacco, "Original and Borrowed," 363 fn 75.

6 For Brussels 4144, RISM gives c.1390. All of the other manuscript sources for the *Ars contrapuncti* date into the fifteenth century.

7 The copy of the *Ars cantus mensurabilis mensurata per modos iuris* in Florence Plut. 29.48 is followed by all three of the treatises comprising the *Ars contrapuncti*, including *Cum notum sit*. In fact, the copyist of these works included the title *Ars contrapuncti secundum Johannem de Muris*, from which Coussemaker derived his title for the composite work. See Balensuela, *Ars cantus mensurabilis mensurata per modos iuris*, 3–10.

8 Ibid., 82. On the motet, see Ursula Günther, *The Motets of the Manuscripts Chantilly, Musée Condé, 564 (Olim 1047) and Modena, Biblioteca Estense, Alpha. M. 5, 24 (Olim Lat. 568)*, Corpus Mensurabilis Musicae 39 ([n.p.]: American Inst. of Musicology, 1965).

42 *The Rules of Counterpoint*

with *Quilibet affectans* on both the number of consonances (six) and their types, retaining the differentiation between the minor and major third and proclaiming that any interval greater than an octave is a replication of these smaller ones. It also provides both the Latin and Greek names for such intervals. For the most part, the interval progressions laid out in Berkeley 2 align with those in *Quilibet affectans*, although Berkeley 2 is unique in referring to the octave as a *dupla* and, despite its reluctance to discuss composite intervals, it does permit the sixth to move to a tenth under certain circumstances. It also retains *Quilibet*'s reference to Boethius within the description of proper motion away from a unison. Other notable expansions of the *Quilibet* material include Berkeley 2's suggestion that a work might begin on an imperfect interval, for example. It also introduces the idea of an intermediary, which would permit the cantus and tenor to approach a perfect consonance by something other than stepwise motion, or to allow for parallel perfect intervals; whether this intermediary is another interval or a type of diminution in the cantus remains unclear. Moreover, Berkeley 2 includes *Cum notum sit*'s explicit instruction that a perfect interval should follow after a short string of imperfect ones. Lastly, Berkeley 2 appears to introduce the idea of oblique motion by permitting the cantus to repeat a pitch, an idea expressly prohibited in *Cum notum sit* and absent in *Quilibet affectans*. Berkeley 2 states that after any interval, one could either remain in the same place (presumably stay on the same pitch) or ascend and descend by any number of pitches, except after the sixth, which must only be left by step. *Quilibet affectans* does not expressly state this latter instruction, although its indication that the sixth must always move to the octave, or in some cases the fifth, implies such motion.

Where *Cum notum sit* and *De diminutione contrapuncti* often follow, Berkeley 2 instead includes a lengthy table of consonances within the hard and natural hexachords, the section on the parts of prolation and the new rhythmic note values discussed in the previous chapter, and a concluding discussion of *verbula*, or florid discant.[9] The table of consonances aside, the remaining two sections on mensural note values and diminutions above a tenor cover the same kind of ground that

---

9 Ellsworth includes a parallel reading of *Quilibet affectans* and the first section of Berkeley 2 in his dissertation; see Ellsworth, "The Berkeley Manuscript," 77–79. On the phenomenon of *verbula*, see Chelsey Hamm, "A Critical Examination of Verbula in the Berkeley Manuscript," in *Histories and Narratives of Music Analysis*, eds. Miloš Zatkalik, Milena Medić, and Denis Collins, 15–30 (Cambridge: Cambridge Scholars Publishing, 2013).

The Rules of Counterpoint 43

De diminutione contrapuncti does, and given that there is at least one nod to material in *Cum notum sit* here that does not appear in *Quilibet affectans*, it could be argued that the whole of Berkeley 2 is actually a version of the entire *Ars contrapuncti*. Once again, then, the *Ars contrapuncti* is found copied contiguously with the *Libellus*, as it is glossed in Berkeley 3. Since the date of January 12, 1375, in the explicit of Berkeley 3 applies to all of the first three treatises, the Berkeley manuscript might therefore be the earliest datable witness to the *Ars contrapuncti* as well as to the *Libellus*.

3.2 *Regulae contrapunctus*

The Berkeley 3 version of the *Libellus*, as well as the section of Berkeley 2 that discusses mensural note values, has a unique concordance in *De arte cantus*. Given the late medieval proclivity to copy the *Libellus* and *Ars contrapuncti* together in some fashion, it is unsurprising, then, to find that both copies of *De arte cantus* are contiguous with a version of the *Ars contrapuncti*.

The first copy of *De arte cantus* is followed directly by what Maria del Carmen Gómez calls *Regulae contrapunctus*: the rules of counterpoint. Berkeley 2 largely expands upon *Quilibet affectans*, while including a small amount of *Cum notum sit* material; *Regulae contrapunctus* appears to be a similar combination.

Both *Quilibet affectans* and *Regulae contrapunctus* begin with a statement of attribution and a declaration of intent for those reading the treatise. Berkeley 2 gives no specific name, but it too appeals to authority, while the much later version in Catania contains a different ascription [emphasis added]:

> *Quilibet affectans*: [The art of counterpoint of magister Johannes de Muris.] Let anyone wishing to understand counterpoint diligently write the following summary, **compiled by Johannes de Muris**. For it first should be known that … six species are included …

> Berkeley 2: Since musicians do not wish to depart from the custom of **ancient philosophers** but try to follow as far as possible their footsteps (as more clearly directed), they take care to present only six species of discant …

> [Catania: … compiled in Paris in the year of our Lord's birth 1385, on the twelfth day of the month of January, **by the excellent Doctor Goscalcus of France.**]

44   *The Rules of Counterpoint*

> *Regulae contrapunctus*: Next, the rules of counterpoint, **made or arranged by the aforementioned magister**, as follows. In order to have knowledge of counterpoint, it should first be known that there are nine names of the species of discant ...[10]

Later in *Regulae contrapunctus*, Copyist A specifies that it is a magister Johannes Pipudi who is responsible for making or arranging these rules; thus, this incipit appears to link him to the preceding *De arte cantus* as well. Since no person is explicitly named in *De arte cantus*, though, the possibility remains that the "aforementioned magister" cited here may be someone else, and it is that person who thus might be responsible for both *De arte cantus* and the first section of *Regulae contrapunctus*, leaving Pipudi responsible only for the rules of oblique motion and the table of consonances. This interpretation of attribution opens the door to the possibility that the "aforementioned magister" could have been Jean des Murs, Goscalcus, or someone else entirely. However, only *Regulae contrapunctus* implies possible authorship by Pipudi, since the other sources indicate that their named authorial figures collected these rules, perhaps for pedagogical purposes.

Just as *Cum notum sit* increased the number of consonances from six to seven by including composite intervals, so too does *Regulae contrapunctus*, although it includes nine intervals up to the fifteenth and refers to them in Latin only, not also in Greek. In these respects, and also in the ordering of some of its topics, *Regulae contrapunctus* differs from Berkeley 2. But its prescriptions for intervallic progressions are similarly expanded. In fact, the only progressions prohibited by *Regulae contrapunctus* are octave reiterations; for example, a unison can move to any consonance except an octave or a fifteenth, and vice versa, while a fifth could move to any consonance but the twelfth. In Berkeley 2, a unison is permitted to move to any kind of third, fifth, or sixth, "or other composite," while a fifth similarly can move to any kind of third, sixth, "or other composite." The only interval routinely left out of these prescriptions is the octave reiteration. In other words, Berkeley 2 spells out which consonances are acceptable, while *Regulae contrapunctus* specifies which are not, with the same results.

Both Berkeley 2 and *Regulae contrapunctus* go into some detail about motion away from a sixth; again, stepwise motion and a progression to the octave are preferred, but *Regulae contrapunctus* follows Berkeley 2 in stating that the sixth could move stepwise upward to

---

10 See Ellsworth, *The Berkeley Manuscript*, 111.

The Rules of Counterpoint   45

form a tenth if the tenor descends by a fourth, or to form a third if the tenor ascends by a fifth.[11] Moreover, *Regulae contrapunctus* includes Berkeley 2's intermediary, which can intervene between two parallel perfect intervals. Lastly, both treatises express a preference for contrary motion but allow for parallel and oblique motion following any kind of consonance.

Regulae contrapunctus concludes the main portion of its text with an expanded explanation of oblique motion. It states that when the tenor (here called cantus or plainchant) ascends or descends by one step, the top voice or discantus should ascend or descend by several steps, and vice versa. This is the segment of the treatise in which Copyist A gives credit to *dominus magister* Johannes Pipudi for arranging such rules—especially, it seems, those of oblique motion, which are not as thoroughly described in any of the prior treatises: "Likewise, magister Johannes Pipudi, canon of Saint-Didier in Avignon, arranged these rules, saying that when the cantus ascends by one pitch ..." It could very well be, then, that such a detailed description was the magister's own contribution to the cause.

Pipudi, "the aforementioned dominus magister Johannes," is also credited with organizing the following table of consonances, itself almost identical to that found in the middle of Berkeley 2. However, in that section of the treatise as elsewhere, the Berkeley 2 author or compiler writes in the first person, appearing to take credit for the organization and possibly even the invention of the material within. Both of these tables lay out pitches comprising the hard (G) and natural (C) hexachords and all of the possible vertical intervals possible for each such pitch.

For Berkeley 2, the hard hexachord ranges from Gamma-ut up an octave and a sixth to E-la-mi *altus*, whereas the natural hexachord also begins on Gamma-ut and progresses up over two octaves to A-la-mi-re *altus*. For each pitch contained within, all possible consonances are laid out both in solmization syllables and in intervals, such that for G-sol-re-ut in the hard hexachord, one could make a unison (ut), third (mi), fifth (sol), or sixth (la), and in the natural hexachord one could make a fifth (re), sixth (mi), or octave (sol). These hexachord tables are presented side by side in two columns. In a nod to the treatise's earlier statement about replication of intervals above the octave, this section

---

11 On this passage, see Bonnie J. Blackburn, "On Compositional Process in the Fifteenth Century," *Journal of the American Musicological Society* 40, no. 2 (July 1987): 210–284 at 235 fn. 41.

46   *The Rules of Counterpoint*

concludes by asserting that the same basic consonances can be made an octave higher, beginning in the hard hexachord on G-sol-re-ut *altus* up to E-la.

The consonance tables in *Regulae contrapunctus* are more involved. Rather than presenting both in columns, Copyist A here presents the hexachord tables one after the other. The language introducing the hard hexachord is identical to Berkeley 2, as is the table itself, although Copyist A has corrected several transcription errors. The language introducing the natural hexachord is slightly different, referring to A-la-mi-re *acutum* instead of *altus*, and also spelling out C as "Ce." From there, however, this table diverges from Berkeley 2, and several errors are left uncorrected. For B-mi, Copyist A includes the possibility of a twelfth (fa), which would ostensibly place an F-natural against a B-natural, creating a tritone. The copyist might have been thinking of B-fa, against which an F-natural would work nicely, but other likelier explanations for this error will be presented momentarily. Copyist A caught their mistake for G-sol-re-ut (here spelled us), lightly dotting out the erroneous fifth (ut) and properly including the fifth (re). But a similar issue occurs for A-la-mi-re, the last pitch included in Berkeley 2's table, where possible intervals are the fifth (re), third (fa), and unison (la). *Regulae contrapunctus* lists an extra sixth (ut), and Copyist A has left no indication that this was done in error.

The tables of consonances do not stop there, as they do in Berkeley 2. Rather, this table continues up another fifth to E-la, at which point Copyist A introduces yet another table, containing all of the consonances from G-sol-re-ut *alto* all the way to E-la. Whereas Berkeley 2 describes the possibility that this phenomenon could occur, *Regulae contrapunctus* actually spells out all such intervals, likely because it distinguishes reiterations above the octave as separate from their smaller intervallic counterparts.

Of all the works concordant with Berkeley 2, two contain similar tables of consonances: London 23220 and Catania D.39, and in the latter lies an intriguing connection with *Regulae contrapunctus*.[12] As Oliver Ellsworth carefully lays out, the Catania version of the tables of consonances is much longer and more detailed than that found in Berkeley 2 or London 23220. Rather than two columns each containing one hexachord, Catania offers seven different consecutive tables,

---

12 See Ellsworth, *The Berkeley Manuscript*, 262. Berkeley 2 is also concordant with Cambridge 410 II and Rome 1146, but neither contain such tables.

The Rules of Counterpoint 47

each called a *"deduccio."*[13] Each table begins on Gamma-ut and offers its own array of possible consonances, but none of them are described as belonging to a particular hexachord. Moreover, Catania permits intervals up to a twentieth.

The table representing the hard hexachord in Berkeley 2 and *Regulae contrapunctus* is the equivalent of Catania's *quarta deduccio*. The subsequent table representing the natural hexachord is also largely concordant across all three sources, and comprises Catania's *quinta deduccio*. However, both *Regulae contrapunctus* and Catania contain the aforementioned "error" of a twelfth (fa) above B-mi, and both add an extra sixth (ut) above the last A-la-mi-re given in Berkeley 2. But *Regulae contrapunctus* continues upward another five degrees, whereas neither Berkeley 2 nor Catania does. It does not match any of the material in Catania's *sexta deduccio*; however, it does match considerably with the *secuda deduccio*. That table begins on Gamma-ut and rises up an octave and a fifth to E-la-mi; with minor exceptions, the pitch names and their respective consonances are quite similar to those in the natural hexachord table beginning on G-sol-re-ut. From E-la-mi to A-la-mi-re, they are an exact match, including the "extra" sixth (ut) on that last pitch. If Copyist A were working from an exemplar, which is almost certain given the running corrections exhibited in these tables, it is easy to imagine that they could have accidentally skipped to an identical passage in a different section and copied its remainder by mistake.

The last table of consonances far surpasses the intervals described elsewhere in either Berkeley 2 or *Regulae contrapunctus*, for like Catania's *septima deduccio*, it includes intervals up to the twentieth. It does not appear that Copyist A is used to documenting such large intervals, since in several cases a Roman numeral "v" is written where it should be an "x." Copyist A mistakenly documents a sixth (vi) instead of a fifth (v) for ut above B-fa and B-mi, and for the same pitch an octave higher accidentally leaves out the unison (mi). Lastly, for the last E-la-mi, they have simply notated a "v" where in fact it should read "iii" for ut. Otherwise, though, this table is concordant with that in Catania. The section ends with a short sigh of relief: "Et est finis, Deo gracias."

Just as *De arte cantus* is a reworking of the *Libellus cantus mensurabilis* in close fashion to Berkeley 3 (and parts of 2), it appears that *Regulae contrapunctus* is a reworking of the *Ars contrapuncti*, very similar

---

13 Ibid., 256–262.

48 *The Rules of Counterpoint*

to Berkeley 2. More specifically, however, the contents of the tables of consonances more closely tie *Regulae contrapunctus* to the version in the later Catania D.39 manuscript. Given the strong similarities between Catania and both *De arte cantus* and *Regulae contrapunctus*, it would not be remiss to revisit Oliver Ellsworth's suggestion that the Catania copyist had access to "some lost fourteenth-century source other than Berkeley" and posit whether that source might have been shared—or even created—by Copyist A.[14]

3.3 *Nota quod novem sunt species contrapunctus videlicet ...*

The second Berkeley treatise and *Regulae contrapunctus* are far from the only extant works to gloss, condense, or expand upon the *Ars contrapuncti*. Another such work, found in several sources, is *Regule contrapuncti* attributed to Philipoctus de Caserta.[15] One source transmits two more counterpoint treatises also attributed to Philipoctus, respectively (and somewhat confusingly) called *Regula contrapunctus* and *Contrapunctum est fundamentum biscanti*.[16] The copies of these three treatises share several segments of text that Giuliano Di Bacco identifies as derivations of *Quilibet affectans* and *Cum notum sit*.[17] Given the disparities among them, it seems unlikely that all could have been authored by the same person, Philipoctus or otherwise. But Di Bacco points out that *Regule contrapuncti* and *Contrapunctum est fundamentum biscanti* share some unique textual concordances that are expanded elsewhere, including in Chicago 54.1, where the name Philipoctus Andree is given. Some of this material might therefore actually have originated with Philipoctus, perhaps in the later fourteenth century.

Di Bacco locates these textual segments not just in the *Ars contrapuncti* treatises and the works attributed to Philipoctus, but in a

---

14 Ellsworth, *The Berkeley Manuscript*, 14.

15 See the edition from Sev in Nigel Wilkins, "Some Notes on Philipoctus de Caserta" and the critical edition of all three sources in Pier Paolo Scattolin, "Le 'Regule Contrapuncti' Di Filippotto Da Caserta," in *L'Ars Nova Italiana Del Trecento*, ed. Agostino Ziino, vol. 5 (Certaldo: Centro di Studi sull'Ars nova italiana del Trecento, 1985), 231–44.

16 Rome B.83 and Sev contain *Regule contrapuncti*, while Florence 1119 contains all three treatises. Di Bacco mentions a variant treatise in Naples VIII.D.12 that could be considered a fourth version of *Regule contrapuncti*. See Di Bacco, "Original and Borrowed," 359.

17 Ibid., 357.

The Rules of Counterpoint   49

number of other related anonymous works. While he does not provide a complete list of such works, noting only that a number of them appear in manuscripts also containing the *Tractatus figurarum*, he does specify one work in Sev.[18] In a short anonymous treatise on folios 110r–v, Di Bacco identifies a version of his segment γ, the mandate to begin with a perfect consonance that occurs in both *Quilibet affectans* and *Cum notum sit*: "And note that we should begin and end all counterpoint with a perfect species."

The same treatise also includes a variant on segment β (β'), which expands *Cum notum sit*'s seven consonances to nine. This expansion, found in *Regulae contrapunctus* in Sev, in the third version of *Regule contrapuncti*, and in *Regula contrapunctus*, is read by Di Bacco as "a significant chronological shift in the evolution of this kind of rules."[19] This expanded statement on consonances acts as the incipit to the treatise *Nota quod novem*.

This short treatise, the first in unit XII and thus immediately preceding the second copy of *De arte cantus*, fills up only one side of folio 110; the verso contains another set of tables of consonances, laid out in a fashion different from the other tables heretofore discussed. Here, Copyist B has cleanly laid out a grid, such that each row contains three pitches and their respective consonances. Only in one place was there insufficient space, and Copyist B was forced to squeeze in two consonances into the same box. At the top of the page, the copyist provides the consonances for the hard hexachord, at the bottom those for the natural hexachord. All of these consonances are identical to Berkeley 2 and *Regulae contrapunctus*, although here the natural hexachord's pitches span only one octave. It too includes the interval of a twelfth (fa) for B, but as this B is not specified as mi, the same concerns about dissonances do not arise.

The treatise's contents are succinct. After the declaration that there are nine consonances in counterpoint, there is a list of precepts about contrapuntal motion, followed by a list of acceptable intervallic progressions. The work concludes with an intriguing description of how to create unnotated counterpoint by mentally transposing clefs: the singer should imagine a clef a fifth apart from the one in which

---

18 Ibid., Table 8/D, 360.
19 Ibid., 357. Some versions of the presumably earlier *Volentibus introduci* also include nine consonances.

50   *The Rules of Counterpoint*

the (presumably notated) music is written and proceed accordingly, though the copyist gives no further instructions.[20]

With the exception of this unique last section, all the material on this folio is derived from the first two *Ars contrapuncti* treatises. As Di Bacco noted, the opening statement about the proper number of consonances is his segment β', which stems from *Cum notum sit*. The statement that the penultimate interval in a given work should be imperfect also occurs in that treatise. Di Bacco's segment γ, that all counterpoint must begin and end with a perfect interval, is found in both *Quilibet affectans* and *Cum notum sit*. The list of intervallic progressions (here expanded to include composite intervals above the octave) and the preference for contrary motion stem from *Quilibet affectans*. The latter is Di Bacco's segment δ, although its presence in *Nota quod novem* went unremarked.[21]

Nota quod novem shares other small connections with *Regule contrapuncti*. After Di Bacco's segment γ, both *Nota quod novem* and *Regule contrapuncti* state that the penultimate interval of a composition should be imperfect, whereas this statement is found later on in *Cum notum sit*. The subsequent directive to avoid parallel perfect intervals is also much closer to *Regule contrapuncti* than to any other work. In *Regule contrapuncti*, examples of such intervals are given smallest to largest: two unisons, two fifths, two octaves, two twelfths, and so forth. *Nota quod novem* does the same, although after the unisons and fifths, it supplies a blanket "etc." for the rest. No examples are given in *Quilibet affectans*, while in *Cum notum sit* the interval examples are given in reverse order, from largest to smallest.

Much of this material is shared with *Regulae contrapunctus*, as well. In particular, both *Nota quod novem* and *Regulae contrapunctus* increase the number of acceptable consonances to nine; the *Regule contrapuncti* attributed to Philipoctus maintains the same seven consonances found in *Cum notum sit*. However, the *Regula contrapunctus* attributed to Philipoctus and found in Florence 1119 also describes

---

20 Given the instructions to mentally imagine a clef a fifth apart, it is tempting to read this section as referring to either a kind of parallel organum or the phenomenon of "fifthing," as laid out in Sarah Fuller, "Discant and the Theory of Fifthing," *Acta Musicologica* 50, no. 1/2 (1978): 241–275, yet the terminology described by Fuller is not present here. See also Cuthbert, "Palimpsests, Sketches, and Extracts," 75.

21 Interestingly, this statement advises that contrary motion should be used such that when the tenor descends, the contrapuntal line ascends, and vice versa. Of all of the sources in which Di Bacco located this segment, only the copy of *Regule contrapuncti* in Rome B.83 describes the tenor descending while the other voice ascends, and not the opposite.

The Rules of Counterpoint   51

nine consonances, as does the related *Regule contrapuncti secundum usum Regni Sicilie* mentioned by Di Bacco, found in Catania D.39. Whereas *Regulae contrapunctus* updates the *Ars contrapuncti* treatises in a manner reminiscent of the Catania version of Berkeley 2, *Nota quod novem* does so in a manner more akin to the counterpoint treatises associated with Philipoctus da Caserta.

To review, *Nota quod novem* opens the penultimate fascicle in Sev, and is followed immediately by the second copy of *De arte cantus*. The entirety of this fascicle—which also includes a copy of the *Tractatus figurarum*, other short anonymous works, an excerpt of Marchetto's *Lucidarium*, and the late fourteenth-century *Compendium artis motectorum Marchecti* by Petrus de Amalfia—appears to be in one hand (Copyist B). In this respect, this fascicle is yet another witness to the practice of contiguously copying the *Ars contrapuncti* and the *Libellus cantus mensurabilis*, here in reworked form, and as with a number of other sources, the *Tractatus figurarum* follows closely behind.

3.4 The Catalan notes

The *Ars contrapuncti* conglomerate consists of three distinct works, two of which present basic rules for two-part counterpoint, while the third provides an overview of the rhythmic note values and their relationships to each other within the four principal mensurations that developed in fourteenth-century France. Berkeley 2 is a version of this conglomerate; its first section updates and expands upon both *Quilibet affectans* and *Cum notum sit*, while its second section treats mensural music, although the new rhythmic note values presented and the expanded discussion of verbula go well beyond the fundamentals documented in *De diminutione contrapuncti*.

While quite similar to Berkeley 2, *Regulae contrapunctus* does not analogously add in a section on mensural music. But immediately after this treatise, Copyist A jots down three pages of notes, basic summaries of some fundamental principles of mensural music, and at its head is a brief discussion of mensuration.[22] Treatises that include such material usually begin by defining their terms: rhythmic note values and their shapes, perfection and imperfection, the four main mensurations, and the constituent parts of larger note values. Here, the copyist organizes the material in reverse of any typical presentation, relating smaller note values to the next larger ones, and then defining that

---

22 See Sachs, *Der Contrapunctus Im 14. Und 15. Jahrhundert*, 86.

52   The Rules of Counterpoint

mensural relationship, beginning with major prolation and ending not with tempus but with perfect and imperfect mode. While exceedingly brief, this portion of the notes was likely intended to supplement the rules of counterpoint in the preceding treatise.

These pages might plausibly represent Copyist A's own attempts to digest, distill, or practice the material they had just copied in the previous treatises. Mensurations are discussed in *De arte cantus*, while the rest of the notes cover topics found in *Regulae contrapunctus*, albeit in a different order and manner. For example, the copyist moves immediately from mensurations to the acceptable consonances in the hard hexachord, albeit without naming it as such. This information is identical to that found in Berkeley 2, *Regulae contrapunctus*, and *Regule contrapuncti*, which also includes tables of consonances.[23] Here, Copyist A does not lay out this information in a table or column, like the others, but rather describes each set of consonances in prose. For Gamma-ut, Copyist A writes: "First, in gamaut there are three consonances, that is to say, ut mi sol. Ut is an octave, mi is a tenth, sol is a twelfth." This requires the copyist to further clarify the differences between B-mi, which has three possible consonances (ut, mi, sol), and B-fa, which has only two (ut, sol).

The next section comprises the basic rules of counterpoint, most of which appear to be drawn from *Cum notum sit*. Here there are only seven species of counterpoint, not the nine found in *Regulae contrapunctus*.[24] This statement is followed by the rule to begin on a perfect interval; only *Cum notum sit* similarly instructs that a work should begin a perfect interval, and places the remainder of the directive to also end on a perfect interval much later in the treatise. The latter instruction is not included in the Catalan notes.

Copyist A also indicates that a larger perfect interval at the beginning is better than a smaller one: starting on a twelfth is preferred over a fifth, which is in turn preferred over a unison. The meaning of this statement is unclear, as no other counterpoint treatise makes such a claim. However, this statement is followed by the prohibition against parallel perfect intervals, which in both *Cum notum sit* and the notes is conditional: parallel intervals such as two twelfths, two octaves, two

---

23 Unlike any of the other tables heretofore described, the *Regule contrapuncti* attributed to Philipoctus names all of the consonances for each pitch from largest to smallest intervallically, such that those possible for A-re are la, fa, re, rather than re, fa, la as in other sources. See Wilkins, "Some Notes on Philipoctus de Caserta," 97–98.

24 In addition to *Cum notum sit*, the *Liber musicalium* attributed to Philippe de Vitry and several versions of both the *Regule contrapuncti* attributed to Philipoctus and the presumably earlier *Volentibus introduci* also name seven consonances.

The Rules of Counterpoint   53

fifths, or two unisons should be avoided, but one can descend from a larger perfect interval to a smaller one. Copyist A included this caveat, and they might have misunderstood it as applying to the beginning interval of a work. Intriguing here is the copyist's inclusion of an intermediary occurring between two parallel perfect intervals, otherwise found only in Berkeley 2 and *Regulae contrapunctus*.

The concluding material lays out the rules of consonance progressions, although in somewhat garbled fashion. Only one interval progression is specified, from smallest to largest, such that a unison moves to a third, then a fifth, a sixth, an octave, a tenth, and finally a twelfth, immediately after which Copyist A repeats that a sixth should always move to an octave. None of the other possibilities for the sixth given in *Quilibet affectans*, Berkeley 2, or *Regulae contrapunctus* are offered here. Parallel imperfect intervals are permissible, and perfect and imperfect intervals should be alternated, each progressing to one of its own best options. Here, more possibilities for intervallic progression are given, such that now a third could move to either a fifth or a unison, and a series of parallel sixths or a tenth could resolve to the octave. The notes end abruptly there, leaving out any instructions to end on a perfect interval or to use contrary or oblique motion. For the most part, then, these notes are derived from *Cum notum sit*, but they include the concept of the intermediary found elsewhere only in Berkeley 2 and in *Regulae contrapunctus*, though not closely enough to the latter to stem directly from it.

Gómez originally suggested that all three treatises represented class notes copied by a Catalan student.[25] The copyist repeatedly refers to "*lo maestre*," or "the teacher," leading Gómez to believe that these notes were taken down during or compiled after lectures by the magister Johannes Pipudi named earlier. The implication now is that Pipudi would have been lecturing from a version of *Cum notum sit*.

Given that there is a second copy of *De arte cantus* just a few short folios away, Gómez's idea that all three treatises were class notes, at least in a modern-day sense, must be revised. In fact, we now have four concordant versions of this reworking of the *Libellus*: the third Berkeley treatise, its later copy in Catania D.39, and the two copies of *De arte cantus* in Sev. Both copies of *De arte cantus* contain the additional mensural note values explained in Berkeley 2 and Catania D.39. The two versions of *De arte cantus* are close enough to each other to demand a common point of origin and, as each copy has its own unique transcription errors and evidence of corrections, such an exemplar or exemplars must have circulated in written form. *Regulae contrapunctus*

25 Gómez, "*De arte cantus ...*," 37.

54   *The Rules of Counterpoint*

is also concordant with both Berkeley 2 and Catania D.39, its tables of consonances in particular. This web of relationships similarly points to a written tradition shared by these heretofore unconnected sources.

In order for the two copies of *De arte cantus* to have so similarly integrated the section of Berkeley 2, the exemplar(s) must have already done so. Neither the Berkeley manuscript nor the version that was copied in Catania D.39 is therefore likely to be the exemplar itself. At some point, then, one of two things must have happened. The first possibility is that someone with access to Berkeley 2 and 3 relocated the section on mensural notation from Berkeley 2 and adapted this new, enhanced version of the *Libellus* into *De arte cantus*, which was then copied at least twice, as Sev attests. The second possibility is that *De arte cantus* is a witness to an expansion of the mensural note values found in the *Libellus* already in circulation prior to 1375, and the author-compiler of the Berkeley manuscript decided to add the section on the newer mensural note values to the end of the Berkeley 2 *Ars contrapuncti* gloss, rather than as an interpolation into Berkeley 3's version of the *Libellus*.[26]

If the former, then perhaps Pipudi himself, if he were the *"maestre"* behind the notes, *Regulae contrapunctus*, and *De arte cantus*, was responsible for this revision. He might also have assigned his students to prepare their own copies of important works, and for at least this Catalan student, those were *De arte cantus* and *Regulae contrapunctus*. This possibility would help to explain the sub-par quality of the Latin in this fascicle, as well as the transcription errors both corrected and unnoticed. There is no reason to exclude the second version of *De arte cantus* as a possible student copy; it too has a number of errors and corrections that evince working from a written exemplar, although the overall quality of its Latin is better. It could be that Copyist B of the later fascicle was also a student of Pipudi, although at a point where other versions of the *Ars contrapuncti* material and even more complicated mensural notation styles were being taught, explaining the presence of *Nota quod novem* and the copy of the *Tractatus figurarum*.

As stated earlier, there is no attribution to the Berkeley manuscript. The later Catania manuscript, however, names a Gostaltus or Goscalcus, and a person by the same name is associated with music theory in later fifteenth-century sources by Florentius de Faxolis and Cristóbal

---

26 See also the discussion and suggested stemma in Gregorio Bevilacqua, "Il Comentum super cantum di Roger Caperon: Introduzione ed edizione critica" (PhD diss., Università di Bologna, 2008), xlviff.

de Escobar.[27] Anna Maria Busse Berger observed that the earliest known theoretical presentation of ciphers placed vertically over one another to indicate tempus and prolation is found in allo Berkeley 3, and that such a mensuration sign is also found in *En nul estat*, a work by the composer Goscalch. Such a unique connection, in her opinion, lends credence to the hypothesis first made by Klaus-Jürgen Sachs that the composer Goscalch is the author-compiler of the Berkeley manuscript.[28] Such a hypothesis is within reason, given the evidence at hand. Several of the composers whose works are found in the Chantilly manuscript alongside *En nul estat* were in residence in papal Avignon in the late fourteenth century. Ursula Günther suggested that Goscalch was perhaps the papal chaplain Petrus de Godescalc, identified in papal records in 1387 and 1394. While she believed this identification would nullify his being the author of the Berkeley-Catania works, the dating alone is insufficient to discount Godescalc as the Goscalcus named in Catania.[29]

The colophon in Berkeley predates Godescalc's time in the papal chapel, and locates the manuscript in Paris. Petrus de Godescalc could, therefore, have compiled the works in Paris in 1375 and later brought them to Avignon, where they came to Pipudi's attention and were taught to the Catalan student and possibly also Copyist B. It is also possible that Godescalc's name became linked to these works only after becoming acquainted with Pipudi, and the attribution in Catania D.39 applies only to that version of the texts. Yet even if this Petrus de Godescalc were without doubt the author-compiler of the Berkeley manuscript, the attribution to Pipudi in Sev likely predates that to Goscalcus in Catania D.39. Pipudi is quite possibly, therefore,

---

27 Ellsworth, *The Berkeley Manuscript*, 13ff; see also Bonnie J. Blackburn and Leofranc Holford-Strevens, *Florentius de Faxolis: Book on Music* (Cambridge, MA: Harvard University Press, 2010), which supersedes Albert Seay, "The Liber Musices of Florentius de Faxolis," in *Musik Und Geschichte, Leo Schrade Zum Sechzigsten Geburtstag* (Cologne: Arno Volk, 1963), 71–95. A Goscalcus, author of a treatise that shares points of contact with Berkeley, is also cited by Cristóbal de Escobar in a 1496 treatise on plainchant. See Bonnie J. Blackburn, "Music Theory and Musical Thinking after 1450," in *Music as Concept and Practice in the Late Middle Ages*, eds. Reinhard Strohm and Bonnie J Blackburn (Oxford: Oxford University Press, 2001), 301–345 at 310; Santiago Galán Gómez, *La teoría de canto de órgano y contrapunto en el Renacimiento español: La Sumula de canto de organo de Domingo Marcos Durán como modelo*, Estudios Sobre Música Antigua (Madrid: Editorial Alpuerto, 2016).

28 Berger, "The Origin and Early History of Proportion Signs," 413.

29 Günther, "Goscalch," in *Grove Music Online*, 2001. https://doi.org/10.1093/gmo/9781561592630.article.11496

56 The Rules of Counterpoint

Table 6 Datable Attributions to Material Concordant with the Three Pipudi Treatises

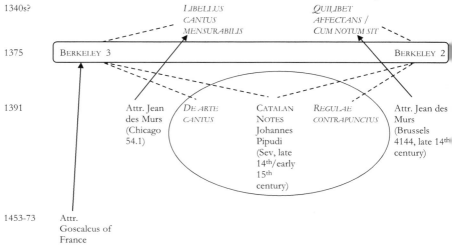

In this table, solid lines with arrows connect the source material with its earliest known attribution, often documented decades after the generally accepted date of composition. Dashed lines connect concordant sources. The three treatises related to Johannes Pipudi are enclosed in the central circle.

the earliest known person linked with certainty to this material, save possibly for Jean des Murs; the next securely datable source for the *Libellus*, and the earliest to carry an attribution to des Murs, is Chicago 54.1, dated to 1391.[30]

To date, the only witness to the existence of dominus magister Johannes Pipudi has been the Catalan Copyist A in Sev. No other sources, including those preserved by Copyist B, contain such a name. But papal records tell the tale of a person who might well be the mysterious theorist. The next chapter provides the first evidence for, and a conjectural biography of, one Johannes Pipardi, chaplain at Saint-Didier in Avignon and skilled in the art of music.

---

30 Karen Desmond has noted that segments of the *Libellus* are highly concordant with the second half of the treatise *Omni desideranti notitiam*, one of the texts comprising the *Ars nova* tradition; its two earliest sources are Chicago 54.1, which attributes the treatise to Philippe de Vitry, and Sev, which does not. See Karen Desmond, "Omni Desideranti Notitiam: A Music Theory Text from the Fourteenth Century," arsmusicae.org, 2011, http://arsmusicae.org/home.xml; "Texts in Play: The Ars Nova and Its Hypertexts," *Musica Disciplina* 57 (2012): 81–153; "Jean Des Murs and the Three Libelli on Music in BnF Lat. 7378A: A Preliminary Report," *Erudition and the Republic of Letters* 4, no. 1 (January 23, 2019): 40–63, esp. the helpful chart on p. 62.

4 Introducing Johannes Pipardi

What little we have known to date about the theorist associated with the treatises discussed in Chapter 3 has come directly from the treatises themselves. The *Regulae contrapunctus* in the eleventh fascicle cites a certain magister Johannes Pipudi, "*canonicus Sancti Desiderii avinionensis*" (Figure 4); later in that treatise, Copyist A also refers to him as "dominus magister Johannes." Outside of that attribution, however, this name is not mentioned in any other extant theoretical literature, nor could I locate anyone named Pipudi, let alone this particular Johannes, in any other Western historical documents. Moreover, "Pipudi" did not appear to be any sort of toponym, patronym, or nickname.

The trail for the mysterious magister could have ended there. But Copyist A did pass on a contextual clue for Pipudi: the name of the church in Avignon with which he was apparently affiliated. Given the dates proposed for the treatises in Chapter 3, it seemed likely that Pipudi could have been in Avignon during the last quarter of the fourteenth century, and therefore might appear in surviving records from the Avignonese popes.

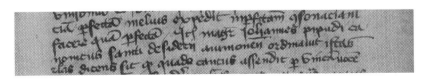

Figure 4 Statement of attribution to magister Johannes Pipudi; Biblioteca Capitular Colombina, sign. 5-2-25, f. 105r, © Cabildo Catedral de Sevilla.

58 *Introducing Johannes Pipardi*

In the supplications to the Avignonese Pope Clement VII, dated from November 24–28, 1378, item 1474 reads[1]:

> *Item Johanni Pipardi, presbytero Cameracensis diocesis, de beneficio ecclesiastico cum cura vel sine cura, spectante communiter vel divisim ad collationem etc. abbatis et conventus monasterii Sancti Petri Lobiensis, ordinis sancti Benedicti, dicte diocesis, providere dignemini. Non obstante quod quondam perpetuam capellaniam sacerdotalem in ecclesia collegiate Sancti Desiderii Avinionensis obtineat. Cum clausulis ut supra.*

May you also deign to provide for Johannes Pipardi, priest of the diocese of Cambrai, to hold the ecclesiastical benefice (with or without residence), considering appointment etc. either jointly or separately, of the abbot and community of the monastery of St. Peter of Lobbes of the order of St. Benedict in the aforementioned diocese, notwithstanding that he maintains a certain perpetual priestly chaplaincy in the collegiate church of Saint-Didier in Avignon. With closing statements as above.[2]

This Johannes Pipardi is called neither magister nor dominus, as in the treatises, nor is he called a canon. Rather, he is described as a priest at the collegiate church of Saint-Didier in Avignon, the very church where Sev tells us the theorist Pipudi held his canonry. "Pipardi" is strikingly similar to "Pipudi"; given Copyist A's flawed Latin and poor handwriting, it is not hard to imagine that a central "-ar-" might have been written down as a "-u-."

On its own, this record put forth a likely candidate for the otherwise unknown Johannes Pipudi. A second, earlier supplication for Johannes Pipardi, however, strengthens an identification as the Sev theorist.[3] In the July 1375 records for Pope Gregory XI, item 3276 reads:[4]

---

1 Karl Hanquet, ed., *Suppliques de Clément VII (1378–1379): Textes et analyses*, vol. 1, Analecta Vaticano-Belgica, Documents relatifs aux anciens diocèses de Cambrai, Liège, Thérouanne et Tournai, vol. 8 (Rome: Institut historique belge de Rome, 1924), 28.

2 I thank Kerry McCarthy for her assistance on the translations of these two supplications.

3 I am grateful to Andrew Hicks for bringing this supplication to my initial attention.

4 Camille Tihon, *Lettres de Grégoire XI (1371–1378): Textes et analyses*, Analecta Vaticano-Belgica, Documents relatifs aux anciens diocèses de Cambrai, Liège, Thérouanne et Tournai, vol. 3 (Bruxelles: Institut historique belge de Rome, 1964), 130. The documentation here that Pipardi was from Cambrai supersedes my earlier speculation that "Pipudi" might have been of Italian origin; see Cook, "Theoretical Treatments …"

Introducing Johannes Pipardi 59

Priori S. Orientii Auxitani et decano S. Petri Avinionensis ac preposito S. Wilheadi Brememsis ecclesiarum mandatur quatenus Johanni Pipardi, presbitero Cameracensis diocesis, qui, ut asseritur, in arte musice peritus existit, conferant, consideratione Johannis, episcopi Sabinensis, pro ipso Johanne Pipardi familiari suo supplicantis, perpetuam capellanium S. Desiderii Avinionensis, vacantem per obitum Guillelmi Blaquerii qui in civitate Avinionensi diem clausit extremum; non obstante quod dictus Johannes beneficium ecclesiasticum cum cura vel sine cura ad collationem thesaurarii ecclesie Cameracensis auctoritate litterarum presentis pape in forma pauperum se asserit expectare; que littere case erunt et irrite.

It is commanded to the prior of St. Orens in Auch, and to the dean of St. Peter in Avignon, and to the provost of St. Willehad in Bremen, that they confer the perpetual chaplaincy of Saint-Didier in Avignon (made vacant by the death of Guillaume Blaquerius, who finished his final day in the city of Avignon) on Johannes Pipardi, a priest of the diocese of Cambrai, who, as it is asserted, proves to be skillful in the art of music; that they confer this chaplaincy on him by the consideration of Johannes, bishop of Sabina, who is making the supplication for the same Johannes Pipardi, his familiar; notwithstanding that the said Johannes asserts that he awaits an ecclesiastical benefice in the manner of poor men with pastoral care or without pastoral care for the collation of the treasury of the church of Cambrai by the authority of a letter of the present pope, a letter which will be useless and invalid.

Just over three years prior to the first supplication, it appears that Johannes, Bishop of Sabina, put forth his familiar Johannes Pipardi for a perpetual chaplaincy. That this proposed chaplaincy was at Saint-Didier in Avignon links the Pipardi in this supplication with the one named in the later record. That this Pipardi is described as "skillful in the art of music" leaves little doubt that he is also the dominus magister Johannes Pipudi, canon at Saint-Didier in Avignon, cited in the Sev manuscript.

This discovery is significant on several fronts. As I will detail in the remainder of this chapter, the new biographical information gleaned from the supplication records points to Johannes Pipardi, as he shall now be called, as someone known for his skill in music. As few people are so described in papal supplications, such a detail requires further inquiry. The dates of the two supplications not only allow a fuller, if still speculative, chronology for Pipardi, but they also shed light onto the possible datings for *De arte cantus*, *Regulae contrapunctus*, and the Catalan notes. Lastly, the 1375 supplication identifies Pipardi

60 *Introducing Johannes Pipardi*

as a familiar in the household of Johannes, Bishop of Sabina. This Johannes is Johannes de Blandiac—in his native French, Jean de Blauzac—one of the most important cardinals under Pope Gregory XI. Locating Pipardi in the household of such an elite member of the papal administration sheds light on networks of patronage and of the transmission of musical knowledge.

4.1 *"In arte musice peritus"*

Even if all that were known of Johannes Pipardi was that he was considered "skillful in the art of music," he would still be of great interest, for a search of extant papal records for the bulk of the fourteenth century reveals that he is one of an extremely small number of people so described.

A priest in the Spanish diocese of Cuenca, one Dominico Fernandi, reserved a canonry and prebend at the church of Badajoz in a 1370 letter to Pope Urban V.[5] In this supplication, he is described as being proficient in canon law, as well as grammar, logic, and music. While music is specifically mentioned, this might have been more to highlight his training in the liberal arts than to signal any particular musical proficiency.

> Dominico Fernandi, *cler. Conchen. dioc., qui in jure can. scolaris existit ac nullum benef. adhuc assecutus existit et per magna tempora tam studendo quam legendo in grammatica et logica et etiam in arte musice laboravit, canonicatus et prebenda eccl. Pacen. ac quoddam prestimonium in eccl. s. Marie de Cafra, Pacen. dioc. (quorum fructus: 40 l.t. secundum communem extimationem), vacat. per provisionem dudum Fernando Fernandi de canonicatu eccl. Elboren. cum reserv. prebende, reservantur.*
>
> For Dominico Fernandi, priest of the diocese of Cuenca, who is a scholar in canon law and has not yet pursued a benefice, and has worked for a long time both studying and reading in grammar and logic, and also in the art of music, a canon and prebend at the church of Badajoz in Extremadura and also a certain priestly fund in the church of Santa María of Zafra in the diocese of Badajoz (the profit of which: 40 l.t. according to general opinion) are reserved, made vacant by means of the recent provision of a canonry and reserved prebend at the church of Évora to Fernando Fernandi.

---

5 Michel Hayez and Anne-Marie Hayez, *Urbain V: Lettres Communes: Analysées d'après Les Registres Edits d'Avignon*, vol. 9 (Rome: École Française de Rome, 1983), 74.

Introducing Johannes Pipardi 61

A similar situation appears in a supplication on behalf of a priest named Robertus de Nathoy.[6] Robertus was a familiar and scribe in the chancellery of Cardinal Gui de Boulogne in 1361; from 1362 to 1364, he was also part of Gui's chapel, and in 1366 he obtained a canonry and prebend in Thérouanne. He is described in this supplication, dated November 1362, as an expert in both grammar and music, though what that means or precisely how he might have used those talents in Gui's household remains unclear.

> *Item* Roberto du Nathoy, *presbitero, in grammatica et musica bene experto, Morinensis diocesis, capellano antiquo dicti cardinalis, de canonicatu sub expectatione prebende ecclesie Morinensis dignemini providere, non obstante quod canonicatum et prebendam ecclesie S. Gaugerici Cameracensis et parrochialem ecclesiam de Edera ac cappellaniam perpetuam de Houvigneul, Parisiensis et dicte Morinensis diocesis, obtinet; que omnia preter canonicatum et prebendam S. Gaugerici paratus est dimittere.*

> Likewise, may you deign to provide a canonicate with the expectation of a prebend in the church of Thérouanne for Robertus du Nathoy, priest, quite expert in grammar and music, of the diocese of Thérouanne, an old chaplain of the aforementioned cardinal, notwithstanding the fact that he maintains a canonicate and prebend at the church of St. Gaugericus of Cambrai and a parrochial church at Edera and a perpetual chaplaincy at Houvigneul, Paris and the aforementioned diocese of Thérouanne; and he is willing to give up all except for the canonicate and prebend at St. Gaugericus.

Musical skill is described in greater detail in the case of Egidius de Flagiaco. In 1336, he received a canonry with an expectation of a prebend at the church of St. Peter in St. Omer in the diocese of Thérouanne. In this document, he too is described as *"in arte musicæ perito."* Unlike Pipardi, though, his expertise is clarified: he is the teacher of the choirboys in the royal chapel at Paris.[7]

---

6 Alphonse Fierens, *Suppliques d'Urbain V (1362–1370): Textes et Analyses* (Rome: M. Bretschneider, 1914), 29.

7 J. M. Vidal, *Benoit XII (1334–1342): lettres communes analysées d'après les registres dits D'Avignon et due Vatican,* vol. 1 (Paris: A. Fontemoing, 1903), 267. See also Alphonse Fierens, *Lettres de Benoit XII (1334–1342): Textes et Analyses* (Rome: M. Bretschneider, 1910), 104–105.

62 Introducing Johannes Pipardi

In ecc. s. Petri Arien., Morinen. di., Ægidio de Flagiaco, in arte musicæ perito, mag. puerorum capellæ regalis Parisien., qui perpet. capellanias de Athies, et de Villaribus Carbonelli, ac s. Mariæ de Soysiaco supra Sequanam, Noviomen. et Parisien. di., dim. tenetur.
[A canon with expectation of a prebend is conferred] in the church of St. Peter of Ariensis, of the diocese of Thérouanne, on Egidius de Flagiaco, skilled in the art of music, *magister puerorum* of the royal chapel in Paris, who has dismissed his perpetual chaplaincy at Athies and at Villaribus Carbonelli and Blessed Marie of Soysiaco supra Secanam, of the dioceses of Noyon and Paris.

Suzanne Clercx and Richard Hoppin suggested this Egidius as a candidate for the author of the short treatise *De modo componendi tenores motetorum*.[8] This work circulated alongside five versions of the *Tractatus figurarum* and, in several of their manuscript sources, one or both of these two treatises was attributed to an Egidius de Murino.[9] As the Latin *Morinensis* or *Morinum* refers to Thérouanne, Clercx and Hoppin discussed the merits of various people named Egidius associated with that area as possible authors of the short treatise. However, since they believed it to share an author with the late fourteenth-century *Tractatus figurarum*, they rejected Egidius de Flagiaco due to the chronological gap between that treatise and the papal record of 1336.

Although Gilbert Reaney later reassessed the biography of Egidius de Murino and discussed several of Clercx's and Hoppin's candidates, he did not mention Egidius de Flagiaco.[10] Alice Clark, however, renewed attention on him in her 1996 dissertation.[11] She points out

---

8 Richard Hoppin and Suzanne Clercx, "Notes biographiques sur quelques musiciens français du XIVe siècle," in *Les Colloques de Wegimont II-1955: L'Ars Nova: Recueil d'études sur la musique du XIVe siècle*, Bibliothèque de la Faculté de Philosophie et Lettres de l'Université de Liège, vol. 149 (Paris: Societé d'Èdition «Les Belles Lettres», 1959), 63–92. The treatise is fully transcribed in Edmond de Coussemaker, *Scriptorum de Musica Medii Ævi* vol. 3 and partially in Daniel Leech-Wilkinson, *Compositional Techniques in the Four-Part Isorhythmic Motets of Philippe de Vitry and His Contemporaries.*, 2 vols., Outstanding Dissertations in Music from British Universities (New York: Garland, 1989).

9 London 4909, Rome 5321, Siena, Wash J6. For a discussion of the authorship of the *Tractatus figurarum*, see Schreur, *Tractatus figurarum*.

10 Gilbert Reaney, "Egidius [Aegidius] de Murino [Morino]," *Grove Music Online*, 2001, https://doi.org/10.1093/gmo/9781561592630.article.08612

11 Clark, "*Concordare cum Materia*: The Tenor in the Fourteenth-Century Motet," PhD diss., Princeton University, 1996.

Introducing Johannes Pipardi 63

that once the attribution of Egidius de Murino is uncoupled from the *Tractatus figurarum*, there is no compelling reason to assume that that treatise shares an author with *De modo componendi tenores motetorum* or that they must be similarly dated. *De modo componendi tenores motetorum* "deals only with the most basic steps for writing a motet," in Clark's words, and might have been written considerably earlier than the *Tractatus figurarum*.[12] If *De modo componendi tenores motetorum* were to be shifted decades earlier, Clark suggests, then its author Egidius de Murino could after all be Egidius de Flagiaco, known for his skill in music. The papal record might actually provide more contextual support for this attribution, which Clercx and Hoppin mention but Clark does not; it specifically labels Egidius de Flagiaco as a teacher of choirboys, and the author of *De modo componendi tenores motetorum* describes the treatise as being "for the teaching of children."[13] It is worth considering, then, that the treatise was written by Egidius de Flagiaco of Thérouanne specifically for pedagogical use in the Parisian royal chapel, perhaps in the 1330s or 1340s.

The papal record for Egidius de Flagiaco is thus the closest relative to the supplication mentioning Johannes Pipardi, for the precision of its wording and perhaps also for its implications. Since Egidius was known to be a teacher, "skillful in the art of music" might suggest some sort of pedagogical practice. If so, then Pipardi might already have been teaching music prior to 1375, and the supplication thus documented his abilities in that area.

The reference to Pipardi as a magister in Sev potentially points to activities as a teacher, as well. The title of magister was awarded to someone who had completed a master's degree at a university, generally in theology or arts; this degree not only imbued a person with the formal right to give lectures on matters in their field, but at some institutions it obligated that person to do so for a period after its conferral.[14] However, the title might have been used by people who were exceptional in their field, regardless of whether they had formally studied at university; it might also have been used by those who wished to confer upon themselves the kind of social standing and intellectual prestige the title carried without having ever obtained a master's degree.[15] While no

---

12 Clark, 5.

13 Clark, 5; Hoppin and Clercx, 85. See Leech-Wilkinson, I.22: "*Sed que scripta sunt superius ad doctrinam parvulorum scriptum sunt.*"

14 Walter Rüegg, "Themes," in *Universities in the Middle Ages*, ed. Hilde de Ridder-Symoens (Cambridge: Cambridge University Press, 2003), 3–34, 21.

15 Jacques Verger, "Teachers," in *Universities in the Middle Ages*, ed. Hilde de Ridder-Symoens (Cambridge: Cambridge University Press, 2003), 144–168,

64   *Introducing Johannes Pipardi*

records have yet been located that identify Pipardi as either a university student or professor, it is possible that he did in fact obtain a master's degree and teach in some official capacity, which would support Maria del Carmen Gómez's suggestion that the treatises mentioning Pipardi in Sev were class notes copied by his Catalan student.[16] Yet, following Joseph Dyer's work on theorist Hélie Salomon, it is unlikely that Pipardi would have had a master's degree by 1375, or even by 1378, for such an official title or rank would have been mentioned in those supplications alongside his status as a familiar.[17]

He could, however, have been teaching choirboys in a manner similar to Egidius, or performing some other sort of pedagogical function within the Bishop of Sabina's household, and the 1375 supplication recognized this skill. The title of magister in Sev could thus apply to a degree earned later, after Pipardi left the Bishop's household, or to his accumulated expertise in music as recognized at Saint-Didier. He could also have been a magister capellae at that church, a position that would often have carried teaching responsibilities.

Another interpretation is that, if Egidius were the theorist behind *De modo componendi tenores motetorum*, "skillful in the art of music" might point to theoretical expertise. In this case, the phrase proves to be even more significant, for it could indicate that Pipardi was already known as a theorist by 1375. As I laid out in the previous chapter, the closest relatives to *De arte cantus* and *Regulae contrapunctus* are the second and third treatises of the Berkeley Manuscript, themselves versions of the *Libellus cantus mensurabilis* and *Ars contrapuncti*, which are frequently attributed to Jean des Murs. The colophon at the end of Berkeley 3 states that it was compiled in Paris in 1375. While it is improbable that the Sev treatises were copied prior to 1375, due to Copyist A's description of Pipardi as a dominus and canon (points I will explain further below), the material was almost certainly in circulation before these earliest copies in Sev and Berkeley were made. It is possible, therefore, that Pipardi's expertise in the kinds of mensural theory and counterpoint documented in Sev was already sufficient enough to earn him praise in the 1375 supplication.

144–145; Olga Weijers, *Terminologie des Universités Au XIIIe Siècle*, Lessico Intellettuale Europeo 39 (Rome: Ed. dell'Ateneo, 1987), 133ff.

16 Gómez, "*De arte cantus …*," 37.

17 Joseph Dyer, *The Scientia Artis Musice of Hélie Salomon: Teaching Music in the Late Thirteenth Century: Latin Text with English Translation and Commentary* (New York: Routledge, 2018), 3.

4.2 The case of *Alma polis religio/Axe poli cum artica*

I first presented my research on Johannes "Pipudi" and *De arte cantus* at the 2013 Medieval-Renaissance music conference in Barcelona. During the ensuing discussion, Margaret Bent raised an interesting question: whether this magister Johannes Pipudi, "*canonicus sancti desiderii*," could perhaps be the "Johannes Desiderii" named in the motet *Alma polis religio/Axe poli cum artica* found in Chantilly.

With this question, Bent echoed the earlier work of Suzanne Clercx and Richard Hoppin; in their report on the biographies of fourteenth-century French musicians, they state outright that the Johannes Desiderii of the motet was the theorist in Sev: "Tel Johannes Desiderii, connu, d'autre part, par la rédaction d'un traité (Conservé à Séville, *Bibl. Colombina*, 5.2.25)."[18] However, they state neither where in the manuscript he is cited, nor that the name given in Sev is Johannes Pipudi, not Johannes Desiderii. Instead, they identify the Johannes Desiderii of the motet, and in their opinion of Sev, as a person named Johannes Desiderii de Latines. He first appears in a supplication to the Avignonese Pope Clement VII in 1378, where he is described as a priest of the diocese of Liège and familiar of Cardinal Gilles de Montaigu of Thérouanne. He reappears in 1410 as a canon and cantor at the church of Notre Dame de Dinant. Clercx and Hoppin also connect this individual to his likely father, a Désiré de Latines, and another potential relative, a Henri Desiderii de Latines (d. 1423) who was a composer, a singer in the chapel of the Roman Pope Boniface IX in Rome, and a canon and singer at the collegiate church of St. Paul in Liège.[19]

It is unlikely that all three could be the same person, for at no point has Johannes Pipudi/Pipardi been referred to as either "de Latines" or "Desiderii." Johannes Desiderii de Latines was named after his father, Désiré, according to Clercx and Hoppin, whereas Pipardi held a position at Saint-Didier in Avignon and his familial ties are unknown. Johannes Desiderii de Latines was a priest of the diocese of Liège, Pipardi a priest from the diocese of Cambrai. Most tellingly, in 1378 Johannes Desiderii de Latines was in the household of Cardinal Gilles de Montaigu, while in the 1378 supplication, Pipardi is not listed as belonging to anyone's household, though he had recently worked for Cardinal Johannes de Blauzac. If the Johannes Desiderii of the motet

---

18 Hoppin and Clercx, 81.
19 Eugeen Schreurs, "Music at the Collegiate Church of Tongeren and the School of Liège in the Late Middle Ages," *Revista de Musicologia* 16, no. 4 (1993): 2476–2494 at 2491.

66 *Introducing Johannes Pipardi*

is in fact Johannes Desiderii de Latines, then neither is likely to also be the theorist Johannes Pipardi.

Johannes Desiderii de Latines was apparently a musician, since he is described as a cantor in the inventory of records for Sainte-Croix of Liège as cited by Clercx and Hoppin. Still, that is not definitive proof that he is the musician mentioned in the motet. The triplum, in particular, singles out the twenty people mentioned in the motet as Augustinian brothers—*fratrum sancti augustini*.[20] Johannes Desiderii de Latines is not affiliated with the Augustinian brotherhood in the records cited above, and although the absence of evidence is not the evidence of absence, an Augustinian connection would give much more weight to Clercx's and Hoppin's identification.

Without a solid link between the Johannes Desiderii of the motet and Johannes Desiderii de Latines, is it possible to reconsider Johannes Pipardi as the musician in *Alma polis*? He would, in many ways, fit quite nicely amongst the others mentioned. The list of musicians in the triplum begins with a "P. de Santo Dionisio," who may very well be the Petrus de Sancto Dionysio responsible for the *Tractatus de Musica*, a gloss of and commentary on Jean des Murs's *Notitia artis musicae*.[21] Immediately after this person are named "Johannes Foreastarii *cum* Nicholao Biohomui, *professores teorici camena*."[22] Whomever these two musicians were, they apparently taught or were known for their expertise in music theory. In this same stanza, "J. Strutevilla, Augustinus de Florentia, [and] Johannes Desiderii" are also mentioned. The next stanza continues the list of musicians: "unioculus Teobaldus, Taxinus de Parisius, [and] Ydrolanus modulator Ciprianus," who have apparently drunk from the fountain of Orpheus. While it seems that only Johannes Foreastarii and Nicholao Biohomui are specifically described as experts in music theory, it is possible that all of the people cited in this stanza, including Johannes Desiderii, are grouped

---

20 Gilbert Reaney, "The Manuscript Chantilly, Musée Condé 1047," *Musica Disciplina* 8 (1954): 59–113 at p. 66; see also Günther, ed., *The Motets of the Manuscripts Chantilly*.

21 Ulrich Michels, *Notitia Artis Musicae, et Compendium Musicae Practicae. Petrus de Sancto Dionysio: Tractatvs de Mvsica.* ([Dallas?]: American Institute of Musicology, 1972); Renata Pieragostini, "Augustinian Networks and the Chicago Theory Manuscript," *Plainsong and Medieval Music* 22, no. 1 (2013): 65–85.

22 The manuscript reads "biohomui," yet Ursula Günther transcribes "bichomui," an emendation that, as Kerry McCarthy pointed out in private conversation (2020), would correct the scansion problem the extra syllable creates. See Günther, ed., *The Motets of the Manuscripts Chantilly*, XLV. I have retained the manuscript reading here.

Introducing Johannes Pipardi 67

together due to some shared prowess in or knowledge of theory. Furthermore, the author of the triplum states that each person described in this motet is a good singer, an excellent musician, and accomplished in both *neuma* and worldly harmonies. Since "*neuma*" can connote not just sung melody but also the system of notation by which it is documented, these musicians are potentially also musically literate.[23] For these reasons, they are labeled *peritos*, skilled in music, as Pipardi is described in the 1375 supplication.

An identification of the Johannes Desiderii in the motet as Johannes Pipardi, placing him in a cohort of other musicians and theorists that likely includes his predecessor Petrus de Sancto Dionysio, a (fellow) glosser of Jean des Murs, is certainly enticing. However, the problem presented earlier for Johannes Desiderii des Latines remains in place for Johannes Pipardi, for the latter is not known to have been an Augustinian brother either. Rather, in the 1378 supplication, Pipardi requests a benefice at St. Peter of Lobbes, a Benedictine monastery. It is unclear whether a person affiliated with the Augustines would have been eligible for such a benefice, although it is possible that Pipardi could have switched allegiances at some point.[24] For the moment, then, it would seem that Johannes Pipardi, *canonicus sancti desiderii*, can neither be conclusively counted nor discounted as one of the musicians extolled in *Alma polis religio/Axe poli cum artica*.

4.3 In the household of Jean de Blauzac

As the fourteenth century progressed, cardinals' households swelled in size and stature. By the 1370s, they rivaled that of the Pope himself. With the rise in both their prestige and their power, cardinals required a household staff that could handle the concomitant increase in personal, administrative, and ecclesiastical responsibilities. The waves of anti-papal sentiment that washed over Western Europe by mid-century, attacking the curia on charges of nepotism, greed, and other spiritual abuses, certainly also included the "Princes of the Church."

---

23 See Charles Atkinson, '*De accentibus toni oritur nota quae dicitur neuma*: Prosodic Accents, the Accent Theory, and the Paleofrankish Script', in *Essays on Medieval Music: In Honor of David G. Hughes*, ed. Graeme Boone (Cambridge, MA: Harvard University Dept. of Music, 1995), 17–42; Atkinson, private communication, 2020.

24 I thank Margaret Bent for drawing my attention to the slightly later composer Beltrame Feragut, who might have changed his allegiance from one brotherhood to another; personal communication, 2019.

68 *Introducing Johannes Pipardi*

After electing Pope Urban VI in 1378, the cardinals were soon distressed to find that he sympathized with the reformers, as immediately after his election he moved to curtail their lavish lifestyles. Shortly thereafter, those cardinals fled Rome, deposing Urban and electing Clement VII, thus beginning the Papal Schism. Not every cardinal took part in this act of rebellion, however; when Pope Gregory XI began to shift the Curia back to Rome in 1376, he left behind in Avignon a coterie of trusted officials to govern in his stead. At their head, he installed Cardinal-Bishop Johannes de Blandiac, known in French as Jean de Blauzac—the same Johannes listed in the papal supplications as the patron of Johannes Pipardi.

Jean de Blauzac was born in Uzés, in southern France, approximately forty-three kilometers to the west of Avignon, and it appears he never really left the broader area. Little is known about his early years, other than his uncle was Cardinal Bertrand de Deaulx. He was a *doctor utriusque juris*—a doctor of both canon and civil law. By the 1340s, he was a canon at the Cathedral of Aix in Aix-en-Provence, and also a chaplain to Clement VI in Avignon. On September 17, 1348, he was elected Bishop of Nîmes; Pope Innocent VI then elevated him to Cardinal-Priest of San Marco on September 17, 1361. Under Pope Urban V, de Blauzac's expertise in law and, presumably, his administrative acumen were put to good use, as he was charged with reforming the statutes of the University of Paris in 1366.[25] Gregory XI created him Cardinal-Bishop of Sabina in 1372, and when the Pope decided to return the papacy to Rome, he combined the positions of Vicar-General and Rector, leaving de Blauzac in charge of both Papal Avignon and the Comtat Venaissin. De Blauzac remained in these positions of authority for three years, until Clement VII arrived in June 1379, but died shortly afterward, on July 6, and was buried two days later at the church of Saint-Didier.

De Blauzac began to cultivate a household of his own while Bishop of Nîmes; his earliest familiar known to date was with him by 1355. From that point to his death in 1379, fifty-one other members of his household appear in papal records, identified by phrases such as *"dilecto suo," "familiari suo,"* and so forth. He submitted supplications

---

25 Although it is not clear from which university he obtained his degrees, the most likely university for such a course of study, according to Pamela Starr, would have been the University of Paris. His later charge to reform its statutes might be a further link to his having studied there. Starr, personal communication, 2018. His uncle, Cardinal Bertrand de Deaulx, had an affiliation with the University of Montpellier, which remains another possibility.

Introducing Johannes Pipardi 69

for another sixteen people who were not so explicitly named but who might also have been familiars. Yet another seven people can be identified as relatives, and they too might have been part of his household (Appendix 1).

Among these familiars are scribes, notaries, treasurers, chamberlains, and members of the chapel. Certainly those with any ecclesiastical or liturgical duties would have had some basic musical training, but only a few in his household were specifically described as musicians. Henricus Poneti (de Bossuto), for example, was a *servitor, subdiaconus,* and *familiaris* in Clement VII's papal chapel by November 1378, where he was joined by better-known composers such as Matheus de Sancto Johanne.[26] His career is therefore indicative of someone with some musical skill. On the other hand, Johannes Butor was magister capellae for de Blauzac toward the Cardinal's last years, and later became part of the household of the cardinal of Bretagne, but his duties there are unclear. One figure in de Blauzac's household is unambiguously described as a singer: Arnoldo Jocalis is called both a familiar and a cantor in his chapel. Unfortunately, only a single record exists for this person, and so there is little else we can speculate about either his musical training or activities. And while the name Hugo Moteti certainly appears to have musical implications, no indication of musicality has yet arisen in records.

Jean de Blauzac has appeared in musicological literature primarily for his patronage of two other musicians of the late fourteenth century: Richardus de Bozonville and Johannes de Bosco. Andrew Tomasello provides a thorough background for both Richardus and Johannes in his volume on music in papal Avignon.[27] Richardus, papal mag-

---

26 Ursula Günther, "Zur Biographie Einiger Komponisten Der Ars Subtilior," *Archiv Für Musikwissenschaft* 21, no. 3/4 (January 1, 1964): 172–199; Andrew Tomasello, *Music and Ritual at Papal Avignon, 1309–1403*, Studies in Musicology, no. 75 (Ann Arbor, MI: UMI Research Press, 1983), 63–64; Christopher Reynolds, "Musical Careers, Ecclesiastical Benefices, and the Example of Johannes Brunet," *Journal of the American Musicological Society* 37, no. 1 (Spring 1984): 49–97; Giuliano Di Bacco, "Documenti Vaticani per la Storia della Musica durante il Grande Scisma (1378–1417)," *Quaderni storici*, Storia e Musica: Fonti, consumi e committenze,32, no. 95(2) (August 1997): 361–368; Andrew Wathey, "The Peace of 1360–1369 and Anglo-French Musical Relations," *Early Music History* 9 (January 1, 1990): 129–174; see also Margaret Bent, "Mayshuet and the *Deo Gratias* Motets in the Old Hall Manuscript," in *Beredte Musik. Konversationen Zum 80. Geburtstag von Wulf Arlt.*, eds. Martin Kirnbauer, Schola Cantorum Basiliensis Scripta 8 (Basel: Schwabe, 2019), 11–28.

27 Tomasello, *Music and Ritual at Papal Avignon, 1309–1403*. I will be revisiting the biography of Johannes de Bosco in a forthcoming publication.

70   *Introducing Johannes Pipardi*

ister capellae, later became provost of the Cathedral of Apt (where he might have played a role in the compilation or copying of the Apt manuscript), and was the most highly prebended papal musician of his day. Moreover, several other familiars joined the households of other Cardinals, others that of the Pope himself, and still others obtained a number of highly favored canonries or other prestigious positions in religious institutions across Western Europe. Some even went to school, obtaining bachelor's and master's degrees in art, theology, and law.

It seems that the personal household of Cardinal-Bishop Jean de Blauzac was a prestigious and potentially fruitful place to be. While Johannes Pipardi seems not to have joined the papal chapel, perhaps due to lowly beginnings—the first supplication describes him looking for a position in the diocese of Cambrai *"in forma pauperum"*—a person of the musical skill he is stated to have had could have carved out a fine living for himself in another religious establishment, such as a collegiate church like Saint-Didier.

De Blauzac and his natural family already had strong ties to the church of Saint-Didier. His uncle, Cardinal Bertrand de Deaulx, died in October of 1355, and allotted funds in his will to build the church as his future burial place. The church took over three years to build; it was consecrated on September 20, 1359, and the Cardinal was interred in a tomb in the choir on the north side of the altar.[28] When de Blauzac himself died in 1379, he too was interred in the church, in front of the main altar with neither tomb nor epitaph.[29] De Blauzac clearly assisted his familiar Johannes in obtaining the chaplaincy at Saint-Didier in 1375, but his ties to the church might have helped others in his household as well; Willelmus Penninc de Eyck, de Blauzac's *buticularius* and a priest from Liège, gets a chaplaincy there in 1381 and retained that position until at least 1384. While Pipardi would have obtained his canonry there after de Blauzac's death, perhaps the Cardinal-Bishop's particular relationship with this church assisted his former familiar to rise up through their ranks.

---

28 Julian Gardner, *The Tomb and the Tiara: Curial Tomb Sculpture in Rome and Avignon in the Later Middle Ages* (Oxford: Clarendon Press, 1992), 146.

29 François Du Chesne, *Histoire de Tous Les Cardinaux François de Naissance, Ou Qui Ont Esté Promeus Au Cardinalat.* (Paris, 1660), 572. https://gallica.bnf.fr/ark:/12148/bpt6k914067.

4.4 Johannes Pipardi: A conjectural biography

Who was Johannes Pipardi? Much of his biography remains frustratingly vague, and further archival research may never reveal answers to the myriad questions that remain. But the historical records which we do have for him provide us with sufficient information to construct possible scenarios for his life and work.

Johannes Pipardi is first mentioned in a 1375 papal supplication, in which he is listed as a familiar in the household of Jean de Blauzac. He is also listed as a priest from the diocese of Cambrai. The age requirement for priesthood in the later middle ages was twenty-five; presuming that this requirement held true in late fourteenth-century France, Pipardi would have been born at the absolute latest by 1350.[30]

Pipardi was already known for his skill in music by this point, a skill that might have been put to use in de Blauzac's household or perhaps even helped him earn a place there to begin with. While his duties in the Cardinal's household are not described, as a priest he would likely have been involved in liturgical services in which music played a role; he might also have been responsible for some sort of musical instruction.

Due to de Blauzac's intercession on his behalf, Pipardi received a chaplaincy at the collegiate church of Saint-Didier in Avignon at some point between 1375 and 1378, when he requested a benefice at the monastery of St. Peter in Lobbes. In this latter supplication, though, Pipardi is not described as a familiar or member of de Blauzac's household. Nor is Pipardi listed as one of de Blauzac's familiars in the rotulus compiled upon his death a mere year later. This could indicate that Pipardi was successful in his request for the benefice in Lobbes and relocated there, leaving Avignon and de Blauzac behind.[31] But another possibility is more compelling: his chaplaincy at Saint-Didier could have permitted him residence at the church, either upon the latter's death or perhaps even prior to the 1378 supplication, thus explaining why de Blauzac is no longer named as Pipardi's patron.

The attribution to Johannes "Pipudi" in Sev supports theories such as the latter. In the treatise, Pipardi is called a canon at Saint-Didier—a position that is considerably higher than the chaplaincy he obtained

---

30 Robert Norman Swanson, *Church and Society in Late Medieval England* (New York: Blackwell, 1993), 42–43.

31 Pipardus is a common Flemish surname, at least in subsequent centuries; it must remain possible that Pipardi was born in the Low Countries, which might explain his request for a benefice in Lobbes.

72 *Introducing Johannes Pipardi*

prior to 1378, and which would have been obtained after the 1378 supplication, which does not mention it. As Paula Higgins and others have shown, lower-ranked members of a collegiate church such as the Sainte-Chapelle at Bourges could remain at their institution and come to take on positions of greater authority, such as a magister puerorum, magister capellae, or canon.[32] While Pipardi's canonry might not have required residence, it would have been an option, as with the benefice at Lobbes; moreover, without a patron to intercede on his behalf, Pipardi might have had a better chance of obtaining such a canonry with the promise of being a more permanent resident. As a chaplain and later a canon, Pipardi would have had sufficient income there to sustain himself without the continued support of an external patron.

Furthermore, Copyist A also calls Pipardi both magister and dominus. As explained earlier, if Pipardi had obtained the title of magister through university study, then his matriculation must have postdated the 1375 and 1378 supplications, which mention neither enrollment nor conferral of title. Dominus in this instance might be a deferential title often used to refer to a priest or a canon; Eugeen Schreurs points out that in archival records for the collegiate church at Tongrens, the vicar-priests who substituted for the canons in case of absence or non-residence were called domini.[33] In the case of Sev, Copyist A may be reaffirming Pipardi's status as a priest and canon at Saint-Didier.

The titles magister and dominus, when taken together as in Sev, could also potentially mark Pipardi as a magister capellae. See, for example, the references to Simon Haquetin in records from Avignonese Pope Clement VII's chapel (emphasis added):

[September 19, 1379]:
> *Die xix dicti mensis fuerunt soliti xiii capellanis capelle domini nostri pape hic presentibus, videlicet domino Symoni Haquetin ... recipiente domino Symone Haquetin, magistro dicte capelle...*[34]

---

32 See, for example, Paula Higgins, "Tracing the Careers of Late Medieval Composers. The Case of Philippe Basiron of Bourges," *Acta Musicologica* 62, no. fasc. 1 (April 1990): 1–28; Higgins, "Music and Musicians at the Sainte-Chapelle of the Bourges Palace, 1405–1515," in *Atti Del XIV Congresso Della Società Internazionale Di Musicologica*, vol. 3, 3 vols. (Turin: EDT, 1990), 689–701.

33 I thank Jennifer Bain and Paula Higgins for their insight into this matter; personal communication, 2018. See also Schreurs, "Music at the Collegiate Church of Tongeren ...," 2478.

34 Cited in Di Bacco, "Documenti Vaticani ...," 366.

Introducing Johannes Pipardi   73

[December 20, 1382]:
> *Die XX dicti mensis fuerunt solute dominis Symoni Haquetin, magistro ... ascendant dicto domino Symone pro se et aliis recipiente ...*[35]

In both excerpts, Simon Haquetin is referenced as both domino and magistro, with the first record clarifying his position as magister capellae.

Yet another possibility is that Pipardi could have acted as a magister puerorum. While little information remains on the activities of Saint-Didier, musical or otherwise, records from other collegiate churches of the late medieval period shed light on contemporary practices.[36] Such churches were often hubs of music-making, and frequently maintained a choir school or maîtrise in which choirboys were trained. The person responsible for the care and training of the choirboys was typically one of the church's canons, and he was often given the title of magister cantus or magister puerorum. As the fourteenth century progressed into the fifteenth, the music performed at such institutions grew increasingly complex. Reinhard Strohm explains that the music lessons offered in this type of school "would cover plainsong, extemporized discanting techniques, music theory (solmization, mensural notation, counterpoint)...," and as such the magister was knowledgeable of and occasionally authored works on music theory, whether oriented toward plainchant or more cutting-edge mensural music.[37] A collegiate church such as Saint-Didier, bordering the papal court in Avignon, would be a likely home for such a school, and as a chaplain turned canon with musical expertise and theoretical skill, Pipardi could quite possibly have been its magister.

If this were the case, then the treatises copied in Sev reflect this kind of pedagogical context, and in turn shed light onto the circumstances in which treatises such as the *Libellus* and the *Ars contrapuncti* were used. Copyist A could have been one of the choirboys active at Saint-Didier, and might have copied the treatises in the first of the two

---

35 Cited in Günther, "Zur Biographie ...," 180.
36 For information on music in the late medieval collegiate church, see Otto Becker, "The Maitrise in Northern France and Burgundy during the Fifteenth Century" (PhD diss., George Peabody College for Teachers, 1967); Higgins, "Music and Musicians ...;" Alejandro Enrique Planchart, "Institutions and Foundations," in *The Cambridge History of Medieval Music*, eds. Mark Everist and Thomas Forrest Kelly (Cambridge: Cambridge University Press, 2018), 627–673; Schreurs, "Music at the Collegiate Church of Tongeren ...," Reinhard Strohm, *The Rise of European Music, 1380–1500* (Cambridge: Cambridge University Press, 2005).
37 Strohm, 288.

74 *Introducing Johannes Pipardi*

Sev fascicles as part of his training at the choir school. If the treatises in the second fascicle, of better quality overall, were also affiliated with this church, Copyist B might have been an older or more proficient student, or even a scriptor.

Other possibilities for both magister Pipardi and the treatises exist, especially given the absence of any proof that such a choir school existed at Saint-Didier in the late fourteenth century. The simplest answer might be the most obvious: Pipardi, formerly of the household of Cardinal Jean de Blauzac, relocated to another household or chapel, perhaps that of another prominent member of the Church or a noble family. Either of the copyists could easily have been associated with such a chapel, wherein they might have participated in more advanced musical studies or made new copies of existing theoretical works.

Scholars such as Lucia Marchi, though, have suggested that works such as the *Libellus* would fit into a potential university music curriculum, and that glosses such as *De arte cantus* or the Berkeley treatises might speak to such a pedagogical context, at least in any curricula that expanded beyond the traditional quadrivium.[38] If Pipardi did in fact earn a master's degree, then perhaps he fulfilled an obligation to teach at his alma mater; Copyist A could have studied with him there. But which institution this might have been is a matter of speculation. The *rotuli* of students at the University of Paris that were submitted to the Avignonese popes do not contain his name, although that does not preclude him from having taught there later. Other nearby institutions, such as the Universities of Montpellier and Orléans, were better known for their schools of law and medicine. But over the last quarter of the fourteenth century, the University of Avignon grew markedly, its proximity to the papal court making it a potentially advantageous base from which to gain civic or clerical favor.

The changes that the University of Avignon underwent during this time suggest a likely, if not the likeliest, university at which Pipardi might have taught. Already home to considerable faculty of law, its faculty of arts tripled; the total number of faculty and students jumped from eighty-two in 1378–1379 to 254 in 1393–1394.[39] Over the same

---

38 Lucia Marchi, "Music and University Culture in Late Fourteenth-Century Pavia: The Manuscript Chicago, Newberry Library, Case Ms 54.1," *Acta Musicologica* 80, no. 2 (January 1, 2008): 143–164.

39 See Jacques Verger, "L'Université d'Avignon au Temps de Clément VII," in *Genèse et débuts du grand schisme d'Occident: [actes du Colloque international] Avignon, 25–28 septembre 1978*, ed. Jean Favrier (Paris: Centre national de la recherche

Introducing Johannes Pipardi 75

period of time, the number of students attending the University of Avignon from the Iberian peninsula also increased, in the later years likely due to the election of the Aragonese Cardinal Pedro Martínez de Luna y Pérez de Gotor as Avignonese Pope Benedict XIII in October of 1394.[40] Strikingly, two of these Catalan students appear to have been familiars of Jean de Blauzac.[41]

Pipardi, already a known entity in Avignon, might well have joined the ranks of the faculty during this time. Since salaries for teachers were not paid by their university (and would not be until the late fifteenth century), they would have had to rely on a benefice or some other external support for living wages.[42] Pipardi's position at Saint-Didier would have provided him with the salary he would need to take up a teaching position. Furthermore, since the University was not the fixed collection of buildings we presume a modern college to be and did not own its own buildings until the 1430s, Pipardi might even have been able to use space within the church of Saint-Didier for his classrooms.[43] Students in the faculty of arts might have been as young as fourteen to sixteen years old, and not every student would have already been proficient in Latin. If the teaching of the kinds of music theory exhibited in the Sev treatises followed typical late medieval pedagogical practices, then Pipardi would have lectured from these texts, and students would have glossed their own copies of the texts with class notes—copies that they might themselves have made during dictation sessions, or from written exemplars.[44] The Catalan Copyist A's poor Latin, sloppy handwriting, and general inaccuracies (misspelling the name of his ostensible "*maestre*" among them) could very well be explained by such youth and inexperience, while the better quality of the works found in the second Sev fascicle might reflect

---

scientifique, 1980), 185–200, especially Appendix 1 on p. 199. The only two *rotuli* for the University of Avignon to survive are those for these two sets of years; unfortunately, neither mentions Johannes Pipardi by name.

40 Verger, "L'Université d'Avignon ....," especially Appendix 2 on p. 200; Josep Rius Serra, "Estudiants espanyols a Avinyó al secle XIV," *Analecta sacra tarraconensia* 10 (1934): 87–122.

41 Rius Serra, "Estudiants espanyols ..."

42 Verger, "Teachers," 152.

43 Ibid., 157.

44 Rainer Christoph Schwinges, "Student Education, Student Life," in *Universities in the Middle Ages*, ed. Hilde de Ridder-Symoens (Cambridge: Cambridge University Press, 2003), 195–243, 232.

76 *Introducing Johannes Pipardi*

an older or more experienced student, or perhaps a person preparing copies for personal use outside of a pedagogical scenario.[45]

4.5 Sev revisited

But must Johannes Pipardi have taught Copyist A directly? More to the point, how does this conjectural biography for Pipardi align with what we already know, and what we could still learn, about Sev?

As the first chapter explored, the composite nature of Sev means that it is typically dated broadly, from the mid-fourteenth century to the early fifteenth century. The only date given within the manuscript itself is found on folio 65: *"copiate per me fratrem Bernardum de Sancta Cruce de Veneciis, Ordinis Predicatorum in civitate Verone, 142[?] de mense Januarii."*[46] But such a date can apply only to the works in Bernard's hand. The treatises in the two fascicles at the heart of this study were first authored or compiled, to the best of our current knowledge, across the fourteenth century, but the fascicles themselves are a different piece of the puzzle. Nothing about the paleography in either fascicle narrows down a more specific date than what is already given for Sev as a whole. The array of newer mensural note values in *De arte cantus* points to ideas developing after the 1340s or 1350s, and more likely closer to the last quarter of the century, especially given Desmond's and Zayaruznaya's recent claims; this dating would be plausible for the other treatises in question here, as well as for the copying of the two fascicles themselves.[47] The void notation in the second copy of *De arte cantus*, as well as in the subsequent copy of the *Tractatus figurarum*, might even suggest an early fifteenth-century hand. Given the first fascicle's description of "Pipudi" as a canon and a dominus magister, these treatises would have had to be copied long enough after 1378 for Pipardi to have attained such positions. A dating of c.1380s–early 1400s for both fascicles therefore seems appropriate.

---

45 See Rainer Christoph Schwinges, "Admission," in *Universities in the Middle Ages*, ed. Hilde de Ridder-Symoens (Cambridge: Cambridge University Press, 2003), 171–194; Schwinges, "Student Education, Student Life."

46 RISM B III 5, 110–120.

47 Of course, the dating of the *Libellus* itself also remains uncertain; if authored by des Murs, then it might still have been written after c. 1340—perhaps even as late as the 1370s, in time to be copied into the Berkeley manuscript in 1375, if des Murs managed to live that long while avoiding any documentation in the historical record after 1345. But if not authored by des Murs, then the possibility that the *Libellus* was a later compilation persists, especially given the dating of the Berkeley manuscript.

Introducing Johannes Pipardi 77

The watermarks for the first of these two fascicles, and possibly for the second, support and clarify this suggestion.[48] A watermark in the shape of a chariot or wheeled vehicle with two wheels, each of which has three bisecting lines creating six spokes, is visible on bifolios 103–104 (Figure 5) and 100–107 (Figure 6), though damage and text hide potential differences.[49] The image on bifolio 103–104 shows that the vehicle's body has a flatter bottom that arches up at an angle on either side, and an upside-down U or pitchfork-shaped decoration underneath the wheels; damage in the fold of bifolio 100–107 makes it impossible to ascertain the shape of the vehicle's bottom, while the heavy text obscures a clear view of the upside-down U. Similarly, some sort of decorative element at the top of the triangular body of the chariot can be seen on bifolio 100–107, but not through the text on bifolio 103–104.

Similar watermarks are visible in the vast catalog compiled by Charles Briquet.[50] His items 3527 (Figure 7) and 3542 (Figure 8) appear to be the closest to the watermarks in Sev; the former has the flat base of the vehicle, but not the six spokes, while the latter shows the reverse.[51] He notes that both tend to be found in early fifteenth-century sources. The former he traces as early as 1412, the latter possibly as early as 1398. The sources in which he finds such watermarks tend to border the Mediterranean, and in both cases he identifies the earliest sources as originating in Perpignan, part of the Principality of Catalonia until 1659. He also documents similarly dated paper with these watermarks in northwestern Italy (Genoa and Lucca), Brussels, northern Holland, and various locations throughout south-central France.

Such watermarks have also been traced in other databases, namely, BITECA (La BIbliografia de TExtos antics CAtalans).[52] Noting the similarities to Briquet's 3542, BITECA offers two additional

---

48 I thank David Catalunya and DIAMM for sharing these images with me.

49 Giuliano Di Bacco first noted this watermark in his 2009 codicological study, where he described it as "a triangle and two wheels?" See Di Bacco, "Original and Borrowed," 354.

50 See Charles-Moïse Briquet, *Les filigranes. Dictionnaire historique des marques du papier dès leur apparition vers 1282 jusqu'en 1600 avec 39 figures dans le texte et 16 112 fac-similés de filigranes* (Paris: Alphonse Picard et fils, 1907). My research in this project was done using the online catalog version BO—Briquet Online (v. 1.2 – 2017-01-17). http://www.ksbm.oeaw.ac.at/_scripts/php/BR.php

51 http://www.ksbm.oeaw.ac.at/_scripts/php/BR.php?IDtypes=32&lang=fr

52 http://stel.ub.edu/biteca/html/ca/presentacio.html

78 *Introducing Johannes Pipardi*

Figure 5 Watermark on bifolio 103–104; Biblioteca Capitular Colombina, sign. 5-2-25, f. 104r, © Cabildo Catedral de Sevilla.

Figure 6 Watermark on bifolio 100–107; Biblioteca Capitular Colombina, sign. 5-2-25, f. 107r, © Cabildo Catedral de Sevilla.

80 *Introducing Johannes Pipardi*

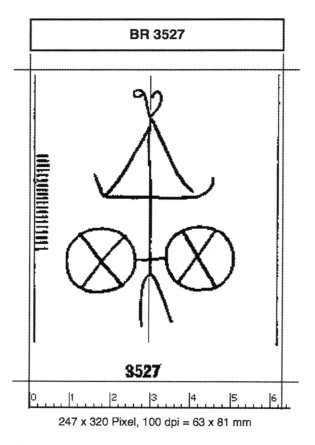

Figure 7 Briquet, watermark 3527.

watermarks: items 067017 (Figure 9) and 067002 (Figure 10).[53] Neither of these has the flatter bottom of the vehicle as seen in the Sev bifolio 103–104, and neither does Briquet 3542, yet the 067002 watermark is also found in another manuscript in the Biblioteca Colombina: Seville 5-4-29, a dictionary of rhymes written in 1371 by Catalan poet Jaume

---

53 http://stel.ub.edu/biteca/filigranes/ca/067017.html; http://stel.ub.edu/biteca/filigranes/ca/067002.html

Introducing Johannes Pipardi 81

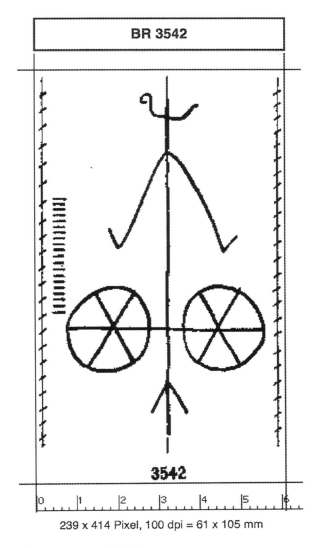

Figure 8 Briquet, watermark 3542.

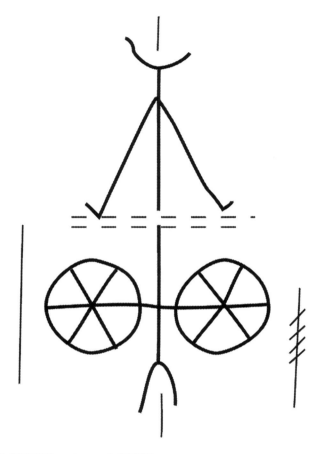

Figure 9 BITECA watermark 067017.

March and copied at some point during the late fourteenth or early fifteenth century.[54]

If the watermarks in this fascicle of Sev are contemporaneous with those noted by BITECA and Briquet, then these treatises might have been copied around 1397 or 1398. Twenty years after his last dated supplication is a more than sufficient window of time for Pipardi to have received a master's degree or to have achieved employment for

---

54 See http://philobiblon.upf.edu/saxon/SaxonServlet?source=BITECA/Display/
1112AnalyticCopy.xml&style=BITECA/templates/AnalyticCopy.xsl&gobk

Introducing Johannes Pipardi 83

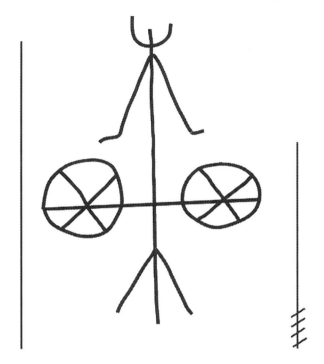

Figure 10 BITECA watermark 067002.

which he would have been called magister, and to have been appointed a canon at Saint-Didier. He might only have been in his late forties or fifties, so it is certainly within the realm of possibility that he could have been working as some sort of teacher at that point, perhaps even with Copyist A directly. Paper with these watermarks would have been available to the copyist either in their home nation or likely also in Avignon.

Yet such watermarks remain in use throughout much of the fifteenth century, and paper can be used years after its making, so it must remain possible that Copyist A was at some remove from Pipardi, chronologically or geographically. Such a distance would explain why the copyist misspelled Pipardi, although there must have been an exemplar, now lost, that contained his name and biographical information and that was considered to be authoritative for mensural and contrapuntal theory. This might also explain why the phrase "the teacher"

84 Introducing Johannes Pipardi

("*lo maestre*") is used in the concluding notes and not "my teacher," and suggests either that the copyist's exemplar contained references to a teacher, Pipardi or otherwise, or that the copyist was himself working with another teacher and did not have a direct relationship with Pipardi himself.

The second watermark is much clearer, for it is visible without ultraviolet light on the blank folio 120r–v[55] (Figure 11). This watermark is of an arrow nocked in a tightly drawn bow. The arrow has no fletching at its base, and its double-lined head is sharply pointed at both tip and base. The bow is similarly double-lined, and its tips curve out to the sides. The watermark is centered in the middle of the page, facing horizontally such that the arrow points toward the outer edge. Briquet identifies four such horizontal watermarks in French and Italian sources, ranging in date from 1360 to 1433, yet none of them quite match this one; none of the bows are drawn tightly enough, and the arrowheads are the wrong shape. The Sev watermark much more closely matches some of the vertical watermarks listed in Briquet's work, which range in date from as early as 1333 to around 1435.[56] Briquet notes that the popularity of this watermark makes it difficult to attribute its different variants to specific paper-makers, but that it likely had its origins in Italy and soon thereafter spread into France.[57] Similar watermarks are identified in databases such as BITECA and the Wasserzeichen-Informationssystem; the former contains watermarks such as 030020, but no dating, provenance, or other identifying information is given there, while the latter suggests perhaps the most similar watermark, found in a manuscript from Florence dated to 1440.[58] When looking holistically at the otherwise Italianate theoretical works found in this fascicle, the paleographical and notational evidence, and this particular watermark, a late fourteenth- or early fifteenth-century Italian origin is likely. If so, though, that puts Copyist B at a potential remove from Pipardi himself, and once again points not only to a possible international popularity for his particular approach to Murisian theory but to the continued interest in French musical practice in Italy throughout the fifteenth century.

---

55 David Catalunya reports in private conversation (2019) that the same type of watermark is found throughout the fascicle, and the paper used is consistent throughout.
56 http://www.ksbm.oeaw.ac.at/_scripts/php/BR.php?IDtypes=9&lang=fr
57 Briquet, *Les Filigranes*, 53.
58 http://stel.ub.edu/biteca/filigranes/ca/030020.html#; https://www.wasserzeichenonline.de/?ref=DE4620-PO-123599. The Wasserzeichen-Informationssystem contains all of the watermarks found in the Piccard Online database.

Figure 11 Watermark on f. 120v; Biblioteca Capitular Colombina, sign. 5-2-25, f. 120v, © Cabildo Catedral de Sevilla.

86 *Introducing Johannes Pipardi*

Regardless of when or where these two fascicles were copied, the fact still remains that the close relationship between *De arte cantus* and the Berkeley-Catania version of the *Libellus cantus mensurabilis* throws a monkey wrench into our current understanding of the different textual traditions of the *Libellus*. If, as Christian Berktold has so thoroughly laid out, the Berkeley manuscript is part of the *Recensio minor*, which otherwise only circulated in England and northwestern France, how then might it have come to the attention of Johannes Pipardi, and thus branched off uniquely into Avignon, eventually to Italy and Spain? Pipardi was, after all, a priest of the diocese of Cambrai; if he joined the retinue of Jean de Blauzac in 1375, the year in which he is first documented as part of the then-Bishop's household, then perhaps while en route to Avignon this already skilled musician obtained a copy of the Berkeley treatises, compiled in Paris early that same year. It is certainly a plausible theory, although this timeline is tight. Another is that if the author-compiler of the Berkeley manuscript is the Goscalcus attributed in Catania, and this Goscalcus is also the composer whose only work is preserved in the Chantilly Codex, he and Pipardi might have been acquaintances, even colleagues, and the treatises were passed on in that fashion. The continued traffic between Avignon, Italy, and Spain throughout the late fourteenth and fifteenth centuries points to the ease with which works copied or taught in Avignon could have been transmitted elsewhere.[59] Given the similarities to the Berkeley manuscript, combined with the paleography, notation, and watermark evidence, it might very well be that these two copies of *De arte cantus* are not just witnesses to the *Libellus*, but among the earliest versions now known; if so, the reference to the authority of Johannes Pipardi almost certainly predates the attribution to Goscalcus, and might also predate that to Jean des Murs.

Clearly, there is more work to be done on such patterns of transmission; for now, it remains sufficient to point to Johannes Pipardi, dominus magister, priest of the diocese of Cambrai, canon of Saint-Didier in Avignon, and skillful in the art of music, as an important figure in the teaching of French-Murisian mensural and contrapuntal theory and its dissemination into late medieval Italy.

---

59 This web of contacts could thus explain why a theorist named Goscalcus becomes so prominent in later Spanish theory, as Santiago Galán observed in private conversation (2019).

Epilogue

Further documentation for the life and career of Johannes Pipardi might never be found. Wars, fires, floods, and the natural deterioration of time have destroyed precious historical materials over the past six centuries. Still, what we do know about him, combined with knowledge of the kinds of institutions and musical developments of the late fourteenth century in which he lived and worked, offers several plausible biographical scenarios. Likely born around the mid-fourteenth century, he was ordained a priest in the diocese of Cambrai at some point prior to 1375, by which time he had also developed a reputation for musical skill that might have helped him earn a position in the household of one of the highest ranked cardinals of his day.

Such a position clearly helped him achieve a chaplaincy at the collegiate church of Saint-Didier in papal Avignon, which in turn appears to have led to a prestigious canonry there. At some point afterward, he might have taught versions of the popular treatises *Libellus cantus mensurabilis* and *Ars contrapuncti*, often attributed to Jean des Murs, to which he might have contributed his own particular rules of counterpoint, if not wholescale revisions of the entire works. Without a clearer idea of dating, transmission, and authorship, it is difficult to say with precision just how innovative or derivative Pipardi's theories are, or even which are of his own design. The close and in many cases unique connections that *De arte cantus*, *Regulae contrapunctus*, and the Catalan notes have to the second and third Berkeley treatises and their Catania concordances, however, signal Pipardi's involvement in new and exciting developments to mensural and contrapuntal theory in the later fourteenth century, including a host of new rhythmic note values, major modus, ciphers, and, in one copy, the backward-semicircle tempus sign. Given the newly discovered dates for Pipardi's activity in Avignon, it might now be possible that Pipardi is the person first

88 *Epilogue*

named in connection with this material elsewhere attributed to the authorship or compilation of Jean des Murs.

The treatises documented by Copyists A and B, including the three here associated with Pipardi, were preserved by Hernando Colón, being bound much later next to one another in the composite manuscript Seville 5.2.25. At least one of these fascicles might have been made in Pipardi's Avignon, but Italy or perhaps even Catalonia are also possibilities, while the other might more clearly reflect an Italian provenance, thus documenting not only Pipardi's authority on mensural and contrapuntal matters but also the continued influx of popular French musical theory into Italy throughout the late medieval period.

While we do not know for sure if or where he taught this material, it is plausible that such activity took place at the church of Saint-Didier, at the University of Avignon, or in the household of another élite figure, where he or his materials encountered at least one student more fluent in Catalan than Latin. Were it not for this student recording the name of the magister associated with this material, we would have no reason to look more closely at Johannes Pipardi, skillful in the art of music; were it not for this student misspelling his name as Pipudi, we would have looked more closely at him much earlier than this.

Appendices

Appendix 1

A preliminary list of members of Jean de Blauzac's household

Key:
Year indicates the first known association with Jean de Blauzac
Bold indicates a (possible) blood relative
Italics indicates a (possible) familiar

1355:
Ade Lascini

1362:
Andreas Rovayroli
Egidius Bourgois
Henrico de Bunde
Johannes Barrerie
Johannes Caneti

Johannes Dominicano
Decani de Tongris
Johannes Pauli
Johannes de Ripis
Johannes Stephani de
Rambertivilla
Petrus Bruni
Petrus Sardi
Petrus de Sancto Petro

Petrus de Teulenco
Philippus de Alayraco
Rostagnus Omagii
Stephano de Plancerio
Thome Richardi de Thilon de
Gembertees
Guirando de Posilhaco

Bertrandi Helie
Gaucelmus de Genestosio
Berengario de Lodeva

Bernardo Rogerii
Hugoni Gilberti

1363:
Lambertus de Frangnees
Raymond Marcelli
Roberto de Blandiaco

Alamando Grandis
Hugo de Aussaco

1364:
Didac. Alfonsi

90   *Members of Jean de Blauzac's household*

1365:
Johannes de Goeria
Egidius de Curtibus
(Gilles de Lescours)

Guillelmus Tebardi

1366:
Arnoldus Prel de Heppenet
Franciscus Boudrici de Bona

Johannes Boylewe de Monte

1367:
Hugo Moteti

1371:
Adulphus Vridach
Bertrandus de Orceto
Jacobus de Ruffo
Jacobus Wolf (Lupi)
Johannes de Bosco
Johannes Butor
Johannes Ermengaudi
Johannes La Buffe
Henricus Poneti

Martiali Cobrerii
Nicolaus Taverii (Caverii)
Nicolaus Papilionis
Richardus de Bozonville
Rostagno Martini
Wilhelmo de Renensis
Petrus Boudrandi
Petrus de Pradis

1372:
Benedicto Petri

Fernando Didaci de Valcanas

1373:
Petrus natum Raymundi
    Garini de Bolena
Willelmus Penninc de Eyck

Gaucelmo de Bariaco

1374:
Johannes de Mandagoto
Ade Robelyn
Armando de Balma

Bernardo Sigerii
Johannes Peregrini
Aymeric Helie

1375:
Hemenoto Ausselini
Arnoldo Jocalis

JOHANNES PIPARDI
Johannes de Trulhatio

1379:
Egidio Archiepiscopi
Johannes Martini
Jacobo Tasketi

Johannes Welsken
Amelio de Wonk

Appendix 2
Texts and translations

Editorial principles:

1 Within reason, and excluding the marking of expanded abbreviations, I have tried to adhere to certain editorial conventions:

   a   *om* = omitted; indicates that certain words or phrases are not included in that master text. Dashes subsequent to *om* indicate length of phrase; if a single word, that word is specified after *om*.

   b   *vac* = areas of the parchment/paper left blank; not ruined or otherwise missing. Dots subsequent to *vac* indicate the range of the vacancy.

   c   ...... = ruined or incomprehensible text.

   d   [...] = text missing due to page damage.

   e   [[X]] = corrections or deletions made by the original copyist.

   f   <X> = letters left out by the original copyist.

   g   \X/ = letters or words inserted as corrections by the original copyist.

   h   {X} = letters, words, or phrases included by the original copyist that are superfluous.

2 A word on notation:

   a   These musical examples have been set contiguously with the prose, and therefore do not necessarily reflect the mise-en-page of the original sources.

   b   The musical notation font used in the appendices and throughout the main text is of my own creation.

92 *Texts and translations*

3   About De arte cantus:

   a   The two texts of *De arte cantus* are highly concordant, but for the most part, *DAC 2* is the more reliable source, although the careful reader will notice that in many cases neither text is any better or worse than the other. Where the two texts vary, even in small matters such as spelling or word order, I have placed the alternate text in the two columns on either side; *DAC 1* variants are to the left, *DAC 2* variants to the right.

   b   There are two places where the original copyist of *DAC 2* accidentally moved on to another section of text before finishing a particular section, and thus copied the remainder of the first section at the bottom of the page or in a different place. I have relocated those texts to their proper place and marked them with * and ^. The treatise concludes with a supplementary paragraph only present in *DAC 2*.

   c   Section numbers are an editorial insertion.

4   About the Catalan notes:

   a   I am grateful for the help of David Catalunya for this section, and give him equal credit both for the transcription and for the translation.

Appendix 2a: De arte cantus

	De arte cantus	
DAC 1		*DAC 2*
[99v] *valloribus*		[111]
	Pro introducione cogniciones habende de valoribus notularum.	
scilicet	1. Primo sciendum est quod quinque sunt figure in cantibus usitate, videlicet maxima, longa, brevis, semibrevis, et minima ut hic: ■ ■ ♦ •	♦ ♦ *massima* ♦ ■
[impl]] imperfecta	Item sciendum est quod maxima est duplex, scilicet perfecta et imperfecta. Perfecta est quando valet tres longas autem earum valorem ordinatam ut hic:	*duples* om *est* *ordinata* om *est*
vallet	■ ■ • ■ ■ ■ ■ ■ ■ . Imperfecta est quando valet duas tantum ut hic: ■ ■ • Item longa est duplex, scilicet perfecta et imperfecta. Perfecta est quando valet tres breves ut hic: ■ ■ • Item brevis est duplex, scilicet perfecta et imperfecta. Perfecta est quando valet tres semibreves ut hic: ■ ♦ ♦ • Imperfecta est quando valet duas ut hic: ■ ♦ ♦ •	om *est*
om *Imperfecta ...* ■ • |scilicet| [...] *val[et]* [...] *-breves* hic: vac [...] |*quando* *tantum* [...] ■ •	Item semibrevis est duplex, scilicet perfecta et imperfecta. Perfecta quando valet tres minimas ut hic: ♦ ♦ ♦ • Imperfecta quando valet duas ut hic: ♦ ♦	om *est*
Item [...] *et imperfecta* [...] om *Perfecta ... duas ut hic:* [...]		*duples*
[...] [...] *brev[es]* [...] *t* [...] [———]	Item sciendum est quod maxima non potest alterari neque minima imperfici. Notule vero medie, scilicet longa, brevis, et semibrevis, imperfici possunt et etiam alterari et de hiis inferius plus dicetur.	*poxunt*

As an introduction: the knowledge to be had concerning the values of notes.

1. First, it must be known that there are five figures used in song, namely, the maxima, long, breve, semibreve, and minim, as here: ■ ■ ■ ♦ ♦ ·

It must also be known that the maxima is twofold, namely, perfect and imperfect. Perfect is when it is worth three longs or their value arranged, as here: ■ ■ ■ ■ · ■ ■ ■ ■ ■ ■ ■ ■ ■ . Imperfect is when it is worth only two, as here: ■ ■ ■ · Likewise, the long is twofold, namely, perfect and imperfect. Perfect is when it is worth three breves, as here: ■ ■ ■ ■ · Imperfect, when it is worth two, as here: ■ ■ ■ . Likewise, the breve is twofold, namely, perfect and imperfect. Perfect is when it is worth three semibreves, as here: ■ ♦ ♦ ♦ . Imperfect is when it is worth two, as here: ■ ♦ ♦ ·

Likewise, the semibreve is twofold, namely, perfect and imperfect. Perfect, when it is worth three minims, as here: ♦ ♦ ♦ ♦ . Imperfect, when it is worth two, as here: ♦ ♦ ♦ ·

It must also be known that the maxima cannot be altered, nor can the minim be imperfected. All notes in between, namely, the long, breve, and semibreve, can be imperfected and also altered, and about this more will be said below.

DAC 1		DAC 2
[99v] *cantatores alliqui*	Item cantores aliqui ponunt iiiior tales figuras additas ♪♪♪♪◆◆◆◆ appellatas et biscantatas pro tribus minimis. Item duas	♪♪♪♪◆◆◆◆ om *appellatas et biscantatas*
tales [[et semi]] fusatis ponunt quia una	fusas tales ◆ etiam ponunt pro tribus minimis. Item duas tales ♪♪◆◆ seminas appellatas vel tales ◆◆ ponunt pro una	om *etiam* ◆◆ om *seminas appellatas vel tales* ♪♪◆◆
◆◆ *figuras minoris*	minima. Item duas tales figuras ◆◆ semibreves caudatas appellatas ponunt pro tribus semibrevibus maioris prolationis.	
*Insuper (MS Inpuper) nota prolacio.	videlicet [[ma]] attenditur videlicet*	2. Item nota quod in cantibus habetur modus, tempus, et prolatio. Modus est duplex, scilicet maior et minor. Modus maior attenditur penes maximas in habitudine ad longas et est duplex, scilicet perfectus et imperfectus. Perfectus est quando maxima de se valet tres longas et ipse per eas computatur. Imperfectus quando duas tantum. Modus minori attenditur penes longas in habitudine ad breves et	*duples*
minor [...] attenditur habitudine ad bre- *[...] etiam* *per- [...] de se [[va]]	breve* *[...] [im]perfectus*	est etiam duplex, scilicet perfectus et imperfectus. Perfectus quando longa de se valet tres breves et ipse pro ea ponatur. Imperfecta quando duas tantum.	*duples	om est*

Likewise, some singers place four such figures, called additas ♦♦♦♦, and sing them for three minims. Likewise, two such fusas ♦♦ are also placed for three minims. Likewise, two such ♦♦ called seminas, or such ♦♦, are placed for one minim. Likewise, two such figures ♦♦, called semibreves caudatas, are placed for three semibreves in major prolation.

2. Likewise, note that in song there exist mode, tempus, and prolation. Mode is twofold, namely, major and minor. Major mode extends to the relationship of maximas to longas and is twofold, namely, perfect and imperfect. Perfect is when the maxima in and of itself is worth three longs and it is reckoned according to them; imperfect, when only two. Minor mode extends to the relationship of longs to breves and is also twofold, namely, perfect and imperfect: perfect, when a long in and of itself is worth three breves, and should be placed according to it [them]; imperfect, when only two.

DAC 1 | **DAC 2**

Item tempus attenditur respectu brevium penes earum in habitudinem ad semibreves et est similiter duplex, scilicet perfectum et imperfectum. Perfectum quando brevis de se valet tres semibreves. Imperfectum quando duas. Item prolacio attenditur respectu semibrevis penes earum in habitudinem ad minimas et est etiam duplex, scilicet perfecta et tunc dicitur maior, et imperfecta quando duas minori. Perfecta seu maior prolatio est quando semibrevis de se valet tres minimas. Imperfecta seu minori quando valet duas. Exempla patent ex predictis.

3. Item etiam patet ex predictis quod omnis perfecto consistit in numero ternario et inperfecto in numero binario.

Item notule perfecte possunt imperfici et hoc per abstractione\<m\> tertie partis sui valoris et non aliter. Et notule imperfecte possunt perfici et hoc per additionem medietatis sui valoris quod fieri solet per appositionem punctus ad ipsam immediate ut hic:

○ ■ ■ ♦ ♦ ♦ ♦ ♦ ♦ ·· ♦
Et de hiis plus infra.

De imperfectione vero notularum primo sciendum est quod maxima perfecta in toto et in partibus omnibus suis potest imperfici ab una longa vel eius valore sequente a

---

DAC 1

Item [...] [bre]vium | om in habitudinem [...] duples et [...]
se- [...]s tantum. Item [...] [p]enes [...]est [...]
...
...
...
...

...
...
[100] [[in]] \binario\ (MS dunario) numero.

per [[im]]perfecte [[im]]perfici astractionem [[partes]] | partis de sui valore medietatem

puncti | hic sequitur:
■ ○ ♦ ♦ ♦ ♦ ■ · ♦ ♦ ♦ ♦ ♦ ♦

imperfectione nota
unam longam | valloris sequens

DAC 2

addicionem apposicionem puntus | imedietate

om Et

[111v] omnibus partibus ad una

Likewise, tempus extends to the relationship of breves to semibreves, and it is similarly twofold, namely, perfect and imperfect: perfect, when the breve in and of itself is worth three semibreves; imperfect, when two. Likewise, prolation extends to the relationship of semibreves to minims, and is also twofold, namely, perfect and then it is called major, and imperfect, when two, minor: perfect or major prolation is when the semibreve in and of itself is worth three minims; imperfect or minor, when it is worth two. Examples are shown from the preceding.

3. Likewise, also, the preceding shows that each perfect thing consists of the number three, and imperfect of the number two.

Likewise, perfect notes can be imperfected, and this by the subtraction of a third part of their value and none other. And imperfect notes can be perfected, and this by the addition of half of their value, which is made by placing a dot next to them, as here[2]: ○ ■ ◆ ■ ◆ ◆ ◆ ■ ◆ ■ ◆ ◆ · · ◆ And of these, more below.

Concerning the imperfection of notes, it must first be known that the perfect maxima, in its whole and in all of its parts, can be imperfected by a long or by its value,

---

2 The musical examples in neither source appear to actually contain dots of addition.

DAC 1		DAC 2
		precedentis ■ ■ ■ ■
brevi | eius unam *[[lo]] longam. Sed hoc |* *[[improprie]] inproprie* *locutum tunc*	parte post vel precedente a parte ante et hoc quoad totum eius corpus, ut hic: ■ • ■ ■ ■ ■ • . Item potest imperfici ab una brevis secundum dictum aliquorum quoad unam eius longam. Scilicet hoc est nimis improprie locutus quia tunc	
una erum longa | om ipsa *non eius maxima*	una longa imperficitur et non ipsa maxima. Item a duabus	
■ ■ ■ ■ ■ • ■ • ■ • ■ ■	brevibus quoad duas eius longas ad intellectum iam dictum et hoc a parte post vel a parte ante ut hic: ■ ■ • ■ • ■ • . ■ .	
Semibrevi quoad eius unam ◆ ◆ ◆ ◆ ■ ◆ ◆	Item ab una semibrevis quoad unam eius brevem, etiam a duabus semibrevibus quoad duas eius breves ad intellectum predictum et hoc similiter a parte post et a parte ante ut hic: ◆ ■ ◆ ◆ ◆ ◆ • .	*quoad \unam|* *[|semibrevis minimis|]* *semibreves*
et *duas eius*	Item ab una minima quoad unam eius semibrevem, etiam a duabus minimis quoad duas semibreves ad intellectum	
sepe dictum et hoc etiam *post vel a parte* ■ • ◆ • • ◆ • | ◆ • ◆ ■	etiam sepe supra dictum et etiam a parte post et a parte ante ut hic: ■ • ◆ • • ◆ • ◆ • ◆ • . ◆ .	
[100v]	Item ab una minima quoad duas eius semibreves ad intellectum etiam sepe dictum et hoc etiam aparent post vel aparent ante ut hic: ■ • ◆ • ◆ • • ◆ • | ◆ • . ■ .	om : : : :
sic minima que debet | *minimas*	Et sicut maxima que deberet valere lxxxi minime potest	
decem | sexdecim minimas	imperfici donec tantum modo valeret xvicim minime.	*[[x]] xvicim*

following by a part after or preceding by a part before, and this with respect to the whole of its body, as here: ■ ■ · ■ ■ ■ ■ . Likewise, it can be imperfected by a breve, as some say, with respect to one of its longs. Certainly, this is very improperly stated, because then a long is imperfected, and not the maxima itself. Likewise, [it can be imperfected] by two breves with respect to two of its longs, according to the aforementioned reasoning, and this by a part after or a part before, as here: ■ ■ · ■ ■ · ■ ■ ■ · ■ ■ ■ · ■ ■ .

Likewise, by a semibreve with respect to one of its breves, also by two semibreves with respect to two of its breves, according to the aforementioned reasoning, and this similarly by a part after and a part before, as here: ♦ ■ ♦ ■ ♦ ♦ · ♦ ♦ ■ .

Likewise, by a minim with respect to one of its semibreves, also by two minims with respect to two of its semibreves, again often according to the reasoning above, and also by a part after and a part before, as here: ■ ♦ · ♦ ■ · ♦ ■ ♦ · ■ ♦ ♦ · ♦ ♦ ■ ·

Likewise, by one minim with respect to two of its semibreves, also often according to the aforementioned reasoning, and this also by a part after or a part before, as here: ■ ♦ · ♦ ■ · ♦ ■ ♦ ■ ♦ ♦ |♦ ♦ ■.

And thus the maxima, which should be worth 81 minims, can be imperfected until it is only worth sixteen minims.

DAC 1		DAC 2
	Item longa perfecta in toto et in omnibus partibus suis potest imperfici ab una brevi vel eius valoris quoad totum eius corpus et hoc a parte post vel a parte ante ut hic:	
valorem		
■ ■ · ◆ ◆ · ■	■ ■ · ◆ ◆ ■ ·	
[[t]] Item semis brevibus	Item ab una semibrevi quoad unam eius brevem, etiam a duabus semibrevibus quoad duas eius breves ad intellectum predictum et hoc a parte post vel a parte ante	*quo duas*
■ ◆ · ◆ ■ ◆ ■ ◆ ■ ◆ · ◆ ◆ ■	ut hic: ■ ◆ · ◆ ■ ◆ · ■ ◆ · ◆ ◆ ■ ·	
	Item ab una minima quoad unam eius semibreves, etiam a duabus minimis quoad duas eius semibreves ad predictum intellectum et hoc similiter a parte post vel a parte ante ut hic: ■ ◆ · ◆ ■ ◆ · ◆ ■ ◆ · ■ ◆ ◆ · ◆ ◆ ■ ·	
*deberet	minimas perfici	valet	viii° tantum*	Et sic longa que debet valere xxvii minime potest imperfici quousque non valeat nisi octo minime tantum.	
[[interfici]] interfici valoris eius	Item brevis perfecta maioris prolationis potest imperfici ab una semibrevi vel eius valoris quoad totum eius corpus et hoc a parte ante vel a parte post ut hic: ■ ◆ · ◆ ◆ ■ ·	■ ◆ · ◆ ◆ ■
*minori	[[unum]] unam eius* [101] om *duas prepositum	om similiter ut sic:*	Item ab una minima quoad una eius semibrevem etiam a	
	duabus minimis quoad duas eius semibreves ad intellectum predictum et hoc similiter a parte ante vel a parte post ut hic: ■ ◆ · ◆ ■ · ◆ ■ ◆ ■ ◆ · ◆ ◆ ■ ·	■ ◆ · ◆ ■ ◆ ■ ◆ ◆ · ◆ ◆ ■
*Item	ipsam breve ad dictum et a duabus set*	Et sic ipsa brevis a dictum intellectum potest imperfici ab una minima et duabus minimis et a tribus et a quatuor et a quinque sed non plus.	

Likewise, a perfect long in its whole and in all of its parts can be imperfected by a breve or by its value with respect to its whole body, and this by a part after or a part before, as here: ■ ■ · ◆ · ◆ .

Likewise, by a semibreve with respect to one of its breves, also by two semibreves with respect to two of its breves, according to the aforementioned reasoning, and this by a part after or a part before, as here: ■ ◆ · ◆ ■ · ■ ◆ · ◆ ■ · .

Likewise, by a minim with respect to one of its semibreves, also by two of its minims with respect to two of its semibreves, according to the aforementioned reasoning, and this similarly by a part after or a part before, as here: ■ ◆ · ■ ◆ · · ◆ · ◆ · ■ · · ◆ · .

And thus the long that should be worth twenty-seven minims can be imperfected until such a point when it is not worth more than only eight minims.

Likewise, a perfect breve of major prolation can be imperfected by a semibreve or by its value with respect to the whole of its body, and this by a part before or a part after, as here: ■ ◆ · ◆ ■ .

Likewise, by a minim with respect to one of its semibreves, also by two minims with respect to two of its semibreves, according to the aforementioned reasoning, and this similarly by a part before or a part after, as here: ■ ◆ · ◆ · ■ ◆ · ◆ · ■ .

And thus this breve, according to the stated rationale, can be imperfected by a minim, and by two minims, and by three and by four and by five, but no more.

DAC 1	DAC 2
	[112]
[|mimo]] minoris	Item brevis perfecta minoris prolationis potest imperfici ab una semibrevi vel a duabus minimis et hoc quoad totum ut hic: ■ ◆ ◆ ◆ ■ ◆ . Item brevis imperfecta maioris prolationis potest imperfici ab una minima quoad
prol[ation]is *[...] om intellectum ...*	intellectum prefatum ut hic: ◆ ◆ ◆ ■ ◆ .
	[[Item brevis imperfecta minoris]] Sic etiam
... [un]–am eius *m[inimi]s* *in[...]um prefactum*	Sic etiam ad unam eius semibrevem etiam a duabus minimis quoad ambas eius semibreves ad intellectum prefatum ut sic: ■ ◆ ◆ ◆ ■ ◆ .
	prefatum ut dictum est supra om sic: ■ ◆ ◆ ◆ ■ ◆
It[em] [...][fecta m[...] *potest im [...] et*	Item brevis imperfecta minoris prolationis nullo modo potest imperfici. Item semibrevis minoris prolationis etiam non potest imperfici. Sed maioris prolationis semibreves imperfici potest ab una minima ut hic: ◆ ◆ ◆ ◆ .
imperfici non potest	◆ ◆ ◆ ◆	*Set*
om	Et nota quidem cantores Guillelmus de Mascandio et
...	nonnulli alii, imperficiunt brevem perfectam minoris
...	prolationis ab una sola minima, et brevem perfectam
...	maioris prolationis a duabus minimis, simul sequentibus
...	vel precedentibus. Et dicunt ibi mutari qualitatem,
...	capientes enimque brevem perfectam minoris prolationis
...	ac si esset brevis imperfecta maioris prolationis et e
...	converso, brevem imperfectam maioris prolationis ac si
...	esset brevis perfecta minoris prolationis. Brevis perfecta
...	maioris prolationis potest imperfici ab una sola minima
...	precedens et alia sequentibus, quo ambabus precedentibus
...	vel sequentibus, et a tribus minimis vel earum valoribus
...	quoad totum, et quatuor minimis vel earum valoribus

Texts and translations 105

Likewise, a perfect breve of minor prolation can be imperfected by a semibreve or by two minims, and this with respect to the whole, as here: ■ ♦ ♦ ♦ ■ ♦ ■ ♦ . Likewise, an imperfect breve of major prolation can be imperfected by a minim with respect to the aforementioned reasoning, as here: ■ ♦ ♦ ■ ♦ ■ ♦ .

Thus, also, by one of its semibreves, also by two minims with respect to both of its semibreves, according to the aforementioned reasoning, as here: ■ ♦ · ♦ ■ ♦ .

Likewise, an imperfect breve of minor prolation can in no way be imperfected. Likewise, a semibreve of minor prolation also cannot be imperfected. But semibreves of major prolation can be imperfected by one minim, as here: ♦ ♦ · ♦ .

And note that some singers, Guillaume de Machaut and several others, imperfect the perfect breve of minor prolation by one single minim, and a perfect breve of major prolation by two minims, either following or preceding. And they call this "to change the quality," namely, treating the perfect breve of minor prolation as though it were an imperfect breve of major prolation, and vice versa, an imperfect breve of major prolation as though it were a perfect breve of minor prolation. The perfect breve of major prolation can be imperfected by one single minim preceding and by another following, or by both preceding or following, and by three minims or their value with respect to the whole, and four minims or their value with respect to the whole,

106   *Texts and translations*

DAC 2

∴

* {*modum perfectum remanet sola brevis perfectione computata si plures fuerint tunc illa imperficit longam precedentem nisi per punctum aut aliud impediatur. Idem est de semibrevi inter breves maioris prolationis ut hic:*

imperfici quod

Item novetur

DAC 1

:⋯
:⋯
:⋯
:⋯
:⋯

quoad totum, et quinque minimis vel earum * ^ valorem quoad totum vel ad ambas partes remanentes. Et non potest plus imperfici quia non remanet [...] nisi valor brevis imperfecta minoris prolationes quia non potest imperfici ut dictum est.

Nota breviter quod quidquid est divisibile in tres principales et equales partes hoc potest imperfici et quod non non. Et quamdiu atque quotiens dividi, sic potest tamdiu et totiens imperfici et non plus. Item nota breviter:

regule que secuntur:

Prima regula est quod longa ante longam in minori modo perfecto semper est perfecta quoad totum. Similiter brevis

ante brevem in tempori perfecto quoad totum est perfecta. Et semibrevis ante semibrevem in maiori prolatione

perfecta est ut hic: ■ ■ ○ ■ ■ ↄ ■ ♦ ♦ .[1]

quod [[quoquid]] quidquid et ...tes hoc
Et qu... dividi
Imperfici ... [non] plus. Item [[no...ter]] nota

perfect ... est |Similiter [[...]] brevis
... [per]fectionis quoad
Et [semibrevis ante]
[10v] minori prolatione
est perfecta

1 In *De arte cantus* 1, the graphemes ↄ ■ are hard to read due to bleedthrough; the ↄ might be a ○, while the breve might be a square mensuration sign with a slash or dot in it.

Texts and translations 107

and five minims ^ * or their value with respect to its whole or to both of its remaining parts, and it cannot be further imperfected because nothing remains but the value of an imperfect breve of minor prolation, which cannot be imperfected, as has been said.

Note briefly that anything that is divisible into three principal and equal parts can be imperfected, and that that is not, cannot. And as long as and as often as it can be [so] divided, thus so long and so often it can be imperfected, and no more. Likewise, note briefly the rules that follow:

The first rule is that a long before a long in minor perfect mode is always perfect with respect to the whole. Similarly, a breve before a breve in perfect tempus is perfect with respect to the whole. And a semibreve before a semibreve in major prolation is perfect, as here. ■ ■ ○ ■ ■ ◗ ■ ◆ ◆.

DAC 1	DAC 2

DAC 2

Secunda regula: post ommem notam que imperficitur, si aliud oportet sequi notulam vel pausam maioris vel minoris forme quia similis ante similem non potest imperfici ut hic: ■ ■ ■ ○ • • ◆ • ◆ ■ •

[112v]

Tertia regula est quando post longam minori modi perfecti secuntur due vel tres breves tantum tunc ipsa longa non potest ab aliqua ipsarum imperfici, quia quando due vel tres notule vel earum valorem inveniuntur simul sine puncto in medio tunc ille non debent partiri sed in

Tercia

simil

simul computari. Sed si punctus divisionis poneretur inter primam brevem et aliam vel aliam sequentes, tunc ipsa

prima brevis imperficiter longam precedentem ut hic:

■ • ■ • ■ ■ • . Item est de brevi temporis perfecti respectu semibrevium, et de semibrevis maioris prolationis respectu minimarum ut hic: ■ ◆ • ◆ • ◆ • ◆ ■ .

Idem

Quarta regula est quando inter duas longas minoris * modum perfectum remanet sola brevis perfectione computata, si plures fuerint tunc illa imperficit longam precedentem, nisi per punctum aut aliud impediatur. Idem est de semibrevi inter breves temporis perfecte et de minima inter semibreves maioris prolationis ut hic:

see above *

om temporis …
… semibreves

DAC 1

perficitur
alliquid sequitur a parte sequi
figure quia

ipsam
alliquid aliarum (allarum)
valor
sine medio puncto tunc |
partiri | om in

et alliam [vel ali]as
[sequen]tes tunc ipsam
imperfici[…] lon[gam]
precedente

res[…] | maioris … s
ut hic:

Quarta … quando
modi perfecti

alliud | Item
… semibrevi

The second rule: after all notes that are imperfected, if another follows, it must be a note or rest greater or smaller in figure, because like before like cannot be imperfected, as here:

■ ■ ■ ■ ○ ■ ♦ · ♦ ■ ■ ♦ ♦ ♦ ■ .

The third rule is when two or three breves follow after a long of minor perfect mode, then such a long cannot be imperfected by any of them, because when two or three notes or their value are found simultaneously without a punctus in the middle, then they cannot be parted but must be computed together. But if the dot of division is placed between the first breve and the other, or another following, then that first breve imperfects the preceding long, as here: ■ ■ · ■ ■ · ■ ■ ■ · ■ ■. Likewise, the same applies to a breve of perfect tempus with respect to semibreves, and to a semibreve of major prolation with respect to minims, as here: ■ ♦ ♦ ■ ♦ ♦ ♦ ■ ♦ · ♦ ■ ■ · ♦ ♦ ♦ ♦ ♦ ♦ ♦ ♦ · ♦ ♦ ♦ ■ .

The fourth rule is when, reckoned by perfection, a single breve * remains between two longs of minor perfect mode, if there are more, then it imperfects the preceding long, unless it is impeded by a punctus or something else. Likewise, the same applies to a semibreve between breves of perfect tempus, and to a minim between semibreves of major prolation, as here: ■ ■ ■ ■ ■ ■ ■ · ■ ■ ■ ○ ■ ♦ ♦ ♦ ♦ ■ ♦ ■ · ♦ ■ ■ ♦ ♦ ♦ ♦ ♦ ♦ · ♦ ♦ ♦ ♦ ■ *

Texts and translations 109

DAC 1

pr...qu... propinquiori
inferfectione imperficiente, si
etiam... imperficiente om et
quem ...
potest ...
[...] ■ [...] ♦ • • ■ ♦ ♦ ○
♦ [...]
[102]

notatur sincopa
| imperfectis suficerit

notula alterare
duplicare
semibrevis ante semibrevem vel
ante pausam brevis
vel ante pausam longam
longa

punctum

vallet

om Idem...
... in tempore | om de
maiori

om patet

DAC 2

si plura imperfici[...]cia

Quinta regula: quidquid imperficitur, imperficitur a propinquori inperficiente, si plura imperficiente, et omnis

figura sola reduci debet ad priorem locum quem comode potest habere ut hic:

[4] Item nota quod omnis reducio notularum ad invicem vocatur sincopa. Et hoc de imperfectione sufficit.

altaratione

5. Sequitur de alteratione, unde notula alterata est eius valorem dupplicatarum. Item minima potest alterari ante semibrevem vel eius pausam, semibrevis ante brevem vel eius pausam, brevis ante longam vel eius pausam longe, et longam ante maximam et non aliter. Item quando inter duas longas in minore modo perfecto vel pausas longarum vel inter puncta et longam aut in principio ante longam inveniuntur simul due breves sine puncto in medio tunc secunda brevis alteratur id est valet duas breves.

breve...

Idem est de duabus semibrevibus ante brevem vel inter breves in tempore perfecto et de duabus minimis inter semibreves vel ante semibrevem in minori prolatione et de duabus longis inter maximas vel ante maximam in maiori modo perfecto ut hic patet:

Texts and translations 111

The fifth rule: whatever is imperfected is imperfected by the nearest imperfecting note, if there are several such imperfecting notes, and each lone figure should be reduced to the nearest place that it can conveniently have, as here:

■ ■ ■ ■ · ▪ ▪ ✦ ✦ · · ▪ ✦ ◆ · ✦ ■ ▪ ◆ ◢ ◯ ◆ ✦ · ✦ ◢ ✦ · ◆ ◆ | ○ ◆ ✦ · · ◆ · ◆ ◆ ▼ .

4. Likewise, note that all reduction of notes to each other is called *sincopa*. And this is sufficient for imperfection.

5. What follows is of alteration, in which an altered note is double its own value. Likewise, a minim can be altered before a semibreve or its rest, a semibreve before a breve or its rest, a breve before a long or its long rest, and a long before a maxima, and none other. Likewise, when two breves are found simultaneously between two longs in minor perfect mode or long rests, or between a punctus and a long, or in the beginning before a long, without a punctus in the middle, then the second breve is altered, that is, it is worth two breves.

Likewise, the same is applied to two semibreves before a breve or in between breves in perfect tempus, and to two minims between semibreves or before a semibreve in minor prolation, and to two longs between maximas or before a maxima ^ in major perfect mode, as shown here: ■ ■ ■ ▪ · ■ ■ ▪ ■ ○ | ◢ ▪ ✦ · ◆ ◆ ◥ ○ ✦ ◆ ◢ ✦ ◆ ✦ ◆ ✦ · · ◆ ✦ ◆ ○

■ ▪ · ▪ · ✦ ▪ ■ ◆ ✦ ■
■ ✦ ✦ ◆ ✦ ▪ ■

DAC 1

[musical notation]

tempus brevis modi

*et minore
alliquod*

perfectionis et divisionis

*notulam de sua natura
imperfectam perficit
addendo super medium
[102v] est converso
alteram notulam
ipsam*

[musical staff notation]

*om mensurabile
ut retro et hic:*

DAC 2

[[musical notation]]

*prolatione
om ad perficiendum*
[113]

[[aliquo]] aliquo

punto | puntus

Puntus

Et nota quod notula alterata potest inperfici ut hic:
[musical notation]

Item minima alteratur ad perficiendum prolationem, semibrevis ad perficiendum temporis, brevis ^ modus minorem, et longa modum maiorem. Item nota quod reducio non impedit neque iuvat alterationem in aliquo.

6. Sequitur de puncto. Unus punctus est duplex, videlicet punctus perfectionis et punctus divisionis.

Punctus perfectionis de sui natura notulam perfectam facit adendo sibi medietatem sui valoris. Punctus autem divisionis e contrario. Notulam perfectam facit quomodocumque imperfici faciendo cum eo aliam notam computari que non computaretur cum ipsa si talis punctus non esset.

Item omnis punctus post minimam positus et etiam post quamcumque pausam mensurabile positus est punctus divisionis ut hic:

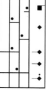

And note that an altered note can be imperfected, as here:

❖ ❖ ❖ ❖ ❖ ❖ ▪ ▪ ❖ ❖ ❖ ❖ ❖ ❖ ▪ ▪ ❖ ▪ ▪

Likewise, a minim is altered to perfect the prolation, the semibreve to perfect the tempus, the breve ˄ the minor mode, and the long the major mode. Likewise, note that reduction does not impede nor assist alteration in anything.

6. The following concerns the punctus. A punctus is twofold, namely, the punctus of perfection and the punctus of division.

The punctus of perfection, by its nature, makes a note perfect by adding half of its value to itself. But a punctus of division is the opposite. It makes a perfect note imperfect in some degree by making it to be calculated with another note and not calculated by itself, [as it would be] if such a punctus were not there.

Likewise, every punctus placed after a minim and also placed after any measurable rest is a punctus of division, as here:

114   *Texts and translations*

DAC 1		DAC 2
minoris perfecta	Item quando inter duas longas modi minorum perfecti sunt due breves et punctus ponatur inter illas breves, tunc	
est punctus	ille punctus est divisionis ut hic: ■ ▪ • ▪ nisi breves ille sint temporis imperfecti, et ante vel post eas sequatur sola semibrevis, tunc enim punctus ille erit punctus perfectionis ut hic: ■ ▪ • ♦ ▪ •	*om erit*
om sint	Idem est de brevibus temporis perfecti inter quas sint due semibreves et punctus inter eas ut hic sequitur: ▪ • ♦ ▪ •	*inter ipsas* *om ut ... ▪ • ♦ ▪ •*
*per se sequitur	ligaturis*	7. Dicto de notulis per sequitur de ipsis ligaturarum. Una ligatura est duplex, scilicet ascendens et descendens.	
atior est priori	Ascendens quando secunda notula altior est prima, descendens de se converso, videlicet quando prima notula altior est secunda. Et de hoc nota que secuntur.	*om de ... videlicet*
omnis prima brevis breves ... *cum*	Primo scilicet quod omnes prime breves dicuntur cum	
...te et	proprietate et omnis prime longe dicuntur sine proprietate.	*probrietate	om et ...* *... proprietate.*
	Omnis prime semibreves dicuntur cum opposita proprietate. Item omnis ultime breves dicuntur sine perfectione. Et omnis ultima longe dicuntur cum perfectione.	
om De ligaturis	De ligaturis.	
prime breves [notation] [103]	Item omnis prima longe ut hic: [notation]	
prime longe [notation]	Item omnis ultima longe ut hic: [notation]	
ut sequitur: [notation]	Item omnis prime due semibreves ut hic: [notation]	

Likewise, when two breves are between two longs of minor perfect mode and a punctus is placed between those breves, then that punctus is one of division, as here: ■ ■ · ■ ■ unless those breves are of imperfect tempus, and a single semibreve should occur before or after them, then in fact that punctus is a punctus of perfection, as here: ■ ■ · ■ ◆ ■.

Likewise, the same applies to breves of perfect tempus between which are two semibreves and a punctus between them, as follows here: ■ ◆ · ◆ ■ .

7. Having spoken of notes, what follows concerns ligatures themselves. A ligature is twofold, namely, ascending and descending. Ascending, when the second note is higher than the first; descending, the inverse, namely, when the first note is higher than the second. And of this, note what follows: first, namely, that all first breves are called "with propriety" and all first longs are called "without propriety." All first semibreves are called "with opposite propriety." Likewise, all last breves are called "without perfection." And all last longs are called "with perfection."

Of ligatures.
Likewise, all first longs, as here:

Likewise, all last longs, as here:

Likewise, all first two semibreves, as here:

116 *Texts and translations*

DAC 1	DAC 2
ultime breves	Item omnis prime breves ut hic:
Ultime omnes longe	Item omnis ultime breves ut hic:
[103v] *esset etiam*	Item omnis medie sunt breves. Si plures sint breves. Si plures sint quam due simul ligate nisi prima esset semibrevis quia tunc secunda esset semibrevis.
[[p]] temporam ocupat | ocupat valet temporam. | pluram debe vac vac. nam | om pausa temporum temporum	8. Sequitur de pausis. Una pausa valet tot tempora quot occupat spatia, si igitur occupat tria spatia tria tempora valet. Si vero plura tunc est comunis et in mensurabilis, nam maior pausa trium tempore non est ponenda. Si autem occupat duo spatia duo valet tempora et si unum unum. Item pausa semibrevis incipere debet in linea et descendere debet usque ad medium spatii. Pausa vero minimarum et converso incipiendo etiam in linea a [113v] *Si plura sint quaque simul*
om *debet | spatium vel spatii [...]mine de converso incipiens [in] linia attendit*	adscendere usque ad medium spatii.
om *Exempla de pausis imperfici nec etiam alterari*	Exempla de pausis. Et nota quod pausa non potest alterari neque imperfici. De pausis omnibus ut hic:  Om *De ... hic:*

Likewise, all first breves, as here:

Likewise, all last breves, as here:

Likewise, all middle notes are breves, if more than two simultaneously are ligated, unless the first is a semibreve, because then the second is a semibreve.

8. The following concerns rests. A rest is worth, however, many tempora as spaces it occupies. If it occupies three spaces, it is worth three tempora. If more, then it is joint and immeasurable, for no rest greater than three tempora is to be placed. If, however, it occupies two spaces, it is worth two tempora, and if one, one. Likewise, the semibreve rest should begin on the line and should descend to the middle of the space. But the minim rest is the opposite, also beginning on the line and ascending to the middle of the space.

Examples of rests. And note that a rest cannot be altered nor imperfected. Of all rests, as here:

118   *Texts and translations*

DAC 1		*DAC 2*
discurrere discernere imperfecto *est sciendum quod* *quominus convenienter potest | ibi debent* *fuit per aliud spatius*	9. Restat nunc discernere perfectum ab imperfectum pro quo sciendum est primo quod quomodocumque quominus tunc potest fieri computatio per tria, tunc ibi debet indicari	*Extat et nunc |* *imperfe[…] pro* *quomodocumque qu[…]*
	perfecto nisi hoc fiat per aliud specialiter impedimentum.	*aliut*
minor	Item si post pausam longam punctus habeatur, signum est quod maior modus est perfectus. Item si inveniatur pausa trium temporum signum est quod maior modus est perfectus in illo genere. Similiter si post pausam unius temporis	*longe* *maior \[[de]] modus*
signum	punctus habeatur signis est etiam quod minor est perfectus.	
tempus est p…f…tum et … *etiam post [m]inimam* *p…tus i…niatur*	Item si post pausam semibrevis habeatur punctus signum est quod tempus est perfectus et si post minimam vel	*pausa*
	pausam minime punctus inveniatur signum est maioris prolationis.	*interveniatur*
et nig… longe longe [104] */[perfecte]] perfecti | allie*	Item si rubee sint et nigre. Longe nigre dicuntur modi perfecti et rubee imperfecti. Si vero breves nigre sunt perfecti temporis, alie imperfecti, sique semibreves nigre	*sicque semibrevis*
minoris prolationis maioris *prolationis allie | alii* *fiant hec omniam*	sunt maioris prolationis, alie minoris, licet aliquando hec	
	omnia fiant est converso.	*[[omnia]] omnia*
	Item bene inspiciendum est ad canones seu subscriptiones	*incipiendo | om canones* *seu*
canendum *fuerint*	sique sint quia prout incipis continetur, ita est cantandum etiam si fiunt contra artem.	

Texts and translations 119

9. Now it remains to discern perfect from imperfect, about which it should first be known that wherever a calculation can be made by three, then there it should indicate perfect, unless this is done specifically by another impediment.

Likewise, if a punctus is placed after a long rest, it signifies that the major mode is perfect. Likewise, if a rest of three tempora is found, it signifies that the major mode is perfect in that genus. Similarly, if a punctus is placed after a rest of one tempus, it too is a sign that the minor [mode] is perfect.

Likewise, if a punctus is placed after a semibreve rest, it is a sign that the tempus is perfect, and if a punctus is found after a minim or a minim rest, it is a sign of major prolation.

Likewise, if there are red and black, black longs designate perfect mode and red imperfect. If, though, black breves are of perfect tempus, the others are imperfect; and if black semibreves are of major prolation, the others are minor, although at any point these can be made in reverse.

Likewise, rightly canons and written instructions should be observed (if they be there, because just as you begin, you continue), they must be sung, even if it is made against art.

DAC 1		DAC 2
talis ⊃ talis	Item circulus talis ○ vel similis designat perfectionem. Et semicirculus talis ⊃ vel similis designant imperfectionem.	om *talis* ○ *vel similis* om *talis* ⊃ *vel similis* *designant*
vel om in *punctum signum tria*	Item ponuntur aliquando in circulo vel in semicirculo puncti signi. Si tres fuerint prolatio erit maior: ⊙ ꜩ et si duo minor ⊙ ꜩ	om ⊙ ... ꜩ
vifre *binaria*	Item cifre numeri ternarii designant perfectionem ternaria est ist(t)a: 3 et binarii imperfectionem inferioris in tempore et superioris in prolatione binaria est ista: 2.	[*ci⌐fre⌐	perfectione* om *ternaria est ista: 3* om *binaria est ista: 2*
modernorum	10. Sequitur de diminutione que sepe fit in tenoribus motetorum.	*mutectorum*
Et primo nota quod pro *maximas ponatur* *diminutionem	pro brevis*	Et nota primo pro maxima ponitur longa in diminutione pro longa, brevis; pro brevi, semibrevis; et pro semibrevi, minima. Idem est de pausis suo modo.	
diminutionem est de minori	Item quando tenor habens diminucionem est diminutio modo imperfecto cuiuscumque temporis fuerit tunc eius diminutio fit directe per medium notarum vel pausarum.	*est	[d]	* [114] *medius*
*est de modo minori	om* *tempore ...*	Item si est diminutio minorem perfecto et tempore	
*...perfecto	tempore etiam* *perfecto tunc cius	trium*	imperfecto diminutio eius etiam fit per medium. Item si est diminutio minorem perfecto tempore perfecto etiam tunc eius diuinutio fit per tertium. Exempla patent in tenoribus motetorum.	*mutectorum*

Texts and translations 121

Likewise, such a circle, ○, or similar, designates perfection. And such a semicircle, ○, or similar, designates imperfection. Likewise, at times puncti are placed in the circle or in the semicircle as a sign. If three are placed, the prolation is major: ⊙ ⊃ and if two, minor: ⊙ ⊃

Likewise, a cipher of the number three designates perfection; ternary is this: 3. and the number two [designates] imperfection—the lower in tempus and the upper in prolation—binary is this: 2.

10. The following is on diminution, which often occurs in tenors of motets.

And first note that in diminution a long is placed for a maxima; a breve for a long; a semibreve for a breve; and a minim for a semibreve. Likewise, it applies to rests in their mode. Likewise, when a tenor having diminution is in imperfect mode, regardless of tempus, its diminution then is made directly by half [the value] of the note or rest. Likewise, if it is diminution of perfect mode and imperfect tempus, its diminution also is made by half. Likewise, if diminution is of perfect mode, also perfect tempus, then its diminution is made to the third. Examples are shown in the tenors of motets.

DAC 1   *DAC 2*

11. Item nota quod color in musica largo modo dicitur
quando eedem voces vel eedem significata figuram in

om *sed …*   eodem cantu plures repetuntur, ^ sed stricto modo color
  … etiam | et   dicitur quando repetuntur eodem voces etiam si sint
eedem   diversarum figurarum. Et tunc quando repetuntur eodem
figure | notum hoc | taylla figuram etiam si sint diversarum vocum hec vocatur talla.
in pluribus   Et ista differentiam servatur in quampluribus tenoribus
om *et … cantus*   motetorum et cetera. Et per hoc sit finis de arte cantus.
[104v]
^*Set corto modo color quando*
repetuntur eedem voces. Et per
hoc sit finit abreviacionem de
arte cantus.

om *largo modo*
om *quando | eodem voces vel*
  eodem | om *significate*
plurores

[[vocum]] vocum

om *…*   Pro quo nota quod non [[n]] nulli cantores ponunt
…   differenciam inter colorem et tallam. Unam color [[in
…   musica ta]] in musica vocatur similium figurarum unius
…   processus pluries repe[…] positus in eodem cantu. Pro quo
…   nota quod nulli cantores ponunt differentiam inter colorem
…   et tallam. Nam vocatur vero colorem quando repetuntur
…   eodem voces. Talla vero quando repetuntur similes figures
…   et sunt diversarum vocum que differencia licet consuetur in
…   quampluribus tenoribus mutectorum non tamen servatur in
…   motectis.

11. Likewise, note that in general it is called color in music when the same pitches or the same figures are repeated many times in the same melody, but more strictly it is called color when the same pitches are repeated, even if they have different figures. And then when the same figures are repeated, even if they have different pitches, that is called talea. And this difference is observed in many tenors of motets, etc. And by this is made the end of the art of song.

On this, note that some singers differentiate between color and talea. The placement of one series of similar figures, repeated many times in the same melody, is called color in music. On this, note that [some] singers differentiate between color and talea. They call it color when the same pitches are repeated; talea, when the same figures are repeated, [even] if they are of different pitches. This differentiation can be observed in many tenors of motets, but not in the motets.

124   *Texts and translations*

Appendix 2b: Regulae contrapunctus

Regulae contrapunctus

[104v] Secuntur regule contrapunctus per supradictum magistrum facte sive ordinate ut sequitur.

Pro noticia contrapunctus habenda primo sciendum est quod {nomen} novem sunt species discantus, scilicet unisonus, tercia (MS dercia?), quinta, sexta, viii, xa, duadecima, xiiia, et quintadecima, quarum quinque sunt perfecte et quatuor imperfecte. Quinque perfecte sunt unisonus, quinta, octava, duodecima, quintadecima {quatuor decima}. Imperfecte sunt tertia, sexta, decima, tertiadecima.

Item omnes cantus incipi debent et finiri in consonantia perfecta. Item cantus ascendit, discantus debet descende vel stare in eodem loco. Item bene possunt fieri due vel tres vel iiiior tertie una post alliam gradatim omnes ascendendo vel omnes descendendo et tot idem sexte, tot idem decime iiie decime. Item numquam debent fieri duo unisoni nec due de supradictis perfectis una post alliam sine me[dio].

Item semper post sexta et terdecima opportet ascende vel descende et hoc per unam vocem tantum. Sed post allias consonantias omnes licet ascendere et descendere per plures voces, etiam in eodem loco remanere. Item discantus potest ascendere [105] et descendere cum plano cantu per unam vocem tantum tamquam ad faciendam consonantiam perfectam. Sed ad faciendum consonantia imperfectam {non} potest ascendere vel descendere cum tenore discantus per tot voces quolibet volueris.

Item post unisonum quelibet allia consonantia preterquam octava et vxa. Item post tertiam potest fieri quelibet allia consonantia preterquam decimam. Item post quintam potest fieri quelibet alliam consonantia preterquam xiia. Item post sextam debet fieri viiia per proximiorem \notam/ sequentem et non alliter. Potest etiam fieri decimam post ipsam et hoc si tenor descendit ad [[qutam]] quartam vocem vel tertia simplex si tenor ascendit quintam vocem.

Item post octavam potest fieri quelibet allia consonantia preterquam unisonus et vxa. Item post decimam potest fieri quelibet allia consonantia preterquam tertia. Item post xiia potest fieri quelibet allia consonantia preterquam quinta.

Texts and translations   125

The rules of counterpoint

Next, the rules of counterpoint, made or arranged by the aforementioned magister, as follows.

In order to have knowledge of counterpoint, it should first be known that there are nine species of discant, namely, the unison, third, fifth, sixth, eighth, tenth, twelfth, thirteenth, and fifteenth, of which five are perfect and four imperfect. The five perfect species are the unison, fifth, octave, twelfth, fifteenth {fourteenth}. The imperfect [species] are the third, sixth, tenth, thirteenth.

Likewise, all songs should begin and end on a perfect consonance. Likewise, when the cantus ascends, the discant should descend or stay in the same place. Likewise, there can well be two or three or four thirds, one after another, step by step, all ascending or all descending, and the same number of sixths, the same number of tenths or thirteenths. Likewise, there ought never to be two unisons nor two of the aforementioned perfect [intervals] one after the other without an intermediary.

Likewise, one should always ascend or descend after a sixth and a thirteenth, and this by only one note. But after other consonances, one can ascend or descend by many notes, as well as remain in the same place. Likewise, the discantus can ascend or descend with the cantus [plainchant] by one note, so as to make a perfect consonance. But to make an imperfect consonance, the discant can {not} ascend or descend with the tenor by however many notes you want.

Likewise, after a unison can be made whichever other consonances except the octave and fifteenth. Likewise, after the third can be made whichever other consonances except the tenth. Likewise, after the fifth can be made whichever other consonances except the twelfth. Likewise, after the sixth, an octave should be made with the nearest following note and none other. Also, a tenth can be made after it, and this if the tenor descends to the fourth note, or a simple third if the tenor ascends to the fifth note.

Likewise, after the octave can be made whichever other consonances, except the unison and the fifteenth. Likewise, after the tenth can be made whichever other consonances except the third. Likewise, after the twelfth can be made whichever other consonances except the fifth.

126   *Texts and translations*

Item post xiiia potest fieri quelibet o[ctava] debet proportionaliter sicut post sextam. Item etiam post quintamdecimam potest fieri quelibet allia consonania preterquam unisonus et viii. Item post qualibet alliam consonantiam perfectam melius expedit imperfectam consonanciam facere quam perfectam.

Item magister Johannes Pipudi, canonicus Sancti Desiderii avinionensis, ordinavit istas regulas dicens sic quod quando cantus ascendit per unicam vocem discantus potest ascendere per plures voces. Et quando cantus ascendit per plures voces discantus non debet ascendere nisi per unam. Et e converso quando cantus descendit per unam vocem discantus potest descendere per plures. Et quando cantus descendit per plures voces discantus potest descendere per unam vocem tantum et est finis.

Item dictus dominus magister Johannes ordinavit regulas sequentes pro [[contrapuc]] contrapuncto sciendo ut sequitur.

Exempla b quadri incipiendo in g-sol-re-ut basso usque ad e-la-mi altum:
[105v]

	viii	x	xii [xiii]	xiii
gamaut	ut	mi	sol	la
	viii	x	xii	
A-re	re	fa	la	
	via	viiia	xa	
B-mi	ut	mi	sol	
	v[i]a	via	viii	x
C-fa-ut	ut	re	fa	la
	v	via	viii	
D-sol-re	re	mi	sol	
	iii	va	via	viii
E-la-mi	ut	mi	fa	[sol] la
	iii	v	vi	
F-fa-ut	re	fa	sol	

Texts and translations 127

Likewise, after the thirteenth can be made whichever octave should proportionally [be made], as after the sixth. Likewise, also, after the fifteenth can be made whichever other consonances except the unison and the octave. Likewise, after whichever other perfect consonances, it is better to make an imperfect consonance instead of a perfect one.

Likewise, magister Johannes Pipudi, canon of Saint-Didier in Avignon, arranged these rules, saying that when the cantus ascends by one note, the discant should ascend by several notes. And when the cantus ascends by several note, the discant should not ascend unless by one. And vice versa, when the cantus descends by one note, the discantus can descend by several. And when the cantus descends by several notes, the discantus can descend by one note only, and it is done.

Likewise, the aforementioned dominus magister Johannes organized the following rules for understanding counterpoint, as follows:

Examples of B quadrum, beginning on G-sol-re-ut bassus up to E-la-mi altus:

	8	10	12	13
gamaut	ut	mi	sol	la
	8	10	12	
A-re	re	fa	la	
	6	8	10	
B-mi	ut	mi	sol	
	5	6	8	10
C-fa-ut	ut	re	fa	la
	5	6	8	
D-sol-re	re	mi	sol	
	3	5	6	8
E-la-mi	ut	mi	fa	la
	3	5	6	
F-fa-ut	re	fa	sol	

128   *Texts and translations*

	unisonus	iii	v	vi
G-sol-re-ut	ut	mi	sol	la

	unisonus	iii	v
a-la-mi-re	re	fa	la

	iii	iii
b-fa	ut	sol

	iii	unisonus	iii
b-mi	ut	mi	sol

\t/	iii	unisonus	iii
c-sor-fa-u[s]	re	fa	la

[106]	v	iii	unisonus
de-la-sor-re	ut	mi	sol

	vi	v	iii	unisonus
e-la-mi	ut	re	fa	la

Exempla nature incipiendo in ce-sol-fa-ut usque ad a-la-mi-re-acutum:

	xii	xiii	[vx] xv	
gamaut	re	mi	sol	

	x	xii	xiii	xv
A-re	ut	mi	fa	la

	x	xii	xiii	
b-mi	re	fa	sol	

	viii	x	xii	xiii
c-fa-ut	ut	mi	sol	la

	viii	x	xii	
de-sol-re	re	fa	la	

	vi	viii	x	
e-la-mi	ut	mi	sol	

	v	vi	viii	x
f-fa-ut	ut	re	fa	la

	1	3	5	6
G-sol-re-ut	ut	mi	sol	la
	1	3	5	
a-la-mi-re	re	fa	la	
	3	4		
b-fa	ut	sol		
	3	1	3	
b-mi	ut	mi	sol	
	3	1	3	
c-sol-fa-ut	re	fa	la	
[106]	5	3	1	
d-la-sol-re	ut	mi	sol	
	6	5	3	1
e-la-mi	ut	re	fa	la

Examples of the natural [hexachord] beginning on C-sol-fa-ut all the way to acute a-la-mi-re:

	12	13	15	
Gamaut	re	mi	sol[vx]	
	10	12	13	15
A-re	ut	mi	fa	la
	10	12	13	
b-mi	re	fa	sol	
	8	10	12	13
c-fa-ut	ut	mi	sol	la
	8	10	12	
de-sol-re	re	fa	la	
	6	8	10	
e-la-mi	ut	mi	sol	
	5	6	8	10
f-fa-ut	ut	re	fa	la

130   *Texts and translations*

g-sol-re-us	[[v]] / [[ut]]	v / re	vi / mi	viii / sol
a-la-mi-re	iii / ut	v / mi	vi / fa	viii / la
b-fa	iii / re	v / fa	vi / sol	
b-mi	iii / re	vi / sol		
c-sol-fa-ut	unisonus / ut	iii / mi	v / sol	vi / la
d-la-sol-re	unisonus / re	iii / fa	v / la	
e-la-mi	iii / ut	unisonus / mi	iii / sol	
[106v] f-fa-ut	iii / re	unisonus / fa	iii / la	
g-sol-re-ut	v / ut	iii / mi	unisonus / sol	
a-la-mi-re	vi / ut	v / re	iii / fa	unisonus / la
b-fa	vi / re	iii / sol		
b-mi	vi / re	v / mi	iii / sol	
c-sol-fa	viii / ut	vi / mi	v[i] / fa	iii / la
d-la-sol	viii / re	vi / fa	v / sol	
e-la	x / ut	viii / mi	vi / sol	v / la

Texts and translations 131

g-sol-re-us	5 ut	5 re	5 mi	8 sol
a-la-mi-re	3 ut	5 mi	6 fa	8 la
b-fa	3 re	5 fa	6 sol	
b-mi	3 re	6 sol		
c-sol-fa-ut	1 ut	3 mi	5 sol	6 la
d-la-sol-re	1 re	3 fa	5 la	
e-la-mi	3 ut	1 mi	3 sol	
[106v] f-fa-ut	3 re	1 fa	3 la	
g-sol-re-ut	5 ut	3 mi	1 sol	
a-la-mi-re	6 ut	5 re	3 fa	1 la
b-fa	6 re	3 sol		
b-mi	6 re	5 mi	3 sol	
c-sol-fa	8 ut	6 mi	5 fa	3 la
d-la-sol	8 re	6 fa	5 sol	
e-la	10 ut	8 mi	6 sol	5 la

132 Texts and translations

Exempla B quadri incipiendo in g-sol-re-ut alto usque e-la etc.

gamaut	xv [u] ut	xvii mi	xix sol	xx la
a-re	xv re	xvii fa	xix la	
b-mi	xiii ut	xx mi	xvii sol	
c-fa-ut	xii ut	viii re	xv fa	xiii la
d-sol-re	xii re	xiii mi	xv sol	
e-la-mi	x ut	xii mi	xiii fa	xv sol
[107] f-fa-ut	x re	xii fa	xiii sol	
g-sol-re-ut	viii ut	x mi	xii sol	xiii la
a-la-mi-re	viii re	x fa	xii la	
b-fa	vi ut	x sol		
b-mi	vi ut	viii mi	x sol	
c-sol-fa-ut	v ut	vi re	viii fa	x la
d-la-sol-re	v re	vi mi	viii sol	
e-la-mi	v	v mi	vi fa	viii la

Texts and translations   133

An example of square B beginning on high g-sol-re-ut all the way to e-la, etc.

	15	17	19	20
gamaut	[u] ut	mi	sol	la
	15	17	19	
a-re	re	fa	la	
	13	20	18	
b-mi	ut	mi	sol	
	12	13	15	13
c-fa-ut	ut	re	fa	la
	12	13	16	
d-sol-re	re	mi	sol	
	10	12	13	15
e-la-mi	ut	mi	fa	sol
[107]	10	12	13	
f-fa-ut	re	fa	sol	
	8	10	12	13
g-sol-re-ut	ut	mi	sol	la
	8	10	12	
a-la-mi-re	re	fa	la	
	6	10		
b-fa	ut	sol		
	6	8	10	
b-mi	ut	mi	sol	
	5	6	8	10
c-sol-fa-ut	ut	re	fa	la
	5	6	8	
d-la-sol-e	re	mi	sol	
	5	5	6	8
e-la-mi		mi	fa	la

	iii	v	vi	
f-fa-ut	re	fa	sol	

	unisonus	iii	v	vi
g-sol-re-ut	ut	mi	sol	la

	unisonus	iii	v
a-la-mi-re	re	fa	la

	iii	iii
b-fa	ut	sol

	iii	iii
b-mi	ut	sol

	iii	unisonus	iii
c-sol-fa	re	fa	la

	v	iii	[uni] unisonus
d-la-sol	ut	mi	[fa] sol

	vi	v	iii	unisonus
e-la	ut	re	fa	la

Et est finis deo gratias.

Texts and translations 135

	3	5	6	
f-fa-ut	re	fa	sol	
	1	3	5	6
g-sol-re-ut	ut	mi	sol	la
	1	3	5	
a-la-mi-re	re	fa	la	
	3	3		
b-fa	ut	sol		
	3	3		
b-mi	ut	sol		
	3	1	3	
c-sol-fa	re	fa	la	
	5	3	[1] 1	
d-la-sol	ut	mi	[fa] sol	
	vi	v	3	1
e-la	ut	re	fa	la

And it is finished, thanks be to God.

136   *Texts and translations*

Appendix 2c: Catalan notes

Notes

Edited by
Karen M. Cook and
David Catalunya

[107v] Quando tres minime pro semibreve, tunc est maior prolatio, ut hic: ♦♦♦ ♦ maior prolatio.
Quando due minime ordinatur pro semibreve, tunc est minor prolatio, ut hic: ♦♦ ♦ minor prolatio.
Quando tres semibreves ordinatur pro breve, tunc est tempus perfectum, ut hic: ♦ ♦ ♦ ■ tempus perfectum.
Quando due semibreves ordinatur pro breve, tunc est tempus imperfectum, ut hic: ♦ ♦ ■ tempus imperfectum.
Quando tres breves ordinatur pro longa, tunc est modus perfectus, ut hic: ■ ■ ■ ■ modus perfectus. Quando due breves ordinatur pro longa, tunc est modus imperfectus, ut hic: ■ ■ ■ modus imperfectus.

Primo, en gamaut ha tres consonantes, so es a saber, ut mi sol. Ut es octava, mi es x^a, sol es xii^a.
En a-re a tres consonantes, es saber, re fa la. Re es viii, fa x^a, la xii^a.
En be-mi a tres consonantes, so es saber, ut mi sol. Ut e vi, mi viii, sol, x^a.
En ce-fa-ut a iiii consonantes, es saber, ut re fa la. Ut es quinta, re vi, fa viii, la x^a.
En de-sol-re a tres consonantes, so es saber, re mi sol. Re quinta, mi vi, sol viii.
En e-la-mi a iiii consonantes: ut mi fa la. Ut es tercia, mi quinta, fa vi^a, la viii.
En f-fa-ut a tres consonantes: re fa sol. Re es iii^a fa v, sol vi^a.
En ge-sol-re-ut a iiii consonantes, es saber, ut mi sol la. Ut es unisonus, mi iii^a, sol v, la vi.
[108] En a-la-mi-re a iii consonantes, so es a saber, re fa la. Re es unisonus, fa iii^a, la v.
En b-fa be-mi a tre consonantes com lo cant se cante per be-cayre, so es saber, ut mi sol. Ut es tertia de jus, mi unisonus, sol tertia de jus; et quant lo cant se canta per be-mol non ha si non duas consonantes, so es saber, ut sol. Ut es terça de jus, e sol terça de jus.
En ce-sol-fa-ut a tres consonantes, es a saber, re fa la. Re es terça de jus, fa unisonus, la iii^a de jus.

Texts and translations 137

Notes

*Translated by
Karen M. Cook and
David Catalunya*

When three minims [are ordered] for a semibreve, that is major prolation, as here: ♦♦♦ ♦ maior prolatio.
When two minims are ordered for a semibreve, that is minor prolation, as here: ♦♦ ♦ minor prolatio.
When three semibreves are ordered for a breve, that is perfect tempus, as here: ♦♦♦ ■ tempus perfectum.
When two semibreves are ordered for a breve, that is imperfect tempus, as here: ♦♦ ■ tempus imperfectum.
When three breves are ordered for a long, that is perfect mode, as here: ■■■ ■ modus perfectus.
When two breves are ordered for a long, that is imperfect mode, as here: ■■ ■ modus imperfectus.

First, in gamaut there are three consonances, that is to say, ut mi sol. Ut is an octave, mi is a tenth, sol is a twelfth.
In A-re are three consonances, that is, re fa la. Re is an octave, fa a tenth, la a twelfth.
In B-mi are three consonances, that is, ut mi sol. Ut is a sixth, mi an octave, sol a tenth.
In C-fa-ut are four consonances, that is, ut re fa la. Ut is a fifth, re a sixth, fa an octave, la a tenth.
In D-sol-re are three consonances, that is, re mi sol. Re is a fifth, mi a sixth, sol an octave.
In E-la-mi are four consonances: ut mi fa la. Ut is a third, mi a fifth, fa a sixth, la an octave.
In F-fa-ut are three consonances, re fa sol. Re is a third, fa a fifth, sol a sixth.
In G-sol-re-ut are four consonances, that is, ut mi sol la. Ut is a unison, mi a third, sol a fifth, la a sixth.
In A-la-mi-re are three consonances, that is, re fa la. Re is a unison, fa a third, la a fifth.
In B-fa B-mi are three consonances as song is sung with square B, namely, ut mi sol. Ut is a third, mi a unison, sol a third; and when song is sung with soft B, you have nothing but two consonances, that is, ut sol. Ut is a third and sol a third.

138   *Texts and translations*

En de-la-sol-re a tres consonantes, so es saber, ut mi sol. Ut es v de jus, mi terça de jus, sol unisonus.

En e-la-mi acut a iiii consonantes, so es a saber, ut re fa la. Ut es vi^a de jus, re quinta de jus fa iii de jus, la unisonus. Et deves saber que tot aquest contrapunt se content de ge-sol-re-ut b-[c]ay[re] entro jus en e-la-mi acut.

Item diu lo mestre [que] nosaltres avem vii^a species de contrapunt, las qual sunt aquestas: unisonus, terça, quinta, sesta, octava, x^a, xii^a, las quals las iiii sunt perfectas et las tres imperfectas. Les perfectas sunt aquestas: unisonus, quinta, octava, xii^a. Las iii imperfectas sunt aquestas: sexta, iii, x^a. Per que pose lo maestre tal regla que tostem[ps] que tu boyles comenssar contrapunt, comensseras per la plus alta especia plus perfecta que sia en tota la guama, et si po[t]s en comenssar per xii^a non en comensseras per v^a, et si po[t]s comenssar per v non comensseras per unisonus.

Item diu lo maestre que jamays non feras duas xii^a ni duas viii^a ni duas v ni duas unisonus un apres de altres ni jamays non feras duas species perfectas una darere altre sens algun mi[t]gen.

Item diu lo maestre que tostem[ps] ordeneras ton [108v] contrapunt a donar la {propria} plus propria especia la una d.altra, a si com diu: apres unisonus iii^a en apres iii v, en apres v vi, en apres vi^a viii^a, en apres viii dehena, en apres x^a xii^a, et e converso et gemay non daras vi^a que viii^a non venga apres.

Item diu lo maestre que les iii especies imperfectas post pujar et devalar ap lo cant pla en desem. En apres les especies perfectas daras tostem[p]s lo contraria de las altras. Item tostemps entre duas perfectas daras la una imperfecta, o ii, o iii^a, pero que apres les imperfecta[s] daras les perfectas que si mericen a quascuna per deles perfectas iii^a imperfectas, asi com dey(e)m apres una iii, daras v^a o unisonus. Se la terça es perfecta daras v^a e se la terça es imperfecta dara unisonus. Apres una vi^a, o duas, o tres, daras octava. Apres ii [o] tres dehena[s], daras xii^a, et apres x^a, po[t]s fer octava.

In C-sol-fa-ut are three consonances, that is, re fa la. Re is a third, fa a unison, la a third.

In D-la-sol-re are three consonances, that is, ut mi sol. Ut is a fifth, mi a third, sol a unison.

In E-la-mi acute there are four consonances, that is, ut re fa la. Ut is a sixth, re a fifth, fa a third, la a unison. And you must know that all of this counterpoint consists of G-sol-re-ut through E-la-mi acute.

Likewise, the master says that we have seven species of counterpoint, which are these: unison, third, fifth, sixth, octave, tenth, twelfth, of which four are perfect and three imperfect. The perfect ones are these: unison, fifth, octave, twelfth. The three imperfect ones are these: sixth, third, tenth. Because the master has set such a rule that anytime you wish to begin a counterpoint, you will begin with the highest and more perfect species of the scale, and if you can begin with a twelfth, you will not begin with a fifth, and if you can begin with a fifth, you will not begin with a unison.

Likewise, the master says that you should never make two twelfths, nor two octaves, nor two fifths, nor two unisons one after the other, nor should you ever make two perfect species one after the other without some kind of intermediary.

Likewise, the master says that you will always organize your counterpoint in order to give the most appropriate species one after another, as it is said: after a unison, a third; and after a third, a fifth; and after a fifth, a sixth; and after a sixth, an octave; and after an octave, a tenth; and after a tenth, a twelfth, and vice versa; and you should never give a sixth that an octave does not immediately follow.

Likewise, the master says that three imperfect species can proceed up and down with the cantus in tenths. And after the perfect species, you will always give the contrary of the others. Likewise, between two perfects you will always give one imperfect, or two or three, but that after the imperfect ones you will give the perfect ones that belong to each of the three imperfects, as we were saying, after a third, you will give a fifth or a unison. If the third is perfect, you will give a fifth, and if the third is imperfect, you will give a unison. After a sixth, or two, or three, you will give an octave. After two or three tenths, you will give a twelfth, and after a tenth, you can make an octave.

140　*Texts and translations*

Appendix 2d: Nota quod novem sunt species contrapunctus videlicet ...

Nota quod novem sunt species contrapunctus videlicet ...

[110]　　　　　　　　　Jhesus Christus

Nota quod novem sunt species contrapunctus, videlicet unisonus, tercia, quinta, sexta, octava, decima, duadecima, terciadecima, e: quintadecima. Quarum quinque sunt perfecte et quatuor imperfecte. Perfecte sunt videlicet unisonus, quinta, octava, duadecima, et quintadecima. Imperfecte sunt videlicet tercia, sexta, decima, et terciadecima.

Et nota quod nos debemus incipere et finiri omnes contrapunctus per species perfectas. Penultima, vero, debet essere imperfecta. Item nota quod nos non possumus pronunciare duas species perfectas consimiles, uniam post aliam, scilicet unisonus et unisonus, vel duas quintas, etc. Set possumus pronunciari duas species imperfectas vel tres vel quatuor unam post aliam. Item nota quod quando cantus planus descendit nos debemus ascendere per contrapunctum et sic e contrario. [[Item nota quod bene possumus faceri dissimiles perfectas scilicet post unisonus quintam post quintam octavam et sic de siglis?]]

Item post unisonus possumus \facere/ quintam sextam et decimam.
Item post terciam possumus facere quintam sextam et decimam octavam.
Item post quintam possumus facere unisonus terciam sextam octavam et decimam.
Item post sextam semper debemus facere octavam in suo gradu in terciadecimam in quintadecimam.
Item post terciadecimam semper debemus facere quintadecimam.

Nota quod unisonus reputate octava, tercia reputate decima, quinta reputur duodecima, sexta reputatur terciadecima, octava reputatur quintadecimam.[3]

---

3 "Reputate," "reputur," and "reputatur" are all better read as "re=etit" or "repetebat."

Texts and translations   141

Note that there are nine species of counterpoint, namely ...

Jesus Christ

Note that there are nine species of counterpoint, namely, the unison, third, fifth, sixth, octave, tenth, twelfth, thirteenth, and fifteenth, of which five are perfect and four imperfect. The perfect ones are, namely, the unison, fifth, octave, twelfth, and fifteenth. The imperfect ones are, namely, the third, sixth, tenth, and thirteenth.

And note that we should begin and end all counterpoint with perfect species. The penultimate [species] should be imperfect. Also note that we cannot express two identical perfect species one after the other, namely, a unison and a unison, or two fifths, etc. But we can express two imperfect species, or three, or four, one after the other. Also note that when the tenor (plain chant) descends, we must ascend in counterpoint, and thus vice versa.

Likewise, after a unison, we can make a fifth, sixth, and tenth.
Likewise, after a third, we can make a fifth, sixth, octave, and tenth.
Likewise, after a fifth, we can make a unison, third, sixth, octave, and tenth.
Likewise, after a sixth, we should always make an octave; similarly, from a thirteenth to a fifteenth.[4]
Likewise, after the thirteenth we should always make a fifteenth.

Note that a unison repeats at the octave, the third repeats at the tenth, the fifth repeats at the twelfth, the sixth repeats at the thirteenth, the octave repeats at the fifteenth.

---

4 The translation of the concluding clause is a best guess for the nonsensical original, which may have been a redundant anticipation of the subsequent statement.

Nota quod si volumus facere contrapunctum finite musice debemus fingere clave de c acutum ac si esset clavis de ef gravis et desuper cantare ac si esset contrapunctum. Item nota quod si volumus facere contrapunctum be quatrati super clavem de c gravi debemus enim convertere ac si esset clavis de ef gravi et cantari super eam ac si esset {ac si esset} contrapunctus de natura.

De be quatrato: ♮

[Gamma-ut]	viii / ut / v	x / mi / vi	xii / sol / viii	xiii / la / x	viii / A-re / v	x / fa / vi	xii / la / viii
					vi / B-ut / iii	x / sol / vi	xii / la / viii
C	x / fa / vi	xii / la / viii	xiii / D-re / v				
F	viii / vi	xiii / la	x / la	unison / G-ut	iii / E-ut	unisonus / A-re	v / ut
B	sol / iii	mi / sol	sol / iii	mi / v vi	viii / mi	x / sol	xii / la
				D / la			
E	fa / iii	re / ut	unisonus / fa	la / v vi	viii / la	x / mi	unisonus / sol

De natura:

[Gamma-ut]	xii / re / x	xiii / mi / xii	xv / sol / xiii	a	x / ut / viii	xii / mi / x	xiii / fa / xii
					xv / la / xiii	C-ut	F-ut
B	x / re / mi	xiii / fa / mi	xv / la / fa	viii / C-ut / sol	x / ut / viii	xii / mi / x	xiii / fa / xii
					D-re / la	la / x	xv / la / xiii
E	xii / re / ut	x / fa / mi	viii / la / mi	v / F-ut / re	vi [[xi]] / mi	G-re / v	la / la
					x / fa / vi	xii / la / viii	sol

Note that if we wish to make counterpoint to the end of the music, we should imagine the clef of c acute as if it were the clef of f gravis, and to sing above as though it were counterpoint. Likewise, note that if we wish to make counterpoint in B-square over the clef of c gravis, we must indeed transpose it as though it were the clef of f gravis and to sing above it as though it were {as though it were} counterpoint of the natural [hexachord].

Of the hard hexachord: ♮

[Gamma-ut]	viii ut	x mi	xii sol	xiii la	viii A-re	x fa	xii la	vi B-ut	viii mi	x sol
C	v v	vi re	viii fa	x la	v D-re	vi mi	viii sol	iii E-ut	v vi / mi fa	viii la
F	iii re	v fa	vi sol	unison G-ut	iii mi	v sol	vi la	unisonus A-re	iii fa	v la
B	iii ut	unison mi	iii sol	iii C-re	unisonus fa	iii la	D	v ut	iii	unisonus
E	vi ut	v re	iii fa	unisonus la				ut	mi	sol

Of the natural hexachord:

[Gamma-ut]	xii re	xiii mi	xv sol	viii A	x ut	xii mi	xiii fa	xv la
B	x re	xii fa	xiii sol	viii C-ut	x mi	xii sol	xiii la	viii D-re
E	vi ut	viii mi	x sol	v F-ut	vi [[xi]] re	viii fa	x la	v G-re

Works cited

Aluas, Luminita Florea. "The *Quatuor principalia musicae*: A Critical Edition and Translation, with Introduction and Commentary." PhD diss., Indiana University, 1996.

Anglès, Higini. "Die Mehrstimmige Musik in Spanien vor dem 15. Jahrhundert." In *Beethoven-Zentenarfeier Vom 26. Bis 31. März 1927*, edited by Michael Hainisch, 158–163. Vienna: Universal-Edition, 1927.

———. "La Música a Veus Anterior al Segle XV dins l'Espanya." *Revista Musical Catalana* 24 (1927): 138–144.

———. "La Música Conservada en la Biblioteca Colombina y en la Catedral de Sevilla." *Anuario Musical* 2 (1947): 3–39.

Atkinson, Charles. "*De Accentibus Toni Oritur Nota Quae Dicitur Neuma*: Prosodic Accents, the Accent Theory, and the Paleofrankish Script." In *Essays on Medieval Music: In Honor of David G. Hughes*, edited by Graeme Boone, 17–42. Cambridge, MA: Harvard University Dept. of Music, 1995.

Balensuela, C. Matthew, ed. *Ars Cantus Mensurabilis Mensurata per Modos Iuris = The Art of Mensurable Song Measured by the Modes of Law*. Greek and Latin Music Theory 10. Lincoln: University of Nebraska Press, 1994.

Becker, Otto. "The Maitrise in Northern France and Burgundy during the Fifteenth Century." PhD diss., George Peabody College for Teachers, 1967.

Bent, Margaret. "A Postscript on the Berkeley Theory Manuscript." *Acta Musicologica* 40, no. 2/3 (Apr.–Sept. 1968): 175.

———. "Mayshuet and the *Deo gratias* Motets in the Old Hall Manuscript." In *Beredte Musik. Konversationen zum 80. Geburtstag von Wulf Arlt*, edited by Martin Kirnbauer, 11–28. Schola Cantorum Basiliensis Scripta 8. Basel: Schwabe, 2019.

Berktold, Christian. *Ars Practica Mensurabilis Cantus Secundum Iohannem de Muris: Die Recensio Maior des Sogenannten "Libellus Practice Cantus Mensurabilis"*. München: Verlag der Bayerischen Akadamie der Wissenschaften, 1999.

Besseler, Heinrich. "Johannes de Muris." In *Die Musik in Geschichte Und Gegenwart*, edited by Friedrich Blume, 7: 105–115. New York: Bärenreiter Kassel, 1958.

146 *Works cited*

Bevilacqua, Gregorio. "Il Comentum super cantum di Roger Caperon: Introduzione ed edizione critica." PhD diss., Università di Bologna, 2008.

Blackburn, Bonnie J. "On Compositional Process in the Fifteenth Century." *Journal of the American Musicological Society* 40, no. 2 (July 1987): 210–284.

———. "Music Theory and Musical Thinking after 1450." In *Music as Concept and Practice in the Late Middle Ages*, edited by Reinhard Strohm and Bonnie J Blackburn, 301–345. Oxford: Oxford University Press, 2001.

Blackburn, Bonnie J., and Leofranc Holford-Strevens. *Florentius de Faxolis: Book on Music*. Cambridge, MA: Harvard University Press, 2010.

Briquet, Charles-Moïse. *Les filigranes. Dictionnaire historique des marques du papier dès leur apparition vers 1282 jusqu'en 1600 avec 39 ntro figures dans le texte et 16 112 fac-similés de filigranes*. Paris: Alphonse Picard et fils, 1907.

Busse Berger, Anna Maria. "The Origin and Early History of Proportion Signs." *Journal of the American Musicological Society* 41, no. 3 (Autumn 1988): 403–433.

———. "The Evolution of Rhythmic Notation." In *The Cambridge History of Western Music Theory*, edited by Thomas Christensen, 628–656. Cambridge: Cambridge University Press, 2002.

Clark, Alice. "*Concordare Cum Materia*: The Tenor in the Fourteenth-Century Motet." PhD diss., Princeton University, 1996.

Clercx, Suzanne, and Richard Hoppin. "Notes Biographiques Sur Quelques Musiciens du XIVe Siècle." In *Les Colloques de Wegimont II: 1955, L'Ars Nova: Recueil d'études Sur La Musique Du XIVe Siècle* Paul Collaer, rédacteur en chef, 63–92. Paris: Les Belles Lettres, 1959.

Cook, Karen M. "Theoretical Treatments of the Semiminim in a Changing Notational World, c.1315–c.1440." PhD diss., Duke University, 2012.

Coussemaker, Charles Edmond Henri de. *Scriptorum de Musica Medii Aevi*. Hildesheim: G. Olms, 1963.

Cuthbert, Michael Scott. "Palimpsests, Sketches, and Extracts: The Organization and Compositions of Seville 5-2-25." In *L'Ars Nova Italiana Del Trecento VII. Dolce e Nuove Note: Atti Del Quinto Convegno Internazionale in Ricordo Di Federico Ghisi (1901–1975), Certaldo, 17–18 Dicembre 2005*, edited by Agostino Ziino, 57–78. Lucca: Libreria musicale italiana, 2009.

DeFord, Ruth I. "On Diminution and Proportion in Fifteenth-Century Music Theory." *Journal of the American Musicological Society* 58, no. 1 (Spring 2005): 1–67.

Desmond, Karen. "Omni Desideranti Notitiam: A Music Theory Text from the Fourteenth Century." arsmusicae.org, 2011. http://arsmusicae.org/home.xml.

———. "Texts in Play: The Ars Nova and Its Hypertexts." *Musica Disciplina* 57 (2012): 81–153.

———. *Music and the Moderni, 1300–1350: The Ars Nova in Theory and Practice*. Cambridge: Cambridge University Press, 2018.

———. "Jean Des Murs and the Three Libelli on Music in BnF Lat. 7378A: A Preliminary Report." *Erudition and the Republic of Letters* 4, no. 1 (January 23, 2019): 40–63.

Works cited 147

Di Bacco, Giuliano. "Documenti Vaticani per la Storia della Musica durante il Grande Scisma (1378–1417)." *Quaderni storici, Storia e Musica: Fonti, consumi e committenze*, 32, no. 95 (2) (August 1997): 361–386.

———. *De Muris e Gli Altri: Sulla Tradizione di un Trattato Trecentesco di Contrappunto*. Lucca: Libreria musicale italiana, 2001.

———. "Original and Borrowed, Authorship and Authority. Remarks on the Circulation of Philipoctus de Caserta's Theoretical Legacy." In *A Late Medieval Songbook and Its Context: New Perspectives on the Chantilly Codex (Bibliothèque Du Château de Chantilly, Ms. 564)*, edited by Anne Stone and Yolanda Plumley, 329–364. Epitome Musical. Turnhout: Brepols, 2009.

Du Chesne, François. *Histoire de Tous Les Cardinaux François de Naissance, Ou Qui Ont Esté Promeus Au Cardinalat*. Paris, 1660. https://gallica.bnf.fr/ark:/12148/bpt6k914067.

Dyer, Joseph. *The Scientia Artis Musice of Hélie Salomon: Teaching Music in the Late Thirteenth Century: Latin Text with English Translation and Commentary*. New York: Routledge, 2018.

Earp, Lawrence. *Guillaume de Machaut: A Guide to Research*. Garland Composer Resource Manuals 36. New York: Garland, 1995.

Ellsworth, Oliver B. "The Berkeley Manuscript (Olim Phillipps 4450): A Compendium of Fourteenth-Century Music Theory." PhD diss., University of Michigan at Ann Arbor, 1969.

———, ed. *The Berkeley Manuscript: University of California Music Library, Ms. 744 (Olim Phillipps 4450)*. Greek and Latin Music Theory 2. Lincoln: University of Nebraska Press, 1984.

———, ed. *Johannes Ciconia: Nova Musica and De Proportionibus*. Greek and Latin Music Theory 9. Lincoln: University of Nebraska Press, 1993.

Fierens, Alphonse. *Lettres de Benoit XII (1334–1342): Textes et Analyses*. Rome: M. Bretschneider, 1910.

———. *Suppliques d'Urbain V (1362–1370): Textes et Analyses*. Rome: M. Bretschneider, 1914.

Fuller, Sarah. "Discant and the Theory of Fifthing." *Acta Musicologica* 50, no. 1/2 (1978): 241–275.

———. "A Phantom Treatise of the Fourteenth Century? The Ars Nova." *The Journal of Musicology* 4, no. 1 (December 1, 1985): 23–50.

Galán Gómez, Santiago. *La teoría de canto de órgano y contrapunto en el Renacimiento español: La Sumula de canto de organo de Domingo Marcos Durán como modelo*. Estudios Sobre Música Antigua. Madrid: Editorial Alpuerto, 2016.

———. "Estudiando Música en la España Bajomedieval: El Ms. 2044 de la Universidad de Barcelona." *Estudios sobre Patrimonio, Cultura y Ciencias Medievales* 19 (2017): 385–414.

Gallo, F. Alberto. "Alcune Fonti Poco Note Di Musica Teorica e Pratica." In *L'Ars Nova Italiana Del Trecento: Convegni Di Studio 1961–67*, edited by F. Alberto Gallo, 49–76. Certaldo: Centro di Studi sull'Ars nova italiana del Trecento, 1961.

———. *La Teoria della notazione in Italia dalla fine del XIII all'inizio del XV secolo*. Bologna: Tamari, 1966.

148   *Works cited*

———, ed. *Prosdocimi de Beldemandis opera: Expositiones tractatus practice cantus mensurabilis magistri Johannis de Muris.* Vol. 3. Antiquae musicae Italicae scriptores. Bologna: Università degli Studi di Bologna, Istituto di Studi Musicali e Teatrali, 1966.

Gardner, Julian. *The Tomb and the Tiara: Curial Tomb Sculpture in Rome and Avignon in the Later Middle Ages.* Oxford: Clarendon Press, 1992.

———. "The Cardinals' Music: Musical Interests at the Papal Curia c.1200–1304." *Early Music History* 34 (October 2015): 97–132.

Gómez, Maria del Carmen. "*De Arte Cantus* de Johannes Pipudi, Sus *Regulae Contrapunctus* y Los Apuntes de Teoria de Un Estudiante Catalán Del Siglo XIV." *Anuario Musical* 31/32 (1977 1976): 37–49.

Günther, Ursula. "Zur Biographie Einiger Komponisten der Ars Subtilior." *Archiv Für Musikwissenschaft* 21, no. 3/4 (January 1, 1964): 172–199.

———. *The Motets of the Manuscripts Chantilly, Musée Condé, 564 (Olim 1047) and Modena, Biblioteca Estense, Alpha. M. 5. 24 (Olim Lat. 568).* Corpus Mensurabilis Musicae 39. [n.p.]: American Inst. of Musicology, 1965.

———. "Goscalch." In *Grove Music Online,* 2001. https://doi.org/10.1093/gmo/9781561592630.article.11496.

Gushee, Lawrence, C. Matthew Balensuela, and Jeffrey Dean. "Muris, Johannes De." In *Grove Music Online,* 2001. https://doi.org/10.1093/gmo/9781561592630.article.14237

Gwee, Nigel. "De Plana Musica and Introductio Musice: A Critical Edition and Translation, with Commentary, of Two Treatises Attributed to Johannes de Garlandia." PhD diss., Louisiana State University, 1996.

Hamm, Chelsey. "A Critical Examination of Verbula in the Berkeley Manuscript." In *Histories and Narratives of Music Analysis,* edited by Miloš Zatkalik, Milena Medić, and Denis Collins, 15–30. Cambridge: Cambridge Scholars Publishing, 2013.

Hanquet, Karl, ed. *Suppliques de Clément VII (1378–1379): Textes et analyses.* Vol. 1. Analecta Vaticano-Belgica, Documents relatifs aux anciens diocèses de Cambrai, Liège, Thérouanne et Tournai, Vol. 8. Rome: Institut historique belge de Rome, 1924.

Hayez, Michel, and Anne-Marie Hayez. *Urbain V: Lettres Communes: Analysées d'après Les Registres Edits d'Avignon.* Vol. 9. Rome: École Française de Rome, 1983.

Herlinger, Jan W. *The Lucidarium of Marchetto of Padua.* Chicago, IL: University of Chicago Press, 1985.

Higgins, Paula. "Tracing the Careers of Late Medieval Composers. The Case of Philippe Basiron of Bourges." *Acta Musicologica* 62, no. fasc. 1 (April 1990): 1–28.

———. "Music and Musicians at the Sainte-Chapelle of the Bourges Palace, 1405–1515." In *Atti Del XIV Congresso Della Società Internazionale Di Musicologica,* 3: 689–701. Turin: EDT, 1990.

Huntington, Archer M. *Catalogue of the Library of Ferdinand Columbus.* New York: Kraus Reprints, 1967.

Works cited   149

Izbicki, Thomas M., and Joëlle Rollo-Koster, eds. *A Companion to the Great Western Schism (1378–1417)*. Boston, MA: Brill, 2009.

Katz, Daniel Seth. "The Earliest Sources for the Libellus Cantus Mensurabilis Secundum Johannem de Muris." PhD diss., Duke University, 1989.

Leech-Wilkinson, Daniel. *Compositional Techniques in the Four-Part Isorhythmic Motets of Philippe de Vitry and His Contemporaries*. 2 vols. Outstanding Dissertations in Music from British Universities. New York: Garland, 1989.

Lefferts, Peter. *Robertus de Handlo: Regule / The Rules and Johannes Hanboys: The Summa*. Greek and Latin Music Theory 7. Lincoln: University of Nebraska Press, 1991.

Marchi, Lucia. "Music and University Culture in Late Fourteenth-Century Pavia: The Manuscript Chicago, Newberry Library, Case Ms 54.1." *Acta Musicologica* 80, no. 2 (January 1, 2008): 143–164.

Meyer, Christian. *Jean des Murs: Écrits Sur La Musique*. Paris: CNRS Éd., 2000.

Michels, Ulrich. *Die Musiktraktate des Johannes de Muris*. Wiesbaden: F. Steiner, 1970.

———. *Notitia Artis Musicae, et Compendium Musicae Practicae. Petrus de Sancto Dionysio: Tractatvs de Mvsica*. [Dallas?]: American Institute of Musicology, 1972.

Miller, Clement A. "Early Gaffuriana: New Answers to Old Questions." *The Musical Quarterly* 56, no. 3 (1970): 367–388.

Pieragostini, Renata. "Augustinian Networks and the Chicago Theory Manuscript." *Plainsong and Medieval Music* 22, no. 1 (2013): 65–85.

Plamenac, Dragan. "'Excerpta Colombiniana': Items of Musical Interest in Fernando Colón's 'Regestrum.'" In *Miscelánea En Homenaje a Monseñor Higinio Anglés*, 2: 663–688. Barcelona: Consejo Superior de Investigaciones Científicas, 1958.

Planchart, Alejandro Enrique. "Institutions and Foundations." In *The Cambridge History of Medieval Music*, edited by Mark Everist and Thomas Forrest Kelly, 627–673. Cambridge: Cambridge University Press, 2018.

Reaney, Gilbert. "The Manuscript Chantilly, Musée Condé 1047." *Musica Disciplina* 8 (1954): 59–113.

———. "Egidius [Aegidius] de Murino [Morino]." In *Grove Music Online*, 2001. https://doi.org/10.1093/gmo/9781561592630.article.08612

———, André Gilles, and Jean Maillard, eds. *Philippi Di Vitriaco: Ars Nova*. Corpus Scriptorum de Musica 8. [Rome]: American Institute of Musicology, 1964.

Reimer, Erich. *Johannes de Garlandia: De Mensurabili Musica*. Wiesbaden: F. Steiner, 1972.

Reynolds, Christopher. "Musical Careers, Ecclesiastical Benefices, and the Example of Johannes Brunet." *Journal of the American Musicological Society* 37, no. 1 (Spring 1984): 49–97.

Riaño, Juan Facundo. *Critical & Bibliographical Notes on Early Spanish Music*. London: B. Quaritch, 1887.

150 *Works cited*

Rius Serra, Josep. "Estudiants Espanyols a Avinyó al Secle XIV." *Analecta Sacra Tarraconensia* 10 (1934): 87–122.

Rollo-Koster, Joëlle. *Avignon and Its Papacy, 1309–1417: Popes, Institutions, and Society.* Lanham, MD: Rowman & Littlefield Publishers, 2017.

Rüegg, Walter. "Themes." In *Universities in the Middle Ages*, edited by Hilde de Ridder-Symoens, 3–34. Cambridge: Cambridge University Press, 2003.

Sachs, Klaus-Jürgen. *Der Contrapunctus im 14. und 15. Jahrhundert: Untersuchungen Zum Terminus, Zur Lehre und Zu Den Quellen.* Wiesbaden: F. Steiner, 1974.

Scattolin, Pier Paulo. "Le 'Regule Contrapuncti' di Filippotto Da Caserta." In *L'Ars Nova Italiana Del Trecento*, edited by Agostino Ziino, 5: 231–244. Certaldo: Centro di Studi sull'Ars nova italiana del Trecento, 1985.

Schreur, Philip Evan. *Tractatus Figurarum = Treatise on Noteshapes.* Greek and Latin Music Theory 6. Lincoln: University of Nebraska Press, 1989.

Schreurs, Eugeen. "Music at the Collegiate Church of Tongeren and the School of Liège in the Late Middle Ages." *Revista de Musicologia* 16, no. 4 (1993): 2476–2494.

Schwinges, Rainer Christoph. "Admission." In *Universities in the Middle Ages*, edited by Hilde de Ridder-Symoens, 171–194. Cambridge: Cambridge University Press, 2003.

———. "Student Education, Student Life." In *Universities in the Middle Ages*, edited by Hilde de Ridder-Symoens, 195–243. Cambridge: Cambridge University Press, 2003.

Seay, Albert, ed. *Ugolino of Orvieto: Declaratio Musicae Disciplinae.* Vol. 1–3. Corpus Scriptorum de Musica 7. [Rome]: American Institute of Musicology, 1959.

———. "The *Liber Musices* of Florentius de Faxolis." In *Musik und Geschichte, Leo Schrade Zum Sechzigsten Geburtstag*, 71–95. Cologne: Arno Volk, 1963.

Stoessel, Jason. "The Interpretation of Unusual Mensuration Signs in the Notation of the 'Ars Subtilior.'" In *A Late Medieval Songbook and Its Context: New Perspectives on the Chantilly Codex (Bibliothèque Du Château de Chantilly, Ms. 564)*, edited by Yolanda Plumley and Anne Stone, 179–202. Turnhout: Brepols Publishers, 2010.

Strohm, Reinhard. *The Rise of European Music, 1380–1500.* Cambridge: Cambridge University Press, 2005.

Swanson, Robert Norman. *Church and Society in Late Medieval England.* New York: Blackwell, 1993.

Taycher, Ryan. "*De Fundamento Discanti*: Structure and Elaboration in Fourteenth-Century Diminished Counterpoint." PhD diss., Indiana University, 2019.

Tihon, Camille. *Lettres de Grégoire XI (1371–1378): Textes et analyses.* Analecta Vaticano-Belgica, Documents relatifs aux anciens diocèses de Cambrai, Liège, Thérouanne et Tournai. Vol. 3. Bruxelles: Institut historique belge de Rome, 1964.

Tomasello, Andrew. *Music and Ritual at Papal Avignon, 1309–1403.* Studies in Musicology, no. 75. Ann Arbor, MI: UMI Research Press, 1983.

Verger, Jacques. "L'Université d'Avignon Au Temps de Clément VII." In *Genèse et Débuts Du Grand Schisme d'Occident: [Actes Du Colloque International] Avignon, 25–28 Septembre 1978*, edited by Jean Favrier, 185–200. Paris: Centre national de la recherche scientifique, 1980.

———. "Teachers." In *Universities in the Middle Ages*, edited by Hilde de Ridder-Symoens, 144–168. Cambridge: Cambridge University Press, 2003.

Vidal, J.M. *Benoit XII (1334–1342): lettres communes analysées d'après les registres dits D'Avignon et due Vatican*. Vol. 1. Paris: A. Fontemoing, 1903.

Vivarelli, Carla. "La 'Mutatio Qualitatis' Nella Teoria e Nella Prassi 'Subtilior': Una Regola Disattesa?" *Studi Musicali* 38, no. 2 (2009): 273–308.

Wathey, Andrew. "The Peace of 1360–1369 and Anglo-French Musical Relations." *Early Music History* 9 (January 1, 1990): 129–174.

Weijers, Olga. *Terminologie des Universités Au XIIIe Siècle*. Lessico Intellettuale Europeo 39. Rome: Ed. dell'Ateneo, 1987.

Wilkins, Nigel. "Some Notes on Philipoctus de Caserta (c.1360?–c.1435)." *Nottingham Mediaeval Studies* 8 (1964): 82–99.

Wilson-Lee, Edward. *The Catalogue of Shipwrecked Books: Christopher Columbus, His Son, and the Quest to Build the World's Greatest Library*. New York: Scribner, 2019.

Wolf, Johannes. *Geschichte der Mensural-Notation von 1250–1460*. Leipzig: Breitkopf & Härtel, 1904.

———. "Ein Anonymer Musiktraktat Aus Der Ersten Zeit Der 'Ars Nova.'" *Kirchenmusikalisches Jahrbuch* 21 (1908): 34–38.

———. "Der Choraltraktat des Cristoval de Escobar." In *Gedenboek Aangeboden Aan Dr. D. F. Scheurleer Op Zijn 70sten Verjaardag*, edited by Guido Adler, 383–391. The Hague: M. Nijhoff, 1925.

Zayaruznaya, Anna. *Upper-Voice Structures and Compositional Process in the Ars Nova Motet*. New York: Routledge, 2018.

———. "Old, New, and Newer Still: Situating *Speculum musice*, Book VII." *Journal of the American Musicological Society* 73, no. 1 (2020): 95–148.

Index

Note: **Bold** page numbers refer to tables, *italic* page numbers refer to figures, and page numbers followed by "n" denote endnotes.

additae, additas **23**, 33–34, 96–97
Alma polis religio/Axe polis cum artica 65–67
Andrea da Firenze **36**
Anglès, Higini 5, 5n2, 6, 8, 9
Apta carol/Flos virginum 27n26
Arnoldo Jocalis 69, 90
Ars cantus mensurabilis mensurata per modos iuris 21, 26, 30n28, 33, 41
Ars contrapuncti secundum Johannem de Muris 1, 4, 8n11, 9–10, 13n20, 14–17, 39–56, 64, 73, 87; *see also Cum notum sit*; *De diminutione contrapuncti*; *Quilibet affectans*
Augustines 66–67
Avignon 1, 9, 15, **17**, 38, 45, 55–61, 65, 68–69, 71–75, 83, 86–88

backward-C mensuration sign **24**, 34–35, *35*, 37, 87, 98, 106–107, 120–121
Balensuela, C. Matthew 22n20, 41
Benedict XIII, Antipope 75
Bent, Margaret 65, 67n23
Berkeley manuscript 20, 20n11, 32–33, 37–38, 37n46, 41, 43, 48, 54–56, 64, 74, 76n47, 86; Berkeley 2 **16**, **23**, 33–34, 33n39, 37, 37n46, 41–49, 42n9, 46n12, 51–54, **56**, 64, 86–87; Berkeley 3 **16**, 20–22, **23–25**, 26–28, 26n22, 27n26, **29**, 30–32, 34, 36–37, 37n46, 43, 47, 53–55, **56**, 64, 86–87

Berktold, Christian 4, 18n1, 20, 20n8, 20n9, 21, 22n20, 34, 38, 86
Bertrand de Deaulx, Cardinal 68, 68n24, 70
Besseler, Heinrich 19
Boethius 42
Briquet, Charles-Moïse 77, *80–81*, 80, 82, 84
Brussels 4144 41, 41n6, **56**
Busse Berger, Anna Maria 34–35, 55

Cambrai 58–59, 58n3, 61, 65, 70–71, 86, 87
canon (clerical position) 1, 6, 8n12, 9, 15, **16**, 45, 57–62, 64–65, 67–68, 70–73, 76, 83, 86, 87, 126–127
Catalunya, David 77n48, 84n54, 92, 136–139
Catania D.39 **16**, 20, 32–33, 37, 37n46, 37n47, 43, 46–48, 51, 53–56, 86, 87
Chantilly 27n26, **36**, 55, 65–66, 66n22, 86
Chicago 54.1 20n11, 48, 56, **56**, 56n30
ciphers **24**, 27, 32, 35, 55, 87, 120–121
Clark, Alice 62–63
Clement VII, Antipope 58, 65, 68–69, 72
Clercx, Suzanne 62–63, 65–66
Colón, Hernando (Fernando) 5, 6n2, 9, 37, 88
color and talea 9, **25**, 36–37, 37n45, 122–123

154 *Index*

Compendium artis motectorum Marchecti **3**, 14, 51; *see also* Petrus de Amalfia
Compendium musicae practicae 19; *see also* Murs, Jean des
Compendium totius artis motetorum 33, 33n39
Contrapunctum est fundamentum biscanti 48; *see also* Philipoctus de Caserta
Coussemaker, Edmond de 9, 18, 18n1, 39, 39n1, 41n7
Cristóbal de Escobar 55, 55n27
Cum notum sit 8n11, 10n18, **16–17**, 39–44, 41n7, 48–53, 52n24, **56**; *see also Ars contrapuncti secundum Johannem de Muris*
Cuthbert, Michael Scott 7

De diminutione contrapuncti 10n18, 39–40, 42–43, 51
De modo componendi tenores motetorum 62–64
De proportionibus 35; *see also* Johannes Ciconia
Desmond, Karen 56n30, 76
Di Bacco, Giuliano **3**, 3n1, 4, 7, 8n11, 10n19, 22, 39, 48–51, 48n16, 50n21, 77n49
Domenico Fernandi 60
dragma, fusa **23**, 33, 33n39, 96–97
Dyer, Joseph 64

Earp, Lawrence 4, 14n23, 21n14, 30n30
Egidius de Flagiaco 61–63
Egidius de Murino 62–63
Ellsworth, Oliver 20, 27n26, 32, 37, 42n9, 46, 48
En nul estat 55

Florence 1119 48n16, 50
Florence Plut.29.48 41, 41n7
Florentius de Faxolis 54
Franchino Gafori 21
Franco of Cologne 26

Gallo, F. Alberto 5–6n2, 6–9, 9n12, 9n13, 13, 13n22, 21–22, 26
Gherardello da Firenze **36**

Gómez, Maria del Carmen 1, 9–10, 9n14, 9n17, 13, 13n20, 15–17, 21, 26, 43, 53, 64
Goscalcus (Goscalch, Gostaltus) **16**, 21, 21n13, 43–44, 54–56, 55n27, **56**, 86, 86n59; *see also* Petrus de Godescalc
Gregory XI, Pope 58–60, 68
Gui de Boulogne, Cardinal 61
Guillaume de Machaut (Mastodio, Mascandio) 13, 14n23, **24**, 30, 30n30, 31n31, 104–105; *see also mutatio qualitatis*
Günther, Ursula 55, 66n22

Henricus Poneti (de Bossuto) 69, 90
Higgins, Paula 72
Hoppin, Richard 62–63, 65–66
Hugo Moteti 69, 90

intermediary interval 42, 45, 53, 124–125
Introductio musice 7; *see also* Johannes de Garlandia

Jacobus 19, 33n39; *see also Speculum musice*
Jaume March 80, 82
Jean de Blauzac 59–60, 64–65, 67–71, 74–75, 86, 89–90
Jean des Murs (Johannes de Muris) 1, 7, 8n11, 8n12, 10n18, 13n20, 15, **16–17**, 18–22, 19n4, **23**, 30, 32n33, 39–41, 39n1, 43–44, **56**, 56, 64, 66–67, 76n47, 84, 86–88; *see also Ars contrapuncti secundum Johannem de Muris; Compendium musicae practicae; Libellus cantus mensurabilis; Notitia artis musicae*
Johannes, Bishop of Sabina *see* Jean de Blauzac
Johannes Alanus **36**
Johannes Butor 69, 90
Johannes Ciconia 35, **36**; *see also De proportionibus*
Johannes de Blandiac *see* Jean de Blauzac
Johannes de Bosco 69, 90
Johannes de Garlandia 7; *see also Introductio musice*
Johannes Desiderii de Latines 65–67

Index 155

Johannes Hanboys 34–35; *see also*
  Summa
Johannes Pipardi (Pipudi) 1, 4, 6, 7,
  8n12, 9, 15, 16, **17**, 44–45, 53–61, **56**,
  57, 63–76, 82–84, 86–88, 90, 126–127

Katz, Daniel Seth 4, 18n1, 21–22,
  22n20, 32

Libellus cantus mensurabilis 1, **2**, 4, 7,
  7n8, 8n12, 9–10, 13n20, 15–34, **16**,
  18n1, 19n4, 20n11, 22n20, **23–25**,
  27n26, **29**, 31n31, 36–39, 41, 43, 47,
  51, 53–54, **56**, 56, 56n30, 64,
  73–74, 76n47, 86–87; *see also*
  Murs, Jean de
London 23220 33, 37n46, 46
Lucidarium **2–3**, 7, 14, 51; *see also*
  Marchetto of Padua

magister 1, 4, 8n12, 9, 15, **17**, **23**,
  31n31, 43–45, 53, 56–59, *57*, 62–65,
  69–70, 72–74, 76, 83, 86, 88, 124–127
maîtrise 73
Marchetto of Padua **2–3**, 7, 14, 41,
  51; *see also Lucidarium*
Marchi, Lucia 74
Matheus de Sancto Johanne **36**, 69
mental transposition 49–50, 142–143
Meyer, Christian 4, 21, 22n20
modus **23**, 32, 87, 96–97
mutatio qualitatis 14, **24**, 30,
  30n30, 31n31; *see also* Machaut,
  Guillaume de

neuma 67
Notitia artis musicae 19, 30, 41, 66;
  see also Murs, Jean de

Omni desideranti notitiam 7, 56n30

Paolo Tenorista **36**
Petrus de Amalfia **3**, 14, 51; *see also*
  Compendium artis motectorum
  Marcheti
Petrus de Godescalc 55; *see also*
  Goscalcus
Petrus de Sancto Dionysio 41, 66–67;
  see also Tractatus de musica
Philipoctus de Caserta (Philipoctus
  Andree) 8n11, **16**, 48, 50–51,

52n23, 52n24, *see also*
  Contrapunctum est fundamentum
  biscanti; Regula contrapunctus,
  Regule contrapuncti
Prosdocimo de Beldemandis 21

Quilibet affectans 10n18, **16**, 39–43,
  48–51, 53, **56**; *see also Ars*
  contrapuncti secundum Johannem
  de Muris

Reaney, Gilbert 62
Regula contrapunctus **16**, 48–50; *see*
  also Philipoctus de Caserta
Regule contrapuncti 8n11, **16**, 48–50,
  48n16, 50n21, 52, 52n23, 52n24;
  see also Philipoctus de Caserta
Regule contrapuncti secundum usum
  Regni Sicilie 51
Rex Karole/Leticie pacis/Virgo
  prius 41
rhythmic modes 9, 15, **25**, 26–27, 33
Richardus de Bozonville 69, 90
Robertus de Nathoy 61

Sachs, Klaus-Jürgen 55
Saint-Didier (church, *sancti desiderii*)
  1, 6, 8n12, 9, 15, **16**, 45, 56–59,
  64–65, 68, 70–75, 83, 86–88,
  126–127
Schreurs, Eugeen 72
semibreves caudatas **23**, 33, 96–97
seminas, semiminims **23**, 33, 96–97
Seville 5-2-25: Catalan notes 1, **3**, 4,
  6, 8n12, 10, 15, **16**, 17, 51–54, **56**,
  59, 87, 136–139; copyists 1, 3, 9–10,
  13–15, **16**, 34, 37, 44–47, 49–58,
  64, 72–76, 83–84, 88; dating 1–3,
  9–10, 13–15, **16**, 17, 34, 37, 44–47,
  49–58, 64, 72–76, 83–84, 88; *De*
  arte cantus 1, **3**, 4, 6–7, 8n12, 9–10,
  11–12, 13, 13n22, 14–15, **16**, 17,
  21–38, 53–54, **56**, 59, 64–65, 74, 76,
  86–87, 94–123; *Nota quod novem*
  3, 4, 14, **16**, 48–51, 54, 140–143;
  provenance 5, 9, 15, 37–38, 55,
  76–86; *Regulae contrapunctus* 1, **3**,
  4, 6, 8n12, 9–10, 15, **16**, 17, 43–48,
  49–54, **56**, 57, 59, 64, 87, 124–135;
  watermarks 77–86
sincopa **24–25**, 27, 110–111

156 *Index*

Speculum musice 19, 33n39; *see also*
  Jacobus
Stoessel, Jason 34–35
Strohm, Reinhard 73
Summa 34; *see also* Johannes
  Hanboys

Taycher, Ryan 4, 40n4
Tomasello, Andrew 69
Tractatus de musica 66; *see also*
  Petrus de Sancto Dionysio
Tractatus figurarum **2–3**, 7, 14,
  27n26, 33, 41, 49, 51, 54,
  62–63, 76

Ugolino of Orvieto 21
University of Avignon 74–75,
  74–75n39, 88
Urban V, Pope 60, 68
Urban VI, Pope 68

verbula 42, 51

Wash J6 41, 62n9
Willelmus Penninc de Eyck
  70, 90
Wolf, Johannes 18

Zayaruznaya, Anna 19, 33n39

Printed in the United States
by Baker & Taylor Publisher Services

Acknowledgments

The recent interest and enthusiasm among historians of philosophy regarding Shepherd's work have made this book possible in a way that might not have been the case even twenty years ago. I am very grateful to have been able to present earlier versions of the material in this book at a variety of conferences. I am also grateful to David Landy for inviting me to present my work on Shepherd at San Francisco State University in 2019 and to meet on Zoom with his seminar students to discuss Shepherd in 2021, to Aaron Garrett for the opportunity to give a talk on Shepherd at Boston University in 2019, and to Manuel Fasko for inviting me to participate in an online workshop on Shepherd and personal identity at the University of Basel in 2021. At all these events, I benefited immensely from the comments and questions provided by audience members and other participants, especially Thomas Aeppli, Donald Ainslie, Martha Bolton, Olivia Brown, Annemarie Butler, Colin Chamberlain, Patrick Connolly, Becko Copenhaver, Louise Daoust, Keota Fields, M. Folescu, James Foster, Gordon Graham, Giovanni Grandi, Lukas Hilgert, Laura Kämpfen, Muriel Leuenberger, Alison McIntyre, Jelscha Schmid, Lisa Shapiro, Julie Walsh, and Markus Wild. And for their generous comments on earlier drafts of material in this book, I thank Charlotte Alderwick, Margaret Atherton, Becko Copenhaver, Manuel Fasko, David Landy, Antonia LoLordo, Terry Meyers, Alison Peterman, Samuel Rickless, and Alison Stone.

Some of the material in this book, especially Chapter 8, is based on work I first presented at the Early Modern–Saint Louis Conference and the Fifth Annual Lehigh University Philosophy Conference, both in 2017, which then developed into my paper

"Mary Shepherd on Mind, Soul, and Self," *Journal of the History of Philosophy* 58, no. 1 (2020): 93–112. I thank the publisher, Johns Hopkins University Press, for permission to reprint this material. Chapter 4 is based on "Mary Shepherd on the Meaning of 'Life,'" published in the *British Journal for the History of Philosophy* 29, no. 2 (2021): 208–25, copyright British Society for the History of Philosophy, available online at http://www.tandfonline.com/ 10.1080/09608788.2020.1771271. My thanks to the society for permission to reprint. Chapter 5 draws from work I presented at the 2019 meetings of the Canadian Philosophical Association, the Hume Society, and the International Conference on the Enlightenment. Material in chapter 9 was first presented in my papers "Mary Shepherd on Minds, Selves, and the Afterlife" at the 2019 Eastern Division Meeting of the American Philosophical Association and "Lady Shepherd on Divine Creation" at the 2020 Institute for the Study of Scottish Philosophy Conference.

I am indebted to Peter Ohlin and Becko Copenhaver for inviting me to write this book in the first place. Support was provided by a sabbatical from the College of Charleston during the academic year 2020–21, as well as by the American Philosophical Association's Edinburgh Fellowship at the University of Edinburgh's Institute for Advanced Studies in the Humanities. Due to the global pandemic, I was unfortunately unable to go in person to Edinburgh, but Steve Yearley and Ben Fletcher-Watson at the Institute helped me connect with the other fellows, many of whom were also working remotely.

Finally, this project would not have been possible without the patient support of my husband Tim and my daughter Maura, whom I kept waiting far too many times as I told them I just needed to finish writing one more sentence.

Abbreviations

CSEV — Mary Shepherd, "On the Causes of Single and Erect Vision." Cited by page number, using the 1828 *Philosophical Magazine* version.

EASP — Mary Shepherd, "An Essay on the Academical or Sceptical Philosophy." Cited by page number of the 1827 edition.

ECHU — John Locke, *An Essay Concerning Human Understanding*. Cited by book, chapter, and section.

EHU — David Hume, *An Enquiry Concerning Human Understanding*. Cited by section and paragraph.

EIP — Thomas Reid, *Essays on the Intellectual Powers of Man*. Cited by essay and chapter number.

EPEU — Mary Shepherd, *Essays on the Perception of an External Universe, and Other Subjects Connected with the Doctrine of Causation*. Cited by page number of the 1827 edition.

ERCE — Mary Shepherd, *An Essay upon the Relation of Cause and Effect*. Cited by page number of the 1824 edition.

IHM — Thomas Reid, *An Inquiry into the Human Mind, upon the Principles of Common Sense*. Cited by chapter and section.

L — William Lawrence, *Lectures on Physiology, Zoology, and the Natural History of Man*. 3rd ed. Cited by page number.

LMSM — Mary Shepherd, "Lady Mary Shepherd's Metaphysics." Cited by page number of the *Fraser's Magazine* edition.

NTV — George Berkeley, *An Essay Towards a New Theory of Vision*. Cited by section.

OLMS — Mary Shepherd, "Observations by Lady Mary Shepherd on the 'First Lines of the Human Mind.'" Cited by page number of the *Parriana* edition.

ONT — Thomas Brown, *Observations on the Nature and Tendency of the Doctrine of Mr. Hume*. 2nd ed. Cited by page number.

xii   LIST OF ABBREVIATIONS

T   David Hume, *A Treatise of Human Nature*. Cited by book, part, section, and paragraph.

PHK   George Berkeley, *A Treatise Concerning the Principles of Human Knowledge*. Cited by part and section.

Unless noted otherwise, all italics in quotations are in the original texts.

1
Shepherd's Life and Context

Mary Shepherd's Life

Lady Mary Primrose, later Lady Mary Shepherd, was born near Edinburgh in 1777. She was the second of six children of Neil Primrose, 3rd Earl of Rosebery, and Mary Vincent.[1] Unfortunately, we know very little of Shepherd's life; indeed, despite her status as a member of the aristocracy, it seems that there is no surviving portrait of Shepherd as an adult. Our primary source of information about her life is a brief memoir written years later by her daughter Mary Elizabeth Shepherd Brandreth.[2]

According to the memoir, until her marriage in 1808, Shepherd resided primarily at her family home outside Edinburgh, Barnbougle Castle. Many wealthy families around Edinburgh sent their daughters to the city for their education,[3] but Mary and her siblings were educated at home. Mary's two brothers were tutored at home by a fellow of Pembroke College, Cambridge, which they later attended themselves,[4] while Mary and her two sisters were taught by a "dominie," or schoolteacher, named Pillans. Pillans taught the sisters geography, mathematics, history, and, unusually for girls in this period, Latin.[5] Shepherd must at some point also have learned

---

[1] The *Oxford Dictionary of National Biography* lists Shepherd as the second of five children, but Jennifer McRobert notes that the Primroses had a sixth child who died in infancy. See Perkins, "Shepherd (née Primrose), Lady Mary (1777–1847), Philosopher" and McRobert, "Mary Shepherd and the Causal Relation," 9.

[2] Brandreth, *Some Family and Friendly Recollections of Seventy Years*, 26.

[3] Glover, *Elite Women and Polite Society in Eighteenth-Century Scotland*, 33–34.

[4] Brandreth, *Some Family and Friendly Recollections*, 116 and 26.

[5] Glover, *Elite Women and Polite Society*, 45.

Mary Shepherd. Deborah Boyle, Oxford University Press. © Oxford University Press 2023.
DOI: 10.1093/oso/9780190090326.003.0001

2 MARY SHEPHERD

French, since her 1827 book shows she could read French; in late eighteenth-century Scotland, French was viewed as an important component of girls' education.[6] Presumably, Shepherd would also have learned sewing and embroidery, music, and dancing, all important parts of a girl's education at that time. The family attended the local church, then part of the Calvinist Church of Scotland, and Mary Shepherd learned Presbyterian doctrine from her tutor.[7]

In 1808, Shepherd married barrister Henry John Shepherd (1783?–1855).[8] They had three children. While Shepherd and her family made London their primary residence, she typically left London in the autumn, going to Cheltenham, Tunbridge Wells, or Brighton, all popular holiday destinations in early nineteenth-century England. Her comings and goings were duly noted in the society columns of British newspapers throughout the 1810s, 20s, and 30s, as is her attendance at balls, concerts, and dinner parties. Her daughter described the intellectual circles in which Shepherd also moved, writing that her parents "gathered in those days both the scientific and the literary sides of the learned world, into easy and intimate intercourse."[9] Their social circle ultimately included geologist Charles Lyell; Cambridge philosopher of science William Whewell; mathematician Mary Somerville; minister, writer, and early editor of the *Edinburgh Review* Sydney Smith; economist Thomas Malthus; political economist David Ricardo; and Charles Babbage, inventor of the analytical engine and difference engine,

---

[6] Glover, *Elite Women and Polite Society*, 32.

[7] Brandreth, *Some Family and Friendly Recollections,* 27. McRobert notes that Mary's father, as a Scottish nobleman, would have been expected to support the local Presbyterian parish ("Mary Shepherd and the Causal Relation," 23).

[8] The marriage record of Mary Shepherd and Henry John Shepherd lists her as a member of the parish of St. George's Hanover Square, but they married in the Anglican church of St. Clement Danes in London (marriage license no. 749, recorded April 11, 1808; *Westminster Church of England Parish Registers*, City of Westminster Archives Centre London). The entry for Henry John Shepherd at the History of Parliament online says that they eloped; see Thorne, "Shepherd, Henry John."

[9] Brandreth, *Some Family and Friendly Recollections,* 41–42.

SHEPHERD'S LIFE AND CONTEXT   3

early computers.[10] Another notable friend of Shepherd was Mary Shelley.[11]

With this busy family and social life, when did Shepherd find time to write her philosophical treatises? We know little about the circumstances of the writing and publishing of her books. Brandreth mentions that her mother wrote "metaphysical disquisitions" about Hume and Priestley before she was married,[12] contrasting these with the published books, which Brandreth says "were written some years later" and published with Henry John Shepherd's encouragement.[13] The 1824 book, *An Essay upon the Relation of Cause and Effect* (henceforth abbreviated as *ERCE*) was published anonymously; the 1827 book, *Essays on the Perception of an External Universe, and Other Subjects Connected with the Doctrine of Causation* (henceforth abbreviated as *EPEU*) was published under her name.[14] An earlier book, published in Edinburgh in 1819, has sometimes been attributed to Shepherd but is now known to have been written by a James Milne.[15]

---

[10] Brandreth, *Some Family and Friendly Recollections*, 41–42.

[11] See Bennett, ed. *The Letters of Mary Wollstonecraft Shelley*, 2:106n1.

[12] Brandreth, *Some Family and Friendly Recollections*, 28–29. While Shepherd's first book does engage with Hume, the second book has only a footnote referring to Priestley, suggesting that there might have been a separate, earlier essay that engaged more extensively with Priestley. If so, however, it is as yet unknown.

[13] Brandreth, *Some Family and Friendly Recollections*, 29.

[14] The book's publication was announced in the March 19, 1827, edition of *The Morning Post*, under the heading "This day is published." There appear to have been two issues of the book, as the library at the University of Cambridge has two copies that vary in the arrangement and wording of their front matter but not in the main text: one copy includes Shepherd's name on the title page and one does not (Liam Sims, Rare Books Specialist at Cambridge University Library, email message to author, January 9, 2020). Curiously, on April 8, 1831, *The Courier* newspaper included *Essays on the Perception of an External Universe*, with Shepherd cited as the author, in a list under the heading "Books Published This Day." If this was a second printing, it seems that no extant copy survives.

[15] The book sometimes attributed to Shepherd is the *Enquiry Respecting the Relation of Cause and Effect: in which the Theories of Professors Brown, and Mr. Hume, are Examined; with a Statement of Such Observations as are Calculated to Shew the Inconsistency of these Theories; and from which a New Theory is Deduced, More Consonant to Facts and Experience. Also a New Theory of the Earth, Deduced from Geological Observations*, published anonymously by James Ballantyne in Edinburgh in 1819. For discussion, see Boyle, "A Mistaken Attribution to Mary Shepherd."

Shepherd's Two Books

In *An Essay upon the Relation of Cause and Effect*, Shepherd argues that causal principles can be known by reason to be necessary truths. In particular, she argues that we can know through reason alone both that nothing can come to exist without a cause other than itself (which I will refer to as the Causal Principle) and that like causes necessarily have like effects (which I will call the Causal Likeness Principle). Her primary target in *ERCE* is Hume, although she also addresses the views of Thomas Brown, who had written about Hume's causal theory in his 1805, 1806, and 1818 essays on causation, and William Lawrence, who had quoted Brown's Humean account of causation in his *Lectures on Physiology, Zoology, and the Natural History of Man* (1819).

As is clear from the title, *Essays on the Perception of an External Universe, and Other Subjects Connected with the Doctrine of Causation*, Shepherd considered her 1827 book to be an extension of the earlier project on causation. Part 1 of the book is a long essay, comprised of eight chapters, entitled "Essay On the Academical or Skeptical Philosophy" (henceforth abbreviated as EASP). Taking her earlier book to have established both the Causal Principle and the Causal Likeness Principle, Shepherd appeals to those principles in EASP to argue that we can know through reason that an external world of continually existing objects must exist independently of us, as the causes of our sensations. Along the way, she raises objections to various points made by Thomas Reid, George Berkeley, and David Hume; but her primary goal is to argue for her own account of how we know that there is an external world. Her footnotes in this essay draw further connections between her views and those of Berkeley, Hume, and Reid, as well as those of Locke, Joseph Priestley, Dugald Stewart, Kant, and James Mill; the French philosophers Étienne Bonnot de Condillac, Antoine Destutt de Tracy, Joseph Marie de Gérando, and Pierre Jean-Georges Cabanis; and the Swiss physicist Pierre Prévost.

Part 2 of *EPEU* consists of fourteen brief essays on a variety of topics that are, as the title of this part indicates, "Illustrative of the Doctrines Contained in the Preceding One, and in An Essay on the Relation of Cause and Effect." In other words, in part 2 Shepherd explores how her arguments in EASP bear on other philosophical questions. These essays, though short, tend to include various digressions and comments that are not clearly connected to the topics indicated by the essays' titles and in some cases repeat points made in part 1. Shepherd apologizes for this in a footnote to essay 7, saying that the redundancies are because "these minor essays were addressed to several friends who considered some objections overlooked in the larger essays" (*EPEU* 314). Unfortunately, we do not know which friends she means or whether their objections were raised in conversation or some as-yet-undiscovered correspondence with Shepherd.

Broadly speaking, the fourteen short essays in part 2 cover the following topics: Berkeley's idealism (essay 1); the role of the sense-organs in human perception and what distinguishes dreams from reality (essay 2); the role of God (if any) in human perception (essay 3); how we perceive extension (roughly, three-dimensionality) and whether Reid is correct to ascribe a role to "visible figure" in so doing (essay 4); the connections between mathematical reasoning and inductive arguments based on experience (essay 5); the way to understand what Berkeley had called "sensible qualities" (essay 6); how children know the causal principles (essay 7); whether belief in reported miracles is reasonable (essay 8); whether a final cause (God) is needed to explain the existence of the universe (essay 9); why it is necessary to posit a continuously existing mind as a cause of particular sensations, and whether mind survives the death of the body (essay 10); the immateriality of mind and the existence of God (essay 11); why God does not require a body (essay 12); and how mind interacts with body (essay 13). The fourteenth and final essay briefly addresses two puzzles about vision.

6 MARY SHEPHERD

In this *Guide*, chapters 1–4 lead readers systematically through Shepherd's *Essay upon the Relation of Cause and Effect*. Chapter 5 addresses Shepherd's views on sensation and reasoning, which requires jumping ahead a bit, to EASP chapter 6. Chapter 6 of this *Guide* proceeds step by step through the key arguments from chapters 1–3, 5, and 8 of EASP.

The fourteen short essays in the rest of *EPEU* are much less systematic than the chapters in EASP and in some cases reprise material covered in EASP. To avoid redundancy in this *Guide*, some chapters from EASP are treated along with topics covered in the short essays. Thus chapters 7–10 of this *Guide* are organized as follows: chapter 7 discusses Shepherd's views on skepticism and Berkeleyan idealism (covering EASP chapter 4 and short essays 1, 2, and 6); chapter 8 discusses Shepherd's accounts of mind and body (covering EASP chapter 7 and short essay 13); chapter 9 discusses Shepherd's philosophy of religion (covering short essays 8–12); and chapter 10 covers Shepherd's discussion of vision (covering short essays 4 and 14). Readers looking for specific discussions of *EPEU*'s short essays 3, 5, and 7 will find those in this *Guide*'s chapters 6, 3, and 5, respectively.

Shepherd's Minor Works

In 1828, Shepherd returned to the topic of vision, publishing a longer piece, "On the Causes of Single and Erect Vision," in the scientific journal *The Philosophical Magazine and Annals of Philosophy*; this essay was reprinted the following month in two consecutive issues of the popular English weekly magazine *The Kaleidoscope; or, Literary and Scientific Mirror*.

The year 1828 also saw the publication—apparently not authorized by Shepherd—of her critique of the writings of retired naval officer and amateur philosopher John Fearn (1768–1837). Fearn published her critique in *Parriana: Or Notices of the Rev. Samuel*

Parr, along with his much longer and very condescending reply. Shepherd did not let Fearn's attack go unanswered; in 1832 she published the essay "Lady Mary Shepherd's Metaphysics," in which she responded to Fearn.[16] Noting that she had not written her original essay on Fearn for publication, she commented that her surprise at seeing the exchange with Fearn in print "was accompanied by some little anxiety, from the recollection of the haste and incorrectness with which I had written a paper, really not intended for the public eye" (LMSM 697). She undertakes in her "Metaphysics" to show that Fearn's remarks were "unphilosophical" and "inconsistent with each other" (LMSM 697) and, in doing so, provides a clear and concise summary of her own views on extension, sensation, and causation. Although Fearn did publish a further reply,[17] it seems that Shepherd published nothing more after 1832. She died in 1847 in London.

The Philosophical Context

At the turn of the nineteenth century, the most original work in metaphysics and epistemology was being done in Germany. The philosophical scene there was dominated by Immanuel Kant (1724–1804), who had published the *Critique of Pure Reason* in 1781, with the second edition appearing in 1787. The *Prolegomena* was published in English translation in 1819, but little of Kant's work was available in English translation until the 1830s, with the publication of John Richardson's *Metaphysical Works of the Celebrated Immanuel Kant* (1836).[18] Until then, British readers

---

[16] On the exchange between Fearn and Shepherd, see Atherton, "Reading Lady Shepherd."

[17] The month after the appearance of "Lady Mary Shepherd's Metaphysics" in *Fraser's Magazine*, Fearn published "A Reply to Lady Mary Shepherd on Impiety, and Professor Stewart" in the *Metropolitan Magazine*.

[18] This volume reprinted Richardson's 1819 translation of the *Prolegomenon*, along with his translations of Kant's *Logic* (1800) and selections from various Kantian works on the existence of God. For more details, see Naragon, "Kant in Translation."

8 MARY SHEPHERD

interested in Kant's philosophy had to rely on summaries or other essays, such as a review article by Thomas Brown (1778–1820), "Viller's Philosophy of Kant," published in the *Edinburgh Review* (1803).[19] Dugald Stewart (1753–1828) does discuss Kant at various points in his 1810 *Essays*, a book Shepherd mentions (*EPEU* 229n, 271n), but she does not seem to have been especially knowledgeable about Kant; she only mentions him once, in a footnote on his views on space and time (*EPEU* 59).[20]

Meanwhile, philosophers in England, Scotland, and France were more focused on moral, political, and social philosophy than on metaphysics and epistemology. Between roughly 1790 and 1830, those who did do work on metaphysics and epistemology in these places focused on further developing views that had already been put forth earlier, rather than producing any dramatically new systems. In Scotland, Dugald Stewart and Thomas Brown took up and defended the "common sense" philosophy of Thomas Reid (1710–96); Reid himself frequently engaged with the views of David Hume (1711–76), whom he saw as having followed up on the works of Descartes, Malebranche, and Berkeley by having "drowned all in one universal deluge" of skepticism (*IHM* 1.7). English philosophers working in metaphysics and epistemology at this time tended toward idealism; this was true of John Fearn, who embraced a version of Berkeley's idealism,[21] as well as Samuel Taylor Coleridge (1772–1834), although his idealism was more influenced

---

[19] Three additional summaries that might have been available to Shepherd were Friedrich Nitsch's *A General and Introductory View of Professor Kant Concerning Man, the World, and the Deity* (1796), Anthony F. M. Willich's *The Elements of Critical Philosophy* (1798), and Thomas Wirgman's essays on Kant published in the *Encyclopedia Londiniensis* (1812).

[20] As Antonia LoLordo points out, in that footnote Shepherd mischaracterizes Kant's views, claiming that he thought space and time are "modes" of mind (LoLordo, "Introduction," 9). The fact that Shepherd characterizes Kant in this way suggests that her source was Brown's summary in the *Edinburgh Review*, where he writes that Kant thought "space and time . . . are modes of *our own* existence as sentient beings" (Brown, "Viller's Philosophy of Kant," 259).

[21] For a helpful overview of Fearn's philosophical system, see Grandi, "Providential Naturalism and Miracles."

SHEPHERD'S LIFE AND CONTEXT 9

by the German philosophers Kant, Fichte, and Schelling.[22] In France, philosophers who had lived through the French Revolution and the Reign of Terror developed themes found in the earlier work of Étienne Bonnot de Condillac (1714–80).

Since Shepherd engages with Scottish common sense philosophers, with the idealism and immaterialism of George Berkeley (1685–1753), and (briefly) with the French philosophers working in Condillac's tradition, sketches of these three philosophical systems follow, as well as a short account of the contemporary English context of moral philosophy with which Shepherd did *not* engage.

Scottish Common Sense Philosophy

In Scotland between 1790 and 1830, philosophers were grappling with the implications of Hume's skeptical conclusions and Reid's "common sense" responses to skepticism. Hume's arguments in the first part of the *Treatise of Human Nature* (1739–40) and in the *Enquiry Concerning Human Understanding* (1748) had suggested that we lack rational justification for a number of beliefs that are central to daily life.[23] According to Hume, causation should be understood in terms of constant conjunctions of events: causes precede effects in regular patterns, but there is no necessary connection between what we take to be a cause and what we take to

---

[22] See Cheyne, "Coleridge the Philosopher," for a helpful introduction to Coleridge's philosophical thought. Coleridge and Shepherd were apparently acquaintances, for Coleridge wrote two draft poems about her in 1833, not especially complimentary; in one, he describes her as "a desperate Scholar,/Like the Heavens, DEEP BLUE," linking her with the intellectual women of the Enlightenment who were pejoratively called "Bluestockings" (Coburn and Harding, eds., *The Notebooks of Samuel Taylor Coleridge*, Vol. 5).

[23] Of course, Hume wrote on a wide range of topics other than just these two issues, as did the other philosophers covered in this chapter. My account of the philosophical context in which Shepherd was working considers, in broad outline, only the issues with which Shepherd herself engaged.

10 MARY SHEPHERD

be an effect. Causal inferences about how objects and people will behave turn out, on Hume's account, to be simply the result of habitual mental associations formed through experiencing such constant conjunctions. Furthermore, our belief that there is an enduring world of external objects causing our perceptions is no more than a "fiction" that is "without any foundation in reasoning" (*EHU* 12.12). While twentieth- and twenty-first-century scholars have stressed the naturalistic alternative explanations that Hume gives of the sources of these beliefs, Hume's own contemporaries read him as engaged in a purely destructive, entirely skeptical project.[24] Reid, a minister who went on to be a professor at the University of Aberdeen and later at the University of Glasgow, wrote that Hume's system would lead one to be an "absolute Sceptic."[25]

In the *Inquiry into the Human Mind on the Principles of Common Sense* (1764), *Essays on the Intellectual Powers of Man* (1785), and *Essays on the Active Powers of Man* (1788), Reid sought to find a foundation for many of our beliefs—including those Hume had considered to be the results of mental associations formed through experience—in what he called "common sense." In his *Inquiry*, Reid claimed that there are "first principles" which it is in the nature of humans to believe and judge to be true:

> If there are certain principles, as I think there are, which the constitution of our nature leads us to believe, and which we are under necessity to take for granted in the common concerns of life, without being able to give a reason for them; these are what we call the principles of common sense; and what is manifestly contrary to them is, what we call absurd. (*IHM* 2.6)

---

[24] For some examples, see the selections in Fieser, ed., *Early Responses to Hume's Metaphysical and Epistemological Writings*.

[25] Fieser, ed., *Early Responses to Hume's Metaphysical and Epistemological Writings*, 1:157.

SHEPHERD'S LIFE AND CONTEXT   11

Likewise, in the *Essays*, Reid writes of truths that he calls alternately first principles, principles of common sense, common notions, self-evident truths, and axioms (*EIP* 6.4). Such principles are

> propositions which are no sooner understood than they are believed. The judgment follows the apprehension of them necessarily, and both are equally the work of nature, and the result of our original powers. There is no searching for evidence, no weighing of arguments; the proposition is not deduced or inferred from another; it has the light of truth in itself, and has no occasion to borrow it from another. (*EIP* 6.4)

Reid argued that the principles undermined by the philosophies of both Hume and Berkeley are in fact just of this sort: that "every change that happens in nature must have a cause," and that an external world of matter exists, are beliefs that no one can doubt (*EIP* 6.4).

Although Reid was concerned to respond to Humean and Berkeleyan skepticism by positing principles of common sense, his work also had continuities with Hume's. Hume had aimed to provide a "science of human nature" (*EHU* 1.1). Similarly, Reid aimed to lay the basis for "a system of the powers and operations of the human mind, no less certain than those of optics or astronomy" (*EIP* preface). Knowledge of the human mind, Reid writes, is "a subject highly worthy of inquiry on its own account, but still more worthy on account of the extensive influence which the knowledge of it hath over every other branch of science" (*IHM* 1.1).

Just as optics, astronomy, geology, biology, and other subdisciplines of what was known as "natural philosophy" require careful observation and experiment, so too does progress in our understanding of the mind. Thus, Reid writes that "all that we know of the body is owing to anatomical dissection and observation, and it must be by an anatomy of the mind that we can discover its powers and principles" (*IHM* 1.1); but while an anatomist can study many different bodies, the "anatomist of the mind" is confined to studying their own

12 MARY SHEPHERD

consciousness (*IHM* 1.2). Combined with the complexity of mental processes and thoughts, this means that the analysis of the human mind requires "great caution, and great application of mind" (*IHM* 1.2). Suggesting that it is best to begin with the simplest abilities of the mind and work up to the more complicated, Reid begins the *Inquiry* with an investigation of the sense of smell (*IHM* 2), then turns to the other sense modalities of taste, hearing, and touch, ending with the "noblest" of the senses, vision (*IHM* 6.1). In the two later *Essays*, Reid considers not just sensory perception but also memory, conception (roughly, imagination), abstraction, judgment, and will.

Dugald Stewart, briefly a student of Reid at the University of Glasgow, continued in the same tradition of Hume and Reid of elucidating human nature by careful observation and analysis. Avoiding metaphysical questions such as the nature of mind and matter—questions that cannot be answered and that lead to an "inextricable labyrinth"—Stewart sought to identify the "faculties and principles" that make up the "general laws of our constitution."[26] Although he thought it "unfortunate" that Reid had used the phrase "common sense" in the title of the *Inquiry*,[27] Stewart's position was similar to Reid's; indeed, he dedicated his *Elements of the Philosophy of the Human Mind* (1792) to Reid. Thus, Stewart argued that there are "fundamental laws of human belief" that it is equally absurd both to doubt and to try to prove.[28] These include the beliefs that space and time exist independently of the human mind,[29] that the order of nature will continue to follow the same laws,[30] and that every change has a cause.[31]

---

[26] Stewart, *Elements of the Philosophy of the Human Mind*, vol. 1, introduction, part 1. Subsequent references to *Elements* are to chapter and section of volume 1.

[27] Stewart thinks the phrase "common sense" implies "more than due respect for the established opinions" of some "particular sect or party" (*Philosophical Essays* 2.1). References to Stewart's *Essays* are to essay and chapter.

[28] Stewart, *Philosophical Essays* 2.1.

[29] Stewart, *Philosophical Essays* 2.1.

[30] Stewart, *Philosophical Essays* 2.1.

[31] Stewart, *Elements* 1.2. Although Stewart held it to be a "fundamental law of belief" that every change has a cause, he followed Hume's account of causation, writing that

SHEPHERD'S LIFE AND CONTEXT   13

Another Scottish common sense philosopher who shaped Shepherd's thinking was Thomas Brown. After studying at the University of Edinburgh, Brown practiced medicine from 1803 until 1810 and then rejoined the university as chair of moral philosophy. Like Stewart, Brown held that Hume was correct to analyze causation in terms of constant conjunctions of events (*ONT* 47, 80) but incorrect to think that our belief that causes of the same type will always produce effects of the same type is the result of experiencing such constant conjunctions (*ONT* 121–22). Instead, Brown argued that this belief is an "intuitive judgment, that, in certain circumstances, rises in the mind, inevitably, and with irresistible conviction" (*ONT* 369).

While Shepherd shared with Reid, Stewart, and Brown both a commitment to investigating and analyzing the abilities of the human mind and the belief that Hume was wrong to explain many of our beliefs as simply the results of mental associations and habits,[32] she did not think their explanations of those beliefs as principles of common sense, fundamental laws of belief, or intuitive judgments were any better. Instead, as we shall see, she emphasized that certain key beliefs—in the uniformity of cause and effect and in the existence of an external world—are the products of human reasoning, and thus can be given rational justification.

"it seems now to be pretty generally agreed among philosophers, that there is no instance in which we are able to perceive a necessary connexion between two successive events; or to comprehend in what manner the one proceeds from the other, as its cause" (*Elements* 1.2).

[32] In his influential 1875 book *The Scottish Philosophy*, James McCosh identified three features that he thought characterized the school of Scottish philosophy: its use of observation and "the inductive method" in "psychological investigation" (6–8); its use of "self-consciousness as the instrument of observation," using both introspection and examination of the beliefs and feelings expressed by others in speech and writing (8–10); and the belief that "there are laws, principles, or powers in the mind" that are "in the very constitution of the mind" (10). For further discussion of how Shepherd's work fits these criteria, and thus should be considered as belonging to the school of Scottish philosophy, see Boyle, "Expanding the Canon."

14   MARY SHEPHERD

Berkeleyan Idealism

In *Essays on the Perception of an External Universe*, Shepherd's main target is the idealist philosophy of the Irish bishop George Berkeley;[33] she counters his insistence that there is no rational basis to believe matter exists externally to our minds (*PHK* 1.15) with her arguments that reason establishes precisely that there is. Interestingly, she does not entirely reject Berkeley's views. She notes that she agrees with him on a number of points (*EPEU* 6, 72, 127, 197, 296), she praises certain aspects of his philosophical system as "truly consistent, and philosophical, and accordant with experience" (*EPEU* 167), and she suggests that reading Berkeley enabled her to "find the clue to a better theory" (*EPEU* 303). Nonetheless, she also sees his work as full of errors and as the basis on which Hume developed his skeptical conclusions (*EPEU* 5). She mentions Berkeley repeatedly throughout the first long essay of *EPEU*, and she devotes several of the shorter essays specifically to the arguments in his *Treatise Concerning the Principles of Human Knowledge* (1710).[34]

Berkeley had argued in the *Principles* that because objects—such things as "houses, mountains, rivers"—are perceived by our senses, and because we can only perceive our own ideas and sensations, it follows that what we take to be external objects are really just our own ideas (*PHK* 1.4). Thus, houses, mountains, rivers, and other "sensible objects" cannot exist unperceived; as Berkeley famously put it, "Their *esse* is *percipi*," or "their being is to be perceived" (*PHK* 1.3). Berkeley takes this argument to establish that only minds

[33] Margaret Atherton has pointed out that Shepherd's occasional references to "followers" of Berkeley suggest that she had more than just Berkeley in mind in her arguments against idealism (*EPEU* 241–42; see also 25). Atherton plausibly suggests that John Fearn was one such "follower" ("Lady Mary Shepherd's Case," 363). Shepherd does indeed say that Fearn's views "appear too much like a renewal of the Berkeleian theory" (LMSM 697).

[34] Shepherd mentions Berkeley's *Three Dialogues between Hylas and Philonous* (1713) only once (*EPEU* 81); at *EPEU* 68, she alludes to his *Essay Towards a New Theory of Vision* (1709).

SHEPHERD'S LIFE AND CONTEXT 15

and the ideas in those minds exist; this is the doctrine of idealism. Furthermore, he argues that it is "impossible . . . that there should be any such thing as an outward object" (*PHK* 1.15) that is made of an unperceiving material substance; this is the doctrine of immaterialism.[35] This is not to say that Berkeley thinks there are no objects such as houses, mountains, and human bodies; as Berkeley puts it, "Whatever we see, feel, hear, or any wise conceive or understand, remains as secure as ever and is as real as ever" (*PHK* 1.34). Such objects exist, Berkeley insists, just not as material entities that could exist outside a mind (*PHK* 1.34).

According to Berkeley, those who maintain that objects exist independently of being perceived have made this mistake because they think they can separate in their thought the perceived features of objects—sensible qualities such as color, taste, and shape—from the notion of a sensible object itself (*PHK* 1.5). In fact, says Berkeley, "it is impossible for me to conceive in my thoughts any sensible thing or object distinct from the sensation or perception of it" (*PHK* 1.5). Berkeley does not deny that he can concentrate on just one aspect of a thing, to the exclusion of its other qualities; for example, when considering a thing in motion, he can focus just on the speed of the motion or just on whether the motion is curved or straight (*PHK* introduction.10). But he denies that he can thereby form an idea of motion itself, an idea with no other features; that is, he cannot separate the idea of the object from the idea of its sensible qualities. And, Berkeley insists, this is not just because of some limitation in his own thinking abilities. Rather, the supposed ability to separate these things, to conceive of them apart from each other and thereby create "abstract ideas," is an ability he thinks no one actually possesses. Those who maintain that there can be some

---

[35] Samuel Rickless succinctly expresses these two Berkeleyan doctrines thus: "Idealism is the view that sensible objects (such as tables and chairs, apples and pears) and their sensible properties (such as shape and color) are nothing more than mind-dependent entities. . . . Immaterialism is the view that there is no such thing as material substance" (Rickless, *Berkeley's Argument for Idealism*, 1).

16   MARY SHEPHERD

sensible object, material substance, that can exist without being perceived are trying to engage in this impossible abstraction; they assume that one can think of a sensible object (matter) apart from *any* of its sensible qualities (*PHK* 1.5).

Berkeley further notes that appealing to a distinction between primary and secondary qualities does not help establish the existence of matter outside the mind of a perceiver. This distinction, common among seventeenth-century philosophers such as Descartes, distinguished qualities such as color, texture, smell, taste, and sound ('secondary qualities') from qualities such as extension, shape, and motion (the 'primary qualities'). As this distinction was typically understood, secondary qualities were simply sensations existing in the mind, *caused* by matter but not resembling anything in matter itself, whereas primary qualities were thought to exist in the physical world just as we perceive them to.[36] But Berkeley insists that the concept of a material, extended world possessing only primary qualities yet existing independently of minds is incoherent. First, primary qualities, just as much as secondary qualities, are *sensible* qualities, and thus exist only as ideas in the mind (*PHK* 1.9). Second, Berkeley insists that it is impossible to think of something as having only primary qualities and no secondary qualities (*PHK* 1.10). One cannot, for example, think of something as having shape and size but no color at all. Like thinking of a sensible object that exists without being sensed, this would require an impossible abstraction.[37]

---

[36] See Descartes' Sixth Meditation. While Locke, too, distinguished between primary and secondary qualities, he took the *qualities* to be in objects, with *ideas* of the qualities existing in the mind (*ECHU* 2.8.7). A primary quality, for Locke, is a power of a material body to produce ideas of such features of objects as solidity, bulk, extension, figure, motion or rest, texture, and number (*ECHU* 2.8.9–10). A secondary quality is a power of a material body to produce ideas of colors, sounds, tastes, and smells (*ECHU* 2.8.10).

[37] Berkeley offers other arguments against positing the existence of an unperceived substance consisting only of primary qualities, such as one based on the claim that not just secondary qualities but also primary qualities vary relative to perceivers (*PHK* 1.11); a full discussion of Berkeley's arguments would take us too far afield.

SHEPHERD'S LIFE AND CONTEXT   17

Berkeley thus diagnosed the source of the error of belief in an external material world as being the mistaken belief in the possibility of forming abstract ideas. Shepherd rejects Berkeley's rejection of abstract ideas. She thinks we *can* form abstract ideas, such as the idea of existence in general (*EPEU* 83), and she takes abstraction to be "the consideration of any quality apart from others with which it may be usually united, in order to notice what inferences may be drawn from its nature" (*EPEU* 291). Abstraction in this sense is the method she uses to show the mistakes of ordinary people, the "vulgar" who are not trained in philosophy, as well as philosophers. The vulgar, she says, have a natural tendency to associate sensible qualities with the ideas of their causes, and to use the same word to name both the conglomeration of sensible qualities in the mind *and* the external cause of those sensible qualities (*EPEU* 41–42, 210–11, 299). Shepherd sees her project as analyzing this compound idea of the effects (the sensible qualities) and the cause (the external object existing outside the mind) into its component parts, abstracting the ideas of sensible qualities from the ideas of their causes. When we perform this abstraction and consider the component parts separately from each other, we can see (she says) that sensible qualities are *not* out there in the world, even if the sensible qualities and their causes are (as all effects and causes are) necessarily connected. Berkeley's error is, she might say, *over*-abstracting, separating the sensible qualities from the causes and then *discarding* the notion of the causes altogether. As she puts it in her 1832 essay, the mistakes idealists make—"separating the notions of external objects from their internal effects (their partial qualities), and considering that the names of objects merely belong to ideas, and that these ideas are the only physical causes with which they are acquainted"—are all due to "a deficiency in the use of abstraction" (LMSM 705). They have abstracted where they should not have, in considering only ideas and not the external causes that are necessarily connected with them (*EPEU* 207, 68). But they have also *failed* to abstract where they should have, failing to see that some of the qualities they

18　MARY SHEPHERD

ascribe to sensible objects (powers to cause other sensible qualities, in particular) really belong to external objects (*EPEU* 299, 304;
LMSM 705).

The French "Ideologues"

Viewing his work as the successor of John Locke's empiricism,
Étienne Bonnot de Condillac argues in his *Traité des sensations*
(1754) not only that all our *ideas* derive from sensory experience
but that our *mental faculties* also develop through experience; all
of these depend ultimately on our ability to feel pain and pleasure,
which was among the very few abilities that Condillac considered
to be innate. In an example to which Shepherd alludes (*EPEU*
43n and 138–39n), Condillac asks his reader to imagine a statue
with a mind and body like a human's, but without yet having had
any thoughts, and limited to the use of just one sensory modality.
Suppose that first sensory modality is smell; were we to allow the
statue to smell a rose, Condillac says, the statue would feel itself to
be simply the scent of a rose.[38] This scent will also appear either
agreeable or disagreeable to the statue, so the statue would *also*
feel a sensation of either pleasure or pain.[39] But until it actually
felt both pleasure and pain, it would have no inkling of the other;
that is, a statue that had never sensed anything but an unpleasant
odor would have no desire to smell something pleasant, because
it would as yet have no idea of the pleasant.[40] If we then offer the
statue an odor it finds pleasant, the memory of the unpleasant odor
will be present to the statue's consciousness as it experiences that
pleasant odor, and this will teach the statue not only what pleasure
feels like but also the difference between current experience and

[38] Condillac, *Traité de sensations*, 1:17–18.
[39] Condillac, *Traité de sensations*, 1:21.
[40] Condillac, *Traité de sensations*, 1:21.

remembered experience.[41] As the statue's attention shifts from the current sensation to the remembered one, it will realize that the two are different—that is, it will make a comparison, which Condillac characterizes as a judgment.[42] The more the statue makes comparisons, the better it will get at judging, so that it will develop a "habit" of making judgments.[43] As we gradually enable the statue to use more of its organs of sense, it will acquire more and more ideas and further develop its mental faculties.

Condillac's work inspired a number of French philosophers in post-revolutionary France who saw themselves as working in a shared tradition according to which all our ideas derive from sensations.[44] Several of these men were members of the Institute of France, founded in 1795 by the government of the new Republic of France to house the nation's learned societies. In a paper read in 1796 to the members of the Institute, Antoine Destutt de Tracy (1754–1836) stressed the importance of a "science of ideas," which he dubbed *idéologie*.[45] The "Ideologues," as they came to be known, shared de Tracy's belief that a scientific, empiricist approach to human thought was necessary for establishing better (and non-monarchical) moral, legal, and political systems.[46] To study ideas was, for de Tracy, to identify the habitual associations among ideas, their associations with words, the illusions to which these associations can give rise, and the sentiments that result from different ideas.

---

[41] Condillac, *Traité de sensations*, 1:29.

[42] Condillac, *Traité de sensations*, 1:33–34.

[43] Condillac, *Traité de sensations*, 1:34.

[44] A brief account of these thinkers can be found in Jean Lefranc, *La philosophie en France au XIXe siècle*, 8–22.

[45] De Tracy is now perhaps better known for his 1806 analysis of Montesquieu's *Spirit of the Laws*, which Thomas Jefferson translated into English in 1811 as *A Commentary and Review of Montesquieu's* Spirit of Laws. Jefferson also later translated another of de Tracy's works under the title *A Treatise on Political Economy* (1817).

[46] On the political goals of the Ideologues, see Kennedy, "'Ideology' from Destutt de Tracy to Marx," and Welch, *Liberty and Utility: The French Idéologues and the Transformation of Liberalism*.

20 MARY SHEPHERD

Shepherd agrees with de Tracy that our sensations are the starting point of all knowledge, and she occasionally invokes his views as further support for her own (*EPEU* 105n, 170n, 171n, 189n, 316n). However, she disagrees with de Tracy and other Ideologues to whom she refers (Pierre Jean-Georges Cabanis [1757–1808] and Joseph Marie de Gérando [1772–1842]) on two points.[47] First, she thinks that their claims that we know the external world only through certain kinds of judgments about our experience of objects are too narrow; as she puts it, her own theory "enlarge[s] the number of such sorts of judgments, by the comparison of many other ideas" (*EPEU* 105n; see also 177–78n). Second, she maintains that de Tracy's and the Ideologues' arguments establish only the exteriority of the physical world, not its continued existence or its independence from thought (*EPEU* 112n).

British Moral Theories

In England and Ireland, as well as Scotland, philosophers, politicians, and ordinary citizens grappled with the implications of the French and American Revolutions abroad and, at home, the need for reforms to address such problems as uneven political representation, unfair penal codes and a cruel prison system, poverty, prostitution, child labor and educational inequities, and the continued practice of slavery in British colonies. Various approaches competed in the marketplace of ideas, including defenses of the notion of natural rights—such as Mary Wollstonecraft's *A Vindication of the Rights of Man* (1790) and *A Vindication of the Rights of Woman* (1792)—and the utilitarianism advocated in Jeremy Bentham's

---

[47] Shepherd mentions in a footnote that she read de Tracy's work *after* writing a first draft of *Essays*: "Since writing this essay, I find that Mr. Destutt de Tracy has many ideas which I am happy unconsciously to have hit on" (*EPEU* 105n). Since all her references to Condillac and de Gérando are also only in footnotes, it seems likely that she read their works, too, only after writing the draft, adding the references later.

SHEPHERD'S LIFE AND CONTEXT 21

An Introduction to the Principles of Morals and Legislation (1789) and William Godwin's *Enquiry Concerning Political Justice* (1793). Shepherd, however, seems to have had little interest in these issues, although she does acknowledge that people's lives can be improved through improving their environment and education. Referring in the *Essays* to the benefits of her theory of sensation, according to which "the same external causes would yield the same internal sensation to each mind, if the varieties were not in the individuals," she notes that individuals have different perceptions of the same external objects because of facts about the individuals, features "as multifarious as food, medicine, and climate; the circulation of the blood, the passions, the habits of education, and the notions of individuals," all things which "wisdom acting in time might alter with advantage" (*EPEU* 264–65). Thus, she observes that acknowledging the influence of these features "may enable physiologists and physicians, moralists and divines, parents and instructors, better to observe, and more wisely to act than they do, with respect to the health, the opinions, and the practices of those under their care" (*EPEU* 264). But Shepherd never says more about what alterations should be made to improve people's lives and opinions. She is silent on issues that preoccupied many of her contemporaries, such as prison conditions, the status of women, or the abolition of slavery.

The Reception of Shepherd's Work

Shepherd's work seems to have been well received in her own day and shortly thereafter. Her daughter reports that philosopher of science William Whewell used one of her books as a textbook in his courses at Cambridge,[48] and Robert Blakey included an account of Shepherd's work in his *History of the Philosophy of the Mind* (1848),

---

[48] Brandreth, *Some Family and Friendly Recollections*, 29.

22 MARY SHEPHERD

where he praised her as displaying "great acuteness and subtility."[49] In 1868, in a talk regarding the role of philosophy in women's education, Scottish philosopher Alexander Campbell Fraser mentioned Shepherd, saying that in her books she "discusses with great ingenuity and acuteness some of the profoundest questions to which the human mind can be applied."[50] Yet, aside from a mention of her 1824 *Essay* in a 1938 bibliography,[51] Shepherd's work seems to have been effectively erased from the philosophical record until the pioneering work of Eileen O'Neill and Margaret Atherton in the 1990s and Jennifer McRobert in the early 2000s. Since then, historians of philosophy have begun to investigate Shepherd's tightly argued criticisms of Hume, Berkeley, and Reid, as well as her own highly original positive arguments, although this exegetical and evaluative work is only just getting started.

Suggestions for Further Reading

- *Some Family and Friendly Recollections of Seventy Years*, an 1886 memoir by Shepherd's daughter Mary Elizabeth Shepherd Brandreth, contains remembrances of Shepherd and her relatives.
- Jennifer McRobert provides further biographical information about Shepherd and helpfully situates her views in their historical context in "Mary Shepherd and the Causal Relation" as well as in the Introduction to *The Philosophical Works of Lady Mary Shepherd*.
- For discussion of why the 1819 *Enquiry Respecting the Relation of Cause and Effect* should be attributed to Milne rather than Shepherd, see Boyle, "A Mistaken Attribution to Mary Shepherd."
- Facsimile copies of the original editions of *ERCE* and *EPEU* are contained in Jennifer McRobert's *Philosophical Works of Mary Shepherd*. Selections from *ERCE*, *EPEU*, and "Lady Mary Shepherd's Metaphysics," and the complete text of Shepherd's "On the Causes of Single and Erect Vision," are available (organized by topic) in Deborah Boyle, ed., *Lady Mary*

---

[49] Blakey, *History of the Philosophy of the Mind*, 4:40.
[50] Fraser, "The Edinburgh Ladies' Educational Association," 5.
[51] Jessop, *A Bibliography of David Hume and of Scottish Philosophy*.

SHEPHERD'S LIFE AND CONTEXT   23

Shepherd: Selected Writings. Antonia LoLordo's modern edition, *Mary Shepherd's* Essays on the Perception of an External Universe, also contains "Lady Mary Shepherd's Metaphysics."

- On Shepherd's critique of John Fearn and his patronizing reply, see Atherton, "Reading Lady Mary Shepherd."
- For overviews of Shepherd's philosophical work, see Martha Bolton's entry "Mary Shepherd" in the *Stanford Encyclopedia of Philosophy*, Antonia LoLordo's introduction to *Mary Shepherd's Essays on the Perception of an External Universe*. LoLordo's concise *Mary Shepherd* also outlines the main themes of Shepherd's two books.
- The Project Vox website has many materials related to Shepherd's life and work, including essays providing overviews of her philosophical system. See https://projectvox.org/shepherd-1777-1847/

2

Causation

Introduction

David Hume's account of causation and causal inference cast a long shadow. Although he first published this account in the *Treatise of Human Nature* (1739–40), with a revised presentation of it in the *Enquiry Concerning Human Understanding* (1748), debates over the implications of his causal theory were still ongoing in the early nineteenth century. In 1805, Sir John Leslie nearly lost an appointment to the chair of mathematics at the University of Edinburgh because of his endorsement of Hume's causal theory, an incident to which Shepherd alludes (*ERCE* 5). This dispute played out in the Edinburgh newspapers and led to several publications, including Dugald Stewart's defense of Leslie[1] and Thomas Brown's 1805 pamphlet *Observations on the Nature and Tendency of the Doctrine of Mr. Hume, Concerning the Relation of Cause and Effect*, which was published in expanded versions in 1806 and 1818.[2] So Humean causation was still a live topic when Mary Shepherd stepped into the debate in 1824. Shepherd thought Hume's views were deeply misguided, so she devoted her first book, *An Essay upon the Relation of Cause and Effect*, to showing where Hume went wrong and to offering an alternative account of her own. Later in the book, she

---

[1] Stewart, *A Short Statement of some Important Facts, relative to the late election of a mathematical professor in the University of Edinburgh.*

[2] Brown, *Observations on the Nature and Tendency of the Doctrine of Mr. Hume, Concerning the Relation of Cause and Effect* (first edition, 1805; second edition, 1806) and *Inquiry into the Relation of Cause and Effect* (1818).

Mary Shepherd. Deborah Boyle, Oxford University Press. © Oxford University Press 2023.
DOI: 10.1093/oso/9780190090326.003.0002

CAUSATION 25

also responds to Brown and another defender of Humean causation, William Lawrence.

This chapter begins with a brief overview of Hume's account of causation, followed by an examination of the first four of six points Shepherd makes in opposition to Hume: that we know through reason, not "custom," that every object that begins to exist must have a cause other than itself; that we also know through reason, not custom, that causes that are similar to each other will necessarily have effects that are similar to each other; that Shepherd can offer a better definition of 'cause' than Hume; and that Hume's definitions of 'cause' are flawed in several respects. In the course of this rebuttal of Hume, Shepherd lays out her own novel theory of causation as synchronous necessary connection. Shepherd's remaining two claims will be the focus of the next chapter.

Hume's Causal Theory

The first chapter of *ERCE* contains quotations from Hume's *Treatise* and *Enquiry* on the topic of causation.[3] As Shepherd notes (*ERCE* 2), Hume requested that his readers not take the *Treatise* as containing the definitive statement of his views; he states that the *Enquiry* should "alone be regarded as containing his philosophical sentiments and principles," since it corrected "some negligences in his former reasoning and more in the expression" (advertisement to *EHU*). Shepherd dismisses Hume's plea on the grounds that the later essay draws on premises established by arguments (which she characterizes as "sophistical reasonings") in the *Treatise* (*ERCE* 2–3), and so her quotations are drawn from both works. She focuses on two key claims from Hume: first, that we cannot know with certainty the general proposition that "every event must have a cause";

---

[3] Shepherd's quotations in her introductory chapter are drawn from the *Treatise*, book 1, part 3, and from the *Enquiry*, sections 4, 5, and 7.

26   MARY SHEPHERD

second, that in particular arguments regarding causes and effects, our inferences that some cause has been at work or that some effect will occur will always be uncertain (*ERCE* 10–11).

Hume contended that all propositions known (or alleged to be known) by humans fall into one of two classes: relations of ideas and matters of fact (*EHU* 4.1).[4] Claims expressing true relations of ideas are necessarily true; to deny such a claim is to express a contradiction. A relation of ideas can be *known* to be necessarily true (or necessarily false) simply by examining the meanings of the words used. For example, "A unicycle has one wheel" is necessarily true, and can be known to be so, because it is simply part of the definition of "unicycle" that it has one wheel. On the other hand, claims expressing matters of fact are, if they are true, only contingently true. The contrary of such a claim can always (according to Hume, anyway) be asserted without expressing a contradiction; it might be *incorrect* to say (of a book with other than 500 pages) "this book has 500 pages," but there is no self-contradiction involved, as there would be in the claim "This unicycle has two wheels."

Another way Hume puts his distinction between a relation of ideas and a matter of fact is in terms of the *separability* of the ideas included in the proposition—that is, in terms of whether one of the ideas can be conceived of *without* thinking of the other. For example, one cannot think adequately of a unicycle without thinking of it as having one wheel; that is, Hume would say, the idea of having one wheel cannot be separated from the idea of a unicycle. In contrast, he thinks that the ideas in a proposition expressing a matter of fact *can* be conceived independently of each other. Suppose someone asserts "This unicycle has a flat tire." Even if this assertion is true, one can conceive of the unicycle as *not* having a flat tire; that is, the idea of the unicycle can be separated in thought from

---

[4] The distinction between relations of ideas and matters of fact is most clearly spelled out in the *Enquiry*, but the same basic idea is expressed in the *Treatise* (*T* 1.3.6.1–2; see also 3.1.1.18).

CAUSATION 27

the idea of the flat tire. And if these things are separable in thought, then Hume thinks it follows that they are separable in reality; for Hume, the conceivability of something shows us that it is possible, while impossible things (such as a square circle) are inconceivable (*T* 1.3.3.3 and *EHU* 4.18).

Based on his distinction between two kinds of propositions, Hume argues that there are just two kinds of reasoning. Reasoning about relations of ideas is "demonstrative" and a priori; that is, correct inferences based on a relation of ideas can be known with absolute certainty to be true (*EHU* 4.18). Reasoning about matters of fact, however, is "moral" reasoning and a posteriori; it is based on experience (*EHU* 4.18–19), as when we predict that it will rain based on seeing dark clouds of the sort that have generally produced rain in the past.[5] Hume draws on this distinction to examine the basis of our reasoning about causes and effects. Suppose someone receives a postcard of a scene in France, signed by their friend and carrying a French stamp and postmark. They might naturally infer that their friend is in France (an example drawn from *EHU* 4.4). The contrary of their judgment is conceivable, not self-contradictory; that is, it is *possible* that their friend is engaged in some scheme to trick them and is not actually in France. So the judgment "My friend is in France" is not *demonstratively* certain; to put this in terms of separability, the person can think of their friend without thinking of them as being in France.

But nor can they use *moral* reasoning to establish with certainty that their friend is in France, according to Hume. This is because, if we spell out the reasoning involved in making this judgment, we will see that it is based on past experience—in this example, on past experience that postcards carrying stamps and postmarks from another locale were sent by someone in that locale—plus an

---

[5] In the seventeenth and eighteenth centuries, 'moral' had a broader meaning than it does today, referring generally to what pertains to human action and life.

28 MARY SHEPHERD

assumption that our future experience will conform to our past experience.[6] But the very principle that future experience will conform to past experience—or, as Shepherd prefers to express this principle, that similar causes will have similar effects—cannot be justified rationally, according to Hume. It is not *demonstratively* certain because there is no contradiction in suggesting that the future will not conform to past experience. But it is also not *morally* certain because to justify this principle by drawing on past experience—that is, that in the past, future experiences have conformed to past experience—is circular (*EHU* 4.19). Thus, trying to justify "My friend is in France" on the basis of moral reasoning turns out to be circular, too.

Since Hume thinks that all reasoning is either demonstrative or moral, and neither type can justify judgments about cause and effect, he concludes that such judgments are, ultimately, not justified at all. Instead, he offers a psychological account of how we make these judgments, an account that appeals to the mental habits we form on the basis of experience (*EHU* 5.5). Repeated experiences of events or objects of one type being accompanied by events or objects of another type give us a propensity to think of one when we think of the other:

All belief of matter of fact or real existence is derived merely from some object, present to the memory or senses, and a customary conjunction between that and some other object. Or in other words; having found, in many instances, that any two kinds of objects—flame and heat, snow and cold—have always been conjoined together; if flame or snow be presented anew to the senses, the mind is carried by custom to expect heat or cold, and to

---

[6] In the secondary literature on Hume, this is typically characterized as the Uniformity Principle. The problem Hume identifies here with justifying causal inferences is often now known as the Problem of Induction.

CAUSATION 29

believe that such a quality does exist, and will discover itself upon
a nearer approach. (*EHU* 5.8)

This account then gives Hume the basis for a definition of 'cause.'
He actually offers two definitions, writing that "we may con-
sider the relation of cause and effect in either of these two lights"
(*EHU* 7.29):

> We may define a cause to be *an object, followed by another, and*
> *where all the objects similar to the first are followed by objects*
> *similar to the second.* Or in other words *where, if the first ob-*
> *ject had not been, the second never had existed.* The appearance
> of a cause always conveys the mind, by a customary transi-
> tion, to the idea of the effect. Of this also we have experience.
> We may, therefore, suitably to this experience, form another
> definition of cause, and call it, *an object followed by another,*
> *and whose appearance always conveys the thought to that other.*
> (*EHU* 7.29)

Two points should be noted here that will be relevant for considering Shepherd's criticisms. First, Hume emphasizes that causes are
prior in time to effects: a cause is "followed by" an effect. Second,
Hume stresses that he is offering *two* definitions. The first defines
a cause in terms of its membership in a class of events or objects
that have always been accompanied by (or "conjoined with") something that is a member of another class of events or objects. The
second defines a cause in terms of a person's customary thought
patterns upon perceiving some event or object. In this sense, both
definitions are "drawn from circumstances foreign to the cause"
(*EHU* 7.29); that is, 'cause' can only be defined by reference to *other*
objects or to *thinkers*. There is, according to Hume, no way to identify one thing as being the cause of another without locating that
thing in a pattern of other events or in what happens in a perceiver's
thoughts.

30 MARY SHEPHERD

The first issue that Shepherd focuses on in *ERCE* is whether or not everything that comes into existence must have a *cause* for its existence. Shepherd correctly observes that in the *Enquiry*, Hume never actually asserts that things can come into existence without a cause (*ERCE* 19). However, she reads Hume's claim that it is "neither intuitively nor demonstrably certain" that *"whatever begins to exist, must have a cause of existence"* (*T* 1.3.3.1–2) as *entailing* the claim that "beings can begin their existences themselves" (*ERCE* 19–20). Or, as she puts it later, Hume thinks that the idea of a thing beginning its existence can be separated from the idea of a cause (*ERCE* 29). It is to that claim that Shepherd first directs her arguments.

Proving the Causal Principle

The principle that Shepherd considers to be the "key to every difficulty that concerns the sources of our belief or knowledge" (*EPEU* 138) is that *"there is no object which begins to exist, but must owe its existence to some cause"* (*ERCE* 36). Call this the Causal Principle, or CP. This principle indeed plays a central role in Shepherd's philosophy; she will use it to argue that we can also know that similar causes must have similar effects, that an external world must exist, and that God must exist. She maintains that everyone knows the CP implicitly by what she calls "latent reasoning" but that the principle can also be explicitly defended with a *reductio* argument.

Before embarking on this project, however, Shepherd offers a diagnosis of why Hume thinks (mistakenly, in her view) that a cause is separable from its effect. She agrees with Hume that we can *imagine* or *conceive of* a cause separately from its effect (*ERCE* 29). We can, for example, think of a match (or, as Shepherd might say, a flint and steel [*ERCE* 124]) without thinking of the flame that results when it is struck. But Shepherd cautions against being misled by language. As she notes later in the book, just because we can "conceive something in the fancy"—that is, imagine it—does not mean that that

CAUSATION 31

thing is possible (*ERCE* 83).[7] The fact that a cause can be imagined separately from its effect does not entail that the two are actually separable. Indeed, she notes that cause and effect are reciprocally defined, or, as she puts it, "relative" terms (*ERCE* 38); that is, what it means to be a 'cause' is to be a producer of an effect, and what it means to be an 'effect' is to be the result of a cause. So to say that "every effect has a cause" is true simply by definition. For Hume to claim that not every effect has a cause, Shepherd insists, he must be using the term 'effect' in a non-standard way. But we cannot just use words however we want, to suit our own purpose; as she puts it, "if the ideas are altered that lie under [a] term, according as the varied occasion seems to require, there can be no philosophy" (*ERCE* 30–31). Since 'cause' means, by definition, 'something that produces an effect,' Hume is not entitled to say that effects can occur without causes (*ERCE* 32).

The real question, then, is not whether every *effect* that comes into existence has a cause, since that is true by definition, but whether every *object* that comes into existence must have a cause (*ERCE* 34). Shepherd thinks that we can establish that this is indeed true by an argument in the form of a *reductio ad absurdum*. Assume the contrary of the claim to be proven: in this case, suppose that some object *can* come into existence without a cause; suppose it "START[S] FORTH into existence, and make[s] the first breach on the wide nonentity around" (*ERCE* 35). This "starting forth," or coming into existence, is an action, and Shepherd treats an action as a quality of an object. However, no object can have a quality without existing. Thus, in order for an object to have the quality of coming into existence, it must already exist; yet by hypothesis it does not.

---

[7] Indeed, as David Landy points out, Shepherd's argument for the CP involves asking us to imagine a scenario that she then claims is impossible ("Shepherd on Hume's Argument for the Possibility of Uncaused Existence," 4). Following a suggestion made in Bolton's "Lady Mary Shepherd and David Hume on Cause and Effect," Landy argues that Shepherd's claim that conceivability need not imply possibility relies on a very different theory of mental representation than Hume's.

32 MARY SHEPHERD

Given this contradiction, Shepherd writes that "we must conclude *that there is no object which begins to exist, but must owe its existence to some cause*" (*ERCE* 36; see also *EPEU* 290). Sometimes she puts this in terms of *differences* or *qualities* requiring causes for their existence (*ERCE* 58–59). Since (as we will soon see) Shepherd defines objects as bundles of qualities, to cause a new object is also to cause a new quality, something different from what previously existed: "*Cause producing Effect*, therefore, under the strict eye of philosophical scrutiny, is a *new object* exhibiting *new qualities*; or shortly, the formation of a *new mass of qualities*" (*ERCE* 50; see also 57).[8]

The argument that Shepherd offers in *ERCE* explicitly spells out the steps by which the CP can be established, but Shepherd thinks that all perceivers know the CP implicitly even if they never spell it out in quite this fashion. As she puts it in the 1827 book, referring back to this argument, "such is the latent reasoning silently generated in the minds of all men, from infancy" (*EPEU* 14). She says something similar about the "reasoning upon experiment" by which another principle—the Causal Likeness Principle (CLP)—can be justified: "This is an argument, which all persons, however illiterate, feel the force of" (*ERCE* 44). What Shepherd means by "latent reasoning," and why she thinks even infants engage in it, will be discussed in chapter 5 of this *Guide*.

Having offered her argument for the CP, Shepherd returns to Hume, focusing on a passage in the *Treatise* where Hume criticizes the views of Samuel Clarke (1675–1729) and John Locke (1632–1704) on the topic of causation (*T* 1.3.3.5–6). In his *A Demonstration of the Being and Attributes of God* (1704), Clarke had offered a cosmological argument for the existence of God that depended crucially on the principle that "whatever exists has a cause, a reason, a

---

[8] For a reconstruction and discussion of this argument, see Landy, "Shepherd on Hume's Argument for the Possibility of Uncaused Existence."

ground of its existence, a foundation on which its existence relies."[9] In the *Essay Concerning Human Understanding* (1694), also in the service of a proof of God's existence, Locke had asserted that "bare nothing can no more produce any real being, than it can be equal to two right angles" (*ECHU* 4.10.3). Since we know there is something real—our own minds, if nothing else—there must be something, itself uncaused and eternal, that produced it; through a few further steps, Locke argues that this cause is God (*ECHU* 4.10.4–6). Hume accuses both Clarke and Locke of arguing in a circle. Clarke's claim that everything must have a cause because it is impossible for a thing to bring itself into existence simply *assumes* that a thing cannot come into existence without a cause (*T* 1.3.3.5); Locke's claim that a "bare nothing" cannot be a cause, and thus that everything that exists has a cause, *assumes* that everything must have a cause (*T* 1.3.3.6).

Shepherd is unpersuaded by Hume's objections. It is true, she says, that both Clarke and Locke assume that everything must have a cause, but this is because the absurdity of denying it is simply obvious: "these philosophers felt the involved absurdity so great, that they passed over the first question as too ridiculous, probably, to consider formally" (*ERCE* 37). It is in fact Hume, she says, who is arguing in a circle. He claims that we can *imagine* something as simply popping into existence without a cause; but to say that we can imagine this is to say that it is *conceivable* that an event can exist without a cause. This is not the same as conceiving of a particular effect without conceiving of its particular cause, which (as we saw above) Shepherd allows we can do; rather, it is to conceive of something occurring without *any* cause at all. Given Hume's assumption that what is conceivable is possible, Shepherd maintains that Hume is thus *assuming*, rather than proving, that it is possible that something can occur that has no cause (*ERCE* 38).

---

[9] Clarke, *A Demonstration of the Being and Attributes of God and Other Writings*, 8.

34 MARY SHEPHERD

The Causal Likeness Principle and
Its Corollaries

In *ERCE* chapter 1, section 2, Shepherd turns to the issue of causal inference: particular cases in ordinary life as well as in scientific contexts when we make some prediction about an effect based on our observations about causes, or where we infer the operation of a cause from our observation of some effect. In the first sort of case, for example, I might predict, based on past experience, that if I eat two slices of cake, the result will be a stomachache. In the second sort of case, I might infer, when I observe paw prints at the beach, that they were caused by a dog running on the sand. These inferences are based on the Causal Likeness Principle (CLP), which holds that similar effects are the result of similar causes. As Shepherd reminds us (*ERCE* 40–41), Hume had argued that we cannot rationally justify any causal inferences, that our confidence in them derives only from the degree to which we have (for example) observed that eating two slices of cake has been, in the past, associated with a stomachache, or that seeing a dog running on damp sand has been correlated with paw prints in the sand. Hume's reason for this conclusion is that we cannot rationally justify the CLP: again, we believe that the future will be like the past only because we have observed that in the past the future was like the past.

In contrast, Shepherd argues that we *can* rationally prove the CLP and that, far from requiring many cases of experiencing like causes producing like effects, we can know in particular cases that some effect will occur simply on the basis of just one well-constructed experiment, an *"experimentum crucis."* As she puts it, "one trial is enough" (*ERCE* 43). According to Shepherd, we can (in principle, anyway) learn through "reasoning upon experiment" (*EPEU* 45) what the necessary cause is of some given effect. "Reasoning upon experiment" is a process that involves the a priori knowledge of the CP combined with an *"experimentum crucis,"* or "crucial experiment" (*ERCE* 43), an experiment that decisively settles some

CAUSATION 35

scientific question about cause and effect.[10] In this kind of experiment, it must be possible to control all the factors in the environment except one. Shepherd argues like this: suppose that we can control all the factors in the environment in which, say, we close and then open our eyes, restoring "all the objects to view" (*ERCE* 44). The CP tells us that no quality or difference can occur without a cause other than itself. Since seeing objects in our environment (after not seeing them) is a case of a difference, our visual experience of the objects around us cannot have arisen without a cause. But since, by hypothesis, no circumstances changed other than our eyes opening, we know that the *only possible* cause of this difference was the opening of our eyes; in other words, we can infer that opening our eyes *necessarily caused* us to see the objects around us (*ERCE* 47–49 and 73). And since the connection is a necessary one, the next time we open our closed eyes (assuming circumstances are exactly the same as before), we can know that the same effect will occur. So Shepherd thinks, contrary to Hume, that we can, in principle at least, acquire certain knowledge that some future causal inference will be correct even after just one relevant experience. Interestingly, this means that Shepherd thinks that truths about physical causes and their effects turn out to be necessary truths that are known a posteriori, through experience.[11]

And if we can know that, in some particular case, an object A is the cause of some object B, then we can know that A and B are necessarily connected. Shepherd thinks we can *also* know the *general*

---

[10] One well-known example of an *experimentum crucis* is found in Isaac Newton's 1672 letter to the Royal Society of London, in which he describes his use of a prism to establish that white light is composed of rays of different angles of refraction, each of which appears as a distinct color (Newton, "A Letter," 3078, 3081–83). For discussion of this experiment, see Sabra, *Theories of Light*, 239–41 and 248–50. On the history of the phrase "*experimentum crucis*" before Newton, see Dumitru, "Crucial Instances and Crucial Experiments in Bacon, Boyle, and Hooke." The notion of an *experimentum crucis* recurs in works that Shepherd read, such as Reid's *Inquiry into the Human Mind*, where Reid proposes "an *experimentum crucis*, by which the ideal system must stand or fall" (*IHM* 5.7; see *EPEU* 109).

[11] In this respect, Shepherd anticipates arguments made more than a century and a half later by Saul Kripke in his *Naming and Necessity* (1980).

36 MARY SHEPHERD

principle that similar causes must give rise to similar effects (the CLP). This is not because we generalize from particular cases where we observe similar causes giving rise to similar effects; Shepherd emphasizes that one can never decisively establish a general principle simply by generalizing from particular cases (*ERCE* 59). The argument for the CLP, as in particular cases, is demonstratively certain, not merely probabilistic. We establish the CLP using "reasoning upon experiment," just as we do in particular cases. In this case, however, the experiment is a thought-experiment. Suppose there are two qualitatively identical causes in exactly similar circumstances and suppose these two causes give rise to different effects. According to the CP, everything that comes into existence has a cause other than itself; thus, the coming-to-be of a difference between the two effects would require some cause to explain it. But since the only causes posited are qualitatively identical, and the situations in which they act are too, "they must have like effects, or qualities, because there is nothing else given that can be supposed to make a difference" (*EPEU* 56). Thus, Shepherd holds, we can know with absolute certainty that, in general, future causes like those we have already experienced will have effects that resemble the effects of past causes, a point about which Hume had drawn skeptical conclusions.

Note that Shepherd thinks the certain knowledge we acquire through "reasoning upon experiment" is possible *in principle*. The conditions in a scientific setting can be much more strictly controlled than those in ordinary life, of course. Consider learning what temperature will melt gold. According to Shepherd, one carefully controlled scientific experiment, one *experimentum crucis*, is all that is needed. In a laboratory setting, we may well be able to achieve this; so long as we ensure that the only difference between the gold's being solid and the gold melting is that the gold's temperature has reached 1064°, combining that observation with the CP allows us to conclude that heating gold to 1064° causes it to melt; that is, it is a *necessary truth* that gold melts at 1064°. However, in

CAUSATION 37

ordinary life—and even in laboratories—conditions cannot always be controlled so perfectly; we might not realize that some additional factor in the environment has changed, and so we might misidentify a cause. Or, in cases where we are making a prediction, we might mistakenly think two items are similar and incorrectly predict similar effects. For example, the scientist who heats a substance they think is gold, expecting it to melt at 1064°, might actually be dealing with pyrite, "fool's gold," which looks similar to gold but melts at a higher temperature. So, in *practice*, we might not be able to achieve certain knowledge in our causal inferences.

Shepherd is well aware that we make mistakes in causal reasoning; we "too frequently consider objects as similar, upon insufficient data" (*EPEU* 323). Because of this, we need to be cautious about other people's causal inferences as well as our own. Shepherd offers an example of a customer in a pharmacy whose request for Epsom salts is fulfilled by an illiterate shop assistant who merely considers how the substance in the jar looks (*ERCE* 104). Since, Shepherd notes, "oxalic acid [has] the same *apparent* qualities" as Epsom salts, we might want more assurance that the assistant has given us the correct substance.[12] But Shepherd is fairly optimistic about our ability to use "good sense" (*ERCE* 102) to tell whether the observations we rely on in our causal inferences are accurate. She suggests that to help us tell whether two items that look similar *really are* similar, we can consider them as *effects* and ask whether the items were caused in the same way. If the causal histories of the two objects are similar, this is further grounds—beyond just their similar qualities—to think that they will have similar effects in similar circumstances: "When we also know that in the FORMATION of any object no difference took place," she writes, "then, there is no ground whatever, for imagining the possibility of an alteration in the effects of that object" (*ERCE* 56).

---

[12] Apparently, poisonings due to precisely this mistake were common in the nineteenth century; see Campbell, "Oxalic Acid, Epsom Salt, and the Poison Bottle."

38 MARY SHEPHERD

Yet even when we know something of the causal histories of objects we are dealing with, we cannot know their complete causal histories. We are finite knowers, after all. Shepherd concedes this in her second book, writing that "the very comparison of what is like, to like, supposes an ability to perfect comparisons, a subject on which we frequently make mistakes" (*EPEU* 174). We cannot ever be *entirely* sure that two similar-seeming objects or situations are identical in all respects. Thus, Shepherd concedes that in practice our causal inferences give us not complete certainty but only "*high probability* founded on REASONING" (*ERCE* 124). She is untroubled by her concession that actual causal inferences are never in fact completely certain, suggesting that, in practice, a causal inference known with a high degree of probability is just as good as one known with absolute certainty. Most human minds are of a practical rather than skeptical bent. Although a skeptic *could* raise a worry about whether the causes we think were involved really were involved, Shepherd says that "ordinary persons" will settle this question easily (*ERCE* 123). Shepherd's example is of seeing something that looks and feels like fire. A skeptic could ask me how I know that this appearance is not just an illusion and that putting a piece of wood on it would really cause the wood to turn to ash. I could answer that I can know—at least with "high probability"— that the appearance of fire is not an illusion because it resulted from a spark produced by a flint and steel (*ERCE* 124). The skeptic could keep pushing, wondering if the flint and steel are "truly such," but I can test this by seeing if they produce a spark (*ERCE* 124). And here, Shepherd says, "plain understandings" will be satisfied, even if philosophers (like Hume, presumably) try to raise further skeptical doubts about whether the secret powers of the various objects might have changed (*ERCE* 124).

In practice, then, Shepherd actually agrees with Hume: all our causal inferences are merely probable. But this is not for the reasons Hume offered. According to Hume's account, we cannot justify the CLP, and so all our causal inferences have exactly the same rational justification—that is to say, none. Shepherd at least can distinguish between degrees of probability of different causal inferences. In cases where we know a great deal about the objects in our experience, she will say that there is a higher degree of probability that our causal inferences are accurate than in cases where we know less.

Shepherd thinks we rely on the CLP, that like causes must have like effects, all the time in ordinary life when we make predictions about the future effects of objects with which we have had experience. But the principle also has useful corollaries that she herself relies on throughout her 1827 book to draw conclusions about the causes of our sensations. One corollary is that *like effects* must have *like causes*. That is, if an effect A results from a certain cause A', then (because causation is necessary connection) *all* effects that are exactly like A must come from causes exactly like A', and causes of type A' can give rise only to effects of type A. A further implication is that *different effects* must be due to *different causes* (*EPEU* 169). If we know that effects of type A come from causes of type A', and we encounter an effect of type B, we can know that it was *not* produced by a cause of type A'.

Shepherd thus takes herself to have established, against Hume, that we know about the causal powers of objects through reason, not just through a habitual association of ideas (*ERCE* 46). She also denies Hume's claim that causes are antecedent to their effects (*ERCE* 49). Understanding why she denies this requires a closer look at her theory of causation.

Defining 'Cause'

As we have seen, Shepherd insists that a causal relationship is one of necessary connection. One perhaps surprising conclusion that Shepherd draws from this is that causes and effects are inseparable and operate *synchronously* (that is, simultaneously): an effect comes into existence at the *very moment* that the relevant causes interact,

40 MARY SHEPHERD

not afterward.[13] Causation, then, is the mixture or interaction of two or more objects to produce, synchronously, a new object with a new quality, and the conjunction of the causes just *is* the effect.

Most people—Hume included—consider causes to be antecedent to effects; for example, people often say that smoking causes lung cancer, with the cancer occurring after years of smoking.[14] Shepherd would consider this example to be an "incomplete manner of thinking on this subject" (*EPEU* 124) and a sloppy way of speaking; while she would not deny that there might be a *causal chain* in some individual person between smoking and cancer, she thinks it is a mistake to say that smoking is the immediate or proximate cause of the person's cancer. This is because she thinks that one thing being antecedent to another is irrelevant to whether or not it is the immediate cause of that thing (*ERCE* 49 and 67). Indeed, it is not merely irrelevant; Martha Bolton has noted that Shepherd's view of causal connections as necessitated actually *precludes* an antecedent event being a proximate cause of a later event. Since two successive events are, as Bolton puts it, "temporally discrete," even if an event of the first type is *usually* followed by an event of the second type, in any particular case something else might intervene after the first event such that the second event does not occur.[15]

---

[13] Hume had maintained that any account of cause and effect as synchronous would mean that all causation would collapse into a single moment (*T* 1.3.2.7). For an argument that Shepherd's account is not susceptible to this objection, see Landy, "A Defense of Mary Shepherd's Account of Cause and Effect as Synchronous."

[14] An exception, as Martha Bolton notes, is Thomas Hobbes (Bolton, "Lady Mary Shepherd and David Hume on Cause and Effect," 136n23). Hobbes writes that "an entire cause, is the aggregate of all the accidents both of the agents how many soever they be, and of the patient, put together; which when they are all supposed to be present, it cannot be understood but that the effect is produced at the same instant; and if any one of them be wanting, it cannot be understood but that the effect is not produced" (*Elements of Philosophy*, part 2, chapter 9, article 3). The physician Thomas Cogan (1736–1818) also suggests in his 1817 book that cause and effect are synchronous and necessarily connected (*Ethical Questions*, 38). Interestingly, Cogan suggests a biological example for understanding causation: "When the parent gives existence to the child, the two *characters* are created at the same instant, though the *person* of the parent had an existence before the offspring was in being" (39). As we will see, Shepherd uses language connoting reproduction and childbirth to characterize causation.

[15] Bolton, "Causality and Causal Induction," 244.

CAUSATION 41

This would show that there is no necessary connection—and thus, by Shepherd's lights, no causal connection at all—between events of the first type and events of the second type. In the smoking example, a person might smoke for years and yet die before ever developing lung cancer; thus, according to Shepherd, it is not strictly accurate to say that smoking causes lung cancer.

Shepherd thus rejects characterizing a causal relationship between two things A and B as "A followed by B." Effects do not *follow* their causes; rather, an effect occurs simultaneously with causal action. And it is not events but *objects and their qualities* that are causally related. Shepherd writes,

> The really philosophical method of viewing the subject is this: that objects in relation to us, are nothing but masses of certain qualities, affecting certain of our senses; and which, when independent of our senses, are *unknown* powers or qualities in nature. These masses change their qualities by their mixture with any other mass, and then the corresponding qualities determined to the senses must of course also change. These changed qualities, are termed *effects*; or *consequents*; but are really no more than NEW QUALITIES arising from *new objects*, which have been formed by the *junctions of other objects* (previously formed) or might be considered as the *unobserved qualities of existing objects*; which *shall be observed when properly exhibited*. (*ERCE* 46–47)

It is important to note that Shepherd expresses her causal theory in terms of the interactions among *objects*. Indeed, she says that her account of causation cannot really be understood without understanding her concept of an object (*ERCE* 42n). As she puts it, "this part of the subject, is of such moment that a separate consideration of it is intended" (*ERCE* 42n); the promised "separate consideration" is her second book. For now, she offers the following highly compressed account of what it is to be an object:

42 MARY SHEPHERD

Objects are but unknown circumstances in Nature, when unperceived by the senses; which when perceived, exhibit their appropriate qualities accordingly; and which then appear in certain defined masses, as to the different senses they affect, as to their figure, &c.; and receive an arbitrary name for their assemblage. They must have also among each other certain proportions. (*ERCE* 42n)

A few pages later, she says that objects, "in relation to us, are nothing but masses of certain qualities, affecting certain of our senses; and which, when independent of our senses, are *unknown* powers or qualities in nature" (*ERCE* 46; see also 53). Note that Shepherd does not write of objects *simpliciter*: she writes of objects "in relation to us" and objects "when independent of our senses." In either case, they are masses of qualities, but, as we will see in chapter 3 of this *Guide*, the meaning of 'quality' differs depending on whether the object is perceived or not. "In relation to us," that is, when perceived by us, the qualities comprising an object are the sensible qualities that we perceive; for example, an apple, "in relation to us," is a collection of sensory perceptions of redness, roundness, hardness, and so on.[16] The qualities of an object when unperceived by us are simply "*unknown* powers" to bring about these sensory perceptions; these powers *could* affect us, but when the object exists unperceived, these "secret" powers are not, at that moment, affecting us.

Causation, according to Shepherd, involves two (or more) objects interacting, with their "mixture" resulting in the simultaneous production of a new quality (*ERCE* 63). Rather than describing a causal relationship as "A followed by B," she says we should characterize a causal relationship between objects A and B and the quality C that

---

[16] There is an important caveat here, which is that objects "in relation to us" are not *mere* bundles of sensible qualities but also contain an idea of being caused by an external object (*EPEU* 197–98). For more on Shepherd's account of objects, see chapter 3 of this *Guide*.

CAUSATION   43

results from their interaction as "A × B = C" (*ERCE* 141).[17] Thus, when Shepherd writes about the cause of something, she is making no claims about what precedes an event. To identify a cause of a thing is to identify one of the factors that, when combined with other factors, results *synchronously* in a new quality beginning to exist (*ERCE* 50). It is worth noting, too, that while Shepherd's schema uses just "A" and "B," she does not think that causal interactions are limited to the mixing of just two factors; any given production of a new quality will involve *at least* two causal factors, and sometimes "a *vast multitude of objects*" being combined (*ERCE* 166–67; see also *EPEU* 123–24).

Interestingly, Shepherd says we should think of a mixture of causes as already containing their effect (*ERCE* 50; see also 141). Her representation of causal relationships as an *equation*, as "A × B = C," is no accident; A and B (and any other causes that might be involved) are, literally, factors, entities that produce something else when multiplied together, and the very combining of those factors *is* the effect, just as "the results of all arithmetical combinations are included in their statements" (*ERCE* 142).[18] The effect is really something *new* because it does not actually exist until the factors are combined (*EPEU* 124). Yet the effect is also numerically identical to the combination of the factors. As Shepherd puts it, "The *union of these*, is the proximate Cause of, and is *one* with the Effect" (*ERCE* 187).

---

[17] We might ask why Shepherd represents the union of causes as *multiplication* rather than addition. Why not represent causation as A + B = C? Indeed, in the very passage discussing her schema, she refers to "the SUM arising from their union" (*ERCE* 141). But as we will see, Shepherd writes of causes "mixing" and "intermixing" (*EPEU* 56, 63, 217). Perhaps she thought multiplication was a better analogy than addition for the way in which objects must *interact* in order to be causes.

[18] Shepherd argues that causal inferences in science and ordinary life—what she calls "physical inductions"—are analogous to inferences in mathematics; indeed, she sees the latter as a special case of causal inference, for (she maintains) mathematical inferences also depend on the CLP (see *ERCE* 77 and *EPEU* 279). For further discussion, see chapter 3 of this *Guide*.

44 MARY SHEPHERD

Antonia LoLordo has suggested that Shepherd's model for causation is chemical synthesis.[19] As we have seen, Shepherd says that an effect is numerically identical to the combination of its causes, and this is indeed true of chemical mixtures and compounds; for example, when nitrogen and hydrogen combine to produce ammonia, the ammonia just is the compound of hydrogen and nitrogen.[20] Shepherd may have had chemical synthesis in mind in her account of causation, but her descriptions of causation also frequently use *biological* metaphors. She writes of causes as "giving birth to" (*ERCE* 101, 124, 128; *EPEU* 154) and "generating" an effect (*ERCE* 45, 63); in Shepherd's day, "animal generation" meant reproduction, so this too is biological terminology.

To return to our earlier example of smoking and lung cancer, what would Shepherd say about the relationship between these in some individual person? First, Shepherd would note that "having lung cancer" is a *quality* of a human body, but she would also probably find this to be a vague and general designation that could describe various situations. To describe a person as "having lung cancer" is clear enough in ordinary life, but a scientific understanding of the causes of lung cancer would need to be much more precise about the exact quality being explained. In fact, in something as complex as lung cancer, scientists might not yet know exactly how cancerous lungs differ from healthy lungs; it has required a considerable amount of scientific research to identify which cells are involved in various varieties of lung cancer and which genes in those cells have mutations, and this research is still ongoing. To simplify matters for this example, let's say that we want to explain why a given person possesses the quality 'having numerous

---

[19] LoLordo, "Mary Shepherd on Causation, Induction, and Natural Kinds," 5. To help establish her claim that chemical synthesis is the model for Shepherd's account of causation, LoLordo draws on passages from the 1819 *Enquiry Respecting the Relation of Cause and Effect*, a book sometimes attributed to Shepherd ("Mary Shepherd on Causation, Induction, and Natural Kinds," 4). However, that work was not in fact by Shepherd (Boyle, "A Mistaken Attribution to Mary Shepherd").

[20] LoLordo, "Mary Shepherd on Causation, Induction, and Natural Kinds," 5.

nonsmall lung cells with a mutation in gene TP53,' and let's call this the 'TP53 mutation quality.'[21]

Shepherd would note immediately that there is no single cause of a given person having the TP53 mutation quality, for there is no single cause of anything. We might know some of the factors required to produce the TP53 mutation quality, but we might as yet be ignorant of others. At the very least, for this quality to result requires a living organism, lungs with lung cells that contain TP53, and some factor—such as polycyclic aromatic hydrocarbons or another carcinogen found in cigarette smoke—that brings about the genetic changes in those cells. Each factor is necessary, and together (no doubt with other causal factors of which we are still ignorant) they are sufficient to bring about the effect. As these causal factors interact, Shepherd would say that they "instantly, and immediately" bring about the genetic mutation (*ERCE* 50). Of course, while the causal interaction might be instantaneous, the effect can endure.[22]

Once the TP53 mutation quality is present, that quality itself becomes a causal factor. As time passes, the TP53 mutation quality "interacts" (to use Shepherd's terminology) with other features of the cells containing them, preventing the cells from operating as usual. Those cells thus develop different qualities than healthy cells. Each interaction itself is instantaneous in its production of a new quality (according to Shepherd), but as the new qualities persist over time, they interact in other ways with other factors. There is thus a chain of causal interactions going forward in time. Similarly, the causal chain can be traced into the past. Suppose the TP53 mutation quality resulted from the interaction of some polycyclic aromatic hydrocarbon with the DNA in a lung cell; the

---

[21] Information on lung cancer and TP53 in this and the next two paragraphs is drawn from Mogi and Kuwano, "TP53 Mutations in Nonsmall Cell Lung Cancer."

[22] It may seem that Shepherd's claim that causes and effects work instantaneously would result in all causal interactions collapsing into one moment. For a discussion of how Shepherd's view might avoid this and how effects have durations over time, see Landy, "A Defense of Mary Shepherd's Account of Cause and Effect as Synchronous."

46 MARY SHEPHERD

fact that the lung contains this hydrocarbon is itself the effect of various previous causal interactions. Ultimately, there were much earlier interactions between a cigarette and the person's mouth, the smoke and the lungs, and so on. In that loose sense we can say that smoking caused the person's cancer.

In sum, Shepherd thinks we speak inaccurately when we describe some earlier event as a cause of something that occurs later:

> A *chain of conjunctions of bodies*, of course, *occupies time*; and is the reason why the careless observation of philosophers, enabling them to take notice only of some one distinct effect, (after perhaps innumerable successive conjunctions of bodies,) occasions the mistake, by which they consider *subsequency of effect*, as a part of the *essential definition* of that term; and *priority*, as *essential* to the nature of Cause. (*ERCE* 50–51; see also *EPEU* 124)

Shepherd herself illustrates this with the example of being nourished by food: food enters the stomach and ultimately results in "every particle [being] absorbed and deposited in the proper place in the body," but between these two situations is a "continuous chain of causes and effects" (*ERCE* 51). The whole chain occurs over time, since effects endure over time, yet each successive production of an effect is itself synchronous with the action of its causes (*ERCE* 52).[23]

After noting that succession in time is not required for—and is even precluded by—causation, Shepherd notes two more features that she sees as *irrelevant* to an account of causation: first, it makes no difference whether we call something an "effect" or a "quality" of an object (*ERCE* 52). The as-yet-unknown properties of objects may reasonably be called either qualities or—even if they have

---

[23] In her second book, Shepherd says more about why certain series of successive events seem to be (and indeed are) necessary, even though she does not think that there are causal connections between successive events. See *EPEU* 128, 130–31, and 298; for discussion, see chapter 7 of this *Guide*.

CAUSATION 47

not yet been perceived—effects. While we tend to call "qualities" only those effects of an object that we have already experienced, Shepherd maintains that an object's qualities include whatever *further* effects would occur if we were to subject it to some *new* circumstance under which we have not previously experienced it (*ERCE* 52–53). For example, suppose someone has experienced cold, white, watery-tasting stuff falling from the sky but has never looked at it closely. These qualities of cold, white, and so on are, together, the object that person knows as "snow." Now imagine that the person takes this stuff and subjects it to magnification, with the effect that they perceive a certain hexagonal structure. Now they know that this new effect, elicited through the interaction of the white, cold stuff with a magnifying glass and the human perceiver, is another one of the properties that make up what we call "snow." Snow is an object comprised of certain qualities both "*tried* and *untried*; *observed* and *unobserved*; *determined* and *undetermined*" (*ERCE* 53); the proper, real definition of any given object, such as snow, includes *all* of those qualities, even ones we have not yet elicited through interacting with it (*ERCE* 54; see also 157–58).

The third feature that Shepherd sees as irrelevant to an account of causation has to do with "secret powers." In passages that Shepherd quoted in her introductory chapter, Hume had claimed that "Nature has kept us at a great distance from all her secrets" (*ERCE* 22, quoting *EHU* 4.16). We can only observe the "sensible qualities" of objects—that is, the way that objects affect us—and from this we infer the "secret powers" that cause those qualities. Shepherd actually agrees with Hume on this: we do not perceive the inherent causal powers of objects to cause the perceptions that we have of them. But she thinks Hume makes too much of this fact. As she reads Hume, he sees our ignorance of "secret powers" as a reason to define cause and effect simply in terms of correlations among our impressions and ideas; yet, she says, "it is immaterial to the definition of Cause and Effect, that we are not acquainted with the 'secret powers' of natural objects, either before or after any experience"

48 MARY SHEPHERD

(*ERCE* 58). Indeed, she suggests, even if we *were* able, somehow, to perceive the secret powers in various objects whereby we perceive certain sensible qualities, this information would not help us know the general CLP (*ERCE* 59), for this principle is not a generalization from particular cases; a "universal conclusion could not logically be deduced from the particular premises concerning it" (*ERCE* 59–60; see also 62).

Hume had also claimed that two objects that we *think* are like each other—and thus that we take to have the same "secret powers"—might actually have different effects. He asks, "May I not clearly and distinctly conceive that a body falling from the clouds, and which in *all other* respects resembles snow, may have the taste of salt, or feeling of fire?" (*ERCE* 23, quoting *EHU* 4.18). Upon seeing the white stuff falling from the sky, how can we be *sure* that its other qualities will be the same as those we have previously experienced? We cannot be, according to Hume; there is no contradiction in imagining different effects, such as the snow being hot instead of cold, and so (according to his view that conceivability indicates possibility) this is a genuine possibility. In one respect, Shepherd agrees with Hume; she allows that two things that we *take* to be similar to each other could have different effects. However, this is only because of our own epistemic limitations; if the effects are different in the two cases, then some additional, new cause that we simply have not perceived must be at work in one of the cases (*ERCE* 61). As Shepherd stresses, Hume's example simply points to an epistemological problem of how we *detect* similar things, not a metaphysical problem about the relation between causes and effects (*ERCE* 60).

At the end of section 2, Shepherd offers one more criticism of Hume:

Also [Hume's] objection forms an illogical argument in another way. For it virtually draws a general conclusion from *two negative premises*. To assert, that like sensible qualities merely, will NOT

CAUSATION   49

produce like Effects; and, that *like sensible qualities* are NOT *like Causes*, is to separate the middle term both from the subject and from the predicate of the general question. By *such an argument* Mr. Hume is certainly right in supposing, that REASON cannot support "*our conclusions concerning the operations of Cause and Effect.*" (*ERCE* 62)

Shepherd appears to be ascribing the following reasoning to Hume: (1) things with similar sensible qualities do not always produce similar effects; (2) things with similar sensible qualities are not always similar causes (i.e., do not always have similar "secret powers"); (3) therefore, similar causes do not always produce similar effects. As Shepherd notes, these premises do not support the conclusion.[24] Thus, she ends her criticisms with an ironic comment: if this is how Hume reasons, then he is actually *right* to say that reason does not establish a conclusion regarding cause and effect—that is, since his own reasoning is so bad, it does not support his own conclusion that similar causes do not always produce similar effects (*ERCE* 62).

Shepherd finally offers a definition of 'cause' in section 3; this is the third point she wants to make in ERCE chapter 2. Since the hard work of explaining what her definition means has already been done in section 2, she spends little time on it here, announcing just that a cause should be properly defined as "such action of an object, as shall enable it, in conjunction with another, to form a new nature, capable of exhibiting qualities varying from those of either of the objects unconjoined" (*ERCE* 63). Correlatively, an effect is "the produced quality exhibited to the senses, as the essential property of natures so conjoined" (*ERCE* 63). To say that an object has

---

[24] Shepherd objects that Hume "separate[s] the middle term both from the subject and from the predicate of the general question" (*ERCE* 62). This is how one standard textbook of the time (to which Shepherd herself refers at *EPEU* 202n) describes the mistake of trying to infer anything from two negative premises (Watts, *Logic, or the Right Use of Reason*, 248).

50 MARY SHEPHERD

a causal power is just to say that it has a property such that, when it is combined with other objects, that combination produces a new quality (*ERCE* 63–64).

Assessing Hume's Definitions

Shepherd's fourth claim in *ERCE* chapter 2 is that Hume's definitions of 'cause' are mistaken. After giving her own definitions of 'cause' and 'effect', she points out several respects in which she thinks Hume's definitions are "faulty, and not borne out by his own arguments" (*ERCE* 64). These are unlikely to be persuasive to a Humean, however.

First, Shepherd notes that while Hume's first definition states that a cause is "an object followed by another, and where all the objects similar to the first are followed by objects similar to the second," he is unable to establish that *future* objects of one first type will *necessarily* be followed by objects of the second type (*ERCE* 64); he cannot prove the "*absolute* INVARIABLENESS *of phenomena*" (*ERCE* 66). But Hume would no doubt reply that this is exactly right; the whole point of his argument is that necessary connections of the sort that Shepherd is after cannot be known. Shepherd argues that Hume *does* want to establish this kind of necessary connection, and she makes this point by noting that he follows his first definition with the gloss "or in other words *where, if the first object had not been, the second never had existed*" (*ERCE* 65, quoting *EHU* 7.29). However, Shepherd misses the mark here. Hume offers only *two* definitions of 'cause,' one based on constant conjunctions among types of objects or events and one based on a perceiver's movement of thought (*EHU* 7.29). The gloss that Shepherd mentions, and takes to be his second definition out of three, is *not* Hume's own definition of a cause; he is indicating that his two definitions are intended as a *reformulation* of this traditional understanding of what a cause is. In claiming that Hume's (alleged) second definition is not supported by his arguments, Shepherd fails to see that he would in fact agree with her point, since this is not his definition at all.

Shepherd's next group of criticisms focuses on the scope of Hume's definitions. In one respect, she argues, Hume's definition of a cause in terms of constant conjunctions of things is too *broad*. Hume assumes that conjunctions of things are *successive* in time: one thing happens, followed by another. But, Shepherd says, "many objects are invariably antecedents and subsequents, that are not Causes and Effects" (*ERCE* 67). This same criticism of Hume was made by Thomas Reid: "It follows from this definition of a cause, that night is the cause of day, and day the cause of night. For no two things have more constantly followed each other since the beginning of the world."[25] The third (really, Hume's second) definition is also too broad, Shepherd argues. Hume suggests that when one idea leads us to think of another, we take the object represented by the first to be the cause of the object represented by the second. But, Shepherd says, associations among ideas do not always indicate real relationships out there in the world. If I hear the name "Andrew," I might, through habits formed by many Sunday school lessons, think immediately of "Simon Peter's brother." But that does not mean that every person named Andrew is *actually* Simon Peter's brother (*ERCE* 68). The fact that perceiving or thinking of one object leads me to think of another as its cause does not mean that there is an *actual* causal relationship there.

Shepherd also maintains that Hume's definition of a cause as that which "*where, if the first object had not been, the second never had existed*" is both too *narrow* and inconsistent with Hume's other views, because Hume thinks that sometimes similar objects can be brought about in different ways (*ERCE* 67). As we have seen, however, Shepherd is mistaken in ascribing this definition to Hume.

In the remaining sections of *ERCE* chapter 2, Shepherd works to establish two more key claims: first, against Hume, that nature

---

[25] Reid, *Essays on the Active Powers of Man*, essay 4, chapter 9.

52 MARY SHEPHERD

cannot change its course; second, that in daily life, we are guided by rational inferences, not mere custom and habit. Shepherd's arguments for these positions will be examined in the next chapter.

Suggestions for Further Reading

- In "Restoring Necessary Connections: Lady Mary Shepherd on Hume and the Early Nineteenth-Century Debate on Causality," Cristina Paoletti discusses the philosophical context in which Shepherd proposed her theory of causation.
- For a different account of how Shepherd defends the Causal Principle and the Causal Likeness Principle, see M. Folescu, "Mary Shepherd on the Role of Proofs in Our Knowledge of First Principles."
- Jessica Wilson surveys and appraises Shepherd's specific criticisms of Hume's account of causation, as well as Shepherd's own positive account of causation, in "On Mary Shepherd's *Essay upon the Relation of Cause and Effect*."
- Martha Bolton discusses and assesses Shepherd's account of causation in two very helpful articles: "Causality and Causal Induction: The Necessitarian Theory of Lady Mary Shepherd" and "Lady Mary Shepherd and David Hume on Cause and Effect." Bolton's article on Shepherd in the *Stanford Encyclopedia of Philosophy* also covers Shepherd's account of causation, among other topics.
- Some scholars have argued Shepherd begs the question in her argument that no object can begin to exist without a cause (see Paoletti, "Restoring Necessary Connections," and Jeremy Fantl, "Mary Shepherd on Causal Necessity"). David Landy defends Shepherd against this charge in "Shepherd on Hume's Argument for the Possibility of Uncaused Existence."
- David Landy also discusses an objection Hume had raised to any account of cause and effect as synchronous (namely, that all causation would collapse into a single moment) and argues that Shepherd has the resources to respond to such an objection. See "A Defense of Mary Shepherd's Account of Cause and Effect as Synchronous."

3

Induction, Objects, and the Uniformity of Nature

Introduction

In the previous chapter we saw that Shepherd argues in chapter 2 of *An Essay upon the Relation of Cause and Effect* for four theses: (1) that we can know through reason that everything that comes into existence requires a cause other than itself; (2) that we can also know through reason the principle that similar causes will have similar effects, as well as its corollaries, such as that different effects must have different causes; (3) that causation is a synchronous relation among at least two objects that necessarily results in a new quality; and (4) that Hume's definitions of causation in terms of constant conjunction and habit are flawed. But this is not all Shepherd undertakes to prove in her densely argued, ambitious second chapter. She also maintains (5) that her theses imply that nature cannot change its course and (6) that when we make causal inferences, reason rather than custom or habit is our guide. In *ERCE* chapter 3 she offers practical advice for engaging in good causal reasoning, and in chapter 4 she extends her criticisms of Hume to the works of the Scottish philosopher Thomas Brown.

Shepherd's defense of thesis (5), that nature is uniform, depends on her account of effects as *qualities* that are *necessarily* connected with the *objects* that cause them. We need to begin, then, with her account of objects and qualities. This will be the topic of the following section. The section after that considers Shepherd's account of the way names and definitions apply to objects. The chapter then

Mary Shepherd. Deborah Boyle, Oxford University Press. © Oxford University Press 2023.
DOI: 10.1093/oso/9780190090326.003.0003

54 MARY SHEPHERD

turns to her argument for thesis (5) and examines thesis (6), that "Custom and Habit alone are not our guides; but chiefly reason, for the regulation of our expectations in ordinary life" (ERCE 28). Then the chapter examines Shepherd's account of how we succeed in making good causal inferences in ordinary life. The chapter ends with discussions of how Shepherd appeals to Locke's views and how she objects to views espoused by Thomas Brown.

Objects and Qualities

Shepherd emphasizes that understanding what she means by 'object' is important for grasping her account of causation. As she writes in a footnote, she intended a "separate consideration" of what 'object' means (*ERCE* 42n); this was provided in her second book. Here in *ERCE* she only sketches her view:

> Objects are but unknown circumstances in Nature, when unperceived by the senses; which when perceived, exhibit their appropriate qualities accordingly; and which then appear in certain defined masses, as to the different senses they affect, as to their figure, &c.; and receive an arbitrary name for their assemblage. They must have also among each other certain proportions. (*ERCE* 42n)

A few pages later, she says that objects, "in relation to us, are nothing but masses of certain qualities, affecting certain of our senses; and . . . when independent of our senses, are *unknown* powers or qualities in nature" (*ERCE* 46) and then again that "an object is nothing else (in relation to *us*,) than a mass of peculiar qualities" (*ERCE* 53).

Shepherd's distinction between objects "in relation to us" and objects "when independent of our senses" is a key doctrine of her metaphysics. Her second book is largely occupied with establishing

INDUCTION, OBJECTS, AND UNIFORMITY OF NATURE   55

that objects "when independent of our senses" must exist.[1] There, Shepherd often marks the distinction between objects "in relation to us" and objects "when independent of our senses" by calling them "inner" (or "inward") and "outward" objects, respectively.[2] It might have been helpful for Shepherd to more clearly mark this distinction when she refers generically to "objects"; this *Guide* will draw the distinction by using the terms 'internal object' and 'external object.' However, in *ERCE*, Shepherd had good reason not to stress the distinction, for she says that it is best explained through her account of causation: "the doctrine of the relation of cause and effect, as I have considered it in my former essay . . . would, I think, if it once became familiar to the mind, explain the whole mystery of external and internal existence" (*EPEU* 71). Clearly, then, it would have been circular for Shepherd to *rely* on the distinction between internal and external objects in the first book. Thus, while she does *mention* the distinction there, her references to "objects" in that book are generally meant to be neutral between internal and external objects. For example, in the thought-experiment by which she argues for the Causal Principle, she asks us to imagine "the object which we suppose to begin of itself . . . abstracted from the nature of all objects we are acquainted with, saving in its capacity for existence" (*ERCE* 34–35). This use of 'object' does not commit her to any particular account of what an object is. The same is true of her definition of 'cause' as "a *new object* exhibiting *new qualities*; or shortly, the formation of a *new mass of qualities*" (*ERCE* 50). Here, 'object' can apply to both internal and external objects: an object, whether internal or external, is a mass (or bundle) of qualities.

---

[1] The details of these arguments will be addressed in chapter 6 in this *Guide*, after completing our examination of *ERCE* and its arguments about causation, on which Shepherd's defense of the existence of external objects depends.

[2] References to "outward" or "exterior" objects occur throughout *EPEU*. For references to "internal objects" or "inward objects of sense," see *EPEU* xii, 8, and 10. She discusses the differences between inward and outward objects in *EPEU* chapter 2. She also distinguishes between "external or internal things" at LMSM 700.

56 MARY SHEPHERD

However, for Shepherd, the meaning of 'quality' also differs depending on whether she is talking about internal or external objects.[3] In *EPEU*, Shepherd makes it clear that the qualities comprising an internal object are *sensible* qualities (*EPEU* 71–72), that is, qualities that "arise from the use of the organs of sense," such as our perceptions of "blue or red, sweet or sour, hard or soft, beautiful or ugly, warm or cold, loud or low" (*EPEU* 135). Sensible qualities are "always effects in the mind" (*EPEU* 56; see also 32). Berkeley had said of sensations such as odors, sounds, colors, and shapes that their "*esse est percipi*": such sensations exist only insofar as there is a perceiver having them (*PHK* 1.3). Shepherd herself notes her agreement with Berkeley as far as sensible qualities are concerned (*EPEU* 72).[4] Perceived objects are internal objects, existing in the mind; they are masses of *sensible* qualities, and sensible qualities are in the mind.[5]

Strictly speaking, however, Shepherd does not think that perceived objects are *only* masses of sensible qualities. As we will see in chapter 6 of this *Guide*, Shepherd's aim in *EPEU* is to establish, against Berkeleyan idealism, that from our sensations (which are constantly coming into and going out of existence), combined with the knowledge that everything that begins to exist requires a cause, we can infer that there is in fact an independently existing external world. Moreover, she thinks that when we have sensations of sensible qualities that we take to be caused by external objects, this idea of an external world as their cause is bundled along with those sensations. As she puts it,

---

[3] Shepherd also identifies a third kind of quality that applies to both internal and external objects (*EPEU* 182), but in that case she seems to be using the term 'quality' differently—to denote not an *effect* but a characteristic that can be predicated of some object. For discussion, see chapter 6 of this *Guide*.

[4] For discussion of Shepherd's agreement with Berkeley on this point, see Atherton, "Lady Mary Shepherd's Case against George Berkeley," 350.

[5] Locke, Reid, and other early modern philosophers also divided sensible qualities further, into the categories of primary and secondary qualities. Shepherd rejects this distinction; see chapter 6 of this *Guide*.

INDUCTION, OBJECTS, AND UNIFORMITY OF NATURE   57

Yet I do not agree with [Berkeley], in stating, that *objects* are nothing but what we perceive by sense, or that a complete enumeration is made of *all* the ideas which constitute an apple, a stone, a tree, or a book; in the summing up of their *sensible qualities*. For . . . *an object perceived* by the mind is a compound being, consisting of a certain collection of sensible qualities, "mixed with an *idea* the *result of reasoning*" of such qualities being formed by a "continually existing outward and independent set of as various and appropriate causes;" therefore . . . there must be "*an outward object*," existing as a cause to excite the inward feeling. (*EPEU* 197–98)

That is, the bundle of sensible qualities comprising an internal perceived object is joined with a further idea: the idea of an *external cause* of those qualities. Shepherd says that the "genus" of an internal perceived object is that it is "a general effect arising from a *general* cause independent of mind" (*EPEU* 198). An internal perceived object is thus a compound of this idea of the genus with certain specific sensations (sensible qualities) (*EPEU* 198).[6]

In contrast, we do sometimes have sensations that we do *not* take to be caused by outward objects at the time we are having them, such as when we remember something that we previously sensed. Shepherd considers memories to be internal objects comprised of rather fainter sensible qualities plus an idea of having been caused by external objects in the past:

Objects of memory are compounded of the fainter *sensations* of sensible qualities, mixed with the *idea* that the causes of the original impressions are removed; (the which *idea* is the result either

---

[6] Recall that, for Shepherd, causation involves mixing two or more objects. Since she says an internal object consists of various sensible qualities that the mind "*immediately* mixes with" the idea of those qualities as effects of external objects (*EPEU* 67), the internal perceived object is *itself* the (synchronous) effect of that mixture of sensible qualities and idea.

58 MARY SHEPHERD

of observation or reasoning;) these again are united with the perception of the lapse of time, or of our own continuous existence going on between the original moment of the impressions, and the existence of the PRESENT faint sensible qualities. Therefore the *objects* of memory are, *masses of sensible qualities plus* the *idea* of past time, *plus* the *idea* of having been caused by causes now removed. (*EPEU* 137)

What about ideas that I simply make up and ideas of objects that occur in dreams? Suppose I dream of eating some delicious chocolate cake, but upon waking I realize that the cake was just in the dream—or suppose I simply daydream about eating chocolate cake, quite aware that there is no such cake at hand. In cases like these, Shepherd says that what are present in our minds are simply "parcels" or "masses" of sensible qualities, without the addition of an idea of being caused by an external object (*EPEU* 11n; see also 237). While still counting as internal objects, these are merely internal objects of imagination, not of sense (*EPEU* 30) or of memory. In contrast, an internal *perceived* object is a mass of sensible qualities that are the effects of an external object that interacted with our own mind and senses, and the idea of being such an effect is *part* of the bundle that makes up an internal perceived object.

What about cases where I have a bundle of sensible qualities in my mind that I *take* to be the current effects of external objects but which are not, in fact, currently so caused? For example, what if I am dreaming of, imagining, or hallucinating eating some chocolate cake, *and* I (mistakenly) believe that my sensations of the cake are actually being caused by a real cake that exists independently of me? In this case, the sensible qualities of chocolate cake are *incorrectly* bundled with an idea that those qualities are caused by an external object. What can Shepherd say about this kind of case? As we will see in chapter 7 of this *Guide*, she thinks there are ways to tell whether internal objects are "real"—that is, really caused by external objects—and thus whether the sensible qualities composing

INDUCTION, OBJECTS, AND UNIFORMITY OF NATURE   59

that internal object really should be bundled with an idea of being caused by an external object.

External objects, too, are bundles of qualities (*ERCE* 46), but these cannot be sensible qualities, which exist only in the minds of perceivers. 'Quality' must therefore mean something different when Shepherd is discussing external objects. In *ERCE*, Shepherd calls these qualities "unknown circumstances in nature" (*ERCE* 64), "secret constitutions" (*ERCE* 119), and, following Hume, "secret powers" (*ERCE* 60–61). These "secret, external, unknown powers or qualities, in nature . . . determine the sensible qualities as their *effects*, as well as every other effect, or property" (*ERCE* 117). In other words, the qualities comprising an external object are *causal powers*. External objects are the causes of sensible qualities in perceivers—that is, external objects are causes of internal objects. We know through causal reasoning that external objects exist,[7] and "the sensible qualities are only considered as SIGNs of the secret powers" (*ERCE* 123). However, we *only* know about these external objects through their effects on our minds, the sensible qualities they bring about; otherwise, they are unknown to us.

It is worth noting Shepherd's comment that "the *secret powers* are the real external unknown Causes in Nature, which determine the sensible qualities, as well as *every other Effect*" (*ERCE* 60). That is, sensible qualities are not the *only* effects of the causal powers making up external objects. Later she writes:

> Objects, when spoken of and considered as causes, should always be considered as those masses of unknown qualities in nature, exterior to the organs of sense, whose determination of sensible qualities to the senses forms *one class of their effects*. (*EPEU* 127)

She makes this even more explicit in her last published work, "Lady Mary Shepherd's Metaphysics": "those causes can externally

---

[7] This causal reasoning will be the focus of *EPEU*; see chapter 6 of this *Guide*.

60   MARY SHEPHERD

intermix, and in different ways mutually affect each other, whilst the results of such mixtures can again farther determine themselves upon the mind" (LMSM 703). In sum, the qualities that comprise external objects include powers to produce sensible qualities in us, plus other causal powers—powers to produce not just new objects "in relation to us" (masses of sensible qualities) but new external objects, that is, new unperceived bundles of causal powers.[8]

Shepherd does describe external objects as made of "matter" (*EPEU* 242), and she considers matter to be composed of "particles": "it is the *formation* of the particles, (whatever particles may be,) which renders exterior objects such as they are, and of any certain definite constitution" (*EPEU* 304). Still, even matter is itself an "unknown being" (*EPEU* 165), the "real essence" of which is unknown (*EPEU* 244). Nor do we know what particles are in themselves, apart from being perceived; we know only that they have the causal power to make us have various sensible qualities (*ERCE* 118 and 28; *EPEU* 181, 309). Further questions about the causal powers that make up external objects cannot be answered. For example, we might wonder if the causal powers that comprise external objects are simply free-floating or whether they inhere in some further kind of stuff. Sometimes Shepherd suggests the latter, as when she refers in general terms to "nature" or "existence" or "beings" (LMSM 701). But if there is some kind of stuff that is somehow distinct from the causal powers, serving as the substratum of those powers yet not causally interacting with us itself, then we can know nothing about it.

---

[8] Shepherd's account of objects leaves a number of questions unanswered. How are internal objects individuated? For example, why do I consider my sensations of redness, roundness, and sweetness, but *not* the cool breeze that I feel, to be qualities of an apple? And is there any sense in which an internal object endures over time, given that our sensations are constantly changing? Likewise, do we have any way to individuate the bundles of causal powers comprising external objects, especially since we only infer their existence from our sensations? And how could the continually existing objects that cause our perceptions undergo changes in their causal powers yet remain numerically the same over time? Shepherd never explicitly addresses these issues.

Objects, Names, and Definitions

Shepherd notes that after we observe certain sensible qualities occurring together, we *name* or *give a sign to* that assemblage of qualities. For example, having observed that coldness, whiteness, and falling from the sky are properties that occur together, we name that "entire *enumeration of qualities*" 'snow' (*ERCE* 55 and 68–69). As she puts it later, an "arbitrary name is affixed" to such "a combined mass of qualities" (*ERCE* 153). The *choice* of a particular term to signify a certain combination of sensible qualities is contingent, "arbitrary"; English-speakers might have used a term other than 'snow' to stand for that combination. But, having dubbed that combination 'snow', we now have a definition for this term that constrains how we use the word in the future (*ERCE* 47). The assertion "snow is not cold" is not only incorrect, Shepherd thinks, but a *contradiction*; it expresses the claim that "what we perceive as falling from the sky and as being cold and white is not cold." In other words, "snow is cold" is a *necessary* truth, once we have so defined our terms.

Shepherd says more about names and objects in *ERCE* chapter 5, in a discussion of two kinds of necessity (*ERCE* 154–55). While the connection between a *term* like 'gold' and the *definition* of that term as a yellow, ductile substance that is soluble in nitromuriatic acid[9] is necessary, this necessity differs from the necessity between an *object* and its *qualities*. Mapping onto this distinction are two kinds of definitions: definitions of "arbitrary names" and definitions of objects (*ERCE* 157). Shepherd notes that her views about definitions coincide with Locke's views in the *Essay Concerning Human Understanding*, 4.6.8–9, where Locke distinguishes between using the term 'gold' to refer to a "nominal essence" and using it refer to a "real essence" (*ERCE* 158n). To see the distinction

---

[9] That is, nitrohydrochloric acid.

62 MARY SHEPHERD

between definitions that Shepherd is making, a brief digression on Locke might be helpful.

Locke held that the use of general terms such as 'gold' or 'human' is essential to human life. When we use such general terms, we take it that they refer to "sorts" (*ECHU* 3.6.1) or what we would today call a 'natural kind.'[10] That is, we take it that there are groups of entities that share an essence or nature, which is some feature (or set of features) the possession of which is both necessary and sufficient for membership in that group. However, Locke argues that general terms cannot refer to sorts or groupings that exist out there in the physical world, for all the entities that exist in nature are particular: this or that piece of gold, this or that human (*ECHU* 3.3.11). And although particular entities in nature do share similarities, grouping them into types is an activity done by perceivers, not nature (*ECHU* 3.3.13). So, a general term like 'gold' refers not to something out there in the world but to an abstract, general idea in the mind of a particular thinker (*ECHU* 3.3.12). Abstract, general ideas themselves are formed just by "separating from them the circumstances of time and place, and any other ideas that may determine them to this or that particular existence" (*ECHU* 3.3.6). Thus, the abstract, general idea of gold is not an idea of a particular lump of physical stuff at a particular time and place but rather a "complex idea of a body of a certain yellow colour, malleable, fusible, and heavier than any other known" (*ECHU* 4.6.8). Our general term 'gold' just refers to that idea.

How, then should we think of the essence or nature of gold itself? Locke notes that references to the 'essence' or 'nature' of a type of physical substance such as gold or copper are ambiguous. In its "most familiar" use, an essence or nature of a type is really a *nominal* essence or nature—it is no more than the abstract idea associated

---

[10] For discussion of our contemporary concept of a natural kind, see Bird and Tobin, "Natural Kinds." Ian Hacking credits John Stuart Mill for the term 'kind' as a philosophical term of art and mathematician John Venn (1834–1923) for the phrase 'natural kind' ("A Tradition of Natural Kinds," 110).

INDUCTION, OBJECTS, AND UNIFORMITY OF NATURE   63

with the word we use to describe a grouping we have made (*ECHU* 3.3.15). So the nominal essence of gold is just our abstract idea of gold. On the other hand, 'essence' or 'nature' may instead refer to the constituent physical parts that make up a particular thing, the "real constitution of its insensible parts, on which depend all those properties of colour, weight, fusibility, fixedness, &c., which are to be found in it" (*ECHU* 3.3.18).[11] Thus, the *real* essence of gold is the physical microstructure of gold. But even if Locke thinks that "it is past doubt there must be some real constitution, on which any collection of simple ideas co-existing must depend" (*ECHU* 3.3.15), he denies that we can know these real essences, and thus to posit them is "wholly useless and unserviceable to any part of our knowledge" (*ECHU* 3.3.17).

Since Shepherd distinguishes between definitions of "arbitrary names" and definitions of objects (*ERCE* 157) and since she says she follows Locke regarding the signification of terms for nominal essences and real essences (*ERCE* 158n), we can fairly characterize Shepherd's distinction between definitions of "arbitrary names" and definitions of objects as one between *nominal* definitions and *real* definitions. And if Shepherd really does follow Locke, we might expect her to say that nominal definitions define a term by identifying the sensible qualities with which it is associated. And since these sensible qualities are what she calls an "internal object," we might expect her to say that nominal definitions are definitions of internal objects.

However, Shepherd's view is complicated by the double meanings she ascribes to the terms 'object' and 'quality.' A nominal definition relates a *term* and various qualities, while a real definition—or what Shepherd herself calls a "whole definition" (*EPEU* 30, 32, 88, 103)—relates an *object* and its qualities. But if qualities and objects can be

---

[11] There is actually considerable debate in the secondary literature on how to interpret Locke's views on real and nominal essences. For an excellent overview of the various interpretations on offer, see Jones, "Locke on Real Essence."

64 MARY SHEPHERD

either internal or external, then Shepherd evidently must be committed to *four* kinds of definitions: nominal definitions relating a term like 'gold' and *sensible* qualities; nominal definitions relating a term like 'gold' and *causal powers*; real definitions relating *internal* objects with their qualities; and real definitions relating *external* objects with their qualities.[12] However, we need not make the baroque distinctions among additional types of definition to which the ambiguity of 'object' and 'quality' seem to commit Shepherd. Given that the unknown causes in nature (external objects) and the sensible qualities they determine (internal objects) are themselves necessarily connected, the nominal definitions relating a term to an external object and to its correlated internal object are co-dependent, as are the real definitions of an external object and of its correlated internal object.

Regarding nominal definitions, Shepherd says that an "arbitrary name is affixed" to "a combined mass of qualities" (*ERCE* 153) and that "the arbitrary connexion of a name, with a certain number of similar enumerated qualities, requires no proof for its assertion; such qualities shall be gold, and such others lead and copper, if we please to call them so" (*ERCE* 157). Again, since "mass of qualities" could refer to a mass of sensible qualities (an internal object) or to a mass of causal powers (an external object), a nominal definition of a word like 'gold' could refer to either of these. As Shepherd emphasizes, we could have chosen any other word to label the qualities we happen to call 'gold,' but once we do, the connection between the word and the qualities is, albeit arbitrary, nonetheless a necessary one. For example, to assert "gold is not yellow" is a contradiction, since 'gold' is *defined* as yellow. But this necessary connection is not especially informative. It reveals only how we are using words, not anything about how the world actually operates.

---

[12] Of course, in *ERCE*, Shepherd also discusses definitions of the terms 'cause' and 'effect' (*ERCE* 30, 49, 51). However, she characterizes causation as a *relation*, not an object (*ERCE* 52). Her account of nominal and real definitions pertains to the definitions of *objects* and their qualities.

INDUCTION, OBJECTS, AND UNIFORMITY OF NATURE   65

These definitions are necessary and knowable a priori, in that we know the definition is true once we know the meanings of the terms involved.

Shepherd says that such a definition is "*absolute*," "because the proposition in which it is contained is identical; such qualities, are gold—and gold is the enumeration of such qualities" (*ERCE* 157). This same thought seems to be captured by an unusual phrase Shepherd uses: "intuitive proposition." She writes that "intuitive propositions are those *included in the very terms*, given to our impressions" (*ERCE* 145) and that in an intuitive belief, "the truth is contained in the definition of the terms; and cannot be altered without altering the signs of the ideas, which have been just allowed to stand for them" (*ERCE* 138). Shepherd evidently takes intuitive propositions to express nominal definitions (whether the terms are referring to internal or external objects).[13] Again, these propositions express necessary truths, but only because of the way we have stipulated our terms.

What, then, is a definition of an object, or a "real definition"? Contrasting this with the definition of a term as "absolute," Shepherd writes,

But the definition of an object in respect to its exhibition of *further qualities in different combinations with other objects, is conditional*; it being understood that it will not hold, unless the *circumstances are similar* upon each occasion, that have any *power to affect them*. (*ERCE* 158)

Shepherd's claim to be following Locke suggests that a definition of an object is an account of what he calls an object's "real essence," the "real constitution" of a thing's "insensible parts" that produce

---

[13] In calling these propositions "intuitive," Shepherd may be drawing on Locke's account of intuition as a capacity to perceive immediately, without argument, whether or not two ideas agree or disagree with each other (*ECHU* 4.11.1).

66 MARY SHEPHERD

the sensible qualities we experience (*ECHU* 3.3.18)—that is, a real definition would be for Shepherd a definition of the causal powers of an external object. Again, since internal and external objects are necessarily connected, a real definition of an object could also characterize the internal object, the sensible qualities caused by the external object.[14]

The real definitions of objects mark out distinctions among natural kinds for Shepherd. While she does not explicitly commit to the existence of natural kinds, her language clearly shows that she believes natural kinds exist. She writes that things that are alike are "the same kind of object" (*EPEU* 287; see also 286, 288, 350, and 353), and she writes explicitly of kinds when she is discussing geometry; the category of circles is a kind, for example (*ERCE* 92). Other examples of entities that she seems to think are natural kinds include fire, snow, and bread (*ERCE* 55),[15] Chinese roses and holly (*ERCE* 85), water and spirits of ammonia (*ERCE* 102), Epsom salts and oxalic acid (*ERCE* 104), gold (*ERCE* 155–56), and wood (LMSM 704). Indeed, if the principle "like causes will always have like effects" is to provide the kind of guidance in religion, practical life, and science that Shepherd insists it has (*ERCE* 194), there need to be genuinely like objects—that is, objects that share the same causal powers. The existence of natural kinds ensures that this will be so; however, Shepherd never provides an argument that natural kinds exist.

Real definitions will never be complete because we cannot put external objects into all the possible situations in which they manifest powers and exhibit qualities. Nonetheless, as we interact with

[14] Shepherd's own distinction between two kinds of necessity at *ERCE* 154–55 slides between these two possibilities for real definitions of objects, because her references to an object's "properties" are ambiguous. The properties of an external object are the causal powers comprising it. But if "its properties" means the *effects* of the external object, these would be its sensible qualities (among its other effects). A real definition of an object can capture either of these.

[15] Bread, we might think, is more properly described as artificial rather than natural. Shepherd probably uses this example because it is one that Hume uses in the first *Enquiry* (*EHU* 4.16), along with the examples of fire (*EHU* 4.4) and snow (*EHU* 4.18).

INDUCTION, OBJECTS, AND UNIFORMITY OF NATURE 67

an external object and learn what qualities it produces under what circumstances, its powers to produce those qualities under the right conditions become part of its real definition (*ERCE* 55). For example, the real definition of the external object *snow* is established through our experiences as we feel it, taste it, heat it, and so on—that is, as we explore its causal powers.[16] Shepherd seems to give an example of such a real definition when she says that it is "part of the definition of fire to burn certain bodies, to melt others; of bread to nourish the human body; of snow to be cold, and white" (*ERCE* 55), for this tells us what those external objects *do*. Unlike Locke, Shepherd does not think real definitions should be given up for nominal definitions, for she thinks we *can* have knowledge of the causal powers of external objects.

As we have seen, Shepherd thinks the connection between a *term* and its definition is necessary but arbitrary—it is stipulative. However, the connection between an *object* and its effects is necessary and *not* arbitrary. And it is not knowable a priori; to know the causal powers of an object requires experience (see *EPEU* 327). Humans could not know that gold is soluble in nitrohydrochloric acid until they actually tried putting the two together. As we *discover* the qualities of an object, those qualities become part of the real definition of that object. This means that definitions of objects, while necessary truths, are *not* known a priori—anticipating Saul Kripke's arguments in his *Naming and Necessity* (1980), Shepherd suggests that such propositions are necessary a posteriori truths.

---

[16] This is not to say that each person creates their own definition of the external object *snow*; Shepherd thinks of definitions of objects as true independently of us, since the external objects themselves exist independently of us (as she argues in *EPEU*). We can thus be wrong about definitions of objects in a way that we cannot be wrong about definitions of terms.

68 MARY SHEPHERD

The Uniformity of Nature

As we saw in the previous chapter, Shepherd argues that we can know with certainty the Causal Likeness Principle, that similar causes have similar effects (*ERCE* 56); this was the second of the six claims she seeks to establish in *ERCE* chapter 2. It follows from this principle that "Nature cannot be supposed to alter her course without a contradiction in terms" (*ERCE* 27–28), which is the fifth claim Shepherd seeks to establish in *ERCE* chapter 2. With an account of Shepherd's views on objects, qualities, and natural kinds in place, we are in a position to understand her view: once we have identified a certain sensible quality as the effect of some external object, we can know that whenever we encounter another external object of the same kind under the same circumstances, we will perceive that same sensible quality. If we do *not* perceive the same quality, then what she calls the "prevening [preceding] causes" must have actually been different; the causal histories of the two apparently similar causes must have differed at some point, so that we made a mistake in thinking they were the same type of object (*ERCE* 70–71). But although "nature . . . cannot, when employing *like* causes in action, alter her course in determining different and contrary '*Effects*' from otherwise similar objects" (*ERCE* 71), this does not mean that nature cannot change, period; Shepherd is not saying that, for example, something that looks like snow but feels hot could never fall from the sky. However, if there *is* a change in nature, it is because the causes operating are new and different from those we have experienced in the past.

Later in the chapter, Shepherd offers a thought-experiment to make her point. Imagine "a receiver . . . void of every substance whatever; and nothing but an *uncoloured space* within it" (*ERCE* 85). The "course of nature" would be "for this uncoloured space to *remain as it is*" (*ERCE* 86). However, suppose the space changes, turning scarlet red. This does not mean nature is altering its course, in the sense of changing what effects are brought about from

INDUCTION, OBJECTS, AND UNIFORMITY OF NATURE   69

identical causes. The natures of objects have not changed. What it means, rather, is that some additional cause must have operated to bring this about (*ERCE* 86). Similar objects in exactly identical circumstances to those that existed in the past will continue to display exactly the same behaviors; any changes in how objects behave mean simply that the objects or circumstances are *not* exactly the same, that other causes are in play, even if we have not been able to detect them.

Returning to her critique of Hume, Shepherd reminds us of a quotation that she included in her introductory chapter: "it implies no contradiction that the course of nature may change, and that an object, SEEMINGLY like those which we have experienced, may be attended with different or contrary effects" (*EHU* 4.18; quoted at *ERCE* 73 and 23). Hume's reference to "an object seemingly like those which we have experienced" could be taken in either of two different ways, Shepherd argues. On each reading of "object seemingly like those which we have experienced," Shepherd says that Hume's claim that it could have effects different than those it has had before is, in fact, "a 'CONTRADICTION TO REASON' and an IMPOSSIBILITY" (*ERCE* 74; see also 134). What she seems to mean is that Hume is contradicting *himself* on either interpretation. We need to consider, then, the two interpretations of Hume's claim that Shepherd identifies.

On the one hand, suppose Hume means that some external object that causes sensible qualities otherwise similar to those produced by another external object we have experienced now produces some effects (that is, some other sensible qualities) *different* from those we have experienced. This seems to be his meaning when he suggests that we might perceive something similar to the external object *snow* in all respects except that it produces a feeling of fire (*ERCE* 74). As Shepherd sees it, Hume is here saying that nature could bring about a change in the effects of external objects, which is to say that nature could *cause* external objects to have different effects. But Hume holds (according to Shepherd, anyway)

70 MARY SHEPHERD

that events and changes occur without truly productive causes; as Shepherd puts it, "as *cause* is not by him granted, nature must be supposed to change her regular march *uncaused*" (*ERCE* 75). So in saying that nature could bring about changes in the effects of external objects, Shepherd thinks he is helping himself to the very notion of 'cause' that he wants to deny: "the *real relation* of Cause and Effect, is *assumed as granted*" (*ERCE* 76; see also 132 and 133–34).

On the other hand, suppose Hume means that an external object changes its "secret powers," which is suggested by his remark that the "secret nature" of objects, "and consequently all their effects and influences, may change without any change in the sensible qualities" (*EHU* 4.21; quoted at *ERCE* 75). For example, suppose one of the "secret powers" of the external object *snow* changes, even though it still produces exactly the same sensible qualities that it did before.[17] What would it take for an external object to have different powers than things of its type previously had? Well, Shepherd notes, there must have been a change in the "prevening *conjunctions of bodies* which produced these secret powers" (*ERCE* 71), for so long as an external object was "*born under like circumstances*" as some other external object, it will be the same kind of thing as that other, and thus have the same "secret powers." In other words, for it to have different causal powers, it must have been produced by different causes. So, again, according to Shepherd, for Hume to say that a secret power of some external object has changed is to say that something *caused* that change. Hume has thus granted to his "adversary" the very point that he sought to refute, the "general principle concerning Cause and Effect" that everything that comes into existence must have a cause (*ERCE* 77). To reach his conclusion that nature can change its course requires conceding the very causal principle that he seeks to deny.[18]

---

[17] Of course, Shepherd thinks this is impossible, since there is a necessary connection between a "secret power" and the sensible quality it brings about.

[18] Appealing to Watts' *Logic*, Shepherd characterizes Hume's error as the fallacy of "ignoratio elenchi," that is, attempting to rebut an opponent but, instead, proving something that is not inconsistent with the opponent's view.

INDUCTION, OBJECTS, AND UNIFORMITY OF NATURE   71

Shepherd imagines one more Humean defense of the claim that effects in nature might change even while identical causes are in operation: perhaps this is possible due to miraculous intervention (*ERCE* 79). But, she says, not even God could use identical causes to bring about varying effects, unless he does so by himself acting as an *additional* cause—in which case the causes are *not*, in fact, identical.[19]

Citing Hume's claim that it is "intelligible" to claim that "all the trees will flourish in December and January, and decay in May and June" (*ERCE* 80 and 23), Shepherd notes that once we have established that the nature of a tree requires warmth for its growth, the tree must always exhibit that quality (*ERCE* 81). The nature of the tree cannot change "without a cause equivalent to the alteration," in which case we are not dealing with the same kind of item after all (*ERCE* 81). In sum, although Shepherd concedes that nature does "vary her operations," this cannot occur through interferences or changes in the effects brought about by exactly identical causes. Whatever variations we see in nature must be the results of *different* causal conditions.

Shepherd concludes by summarizing what she sees as Hume's key errors. He begs the question of whether we can know that like objects will have like effects because he merely *assumes* that there is no necessary connection between cause and effect (*ERCE* 82); of course, if we assume that there is no such connection, then we can imagine that two identical objects might have different effects. He also depends on the false assumption that "what we can conceive in the fancy"—what we can imagine—indicates what is possible in reality. In fact, according to Shepherd, what we can imagine is no guide to the possible; we need *reason* to show us what is possible or impossible (*ERCE* 83). Finally, Shepherd says that Hume only thinks a change in the course of nature is possible because he has

---

[19] Shepherd also discusses miracles in *EPEU*, essay 8. These arguments are covered in chapter 9 of this *Guide*.

72 MARY SHEPHERD

excluded using reason as a guide to knowing anything about causes and effects, depending instead on past experience.[20] But why does he exclude reason as a reliable guide for knowledge about causes and effects? Only because he has *already* assumed that nature can change its course, that there is "no contradiction that the course of nature may change" (*EHU* 4.18). Of course, if we assume there is no contradiction that the course of nature may change, we can conclude that a change in the course of nature is possible, but this is, as Shepherd puts it, "but a circle!" (*ERCE* 87–88).

Custom versus Reason

The final thesis defended in *ERCE* chapter 2 is that "Custom and Habit alone are not our guides; but chiefly reason, for the regulation of our expectations in ordinary life" (*ERCE* 28). As we have just seen, Shepherd argues that Hume's account is circular since he *assumes* that reason *cannot* guide us regarding causal relationships. But she also argues that his positive account of the role of custom in causal inference is flawed: again, either he assumes the very account of causation he seeks to undermine, or he assumes the very theory he is trying to establish.

To show this, Shepherd reminds us of a key principle in Hume's *Enquiry*: the principle that "every idea is copied from some preceding impression" (*EHU* 2.5), or, as he puts it in the *Treatise*, "*that all our simple ideas in their first appearance are deriv'd from simple impressions*" (*T* 1.1.1.7). Shepherd points out that this is *causal* language: "In both works *impressions* are considered as absolutely necessary to cause ideas—to create them; to *produce* them;—they are considered as the truly "productive principle" of ideas—Objects without which they could not exist" (*ERCE* 89n).

---

[20] Hume says that demonstrative reason cannot guide us regarding matters of fact because "it implies no contradiction, that the course of nature may change" (*EHU* 4.18).

INDUCTION, OBJECTS, AND UNIFORMITY OF NATURE   73

Hume maintains that we get the idea of necessary connection from an impression we feel after habit has linked one idea or impression with another idea in our thought; an impression in the mind *causes* the idea of necessary connection. Thus, even to offer an account of the role of custom in our causal inferences, Hume must assume a theory of causation. If he assumes the very theory of causation he rejects, then of course his argument for his own theory fails; if, on the other hand, he assumes his *own* theory of causation, then his reasoning is circular (*ERCE* 90; see also 146–47). Either way, he fails to establish that custom is the basis of our causal reasoning.

Shepherd is not yet done with Hume's arguments. She quotes a passage from Hume's *Enquiry* that she says contains "the whole gist of Mr. Hume's error":

> As reason is incapable of any variation, the conclusions which it draws from one circle, are the same which it would form from surveying all the circles in the universe. But no man having seen one body move after being impelled by another would infer, that every body will move after a like impulse. (*EHU* 5.5; quoted at *ERCE* 91)

But why, asks Shepherd, do we assume that what we prove to be true of one circle (say, that its area is equal to πr^2) will be true of every circle? Because of the principle that like causes will have like effects (*ERCE* 92). So, when we find one body like another,[21] we are similarly justified in concluding that what was true of the first will be true of the second.

In what sense does the above passage contain the "gist" of Hume's error? The problem Shepherd sees is that Hume has not recognized that *causal* reasoning regarding the physical world has the same

---

[21] Shepherd notes that Hume's comparison is not really apt; instead of comparing what is true of *all circles* to what is true of *all bodies*, he should compare what is true of one specific kind of shape (e.g., all circles) to what is true of one *specific kind* of body (*ERCE* 92).

74 MARY SHEPHERD

basis as *demonstrative* reasoning in mathematics: both kinds of reasoning depend on the axioms that nothing can arise without a cause (Causal Principle) and that like causes must have like effects (Causal Likeness Principle). If this is right, then correct causal inferences *can* have the kind of certainty that inferences in mathematical reasoning have.

Indeed, this is a point to which Shepherd returns in her 1827 book. She spells it out in the very title of essay 5: "That Mathematical Demonstration, and Physical Induction, Are Founded upon Similar Principles of Evidence" (*EPEU* 271). Shepherd says she wrote this chapter because, after publishing *ERCE*, she realized how much her views on this topic varied from "almost universal opinions, as to the nature and manner of causation" (*EPEU* 272). The "almost universal opinion" is Hume's view that induction in science and ordinary life does not have the certainty of a mathematical demonstration; Shepherd cites philosopher Dugald Stewart, as well as an article in the *Encyclopedia Britannica* that Stewart had cited in defense of the Humean view.[22] Shepherd quotes passages in which Stewart claims that "the evidence afforded by mathematical induction must be allowed to differ radically from that of physical" (*EPEU* 276), and she counterbalances these with quotations from *ERCE* arguing that both mathematical proofs and induction are based on the principle that like causes must necessarily have like effects (*EPEU* 281–84, quoting *ERCE* 77–78, 141–43, and 57, respectively). That is, inductive reasoning (in ideal cases, anyway) is analogous to mathematical reasoning.

Shepherd's view that mathematical knowledge is absolutely certain was not new, and many philosophers have held that other disciplines should *aspire* to the certainty of mathematical

---

[22] Shepherd quotes from Stewart's essay "The Idealism of Berkeley" in his *Philosophical Essays*. The passage Stewart quotes is from article 57 in George Gleig and John Robison, "Philosophy," *Encyclopedia Britannica* 14:590.

INDUCTION, OBJECTS, AND UNIFORMITY OF NATURE 75

knowledge; Descartes, for example, thought metaphysical proofs should have conclusions as certain as those reached in geometrical reasoning. Shepherd, however, sees *causal* reasoning as the model for mathematical reasoning. She writes,

> *the science of mathematics is truly but one branch of physics*: for that all the conclusions its method of induction demonstrates, depend for their truth upon the implied proposition, "That like cause must have like effect;" a proposition which being the only foundation for the truths of physical science, and which gives validity to the result of any experiment whatever, ranks mathematics as a *species* under the same *genus*. (*EPEU* 278–79; see also 290)

Just as geometrical relationships can be established by reasoning based on a diagram (*EPEU* 285), causal relationships can (at least in theory, if not always in actual practice) be established by *"one simple and judicious experiment"* (*EPEU* 285), what Shepherd calls in *ERCE* an *"experimentum crucis"* (*ERCE* 43).[23]

Shepherd ends *ERCE* chapter 2 by noting how Hume's account of causation applies to religious belief. First, she takes his account to imply that we have no proof that God exists (*ERCE* 93). Second, Hume himself drew on his account of causation to argue that it is not reasonable to believe in miracles, the topic of section 10 of his *Enquiry*. Since Shepherd discusses these arguments in *EPEU*, those arguments will be addressed in chapter 9 of this *Guide*.

---

[23] Shepherd expresses similar views about physical and mathematical induction in a letter to her friend Charles Babbage: "Suffice it to say that the authors who object—to *induction* in Physics being of the same force in its conclusions as those of a mathematical nature, always consider fire as fire—water as water—Man as Man & the mistaken views arise from an ignorance rather of the nature & manner of Cause as a *productive* principle, & as *necessarily* in, & with its Effect" (letter to Charles Babbage of November 18, 1825).

76 MARY SHEPHERD

Causal Inference in Ordinary Life

Shepherd's view is that there are necessary truths about causal connections in the world, but that these truths must be learned through experience. As human observers in the real world, where multiple causes operate at once and our powers of observation are limited, we are never in an ideal position. Learning about causes and effects and making inferences on the basis of our knowledge thus require careful, close, empirical observations. In *ERCE* chapter 3, section 2, Shepherd addresses how we can do this. Hers is primarily a descriptive project; she does not offer anything like the methods of inductive inquiry that John Stuart Mill (1806–1873) would later set forth in his *System of Logic, Ratiocinative and Inductive* (1843).[24] However, since Shepherd thinks we are generally pretty successful at making causal inferences, she also takes her description to show how we can make *good* inferences.

Shepherd begins by rejecting, again, Hume's claim that we make causal inferences on the basis of mental associations formed by habit and custom (*ERCE* 100; see also 105 and 110). She concedes that associations are involved in *memory*, which plays a role in causal inference; after all, we need to remember what we have observed in the past in order to compare it to what we observe in the present. Causal inference is, Shepherd says, a two-step procedure of first observing whether the object in the present case resembles that of some past case and then reasoning on the basis of the Causal Likeness Principle that the effect in the current case will be the same as in the former (*ERCE* 100; see also 108). Everyone is capable of doing this, although the abilities involved in observing and comparing items depend on "good sense," which can vary from person to person (*ERCE* 102).

---

[24] These are Mill's methods of agreement, difference, residues, and concomitant variations. Although Shepherd would deny Mill's view that cause and effect can occur successively, his method of difference echoes Shepherd's description of an *experimentum crucis*; see *A System of Logic, Ratiocinative and Inductive*, 454–55.

INDUCTION, OBJECTS, AND UNIFORMITY OF NATURE   77

Shepherd stresses that the "quick, steady, accurate" observations we make are *not just* observations of the sensible qualities of the objects. Take her example of ordering Epsom salts in a pharmacy (*ERCE* 104). It is not enough just to note that, say, the stuff in this jar is white, crystalline, and odorless, like the Epsom salts in a different jar seen last week. Rather, she says that we observe "*whether the prevening causes are the* SAME, *from which an object is elicited in any* PRESENT *instance, as upon a* FORMER *one*" (*ERCE* 100). Only then can we know that similar sensible qualities do in fact derive from the same kind of cause in each case (*ERCE* 101). To determine whether consuming the white crystalline substance now before me will have the same effects as those that occurred when I consumed a similar substance last week, I need to know something about the causal histories of each substance. Where did each come from? How were they produced? If I don't know these things, it might turn out that while the substance I consumed last week was innocuous Epsom salts, the one in front of me is the highly toxic oxalic acid: both have similar sensible qualities, but those qualities result from very different kinds of things, and one of them can have fatal effects.

Thus, causal inference is not so much a matter of noting similar *appearances* as it is of noting similar *causal histories* (*ERCE* 106). And this explains why we do not, in fact, always expect similar effects from items that appear the same. Shepherd mentions Hume's example of eggs, which look alike yet which we learn from experience may not taste the same (*EHU* 4.20). The lesson Shepherd draws from the example is that relying on appearances in our causal reasoning is not enough. We need to know the causal history of the eggs in question in order to be able to make a prediction about whether they will be fresh or rotten (*ERCE* 109).

What makes a causal inference better or worse thus has little to do with associations of ideas. Some associations of ideas are easily separated in thought, as in two lines of verse by Virgil; a schoolboy who has used repetition and habit to memorize "Arma virumque

78 MARY SHEPHERD

cano, Troiae qui primus ab oris" being followed by "Italiam fato profugus Lavinaque venit"[25] can, nonetheless, think of these lines separately (*ERCE* 111). Mental associations between causes and effects are not so easily pried apart; and even if we are "forced" for some reason or other to think of what is normally a cause without thinking of its effect, this does not mean that one can exist without the other in reality (*ERCE* 112).

What makes a causal inference better or worse are the reasoner's strength of memory and knowledge of the causal histories of the entities in question, as well as the person's abilities to compare objects closely. Shepherd recognizes that judgments about the similarities of objects are only probable, not absolutely certain, and that we are often mistaken about which objects resemble each other (*EPEU* 174). However, she describes various strategies that the mind naturally employs in order to decide whether an object is similar to those we have experienced. In section 1 she notes that we can draw on our own memories of how we and others have acted as causal agents in the past (*ERCE* 113). In section 2 (after a discussion of Locke, to be examined below), she lists four further strategies. First, we can employ "more senses than one" to consider any given object and compare it to our memories of other objects (*ERCE* 118). Second, we can (as we have already seen) examine "the *method* taken by *nature* and *art* in the FORMATION of an object" (*ERCE* 119)—that is, its causal history.

Third, observing repetitions of similar causes producing similar effects can improve our causal inferences. It is not, as Hume would have it, the bare fact of the repeated experiences themselves that matters; if we had not already established the Causal Principle and the Causal Likeness Principle through reasoning, "frequency of repetition" alone would never be "a circumstance sufficient to generate such a principle" (*ERCE* 120; see also 144). However, *knowing* these

---

[25] "Arms and the man I sing, who first from the coasts of Troy/Exiled by fate, came to Italy and Lavine shores" (Virgil, *Aeneid*, 263).

INDUCTION, OBJECTS, AND UNIFORMITY OF NATURE 79

causal principles, we also know that having repeated experiences of similar causes having similar effects is *itself* an effect that requires a cause (*ERCE* 120–21). That is, we come to recognize that "the *invariable regularity* of nature is a POWER that may be depended upon (*ERCE* 125); we form a rationally justifiable belief in the "grand and regular operations of nature" (*ERCE* 123) to which we can appeal in judgments about the probability of some individual object behaving like those experienced in the past. Suppose I see something that has sensible qualities resembling bread; even if I do not know much about the causal history of this particular bread-like item, my knowledge that nature has the power of being uniform *itself* provides a reason for thinking that its causal powers will be the same as those of bread I have experienced in the past.

Fourth, as we saw in chapter 2 of this *Guide*, Shepherd holds that humans do not naturally incline to skepticism about objects in the external world. In any given causal inference, a skeptic *could* question whether the causes we think were involved really were involved, but "ordinary persons" will not be troubled by such worries (*ERCE* 123). A skeptic could ask how someone knows that something that looks and feels like fire really is fire; how can the person be sure that putting a piece of wood on it would really cause the wood to turn to ash? "Ordinary persons" with "plain understandings" would reply that this object that looks and feels like fire is certainly fire, because it resulted from a spark produced by a flint and steel (*ERCE* 124). The skeptic could keep pushing, wondering if the flint and steel are "truly such," but only the skeptic will not be satisfied by being told that if the flint and steel produce a spark, they are real (*ERCE* 124). "Plain understandings" will be satisfied (*ERCE* 124), for the human mind is such that "it cannot stand hesitating, and therefore 'takes a step' (in arguing from the sensible qualities to the future effects of things) governed by a *high probability* founded on REASONING" (*ERCE* 124). This tendency to "consider invariability of recurrence as incapable of arising from *chance*" is "one of the most ordinary modes of reasoning" (*ERCE* 126).

80 MARY SHEPHERD

It should be stressed that Shepherd is *not* saying we have an *instinct* to think that uniformities in nature are not due to chance. As we will see when we consider her fourth chapter, according to Shepherd, instincts are not rationally grounded, and thus cannot provide knowledge in causal inferences. Rather, we see "invariable regularity" as *itself* an effect, a quality that we observe in nature, and so we infer that there must be a cause of this regularity itself (*ERCE* 126); past regularities were not mere "coincidences" (*ERCE* 124). Thus our default approach is to expect regularity. To raise skeptical worries about the regularity of nature is not the "ordinary mode of reasoning," and Shepherd thinks even Hume cannot consistently raise such worries: he himself asserts at the beginning of the *Treatise* that the constant connection between impressions and ideas "can never arise from chance" (*ERCE* 126–27, citing *T* 1.1.1.8). But this non-skeptical attitude is due to implicit causal reasoning, not instinct.

Shepherd's Appeal to Locke

While most of *ERCE* chapter 3, section 2 is concerned with describing how we can make good causal inferences, Shepherd opens the section with quotations from John Locke's *Essay Concerning Human Understanding* (*ERCE* 114–15). We saw above that in her fifth chapter, Shepherd will appeal explicitly to Locke when she distinguishes between definitions of *terms* and definitions of *objects* (*ERCE* 158n). Here she considers a related issue, Locke's views concerning the internal constitutions of things, what he calls their 'real essence.'

As Antonia LoLordo has noted, Shepherd's sudden focus on Locke is "surprising," for

Hume's views on causation are not usually read as responses to Locke. What's more surprising is that the passages Shepherd has

INDUCTION, OBJECTS, AND UNIFORMITY OF NATURE 81

in mind concern real and nominal essences. On the face of it, these passages have nothing to do with causation or induction.[26]

But, as LoLordo also points out, Shepherd had strategic reasons for showing that Locke's view is at least consistent with hers: Locke had a "great deal of authority in early 19th century Britain," and so by showing her philosophical affinities with Locke, Shepherd both "gains rhetorical support for her cause" and shows that "she—and not Hume, Reid, or Stewart—is the legitimate heir of the British tradition of natural philosophy."[27]

Shepherd is indeed concerned that Hume has appropriated Locke's views to bolster his own position. She quotes two passages from Locke that suggest that similar sensible qualities are caused by similar "insensible parts" of objects' "internal constitutions" (*ERCE* 114–15), as well as one passage in which Locke says that we cannot know the "secrets of nature" by which these internal constitutions cause the sensible qualities.[28] Her worry is that Hume has read these passages from Locke as expressing skepticism about whether those powers do in fact cause the sensible qualities of objects (*ERCE* 115–16). However, Shepherd thinks Hume has misread Locke; she writes that Locke's skepticism about our *knowledge* of "real essences," or what Hume calls the "secret powers" of objects, should not be taken as skepticism about whether the sensible qualities we perceive are actually caused by those real constitutions. If Locke did not doubt that real essences cause sensible qualities, then Hume cannot draw on Locke for support.

[26] LoLordo, "Mary Shepherd on Causation, Induction, and Natural Kinds," 5.
[27] LoLordo, "Mary Shepherd on Causation, Induction, and Natural Kinds," 6–7.
[28] Shepherd quotes three passages: *ECHU* 3.10.20, 4.6.9, and 4.6.11 (*ERCE* 114–15). In a footnote, she also quotes *ECHU* 3.10.21.

82 MARY SHEPHERD

Thomas Brown

Shepherd closes *ERCE* chapter 3 by summarizing Hume's views and her major criticisms of them.[29] Her next chapter, the shortest in *ERCE*, examines some of the views of Thomas Brown (1778–1820) on causation.[30] Educated at the University of Edinburgh, Brown was later appointed to the chair of moral philosophy at Edinburgh, after a stint practicing medicine from 1803 to 1810.[31] His lectures at Edinburgh focused on issues related to consciousness, emotions, and other mental phenomena and were published in 1820 (the year of his untimely death) as *Lectures on the Philosophy of the Human Mind*. Brown had made a name for himself at a young age with the publication of his *Observations on the Zoonomia of Erasmus Darwin* (1798), and he became even better known through his intervention into the "Leslie affair" at the University of Edinburgh.

In 1805, Sir John Leslie was a candidate for the chair of mathematics at Edinburgh, but this was challenged by opponents who wanted a clergyman appointed. These opponents seized on a footnote in Leslie's 1804 *An Experimental Inquiry into the Nature and Propagation of Heat*, in which he praised Hume's account of

[29] While Shepherd puts her summary of Hume's views in quotation marks, these are not direct quotations from Hume (*ERCE* 129–31).

[30] An 1814 letter from novelist Amelia Opie to her father reveals that Shepherd had met Brown at a dinner party. Opie wrote,

> Her ladyship fairly threw down the gauntlet, and was as luminous, as deep, as clever in her observations and questions, and her display of previous knowledge of Gall's theory and Hartley's, as any professor could have been. . . . The professor looked alarmed, and put on his pins; and Lady Mary began her dialogue at ten, and it was not over at a little past twelve.
>
> Dr. Brown listened occasionally, and with an anatomizing eye, for he does not like literary women; therefore a woman, entering his own arena, must have called forth all his reviewer bitterness. (Brightwell, *Memorials of the Life of Amelia Opie*, 153)

Opie wrote in a subsequent letter of her next meeting with Shepherd: "She was nervous about her display on Sunday last; but I assured her she was thought to talk well, though I could have added, but not by Dr. Brown" (Brightwell, *Memorials of the Life of Amelia Opie*, 154).

[31] Biographical information on Brown is drawn from Dixon, "Introduction," in *Thomas Brown: Selected Philosophical Writings*.

INDUCTION, OBJECTS, AND UNIFORMITY OF NATURE   83

necessary connection.[32] Maintaining that Hume's causal theory provided a basis for atheism, Leslie's opponents claimed that his endorsement of that theory indicated his unsuitability for a faculty position. Defenders of Leslie—who was, ultimately, appointed—included philosopher Dugald Stewart as well as Thomas Brown. Brown published a short pamphlet, *Observations on the Nature and Tendency of the Doctrine of Mr. Hume, Concerning the Relation of Cause and Effect* (1805), largely defending Hume's account of causation and arguing that it had no pernicious consequences for religious belief. He published a longer, revised edition of the pamphlet in 1806, ultimately expanding it into a book published in 1818.[33]

Shepherd's chapter focuses on the arguments from the 1806 book,[34] in which Brown identifies five key claims in Hume's account of causation. Brown defends three of these claims—namely, that cause and effect cannot be discovered a priori; that even after experience, cause and effect cannot be discovered using reason; and that we can only *believe* in cause and effect and not *know* it.[35] However, Brown takes issue with two further Humean claims: that we only believe in cause and effect after repeated experiences of customary conjunctions between objects and that the idea of necessary connection arises as a copy of the impression of the "customary transition of the imagination from one object to its usual attendant" (*EHU* 7.28).[36] Instead, Brown maintains that "the belief in power is immediately intuitive" (*ONT* 194). This instinctive belief, present

---

[32] For discussion of the broader implications of the Leslie affair, see Bow, "In Defence of the Scottish Enlightenment: Dugald Stewart's Role in the 1805 John Leslie Affair."

[33] Brown, *Observations on the Nature and Tendency of the Doctrine of Mr. Hume, Concerning the Relation of Cause and Effect* (first edition, 1805; second edition, 1806); Brown, *Inquiry into the Relation of Cause and Effect* (1818).

[34] This is clear from the title of her chapter, "Observations on Dr. Brown's Essay on the Doctrine of Mr. Hume," and from the fact that only Brown's 1805 and 1806 works are structured around the five propositions drawn from Hume that Shepherd lists in her discussion. It appears that Shepherd was using the 1806 version because her quotation from Brown's account of Hume's fifth proposition (*ERCE* 146) does not appear in the 1805 edition.

[35] Brown defends these claims at *ONT* 47, 80, and 94, respectively.

[36] Brown's criticism of the former begins at *ONT* 121; of the latter, at *ONT* 142.

84 MARY SHEPHERD

in all humans, exercises an "irresistible influence on our reasoning and conduct" (*ONT* 210; see also 207).

But Brown considers Hume's failure to characterize our belief in causation as instinctive to be a relatively minor problem, and so he ends his book by defending Humean causation against the charge that it leads to atheism. He writes,

> many of Mr. Hume's doctrines are indeed dangerous in the extreme, as destructive of christianity, of belief in a future state, and of every sublime conception of Deity; but it would be difficult to mention any great general theory, either of matter or mind, from which less practical danger can be supposed to flow, than from the preceding simple theory of causation. (*ONT* 204–5)

Indeed, he suggests that the whole controversy over Leslie's appointment was due simply to a misreading of Hume: Leslie's opponents took Hume to be saying we have no idea of power at all and then inferred that Hume "denied, in consequence, the possibility of the belief of divine power" (*ONT* 189n). Brown wryly notes that "it must, therefore, be consoling, to find, that, however false his theory *of the origin of the idea of power* may be, he still asserts, that we have an idea of power, and that, hence, the asserted impossibility of the idea of divine power does not follow from his theory" (*ONT* 189n).

Unsurprisingly, Shepherd praises Brown for his criticisms of Hume on the origins of our idea of causal connection (*ERCE* 144–45). And, in one respect, she agrees with Brown on the first Humean proposition he defends, that cause and effect cannot be discovered a priori, for she thinks this is certainly true of particular cases. However, she notes that the genuinely philosophical question is how "the *general* relation of Cause and Effect" is known (*ERCE* 139). Repeating a point she had made against Hume (*ERCE* 59), she observes that this general question cannot be settled by considering particular cases.

INDUCTION, OBJECTS, AND UNIFORMITY OF NATURE · 85

Shepherd also objects to Brown's treatment of cause and effect as a temporal sequence. Again, we have already seen that she thinks "'*Antecedency* and *subsquency*' are . . . immaterial to the proper definition of Cause and Effect" (*ERCE* 49), so she does not offer any new arguments here. However, it is here that she compares the relation between cause and effect to the relation of a product of multiplication and its factors. She writes,

> to represent the relation of Cause and Effect, as A *followed* by B, is a *false view* of the matter. Cause and Effect, might be represented rather by A × B = C, therefore C *is* INCLUDED *in the* MIXTURE of THE OBJECTS called CAUSE. If C arises once from the *junction of any two bodies*; C must upon every other *like conjunction*, be the *result*; because there is *no alteration in the proportions of the quantities to make a difference;* C is really included in the MIXTURE of A and B, although, to our senses, we are forced to note down (as it were) the SUM arising from their union, *after the observance* of their coalescence. (*ERCE* 141–42)

Composite numbers can be produced by multiplying two or more whole numbers, their factors. In causal relationships, Shepherd suggests, an effect is also composite, the result of the combination of *physical* factors. So, just as "the results of all arithmetical combinations are included in their statements," so too are physical effects included in the combination of their causes (*ERCE* 142).

Regarding Brown's own view that belief in causation is "*instinctive*" (*ERCE* 137, 144) or a "*blind impulse of faith*" (*ERCE* 145),[37] Shepherd maintains that "instinctive belief" can mean one of only two things, neither of which makes it suitable as a basis for knowledge about causation. First, it might mean "the mysterious

---

[37] While Brown does say belief in causation is an "instinctive principle of faith" (*ONT* 94), he does not call it a "blind impulse."

86 MARY SHEPHERD

manner in which animals know of the qualities of bodies previous to experience, by some laws beyond our scrutiny" (*ERCE* 137–38).[38] Shepherd is thinking of cases where animals know instinctively what is safe to eat or what materials to use to build a nest (see *EPEU* 160). It may seem surprising that she allows that non-human animals—but not humans—can know about objects' particular qualities prior to experience, but even Hume conceded the same point.[39] She does not actually argue that humans lack these kinds of instincts; perhaps she thinks it is obvious that we do.

Shepherd then considers another possible meaning for Brown's "instinctive belief"; he might mean "intuitive belief." As we saw earlier, by "intuitive belief" Shepherd means belief in a proposition that is true by definition. Here, Shepherd argues that for a belief to provide conclusive reason for believing anything else requires that there be *evidence* for the former (*ERCE* 138). So even "intuitive propositions" should be based on our experience of objects and their qualities if they are to be usable in inferences—that is, intuitive beliefs should ultimately be based on real definitions, which themselves are based on experience; there must be reasons for the definitions of terms we have made. But as Brown understands instinctive beliefs, they are believed *without* a reason (*ERCE* 138). And to base reasoning on ungrounded propositions is, Shepherd says, "an absolute contradiction to philosophy and common sense" (*ERCE* 145; see also *EPEU* 212).

Finally, Shepherd turns to Brown's contention that Hume's account of the origin of our idea of causal connection, while mistaken,

---

[38] Shepherd says little about how animals think. She says "latent reasoning" about causation is done by "children, peasants, and brutes" (*EPEU* 171; see also 189 and 287); "brutes" refers to non-human animals.

[39] Hume writes that "though animals learn many parts of their knowledge from observation, there are also many parts of it, which they derive from the original hand of nature; which much exceed the share of capacity they possess on ordinary occasions; and in which they improve, little or nothing, by the longest practice and experience. These we denominate *instincts*" (*EHU* 9.6).

INDUCTION, OBJECTS, AND UNIFORMITY OF NATURE 87

need not lead to religious skepticism. Shepherd thinks Brown is simply wrong:

> He seems to think, that as Mr. Hume got hold of the idea of POWER, by *some means or other*, it is immaterial by what means; as any idea of power whatever, would show that a Deity was alike necessary. (*ERCE* 148)

The problem, as she sees it, is that if our idea of causation came merely from an impression in our own minds, we would have no reason to think causation really exists *independently* of us, "and therefore could not draw any conclusion in favour of the necessity of a Creator, as the 'productive principle' of the universe" (*ERCE* 149). Hume's account gives us only a "*fancy of power*, without *knowledge of it*" (*ERCE* 149–50). And without a firm basis in reason for belief in causal power, we will have none of the "consolation, and the peace, and the happiness, and the virtue of a filial confidence in the great Father of mankind" (*ERCE* 150–51, quoting *ONT* 195).

Shepherd evidently thought Brown's defense of Hume was significant enough to require a chapter of its own for an answer. In the next two chapters of *ERCE*, she considers the work of another defender of Humean causation, physician William Lawrence. Here, the consequences she is concerned about are not religious but scientific: how to understand what accounts for the sensitivity of nerves and the irritability of muscles and what distinguishes living from nonliving entities. Shepherd's critique of Lawrence is the topic of the next chapter.

Suggestions for Further Reading

- On Shepherd's account of induction, see Martha Bolton, "Causality and Causal Induction: The Necessitarian Theory of Lady Mary Shepherd."
- Shepherd's bundle theory of objects is discussed in David Landy's "A Defense of Mary Shepherd's Account of Cause and Effect as Synchronous."

88 MARY SHEPHERD

- Jeremy Fantl connects Shepherd's account of causation and bundle theory of objects to contemporary causal accounts of properties and natural kinds in "Mary Shepherd on Causal Necessity."
- In "Mary Shepherd on Causation, Induction, and Natural Kinds," Antonia LoLordo discusses connections between Shepherd's and Locke's accounts of natural kinds.

4

Causation, Sentience, and Life

Introduction

In the final two chapters of the *Essay upon the Relation of Cause and Effect*, Shepherd considers the ramifications of a Humean theory of causation for scientific investigation.[1] Her target here is London surgeon William Lawrence (1783–1867), who was involved in a debate among early nineteenth-century scientists, physicians, and philosophers about the nature of life. Shepherd examines how Lawrence's application of a Humean causal theory led him astray in explaining the nature of sentience or consciousness (in *ERCE* chapter 5) and the nature of life (in *ERCE* chapter 6). In both cases, her point is to show how the right theory of causation is essential not just for "important practical theories" (*ERCE* 159) but also for science (*ERCE* 194).

The debate in which Lawrence was involved concerned whether living organisms have a distinctive *matter* or *structure* that makes them different from non-living things or, alternatively, whether the matter and structure are the same in both living and non-living things so that some extrinsic factor (such as a soul) must be present in the former but not the latter. Following historian Stephen Jacyna, we can call these, respectively, *immanentist* and

---

[1] Shepherd also notes the deleterious effect of Humean theories of causation on science at *EPEU* 129, although she gives no specific examples there. In her second book, she touts the benefits of her theory of causation for "physiology" and "the treatment of mental and bodily disorder, upon the nature of chemical actions, &c." (*EPEU* 307). She writes that "if a scientific knowledge of [the principle of cause and effect] be obtained, we may perhaps be enabled to understand and imitate nature, better than we have hitherto done" (*EPEU* 308).

Mary Shepherd. Deborah Boyle, Oxford University Press. © Oxford University Press 2023.
DOI: 10.1093/oso/9780190090326.003.0004

90   MARY SHEPHERD

transcendentalist theories of life.[2] Immanentists typically did not deny that living bodies contain some sort of vital force, but they saw this force as emerging from the physical or structural features of bodies. Transcendentalists, on the other hand, held that living entities differ from non-living ones because the former contain a vital principle that is not inherent in matter but is, theoretically at least, separable from it.

The transcendentalist approach was defended by (among others) London surgeon John Abernethy (1764–1831).[3] In his 1814 lectures to the Royal College of Surgeons, subsequently published as a book, Abernethy wrote that "the matter of animals and vegetables is ... as we express it, common matter, it is inert; so that the necessity of supposing the superaddition of some subtle and mobile substance is apparent."[4] The book received a scathing review in *The Edinburgh Review*, and in 1816, William Lawrence added to the criticisms in his own lectures to the Royal College of Surgeons, where he rejected Abernethy's defense of a superadded source of life. Abernethy replied, attacking Lawrence, and Lawrence defended himself in another lecture series, published in 1819 under the title *Lectures on Physiology, Zoology, and the Natural History of Man*. It is to this book that Shepherd is responding in her *Essay upon the Relation of Cause and Effect*.[5]

Lawrence's immanentist accounts of sentience and life will be the topic of the next section. The section after that considers Shepherd's objections to Lawrence's account of necessary connections; subsequent sections consider how she objects specifically to his account of sensation and to his account of life. The chapter ends with a

---

[2] Jacyna, "Immanence or Transcendence: Theories of Life and Organization in Britain, 1790–1825," 311.

[3] This account of the dispute between Abernethy and Lawrence relies on Temkin, "Basic Science, Medicine, and the Romantic Era."

[4] Abernethy, *An Inquiry into the Probability and Rationality of Mr. Hunter's Theory of Life*, 41.

[5] Shepherd gives page numbers from the 1819 edition of Lawrence's book (the first edition). However, all citations here are from the third edition (1823).

CAUSATION, SENTIENCE, AND LIFE 91

sketch of Shepherd's own account of what it means to say a creature is living.

William Lawrence on Explaining Sentience and Life

The question of whether or not life can be explained by forces immanent in the matter making up an organism was typically posed as a question about how to explain the "vital processes" of "irritability" and "sensibility." Irritability and sensibility had been key concepts in physiology since the work of Francis Glisson (1599–1677) in the seventeenth century and Albrecht von Haller (1708–77) in the eighteenth, but even in Shepherd's day there was still debate concerning what these terms even meant. As Haller understood 'irritability,' it meant the capacity of muscular tissue (or "living muscular fibres," to use Lawrence's terminology [L 70–71]) to contract when stimulated, allowing an organism to move; 'sensibility' was, roughly, the capacity of nerves ("living nervous fibres") to transmit sensations to the brain when a sensory organ was stimulated.[6]

Lawrence thought the distinction between living and non-living organisms could be explained by understanding these "vital" processes. But for Lawrence, to understand these processes is just to be able to give accurate descriptions, based on dissection, observation, and experiment, of the various structures and processes in the body (L 57). He emphatically rejected the idea that any vital process should be explained by invoking a separable, immaterial soul or principle; in Lawrence's memorable terms, "an immaterial and spiritual being could not have been discovered amid the blood and filth of the dissecting room" (L 7). To use the distinction introduced earlier, Lawrence was an immanentist; he warns his readers not to

[6] See Gambarotto, *Vital Forces*, 36–37.

92   MARY SHEPHERD

commit the "error of viewing the vital manifestations as something independent of the organization [i.e., body] in which they occur" (*L* 53).

Thus, Lawrence thinks that the goal of physiology should be to learn

> whether the internal movements of the animal machine are explicable by the laws of mechanics and hydraulics; whether, like these, they can be subjected to calculation; whether the changes of composition, incessantly going on in all parts of the frame, can be assimilated to the operations of our laboratories, or reduced to the laws of external chemistry; whether any living phenomena can be so far likened to those of electricity, galvanism, magnetism, as to justify us in referring their explanation to the same principles. (*L* 60)

Perhaps surprisingly, though, Lawrence was rather pessimistic about how much knowledge can be gained from observation and experiment. The variety and complexity of forces and motions in animal bodies are so great that he thought it would be impossible to do the calculations needed to explain these forces and motions in mathematical terms (*L* 63). Since complete mechanical or chemical descriptions of vital processes would forever escape our human capabilities, Lawrence thought physiologists, anatomists, and chemists should limit themselves just to the observation that "certain vital manifestations are connected with certain organic structures" (*L* 68; see also 12). In other words, Lawrence said that it is enough to identify certain *constant conjunctions* of processes with structures in living entities. Living beings can be *described* in ways that distinguish them from the non-living, insofar as only the former have "vital processes"—that is, the actions of muscles, nerves, and capillaries (*L* 66, 68).

This is where Hume comes into the picture: in a long footnote, Lawrence approvingly quotes from Thomas Brown's Humean

CAUSATION, SENTIENCE, AND LIFE 93

account of causation (*L* 68–70). For example, regarding the muscles and nerves in particular, Lawrence insists that all the physiologist can say is that living muscular fibers are irritable and living nervous fibers are sensible. As he puts it,

> To say that irritability is a property of living muscular fibres, is merely equivalent to the assertion, that such fibres have in all cases possessed the power of contraction. What then is the cause of irritability? I do not know, and cannot conjecture.
>
> In physiology, as in the physical sciences, we quickly reach the boundaries of knowledge whenever we attempt to penetrate the first causes of the phenomena. (*L* 71)

One might think that Lawrence has misunderstood Hume, for according to Hume, to identify a constant conjunction between two types of entities or events *is* to identify the cause. But when Lawrence says he does not know, and "cannot conjecture" about, the cause of irritability, he means that we cannot know anything about the cause understood in a *non*-Humean way; we cannot know *why* irritability is always found with living muscles and sensitivity with living nerves.

For Lawrence, then, to understand life is to be able to describe the correlations among the structures, functions, and processes displayed by living organisms, including but not limited to irritability and sensibility. Shepherd says almost nothing about irritability, except to note that muscles can exist without being irritable, as they do in a corpse (*ERCE* 162): she focuses on sensibility, although she herself does not use the term 'sensibility'. Where Lawrence says nerves are "sensible," Shepherd prefers to say they are "sentient" (*ERCE* 162, 163) or that they have "sentiency" (*ERCE* 155, 162) or "sensation" (*ERCE* 166).[7] She equates this with

---

[7] This might seem to imply, oddly, that *nerves* have minds and can think. However, as we shall see, Shepherd thinks that to say a nerve is sentient is to say that the nerve has combined with various other *separate* capacities—at the very least, a capacity to sense

94 MARY SHEPHERD

having thought (*ERCE* 166; see also 173–74);[8] in her second book, Shepherd defines 'mind' or 'soul' as the capacity to have thoughts or sensations (*EPEU* 15, 18).

Shepherd also draws a sharper distinction than does Lawrence between sentience and life. She is careful to note that any acceptable account of life should include living organisms that lack sentience altogether, such as plants (*ERCE* 181); in contrast, Lawrence's chapter on the nature of life refers almost exclusively to animals (*L* 80–100). She agrees (with some caveats, to be noted below) with Lawrence's characterization of being alive as having "a constant internal motion, which enables a body to assimilate new and separate old particles, and prevents it from yielding to the chemical affinities of the surrounding elements" (*ERCE* 181; see also 183).[9] However, since this is applicable to living plants as well as living animals, Shepherd suggests that it entails that "either *all living* beings must be *sentient*, or else a *further cause* must be sought for *sensation* than *mere life*" (*ERCE* 181). There is no evidence that Shepherd believed the former was true—she never suggests that plants are sentient, although she does suggest that even worms are (*EPEU* 174). Thus, she holds the latter view: to explain sentience, "a *further* cause must

---

(mind) and a capacity of being alive, and probably with other capacities that we have not yet identified. The *combination* of the nerve with these capacities to sense (and with the capacity to live) is what allows the nerve to transmit sensory information from the sensory organ to the brain. It is nonetheless the mind that has the sensation (of whatever kind corresponds to the sensory organ from which the information came). Nerves can be said to be "sentient" or "sensitive" when they are mixed with mind (and other necessary factors), but that just means that under that condition they are able to transmit sensory information from one part of the body to the brain.

[8] While Shepherd seems to assume that her concept of 'sentiency' (sensation, consciousness) is equivalent to what Lawrence means by 'sensibility,' it is possible she misread Lawrence. To be fair to Shepherd, however, Lawrence never actually defines 'sensibility' in his *Lectures*. In what follows, this *Guide* will use 'sentience' (or, occasionally, 'sensitivity') to refer to Shepherd's 'sentiency' or 'sensation' and Lawrence's 'sensibility.' Furthermore, to avoid any confusion with Shepherd's entirely different usage of 'sensible' (as in her phrase 'sensible qualities'), this *Guide* will use 'sensitive' where Lawrence uses 'sensible.'

[9] Shepherd paraphrases Lawrence (*L* 81) but does not change his meaning.

CAUSATION, SENTIENCE, AND LIFE 95

be sought" (*ERCE* 181) beyond whatever cause explains merely being alive.

Shepherd's Objections to Lawrence's Account of Necessary Connection

Before criticizing Lawrence's accounts of sentience and life, Shepherd devotes sections 1–3 of *ERCE* chapter 5 to examining in more general terms how Lawrence understands 'necessary connection.' Unsurprisingly, given his endorsement of Brown's Humean account, Lawrence thinks that to identify the "necessary connection" between "the properties of sensibility, and irritability, and the structures of living muscular and nervous fibres" is to say no more than that "the living muscular fibre is irritable, and the living nervous fibre is sensible" (*ERCE* 152, paraphrasing *L* 70–71). Equally unsurprisingly, Shepherd thinks this is not nearly enough.

Shepherd opens *ERCE* chapter 5 by paraphrasing a passage from Lawrence and then quoting the passage that leads to her first objection. She cites Lawrence's view that

the only reason we have for asserting in any case that any property belongs to any substance, is the certainty or universality with which we find the substance, and the property in question accompanying each other.—Thus we say that gold is ductile, yellow, soluble in nitro-muriatic acid, because we have always found gold, when pure, to be so.—We assert the living muscular fibres to be irritable, and the living nervous fibres to be sensible for the same reason. The evidence for the two propositions presents itself to my mind as unmarked by the faintest shade of difference. (*ERCE* 153, paraphrasing *L* 69–70)[10]

---

[10] Lawrence assimilates *both* "living muscular fibres are irritable" and "living nervous fibres are sensible" to "gold is ductile, yellow, soluble in nitro-muriatic acid." Although Shepherd says almost nothing about what might cause muscles to be irritable, elsewhere

96 MARY SHEPHERD

However, Shepherd thinks there *is* an important difference in the basis for these two claims. Her argument here is rather difficult to follow, involving some dialectic between her and an imagined defender of Lawrence, but her basic point is that there are two kinds of necessary connection: that between a name and the qualities we associate with it and that between an object and its qualities.[11] Lawrence, she thinks, conflates these two kinds of necessary connection, leading him to claim incorrectly that understanding sentience and life requires merely spelling out what qualities we have come to associate with the terms 'sentience' and 'life.'

Shepherd's first step in her criticism of Lawrence is to remind her reader that she has already offered an account of *objects*. Back in *ERCE* chapter 2 she had said that objects, "in relation to us, are nothing but masses of certain qualities, affecting certain of our senses; and which, when independent of our senses, are *unknown* powers or qualities in nature" (*ERCE* 46); as we have seen, this expresses the distinction she will go on to defend in *EPEU* between internal and external objects, where internal objects are collections of sensible qualities and external objects are collections of causal powers, including the powers to produce the sensible qualities.[12] Shepherd had also noted in *ERCE* chapter 2 that after we observe certain qualities occurring together, we *name* or *give a sign to* that assemblage of qualities (*ERCE* 55). For example, English-speakers

she makes a tripartite distinction, referring to "sensation, life, or action" (see *EPEU* 394–95), suggesting that she thought muscular motion (action) is due to yet another distinct causal factor besides those responsible for sentience and life.

[11] In *EPEU*, Shepherd actually discusses a third type of necessary connection: "the necessary connection of *invariable antecedency* and *subsequency* of successive aggregates of sensible qualities" (*EPEU* 130–31). Although the operations of causes and the effects with which they are necessarily connected occur synchronously, Shepherd acknowledges that certain successive series of events necessarily occur in the order they do. This is not because the earlier and later events are necessarily connected with *each other*, but because a single external object has various effects as it "mixes successively with different organs of sense, or various parts of the human frame, &c." (*EPEU* 131; see also 298; for discussion, see chapter 7 of this *Guide*).

[12] For discussion of this distinction, and the distinction between nominal and real definitions, see chapter 3 of this *Guide*.

CAUSATION, SENTIENCE, AND LIFE 97

dub a certain bundle of sensible qualities 'snow.' Shepherd notes that the *particular name* we choose (whether for an internal or an external object) is arbitrary; we might have called that particular assemblage of sensible qualities something else. Nonetheless, once we have stipulated a name for those sensible qualities, the *connection* between the name and the properties it signifies is not arbitrary but necessary (*ERCE* 154). But, Shepherd says, this is a different kind of necessity than that linking objects and their qualities, where the necessity is not due to how we have decided to use words but to features—causal powers—of the external world that obtain independently of us (*ERCE* 154).

Shepherd claims that when Lawrence says that the connection between gold and the quality of being yellow (and ductile, soluble in nitrohydrochloric acid, etc.[13]) is exactly the same as the connection between a living nerve and the quality of being sensitive, he is conflating (1) the necessary connection between a *name* and its definition and (2) the necessary connection between an *object* and its qualities. According to Lawrence, scientific investigation only tells us what qualities are constantly conjoined in our experience; so, when we say "gold is yellow (etc.)," we are just enumerating the sensible qualities we associate with the word 'gold,' based on the fact that those sensible qualities have always appeared together. Another way to put this is to say that, for Lawrence, scientific investigation gives us information for forming nominal definitions but not real definitions: it does not reveal anything about the causal powers of objects themselves. So, as Lawrence sees it, to say living nervous fibers are sensitive is just to enumerate a quality (sensitivity) that we always find conjoined with the other qualities we experience when we study a living nerve.

However, Shepherd thinks a claim like "living nervous fibers are sensitive" tells us *more* than that. Such a statement identifies an effect that results from a living nervous fiber under certain

---

[13] For convenience, this will henceforth be shortened to 'yellow (etc.).'

98   MARY SHEPHERD

conditions, namely, when it interacts with some other object. It tells us something about the *causal power* of the living nervous fiber itself. The same is true when someone ascribes irritability to living muscles; Shepherd's point is that this is to identify a causal power that muscles in living bodies exercise when they interact with something else. To say that living nerves sense is to report something about objects in the world, not just to report what qualities we have associated with a word. In assimilating "living nervous fibers are irritable" and "living nerves are sensitive" to "gold is yellow (etc.)," Lawrence fails to see that the two former claims actually tell us something important about the necessary connection between an object and the qualities that it can cause.

In *ERCE* chapter 5, section 2, Shepherd continues her argument that Lawrence has confused two kinds of necessary connection. But now she imagines a hypothetical objector, defending Lawrence, who notes that the word 'gold' need not refer to a particular set of sensible qualities caused by some *particular* lump of gold. Such a set of sensible qualities would include not just yellowness and ductility, but also whatever size, shape, texture, etc., are possessed by that particular lump. But (so the imagined objector observes) sometimes we use 'gold' to refer to a *type* of thing, where we mean to convey the "qualities of the genus" (*ERCE* 156)—that is, the qualities shared by all gold, the essence or nature of the natural kind *gold*, excluding the specific properties of particular instances. So, Shepherd imagines her objector saying, perhaps Lawrence is trying to make general claims about the natural kinds *gold* and *living nerves* or *living muscles*; he is not *just* reporting properties we experience in particular interactions with instances of these things.

Shepherd thinks that this objection misses the point. She agrees that we do sometimes use terms to characterize general categories rather than specific instances. Certainly, for Locke, a term like 'gold' refers to a complex abstract idea that includes only the ideas that pertain to 'gold' generally (*ECHU* 3.6.9). But, Shepherd notes, even in this use of 'gold,' the word is just a "sign, merely standing

CAUSATION, SENTIENCE, AND LIFE 99

for the qualities of the genus" (*ERCE* 155–56). This is still a kind of nominal definition, reporting a collection of qualities that we have decided to call 'gold.' And the connection between a word and qualities, though necessary, is still "arbitrary" (*ERCE* 156), whether that word is being used to refer to a particular object or a general type of object. So, to object that Lawrence might be using a word in a general sense still does *not* show that he is engaged in the project of identifying the causal powers of an object; it does not show that he means that "the *mass of qualities*, which combine to form this object, are afterwards necessarily connected as a *Cause*; when, in its conjunction with any other objects, it puts on further qualities, which then are its *effects*, or *properties*" (*ERCE* 156).

But suppose our hypothetical defender of Lawrence insists that Lawrence *does* mean that "gold is yellow (etc.)" ascribes certain causal powers to the external object *gold*, so that Lawrence *is* asserting a necessary connection between the object and the qualities that result from its causal powers. If so, Shepherd concedes, then Lawrence would be correct that the evidence for "gold is yellow (etc.)" and "living nervous fibers are sensible" is of the same type:

> if this should be the sense . . . of Mr. Lawrence in his passage on gold—it is true there may be "no difference between the evidence for the two propositions;" for both objects are necessarily and invariably connected with their effects or properties. (*ERCE* 156)

Such evidence would be empirical investigations in which instances of the types of object in question are put under different circumstances to find out the causal powers that belong to all such instances, and hence to identify the sensible qualities that are *necessarily* connected with the object.

But, Shepherd says, she does *not* think this is what Lawrence means in his passage on gold (*ERCE* 156). She does not offer reasons for her dismissal of the objector's suggestion, but, as we have seen, Lawrence's writings do indicate that he thought the

100 MARY SHEPHERD

search for necessary connections between objects and their qualities is misguided.[14] And, Shepherd notes, even if Lawrence did mean that "gold is yellow (etc.)" is a claim about the causal powers of gold and the effects necessarily connected with it, his claim that this necessary connection is due to *past concurrence* between gold and its qualities (and so between the living nerve and sentience) would still be incorrect (*ERCE* 157).

In *ERCE* chapter five, section 3, Shepherd considers the long footnote in Lawrence's *Lectures* where he approvingly quotes from Thomas Brown's Humean account of causation. It is, of course, Lawrence's acceptance of this account of causation that Shepherd diagnoses as the source of his mistaken thinking about sentience and life. Here, Shepherd identifies what she sees as three errors in Lawrence's footnote. The first two pertain to Brown's definitions of 'cause' and 'property,' with which Lawrence agrees and with which Shepherd has already made clear her disagreement (*ERCE* 159–60). The third point that Shepherd quotes from Lawrence is as follows:

The powers, properties or qualities of a substance are not to be regarded as any thing superadded to the substance, or distinct from it.—They are *only* the substance itself considered in relation to various changes that take place when it exists in peculiar circumstances. (*ERCE* 160, quoting *L* 70n[15])

Shepherd *agrees* with Lawrence on this, but she thinks that he has misunderstood its implications. If a property of a substance is not distinct from the substance but is simply "brought out to view

---

[14] For another example of this, consider his claim that "having found by experience that every thing we see has some cause of existence, we are induced to ascribe the constant concomitance of a substance and its properties to some necessary connexion between them; but, however strong the feeling may be, which leads us to believe in some more close bond, we can only trace, in this notion of necessary connexion, the fact of certainty or universality of concurrence" (*L* 70).

[15] Lawrence himself is quoting Brown, *Inquiry into the Relation of Cause and Effect*, 20–21.

CAUSATION, SENTIENCE, AND LIFE 101

when [the substance is] mixed with the qualities of other objects," then the property does not exist *after* a change in a subject; rather, the property exists *synchronously* as the causal interaction occurs (*ERCE* 162). But, Shepherd notes, this implication contradicts Lawrence's own commitments regarding causation. Lawrence, she implies, is a careless reader who failed to see a contradiction in the very theory of causation that he so lauds.[16]

Implications of Shepherd's Criticisms for Lawrence's Account of Sentience

In *ERCE* chapter 5, section 4, Shepherd shows the implications of Lawrence's confusion regarding the two kinds of necessary connection for his account of the sensitivity of nerves (as well as the irritability of muscles). She opens by noting that irritability and sensitivity are not found in dead bodies but only in living ones: "the muscle and nerve can and do exist as organized beings, without irritability and sentiency when under death" (*ERCE* 162). Or, as she more poignantly puts it later, "many a beautiful and youthful set of organs are perfect, without animation" (*ERCE* 180). In a dead body, the nerves and muscles continue to exist; however, they lack their usual causal powers. Shepherd takes this close relationship between life and the bodily processes of muscles and nerves as evidence that the relationship between life and causal powers is deeper than mere constant conjunction; "it must be by a *truly necessary connexion*, between life and these qualities" (*ERCE* 162). Life must be some kind of productive principle that is *responsible* for muscles and

---

[16] Shepherd's argument amounts to an *ad hominem* argument against Lawrence. Clare Marie Moriarty has noted that *ad hominem* arguments noting inconsistencies in a philosopher's views were not necessarily viewed as fallacious in early modern philosophy. She writes, "rather than an 'abusive ad hominem,' the early modern conception of ad hominem was a catch-all for any arguing that took the circumstances of the disputants into account in attempting to block certain arguments or discredit the neutrality of the opponent" ("The Ad Hominem Argument of Berkeley's *Analyst*," 439).

102 MARY SHEPHERD

nerves having powers (namely, irritability and sensitivity) in living bodies that corpses do not have.

Shepherd imagines Lawrence insisting again that in every case when we ascribe a quality to an object, we are saying *no more* than that our experience of objects of that sort is always accompanied by that quality (*ERCE* 163). As we have seen, Shepherd thinks that if this is how a word is being used—that is, as a kind of short-hand for a certain assortment of properties that always appear together— then to assert of a thing that it has some quality is just to assert something that is true *by definition*; such a claim would indeed be necessarily true, but it would not tell us anything useful. Moreover, she adds now, the very utterance of a statement in which a property is ascribed to an object named by a qualified noun *shows* that the speaker is *not* merely making a definitional claim.

To make this point, Shepherd asks us to consider a "familiar illustration," the claim that "a bilious man is choleric" (*ERCE* 164). This is an unfortunate example, not just because such terms are actually *not* familiar to twenty-first-century readers[17] but because, once we see that "bilious" in her day meant "having too much bile in the body" and that "bile" was called "choler," this looks like a tautology, exactly the kind of definitional claim that she wants to say is *not* the case with the claim "a living nervous fiber is sensitive." Evidently, however, by "choleric" she means "angry," so the claim is ascribing a property (anger) to an object (a bilious man). Shepherd claims that in characterizing (or "qualifying") the word 'man' with 'bilious,' the speaker is thereby implying that the bile is the *cause* of the anger; the very structure of the proposition shows that *more* is being asserted than just what is definitionally true. Analogously, when Lawrence says "a living nerve is sensitive," the very fact that he has qualified 'nerve' with 'living' shows that life is being asserted to be a *cause* of the sensitivity (*ERCE* 164; as we will see, Shepherd

---

[17] Moreover, Shepherd's point is obscured by an unfortunate misprint in the original text, which has "vile" instead of "bile" (*ERCE* 164).

CAUSATION, SENTIENCE, AND LIFE   103

thinks another required cause of sensitivity is mind). As Shepherd sums up this objection to Lawrence, "This distinction between a *qualified*, and *unqualified* noun, on account of the different nature of the *connexion* of the predicate of the proposition, with its subject, Mr. Lawrence did not take notice of; or he would not have thought 'there was not the faintest shade of difference' between the two propositions he states, in this respect" (*ERCE* 165).

Lawrence's "Dangerous" Error Regarding Sentience

Although Shepherd has at this point made several objections to Lawrence, she raises what she takes to be the most serious objection in *ERCE* chapter 5, section 5. There she accuses Lawrence of committing the "dangerous mistake" of *denying* that a cause can be found for qualities such as irritability and sensitivity and, in this denial, thereby assigning them a "false cause" (*ERCE* 165–68; see also *EPEU* 156–57). She writes, "Of all philosophical errors, the substitution of false, partial, or insufficient causes for the production of an end or object, is the most dangerous, because so liable to escape detection" (*ERCE* 167). She admits that being sentient may be the result of many combined causes and that we may never know all the factors necessary for it (*ERCE* 168; see also 191); but that does not mean that there are no such factors. Her suggestion is that this kind of fallacious argument is due to Lawrence's lazy, impatient thinking and pride (*ERCE* 167)—itself an *ad hominem* argument on Shepherd's part.

In the next section (misnumbered as 7 instead of 6), we get some indication of Shepherd's own view about what causes sentience. While a materialist (like Lawrence) might say sentience arises from "the powers of matter in general, (whatever matter may be) . . . when placed under *arrangement* and mixed with life," Shepherd says there is no proof of this (*ERCE* 169). The factors of

104 MARY SHEPHERD

being made of matter and being alive, even if they are necessary for sentience, seem insufficient to bring about "so extraordinary a difference as that between conscious and unconscious being" (*ERCE* 169); after all, plants are made of matter and are alive, yet they are not sentient. Shepherd takes this to show that there must be some other factor involved, some "particular cause" for sentience (*ERCE* 169). According to Shepherd's account of causation, whatever this cause is must combine with properly arranged living matter and, in the very act of combination, thereby produce a new effect, a sensing entity. In other words, in seeking the cause of an organism being sentient, Shepherd is *not* asking what action, event, or state of affairs *precedes* the creature's sentience. Rather, she is seeking the *factor* that, when combined with others, synchronously produces sentience. Since this cannot be proved to be in mere living matter and its structure, she concludes that it must be an "immaterial cause, that is, a *principle, power, being*, an unknown quality *denied* to exist in matter.—This must have a name, and may be called *soul*, or *spirit*" (*ERCE* 169).

Shepherd thus objects to Lawrence's materialism, according to which he denies that "any cause beyond the brain is necessary to thought, on account of the impossibility of assigning the *time* of its union with the body" (*ERCE* 169–70).[18] In a short digression, she suggests that mind or soul (the "capacity of sensation") might have been created when humans were first created, and be, as it were, individually parceled out to each individual (*ERCE* 170); we shall consider this suggestion in chapter 8 of this *Guide*.

Returning to the question of what causes sentience, Shepherd reminds us that, according to her theory of causation, for an effect to occur requires a "*junction or mutual mixture of all* the objects *necessary to it*" (*ERCE* 170). Clearly, a living brain is required for

---

[18] Indeed, one of Lawrence's criticisms of those who posit an immaterial soul is that "they have left us quite in the dark on the precise time at which the spiritual guest arrives in his corporeal dwelling" (*L* 93).

CAUSATION, SENTIENCE, AND LIFE 105

sentience; brain, nerves, mind, and "whatever other powers are also necessary for that result" interact to produce specific sensations (*ERCE* 170–71). Moreover, Shepherd says, *"for each variety of thought and sensation,"* there must be a distinct kind of action in the brain (*ERCE* 171). Her reasoning here is that since like effects come from like causes, *different* effects come from *different* causes. So, if there are different types of sensations, they must be the results of differences in the causes.[19] Unfortunately, she does not say what different types of sensations she has in mind. In *EPEU* she mentions "various classes" of sensation (*EPEU* 7; see also 34), writing that sensations "should be divided into *the sensations of present sensible qualities; sensations of the ideas of memory, sensations of the ideas of imagination, sensations of the ideas of reason, &c."* (*EPEU* 135–36). Since the causes of each of these types of sensations must differ from each other, then "a different action of brain is wanted for each variety of thought and sensation" (*ERCE* 171). For example, sensing a sound or color involves a kind of brain action that differs from the kind of brain action involved in remembering. Here Shepherd introduces an unusual phrase: she says that the brain becomes the "exponent" of the soul or mind (*ERCE* 171). We will consider what she means by this in chapter 8 of this *Guide*.

In another digression from her analysis of the cause of sentience, Shepherd criticizes Lawrence's dismissal of "moral treatment" for the "diseases of an 'immaterial being'" (*ERCE* 171–72, quoting *L* 97). As a materialist, Lawrence maintained that insanity and mental illness had their basis in brain disorders; in postmortem investigations, he says, he has "examined after death the heads of many insane persons, and have hardly seen a single brain which did not exhibit obvious marks of disease," and he thinks "the effect of medical treatment completely corroborates these views" (*L* 99). In a passage to which Shepherd alludes, he insists that "arguments,

---

[19] Shepherd distinguishes between "sensations" and "perceptions." For discussion of Shepherd's usage of these terms, see chapter 5 of this *Guide*.

106 MARY SHEPHERD

syllogisms, discourses, sermons, have never yet restored any patient" (*L* 99, quoted at *ERCE* 172). But, replies Shepherd, even a materialist should acknowledge that physical ailments, including those of the brain, can be improved by friendship, social interaction, beauty, love, "the calm discussions of reason," and "scenes that please the imagination, or enchant the sense" (*ERCE* 172). And although she posits an immaterial soul, she holds that *both* soul and brain are among the causes of thought. They work together simultaneously, and so affecting *either one* will bring about changes in thinking and sensing (*ERCE* 172). Thus, Shepherd makes the case that metaphysics and physiology can each benefit from the influence of the other (*ERCE* 173). Religion, too, will benefit, because a proper appreciation of the roles of mind *and* body in thought would help people realize that an immortal afterlife is not due to intrinsic features of the soul but to the generosity of God (*ERCE* 174–75).[20]

Lawrence's Alleged Inconsistencies about the Nature of Life

In *ERCE* chapter 5, section 8, Shepherd moves from Lawrence's account of sentience to his account of life, a topic to which the entirety of *ERCE* chapter 6 is devoted. As she observes, "the *nature of life* is become a question of great interest" (*ERCE* 175). Just six years before, Mary Shelley had published *Frankenstein*, in which Dr. Frankenstein sought and found "the cause of generation and life" and became "capable of bestowing animation upon lifeless matter."[21] As we saw above, Lawrence had publicly disputed John Abernethy's theory that life must be due to something other than just matter.

---

[20] For further discussion of Shepherd's views on the afterlife, see chapter 9 of this *Guide*.
[21] Shelley, *Frankenstein*, 79.

CAUSATION, SENTIENCE, AND LIFE 107

Shepherd's arguments against Lawrence on the nature of life are primarily *ad hominem*. Quoting six passages drawn from throughout Lawrence's lectures, Shepherd alleges that there are three ways that Lawrence contradicts himself. She does not explain why she thinks the passages are contradictory, and it is not clear that her criticisms are always fair.

First, Shepherd maintains that Lawrence contradicts himself when he says both that life depends on "organization"[22] just as light depends on the sun (see *L* 6 and 81) and that life cannot be said to be a property of an organized body (*ERCE* 179; see *L* 70–71). At first glance, it is hard to see that there is a contradiction here. After all, it seems one thing x can *depend on* another object y, in the sense that y is a necessary condition for the existence of x, without x being a *property, or quality,* of y. For example, the existence of a child requires the existence of its parent, yet we would not say that a child is a quality or property of the parent. However, according to Shepherd's causal theory, the effects of a mixture of causes *are* actually qualities or properties of that mixture, and the qualities or properties of a thing are the effects of it under various causal conditions. So when Lawrence says that life depends on an organized body just as light depends on the sun, Shepherd reads him as saying that life is an *effect* of an organized body, just as light is an effect of the sun. And when Lawrence denies that life is a *property* of an organized body, she reads him as denying what he had just asserted, that life is an *effect* of the organized body. In his defense, Lawrence might deny that a property of a thing should be understood as an effect of that thing.

Shepherd's second charge of contradiction is highly compressed and not entirely clear. She argues:

It is a second contradiction to say, that life is *dependent as a function*, upon an animated body; when the body could not be

---

[22] "Organization" was a nineteenth-century term for an organism or body.

108 MARY SHEPHERD

animated without it; or that as *"assembled functions,"* it is "dependent on organization, as light is dependent on the sun." When life is so far from consisting in "the *assembled functions,"* that none of the functions can take place without life. (*ERCE* 179)

Shepherd is actually attacking a straw man; Lawrence wrote that life depends on an "animal" body, not an "animated" body (*L* 53). However, her point would remain the same even if she had quoted him accurately: the assembled functions of a body must *depend* on a cause—that is, upon life—and so Lawrence should not say that those functions *are* life. But it does not seem apt to claim, as Shepherd seems to be claiming, that this is a contradiction within Lawrence's own views; if anything, his claim is a contradiction with *her* views.

In Shepherd's third allegation of a contradiction in Lawrence's views, she cites Lawrence's claim that "the primary or elementary animal structures are endued with vital properties; their combinations compose the animal organs, in which, by means of the vital properties of the component elementary structures, the animal functions are carried on" (*L* 71). Presumably, by "primary or elementary animal structures" Lawrence means nerves and muscles, which he elsewhere characterizes as having "vital processes." Shepherd also cites his claims that in living beings, "their body is composed of solids and fluids" and that "the component elements, of which nitrogen is a principal one, united in numbers of three, four, or more, easily pass into new combinations; and are, for the most part, readily convertible into fluids or gas" (*L* 80). Her objection is that the first passage (about nerves and muscles having vital properties) is inconsistent with the second (the claim that nerves and muscles can be reduced to "the inorganic matters of nitrogen and gas") (*ERCE* 180).

Again, the inconsistency alleged by Shepherd is not obvious. Lawrence hesitated to claim that vital processes can be explained in chemical terms—but only because he thought the chemistry

CAUSATION, SENTIENCE, AND LIFE   109

involved would be beyond our ability to understand and explain, not because he thought chemistry was *in principle* unable to explain vitality. So Lawrence, as well as other immanentists, would not have seen a contradiction in claiming that vitality can be reduced to inorganic matter, and he might in turn have accused Shepherd of begging the question in claiming that it could not be done.

But what Shepherd might mean is this: if the vital processes of living entities could be *completely* reduced to chemical processes such as those of "nitrogen and gas," then it would follow that other, non-living entities that are also fully explainable in chemical processes are ultimately no different from entities that we characterize as living. In other words, a completely *chemical* explanation of life would eliminate the very distinction between living and non-living organisms, a distinction that Lawrence claimed to accept. The contradiction, in other words, would be between Lawrence's commitment to a distinction between living and non-living organisms and what Shepherd sees as a consequence of the materialist suggestion that life can be fully reduced to chemical processes, which is that there is really no distinction between the living and the non-living.

Shepherd does note one point on which she agrees with Lawrence. She identifies as Lawrence's "only clear and valuable definition" of life his view that "life is a constant internal motion, which enables a body to assimilate new and separate old particles, and prevents it from yielding to the chemical affinities of the surrounding elements" (*ERCE* 181; see also 183).[23] Shepherd praises this definition for being both comprehensive (inclusive of plants as well as animals) and exclusive (not applicable to anything that we would not want to say is alive). According to her own "notion of life," the biblical description of God's breathing life into man can be read as God "giving [the organs] that internal vigour and motion,

---

[23] Shepherd paraphrases Lawrence (*L* 81) but does not change his meaning.

110 MARY SHEPHERD

capable of enabling them to act afterwards for themselves, upon the objects which surrounded them" (*ERCE* 183).

Yet Shepherd's agreement with Lawrence is on a relatively superficial point. She agrees with him that all and only living entities have a certain kind of motion such that they can, on their own, assimilate new particles and separate old particles and not "yield to the chemical affinities of the surrounding elements"—that is, they can persist in their environment, assuming conditions are more or less normal, although of course every living entity dies at some point. Yet Lawrence's definition of life is, to use Shepherd's terminology, merely a description of the *qualities* of living entities. Qualities are effects that require causes, yet Lawrence's definition says nothing about what *causes* living entities to have such motions. Another way to put this is to say that she agrees with Lawrence's *nominal* definition of 'life': she agrees that entities we describe as 'living' have been observed to have certain characteristic motions not found in non-living entities. But this does not undermine her primary objection to Lawrence, that he has failed to offer a *real* definition of life understood as the productive factor that explains *why* an entity has the qualities of assimilating new particles, separating old particles, and not succumbing to the environment. Just as Lawrence's "most dangerous error" regarding sentience was his insistence that we need not seek a *cause* of sentience (*ERCE* 167), so also the root of his mistakes regarding life is "his not supposing that a real efficient cause is necessary to be assigned for life" (*ERCE* 175). And another error that Shepherd identifies in Lawrence's text, that "life must presuppose organization" (*ERCE* 181; see *L* 81), derives from this same mistake: he thinks life is a quality or *effect* of an organized body, instead of realizing that life is one of the *causes* of organized bodies existing, for "without life in the parents, the organs could not have been formed" (*ERCE* 182).

Even if Shepherd's various *ad hominem* objections to Lawrence are not entirely successful, there is a sense in which it wouldn't matter; the failure of one or more of these particular arguments

CAUSATION, SENTIENCE, AND LIFE 111

does not affect the crux of her objection to Lawrence, his "dangerous" mistake of refusing to consider the cause of being alive. And this mistake is due to his Humean conception of causation. As Shepherd puts it toward the end of this chapter, "as long as the notions of Mr. Hume shall prevail, inquiries of this nature shall be instituted in vain" (*ERCE* 186).

Shepherd's Theory of Life

Shepherd has made it clear that a "real efficient cause" (*ERCE* 175) must mix with an organized body to bring about the effect of being alive, just as a separate cause (mind, a capacity to sense) must mix with a living body endowed with nerves to bring about sentience. But what *sort of thing* is this cause that produces the effect of being alive, of having certain characteristic motions whereby a physical body can assimilate new particles and separate old particles and persist in existing (for a time, anyway) even in the face of potentially destructive forces in its environment? Shepherd gives some hints in *ERCE* chapter 6, section 3. She compares life to a spark that starts a fire burning, which, in turn, can ignite further objects and set them aflame:

> Thus combustible matters may be heaped upon each other, yet neither warmth or light succeed; but let an "extra cause" kindle the pile, then the flame may be kept alive for ever, by the constant addition of such substances.—In like manner life as we find it, as a perpetual flame, must be kept up and transmitted, whilst the proper objects for its support are administered: but for its original *Cause* we must go back, until some extraneous power is referred to as its first parent. (*ERCE* 182)

Fire is both a cause and an effect: an initial spark of fire is needed to set a pile of combustible materials burning, to produce fire as

112 MARY SHEPHERD

an effect, which can then cause something else to burn. Thus, fire can be passed from one entity to another, retaining a causal connection with an original source. Shepherd suggests that life is like this: the *state* or *quality* of being alive is passed from parents to offspring, and then the living offspring can *cause* life in the next generation. As she puts it, life is "continually propagated through the species" (*ERCE* 183). But, like fire, there must have been some initial, exogenous power that set the causal chain in motion. Thus, she writes, "the first cause of life, therefore must be 'extraneous' to any of the bodies among which it is found" (*ERCE* 184). This puts Shepherd squarely in the camp of transcendentalists such as John Abernethy: whatever is responsible for an entity being alive (that is, having certain characteristic motions such that it can self-regulate its particles and avoid succumbing to the environment) must be some additional factor above and beyond the matter and structure of the entity. There must be some additional causal power that is able to produce the effect (the quality) of being alive.

Still, Shepherd says almost nothing about what this power is. As we saw above, Shepherd thinks that sentience also requires a cause, which is the soul or mind. In *EPEU*, Shepherd characterizes mind as the "sentient principle and capacity" (*EPEU* 217) that must be "mixed" with already-living nerves (as well as the sense-organs, brain, and external objects) in order for sensory perception to occur.[24] Mind is *"the power of thought and feeling"* (*EPEU* 40), a cause (*EPEU* 155) that, in conjunction with other causes, produces specific conscious sensations. Shepherd likely conceives of life analogously, as a general capacity or power that, when combined with other factors, causes a body to have specific types of environment-resisting motions. An entity with the quality of being alive can then, under the right conditions, produce another entity with that quality: that is, the quality of being alive can serve as a *cause* of another being having that quality. Ultimately, Shepherd traces both

---

[24] For further discussion of Shepherd's account of mind, see chapter 8 of this *Guide*.

CAUSATION, SENTIENCE, AND LIFE 113

life and sentience—indeed, all existing beings, with all their qualities and capacities—back to the divine cause, God (*ERCE* 185). As she puts it in *EPEU*, "the wide universe, with all its gradations of wonderful beings, with all its powers of life and heat, and motion, must have come out from him according to the laws with which they were endowed" (*EPEU* 97).

To say that the cause of being alive is a capacity that, under the right conditions, brings about the effect of being alive may be a disappointment. It seems reminiscent of Molière's satire of Aristotelian philosophers in his 1673 play *The Imaginary Invalid*; when asked why opium makes people sleepy, the Aristotelian philosopher says that it possesses a "*vertus dormitiva*," a "dormitive virtue."[25] But this is circular; to say that the cause of being sleepy is simply the power of producing sleepiness is to explain the cause in terms of the effect. Likewise, on the interpretation offered above, Shepherd explains the cause of being alive in terms of a power of making an entity be alive. But this seems to be no explanation at all.

However, such an explanation is perhaps just what we should expect from a causal theory in which effects are "contained in" their causes. If the effect were completely different from the cause, then cause and effect would be separable, and thus not necessarily connected—and thus not really cause and effect at all, by Shepherd's lights. Suppose we suggest that the cause of the special kind of motion in an organism that constitutes being alive is the motion of some *other* physical entity that preceded it; suppose, for example, we suggest that an embryo is alive because of the precedent motions of sperm and egg. According to Shepherd's account of causation, this suggestion would amount simply to identifying a contingent state of affairs that preceded the existence of the living embryo. To correctly identify the cause of that special kind of motion in an organism that constitutes being alive would be to identify the *various* factors that must combine for that motion to exist,

---

[25] Molière, *Imaginary Invalid*, 134.

114   MARY SHEPHERD

and one such factor is the capacity for such motion to be produced. Such a capacity is *not*, as Molière's satire would have it, the only required factor. But it does seem reasonable for Shepherd to insist that the existence of a quality requires, among other things, a capacity or power for that quality to exist.

In *ERCE* chapter 6, section 4, Shepherd contrasts her theory of causation with Hume's and with other "received doctrine[s] upon the relation of cause and effect" (*ERCE* 196). Other theories inhibit the advancement of science by insisting that causal action must precede an effect, that a single object can be a cause, or (in Berkeley's case) that only spirits can be causes (*ERCE* 186–87). She summarizes her own positive doctrine of causation in eight propositions (*ERCE* 187–89) and concludes by noting that "every science" depends on "the necessary connexion of Cause and Effect, and our knowledge of it, in opposition to mere *fancy* or *custom*" (*ERCE* 192). Mere observation of correlations should not be taken as evidence of necessary connections (*ERCE* 192). Thus, Shepherd's critique of Lawrence stands as a sort of cautionary tale, an example of how misconceptions of something as fundamental as the nature of causation can ramify into errors that infect "scientific research, practical knowledge, and of belief in a creating and presiding Deity" (*ERCE* 194).

Suggestions for Further Reading

- Discussions of the debate between Lawrence and Abernethy can be found in Owsei Temkin, "Basic Science, Medicine, and the Romantic Era."
- For a broad-brush history of neuroscientific concepts leading up to the early nineteenth century, see C. U. M. Smith, "Brain and Mind in the 'Long' Eighteenth Century."

5

Sensing and Reasoning

Introduction

Shepherd's goal in *Essays on the Perception of an External Universe* is, as the title suggests, to show how each of us can know with certainty that there is an independent, continuously existing world of external objects. One of her main targets here is George Berkeley, who argued that there are only minds and ideas in those minds; the external world of spatially extended objects like flowers, mountains, and tables is a world of *ideas*, not a world of matter that could exist independently of a mind. Nonetheless, Berkeley thought objects like trees, mountains, and tables are no less real for being ideas that depend on the existence of a thinking mind; we can still smell a flower, hike a mountain, or put an object on a table.[1] In contrast to Berkeley, Shepherd argues that we can know, through reason, that there is a continually existing external world of objects that does *not* depend on perceivers. This independent, external world, according to Shepherd, is the cause of our sensations of sensible qualities. The first, long essay in the book, "An Essay on the Academical or Sceptical Philosophy," focuses on this argument.[2]

Since Shepherd's argument turns on claims about sensations, it is important to understand what she means by 'sensation,' as well as related terms like 'perception' and 'idea.' These terms will

---

[1] Berkeley makes these arguments in *A Treatise Concerning the Principles of Human Knowledge* (1710) and *Three Dialogues between Hylas and Philonous* (1713). While Shepherd does mention the *Dialogues* in passing (*EPEU* 81), her quotations are all from the *Principles*.

[2] The argument itself will be examined in chapter 6 of this *Guide*.

Mary Shepherd. Deborah Boyle, Oxford University Press. © Oxford University Press 2023.
DOI: 10.1093/oso/9780190090326.003.0005

116 MARY SHEPHERD

be explained in the next section, followed by discussions of her account of sense perception and her view that motion is a kind of sense. The chapter then turns to Shepherd's accounts of other mental faculties: memory and imagination, the will, and, most importantly for Shepherd, reason. Her distinction between demonstrative and probable reasoning will be discussed, followed by a sketch of some suggestions for how to understand Shepherd's account of what she calls "latent" reasoning.

Sensations, Perceptions, Ideas, and Notions

As Shepherd typically uses the term 'sensation,' it means a particular conscious mental state: "in reality, every thought, notion, idea, feeling, and perception, which distinguishes a sentient nature from unconscious existence, may be considered generally as sensation" (*EPEU* 7; see also 135). She does occasionally use 'sensation' to refer to the *capacity* whereby we have sensations; in this case, she refers to it as "sensation in general" (*EPEU* 13, 18), and it is equivalent to the mind or sentience.[3] In the vast majority of cases, however, 'sensation' means a particular effect of the use of the mind.

The category of sensations is very broad for Shepherd. To twenty-first-century readers, 'sensation' may suggest a special connection with sense perception, but it does not have this connotation for Shepherd. To Shepherd's own contemporaries, she notes, the term 'sensation' typically referred to mental states that "are unaccompanied with the notion *of their inhering in an outward object,*" such as pains and pleasures—in contrast to mental states that result from the use of the sense-organs and that purport to be about external objects, which her contemporaries tended to call 'perceptions' (*EPEU* 7).[4] But for Shepherd, 'sensation' means *any* conscious

---

[3] On Shepherd's account of the mind, see chapter 8 in this *Guide*.

[4] Indeed, she maintains that her contemporaries' usage of 'perception' is question-begging, for it implies that there is an external thing that is perceived, when in fact the

SENSING AND REASONING 117

mental state, whether sensory organs were used or not and whether the mental state purports to be about external objects or not.

Shepherd does draw further distinctions *within* the category of sensation (*EPEU* 7). She says that sensations "should be divided *into the sensations of present sensible qualities, sensations of the ideas of memory, sensations of the ideas of imagination, sensations of the ideas of reason, &c.*" (*EPEU* 135–36). "Sensations of sensible qualities" (or, as she usually terms them, "sensible qualities" *simpliciter*[5]) are feelings, just as the passions of joy and sorrow are feelings (LMSM 700): "the sensible qualities have an immediate incontrovertible evidence, from the consciousness of their immediate presence.—They are felt—and the *feelings* are themselves the very existences" (*EPEU* 142). Examples offered by Shepherd include heat, the felt sharpness of a razor, "the noise and coldness of wind," and "my sense of the song of the nightingale" (OLMS 626–27). As we will see in greater detail later, reason is "the *observation of the relation of our simple sensations*" (*EPEU* 19; see also 10). Thus, whenever a thinker compares sensations, draws inferences from sensations, or otherwise relates sensations together, the thinker is using reason—but the thoughts that result from such processes are themselves a variety of sensation.

Shepherd claims that 'perception' has a precise meaning in her system, although in fact she does not always adhere to her stipulation. She says that when she uses the term 'perception,' she means a "'*consciousness of sensation*,' a SENSATION TAKEN NOTICE OF BY THE MIND" (*EPEU* 9). A perception, in other words, is a second-order sensation. According to this account, all perceptions are sensations, but not all sensations are perceptions. That is, every sensation is conscious, but not every sensation is such that the thinker has explicitly noted that they are conscious of it. However, Shepherd does

---

existence of external things is a *conclusion* for which Shepherd wishes to argue, rather than to imply through her terminology (*EPEU* 7–8).

[5] Shepherd says that "the sensations of qualities" are "usually termed sensible qualities" (*EPEU* 25), and the latter is her preferred phrase.

118 MARY SHEPHERD

occasionally use 'perception' in a looser sense, as when she writes that the "*general* notion" of perception "*includes every species of consciousness whatever*" (*EPEU* 203; see also 39). Sometimes, then, 'perception' is interchangeable with 'sensation,' meaning a particular mental state.

Shepherd also specifies a technical sense of 'idea.' Indeed, she devotes all of EASP chapter 6 to elucidating her use of this term. For Locke, an idea is "*whatever it is which the mind can be employed about in thinking*" (*ECHU* 1.2.8). For Shepherd, ideas are, like sensible qualities, a sub-type or species of sensation (*EPEU* 133). But they are importantly different from sensible qualities. Shepherd objects that Berkeley's usage of the term 'idea' is ambiguous, sometimes meaning "the consciousness of the sensible qualities, which arise from the use of the organs of sense" and sometimes meaning "the conclusions of the understanding, after surveying the various relations and circumstances, attendant on these sensible qualities" (*EPEU* 134–35). Shepherd's precise, technical sense of 'idea' corresponds to Berkeley's second sense, although she adds the requirement that an idea is a specific kind of sensation, a "conclusion from reasoning" (*EPEU* 59)—and not just any reasoning, but, specifically, reasoning that shows that there must be a cause of sense perceptions: "I use the word *idea*, as signifying a distinct class of sensations, being the result of that reasoning or observation which shows that there must needs be an existence when we cannot perceive it" (*EPEU* 133–34). In other words, when we *infer* the existence of something, we have an *idea* rather than a *sensation* of that thing (although to have the idea is itself to have a sensation, a sensation of the idea). We do not have *sensations* of the external world,[6] but we do (through inference) have *ideas* that are about the external world (*EPEU* 134), and in having these ideas we are having

---

[6] In her 1832 essay, Shepherd writes that "external perception is a contradictory term—all perception, whether of ideas, of bodies, or facts, the passions of others, &c., all are in a mind, which is in a state of feeling at the moment of perception" (LMSM 700).

SENSING AND REASONING 119

sensations. For example, Shepherd says we do not have sensations of distance, but we do have an *idea* of distance; we infer that such a thing as distance occurs (*EPEU* 59). Having the inferred idea of distance is itself a case of having a sensation of the idea of the distance.

However, Shepherd's own usage is sometimes ambiguous, as she herself acknowledges, for she says that when she is not using 'idea' in her technical sense, she is using it "in a popular manner signifying notion or object of thought, &c" (*EPEU* 134). In this looser sense, 'idea' is equivalent to 'sensation,' which, as we have seen, can include sensations of various sorts.

The word 'understanding' is linked with Shepherd's technical sense of 'idea.' The understanding is the mental capacity that produces ideas (*EPEU* 96, 108, 168); it is an ability to draw conclusions from other sensations (*EPEU* 32, 56, 73, 181).

The term 'notion' appears throughout Shepherd's writings, but she never explicitly defines it. In general, she uses this term to characterize an idea that is inferred through reason, in contrast to sensible qualities: she refers to notions of existence (*EPEU* 162–63), extension (*EPEU* 165), "*unperceived* exteriority" (*EPEU* 175), external objects (*EPEU* 207), and time (*EPEU* 288). But the category of 'notion' seems to be a mixed bag. Sometimes she suggests that notions are concepts, as she refers to "the general notion of perception; *which general* notion *includes every species of consciousness whatever*" (*EPEU* 203), and she suggests that the "ancients," such as Aristotle, "*invented* the notion of sensible species" (*EPEU* 307), a concept she clearly thinks was mistaken. At one point she suggests that the causal principles themselves are notions, since she says that we infer the existence of the external world from "some notions previously in the mind, being mixed with each sensation as it arises" (*EPEU* 169; see also 373). Evidently, then, notions can be either propositions or concepts.

By the time Shepherd was working out her philosophical system, it was a philosophical commonplace to distinguish between primary and secondary qualities, although different philosophers

120 MARY SHEPHERD

understood the distinction differently.[7] Locke's way of drawing the distinction was especially influential on the philosophers to whom Shepherd was responding, Berkeley and Reid.[8] For Locke, both primary and secondary qualities of bodies are powers to produce ideas in perceivers (*ECHU* 2.8.8). *Primary* qualities are "inseparable" from bodies, in the sense that every physical body possesses powers to produce ideas of "solidity, extension, figure, and mobility" (*ECHU* 2.8.9). Bodies have these powers because they actually *are* solid, extended, shaped, and in motion (*ECHU* 2.8.17); according to Locke's mechanistic account of sensory perception, these features of bodies impact our sense-organs and brains through the "impulse" of "insensible particles" (*ECHU* 2.8.11–12), resulting in "ideas of primary qualities" that resemble and thus represent the actual size, shape, motion, and so on of the physical objects (*ECHU* 2.8.15). In contrast, *secondary* qualities are powers of a physical body to produce ideas of colors, tastes, sounds, smells, and so on in us; these powers are derived from an object's primary qualities (*ECHU* 2.8.10). Locke also calls these powers "*sensible qualities*" (*ECHU* 2.8.23). However, our ideas of these secondary qualities do not resemble anything in the physical objects themselves:

> There is nothing like our ideas [of secondary qualities] existing in the bodies themselves. They are, in the bodies we denominate from them, only a power to produce those sensations in us; and what is sweet, blue, or warm in idea is but the certain bulk, figure, and motion of the insensible parts, in the bodies themselves, which we call so. (*ECHU* 2.8.15)

---

[7] For essays on the primary/secondary quality distinction in the history of Western philosophy, see Nolan, ed., *Primary and Secondary Qualities: The Historical and Ongoing Debate.*

[8] For discussion of how Berkeley and Reid interpreted (and perhaps misinterpreted) Locke's account, see Wilson, "Primary and Secondary Qualities."

SENSING AND REASONING   121

Locke also identifies "a third sort" of quality, the powers in objects to produce changes in other objects, such as the power of fire to melt wax, even when this is not perceived by us (*ECHU* 2.8.10).

As we have seen, Shepherd also uses the terminology of 'qualities,' but she draws different distinctions.[9] Qualities comprising external objects are causal powers, like Locke's primary and secondary qualities (powers to produce ideas in us) and his "third sort" (powers to produce changes in other objects). Internal objects are bundles of "sensible qualities," and, for Shepherd, "sensible qualities" are what Locke calls "ideas of primary qualities" and "ideas of secondary qualities." For Shepherd, sensible qualities, such as our sensations of "blue or red, sweet or sour, hard or soft, beautiful or ugly, warm or cold, loud or low" (*EPEU* 135), are in the mind; they "arise from the use of the organs of sense" and other external objects (*EPEU* 56). And, as we will see in the next chapter, Shepherd thinks there is no basis for a distinction between primary and secondary sensible qualities (*EPEU* 180).

Sensory Perception

Shepherd's account of sensory perception depends on her arguments for the existence of the external world, to which we will turn in the next chapter of this *Guide*. However, we can sketch the basic picture here. According to Shepherd, we get particular sensations of sensible qualities when our sense-organs and mind (what she calls our "capacity for sensation in general" [*EPEU* 18]) interact with an external, independent, continually existing object (*EPEU* 71–72). This combination of factors results in a particular

---

[9] On Shepherd's account of internal and external qualities, see chapter 3 of this *Guide*.

122　MARY SHEPHERD

sensation of some sensible quality, such as a sensation of cold or sweetness, the scent of a rose, a shade of green, and so on. These sensible qualities exist only in the mind, although humans have a natural tendency to blend their sensations of the sensible qualities with their ideas of the external causes of those sensible qualities, and thus to think that objects out there in the external world have the very same qualities that we sense—that the bread in itself is sweet and white, for example, when actually the sweetness and whiteness exist only in the mind, as sensible qualities (*EPEU* 127–28).

Again, it is important to note that Shepherd does not think we *sense* the external objects. We do sense our *idea* of the external objects, but this idea is the result of reasoning (to be examined in chapter 6 of this *Guide*); thus, "the perception of external, continually existing, independent objects, is an affair of the understanding" (*EPEU* 168–69).

In sensory perception, Shepherd says that the sense-organs and mind (both being understood as capacities) undergo no changes in this process (*EPEU* 27, 48), and yet we have constantly changing sense perceptions. Since, by a corollary to the Causal Likeness Principle (CLP), different effects require different causes (*EPEU* 169), and the mind and sense-organs remain the same no matter what sensible qualities we have, the only factor that could cause changes in our sense perceptions is the external world itself. Thus, changes in our sense perceptions show us that we are perceiving different external objects. For example, when I glance at a tree and have one set of sense perceptions, then glance at a house and have a different set, the variety shows that I am perceiving objects that themselves are constituted by different bundles of causal powers. However, although we can know that our sensory perceptions are caused by external objects, and we can know that there must be a variety of such objects to explain the variety among our sensory perceptions, the true nature of these external objects is unknown.

SENSING AND REASONING 123

Motion as a Sense

Shepherd's argument for the continuous, independent existence of external objects depends primarily upon her appeal to sensations received via the five senses. Yet throughout *EPEU*, she includes *motion* when she mentions the senses.[10] Motion is "a sort of sense" (*EPEU* 104), and the "power of motion" is "a sixth organ of sense" (*EPEU* 230). What does she mean by this?

Many physiologists today recognize more than just the five senses of sight, hearing, smell, touch, and taste. For example, some argue that proprioception (awareness of the position of the parts of one's body) and equilibrioception (one's awareness of being in motion) should be considered as kinds of senses.[11] Disorders in the vestibular system, which is responsible for proprioception and equilibrioception, can give rise to illusions that one is moving.[12] It could be said, then, that the vestibular system is the sensory system that gives rise to sensations of movement, just as the auditory system gives rise to sensations of sound. In Shepherd's day, however, the vestibular system was not yet understood,[13] so this is not what she was referring to. In fact, while Shepherd often writes of "the organs of sense and motion" (*EPEU* 27, 74, 102), as if there were some specific organ that helps produce the sensation of motion, she never specifies what that might be. Her reference to the "power of motion" as a "method of overcoming distance, and of becoming acquainted with tangible extension" (*EPEU* 230) suggests that it might be the whole body that is the relevant organ in this case.

Shepherd argues that from our sensations we can infer the existence of continually existing external objects; although we do not directly sense these objects, we know of their existence through

---

[10] For passages where she writes of the senses *and* motion, see *EPEU* 27, 40, 41, 77, 88, 89, 102, 103, 176, 181, and 188.

[11] See Macpherson, "Introduction: Individuating the Senses," 16–18.

[12] Macpherson, "Introduction: Individuating the Senses," 17.

[13] See Wiest, "The Origins of Vestibular Science."

124　MARY SHEPHERD

reasoning. Just as our sensations of colors and sounds must have an external source, so too must our sensations of being in motion. This external cause of the motion of our bodies (or, indeed, of the motion of any external body) is, like the external causes of all our perceptions, not something we directly sense; in this unperceived state, it is a "capacity or quality of being, in relation to those various [external] objects" (*EPEU* 175). But it is a mistake to think that "the motion which we feel, is the *real motion*" (LMSM 701).

Among the causes of this sensation is extended space, what Shepherd also calls "outwardness" or "distance"; we could not move if there were no outward space in which to do so. As she puts it,

> Outward existence, is the perception of a *continued independent existence in relation to motion, from our own minds taken as a centre whence we set out*; the which motion is a sort of sense, whose sensible quality merely, could not *immediately* yield the notion of *unperceived* exteriority, unless mixed with the powers of the understanding, which refer its *sensible quality* to an *unperceived cause*. (*EPEU* 174–75)

Thus, if we think of vision as the capacity of an eye to have visual sensations, and thereby to detect that unperceived external objects exist, we can characterize the movement of one's own body as a capacity to feel a sensation of motion, and thereby detect *outwardness* and *distance*.

Memory and Imagination

As we have seen, Shepherd rejects explaining our knowledge of the uniformity of nature in terms of the association of ideas; instead, she says we can be sure that nature will continue as it has because we can know the CLP, which ensures that similar causes will always have similar effects. Yet Shepherd does not reject associationism altogether. She concedes that "custom or an association of ideas, arising from those habits which infix ideas in the mind, is the foundation of all memory" (*ERCE* 110), and she suggests that our ability to associate ideas was "ordained" by God "for practical purposes" (*EPEU* 127). Thus, while my *certainty* that my rose bush will bloom again in the spring (assuming that other causal factors such as the climate, soil quality, and so on remain roughly the same) is due to the CLP, my *thought* of the rose bush blooming again involves a memory that it did so before, and that memory involves an association of thoughts of the spring with thoughts of the blooming rose bush. Since I saw the rose bush blooming several times over the duration of the spring, the repetition of those thoughts has served to "infix" the two ideas together in my mind. Presumably, then, Shepherd would say that events we have experienced more often are more fixed in the memory than those that happened just once.

If this were all Shepherd had to say about memory, it would clearly be an inadequate account. Suppose I plant a rose bush that never blooms, yet each day in the spring I wistfully *imagine* it blooming. Over time, this association of the ideas of springtime and the blooming rose bush might become as habitual as if I really remembered it happening. Shepherd thus needs a way to distinguish memories from mere imagination. Hume had drawn the distinction in terms of the "superior force and vivacity" of remembered ideas (*T* 1.3.5.3). Insisting that there is no difference in the *content* of memory versus a merely imagined idea of the same thing, he says that to remember is to have ideas that are "more strong and *lively*" than one would have when simply imagining the same thing (*T* 1.3.5.5; see also *EHU* 5.12). Shepherd clearly has Hume in mind when she says this kind of account is inadequate: "the objects of memory and imagination differ as to the *nature of their* COMPONENT PARTS, and not *merely* as to the comparatively higher *vivacity* of those of imagination" (*EPEU* 139–40).

Instead, Shepherd distinguishes between imagined thoughts and remembered thoughts by emphasizing that the latter are

126 MARY SHEPHERD

accompanied by a special kind of idea. Recall that internal objects are bundles of sensible qualities, with internal *perceived* objects including as part of that bundle the idea of being caused by an external object (*EPEU* 197–98). Internal *remembered* objects—or, more simply, memories—are bundles of sensible qualities accompanied by the idea that the sensations *were* caused by external objects that are no longer present:

> *Objects of memory* are compounded of the fainter *sensations* of sensible qualities, mixed with the *idea* that the causes of the original impressions are removed; (the which *idea* is the result either of observation or reasoning;) these again are united with the perception of the lapse of time, or of our own continuous existence going on between the original moment of the impressions, and the existence of the PRESENT faint sensible qualities. Therefore the *objects* of memory are, *masses of sensible qualities plus* the *idea* of past time, *plus* the *idea* of having been caused by causes now removed. (*EPEU* 137)

In contrast, "*ideas of imagination* are faint images of sensible qualities *unmixed with any notions concerning time*; whose causes are considered as at present removed from their operation on the senses; and variously compounded by the influence of fancy, or rendered more or less *vivacious* by its power" (*EPEU* 139).

The images we have in dreams also count for Shepherd as being objects of the imagination (*EPEU* 30). Shepherd characterizes the bundles of sensible qualities comprising dreamt-of objects in negative terms: a dreamt-of object is a bundle of sensible qualities that is not combined with an idea of the thinker's location. As she puts it, the sensations in a dream "are combined in the same forms in which they appear in a waking hour," and yet "on account of our ignorance of remaining in the same place during the time of the dream, the *relation of place* is wanting to enable us to correct the false inferences from these vivacious imaginations, and view them in their true character" (*EPEU* 29).

In sum, the images in our waking imaginations are "unmixed" with the idea of being caused by an external object as well as with the idea of *time* characteristic of memories, and the images in our dreams are unmixed with the idea of being caused by an external object as well as with the idea of the thinker's *location* that would (if that idea were present) indicate that we are dreaming.[14]

Will

We have seen how Shepherd understands the mental faculties of sensing, remembering, imagining, and reasoning. Another mental faculty we might expect her to discuss is the will. Yet Shepherd has surprisingly little to say about this, only mentioning will or volition at four points in all her published writings. These passages suggest that Shepherd was a compatibilist about freedom. That is, she does not seem to have believed in the existence of the kind of freedom envisioned by incompatibilist libertarians such that, given a choice between two alternatives, one could choose otherwise than one actually does. Rather, human choices and decisions are thoughts that are the necessary effects of other factors, themselves the necessary effects of other factors, and so on. She does, however, hint that we can have greater or lesser degrees of autonomy in the determinations of our choices.

Shepherd does not discuss human will or volition anywhere in *ERCE*.[15] Her first mention of it in *EPEU* is in a discussion of Berkeley's account of the mind and ideas, where she rejects his claim that the mind is active insofar as it can think of various ideas

---

[14] For further discussion of dreams and Shepherd's criteria for distinguishing real from unreal objects, see chapter 7 of this *Guide*.

[15] She does make a passing reference to "the will and power of the Deity" (*ERCE* 72).

128 MARY SHEPHERD

simply by willing.[16] Shepherd asks a rhetorical question: "how can the will at pleasure, call upon an idea, when before it begins to call, it must know what it wishes to call, and so must have consciousness of the idea in question" (*EPEU* 216)? But even if this makes clear that Shepherd thinks the will cannot choose what ideas the mind thinks of, it tells us little about what she thinks the will is.

Her second and more revealing comment on the will occurs in a discussion of how "the same external causes would yield the same internal sensation to each mind, if the varieties were not in the individuals" (*EPEU* 264). Under ideal conditions, Shepherd holds that any given object would affect all perceivers in the same way: an external object that includes a causal power to produce a sensation of green when a perceiver with healthy eyes interacts with that object under certain lighting conditions should produce that sensation in all such perceivers. But, of course, people do not all perceive objects in the same way; a person with a cold will taste and smell things differently than they do when healthy, and a person with more acute hearing will have aural sensations that others don't experience. Shepherd recognizes such differences, arguing that these must derive from differences in the perceivers' bodily constitutions (*EPEU* 265).[17] Possessed of different sensory perceptions to form the starting points of their reasoning, people may end up holding different opinions on a variety of topics. Some features of our bodily "arrangement" are "stamped by the Deity," and there is often little we can do to change that; for example, a color-blind person will naturally have different visual sensations than someone who is not color-blind. However, Shepherd notes that our sensory perceptions

[16] Berkeley writes, "I find I can excite ideas in my mind at pleasure, and vary and shift the scene as oft as I think fit. It is no more than willing, and straightway this or that idea arises in my fancy" (*PHK* 1.28).

[17] Shepherd's reasoning for this view is as follows. "Sentient capacities seem . . . [to be] the result of an uniform, permanent power in nature" (*EPEU* 265); that is, the mind, the power of sensation, does not vary from person to person. If two perceivers interacting with the same external object under the same conditions have different sensations, the cause of this difference must be something other than the external object or mind, and the only other candidate is the perceiver's "organization" or bodily structure (*EPEU* 265).

SENSING AND REASONING 129

are also affected by factors over which we have some control: "food, medicine, and climate; the circulation of the blood, the passions, the habits of education, and the notions of individuals" (*EPEU* 265). This fact has potentially important consequences: it "may enable physiologists and physicians, moralists and divines, parents and instructors, better to observe, and more wisely to act than they do, with respect to the health, the opinions, and the practices of those under their care" (*EPEU* 264). In other words, society could do a better job of improving people's characters if we paid attention to "food, medicine, and climate; the circulation of the blood, the passions, the habits of education, and the notions of individuals (*EPEU* 265)—that is, if we ensured people had better health and education.

Interestingly, Shepherd also draws a conclusion about freedom of the will. She writes,

> They are wrong, therefore, who, ignorantly taking no notice of these things, expect the *human will*, to be in all circumstances equal to selfcommand. Men make excuse for their actions in dreams and insanity, saying, the essences of things are then different; but never consider, that every degree and variety of their state of mind depends upon analogous laws and causes, which wisdom acting in time might alter with advantage, but which afterwards may lie beyond any human power to ameliorate. (*EPEU* 265)

Two points are worth noting. First, Shepherd says that it is wrong to think people can command their own actions "in all circumstances." This suggests that she thinks there are some cases where we can command our own actions. But, second, if every mental state depends on "laws and causes," then it seems we do not have the kind of freedom envisioned by incompatibilist libertarians; human decisions are necessarily connected with the beliefs, desires, other mental states (and other non-mental factors) which give rise to

130 MARY SHEPHERD

those decisions, and so it seems that, for Shepherd, determinism is true. In writing of "self-command," then, Shepherd means something more like the compatibilist notion of "autonomy": a free action is one which is brought about by internal factors (one's own beliefs and values, for example) rather than external factors (such as being physically compelled or, perhaps, coerced).

The third relevant passage is Shepherd's claim that "*a final cause is the efficient cause that determines the will*; and WHICH WILL, *is the efficient cause that determines the direction of motion upon matter in any given case*" (*EPEU* 360; see also 366 and 404–5). Traditionally, a final cause was understood as the goal or purpose for which one acts. Shepherd collapses that conception of cause into her conception of an efficient cause, the factor that actually produces the effect.[18] Significantly, Shepherd claims not just that the will determines one's action (which of course a libertarian would grant) but that the will is determined (something a libertarian would deny).

The fourth and final passage in which Shepherd discusses the will occurs in "Lady Mary Shepherd's Metaphysics": "Of the influence of the will, indeed, we have immediate consciousness. We feel that it is the cause for the beginning of the change called motion" (LMSM 702). Her example is of seeing a garden of flowers and deciding to walk in it:

What is perceived, are changes of sensations and ideas—are effects; the correspondent causes which determine them are all external, except one, and that is, the beginning of the change from the state of rest in which are those external things, by the impulse with which the will effects the first change of their relative places, and keeps up a succession of similar changes, by the continuance of a similar will. (LMSM 702)

---

[18] Of course, for Shepherd there is never simply one cause; a variety of causal factors interact to bring about the simultaneous effect. Nonetheless, she does say that all the relevant causal factors can be considered as one cause (*EPEU* 360).

This is the closest Shepherd comes to a discussion of autonomy: a recognition that while the vast majority of our sensations come from objects outside us, the will is an internal power, even if it, too, is determined by other internal states.

Reason and Understanding

Shepherd's writings contain many references to both 'reason' and 'understanding,' terms that she seems to use interchangeably. The understanding is the mental "power" (*EPEU* 175) by which we conclude that there are "external, continually existing, independent objects" (*EPEU* 168); similarly, "*Reason* has power to deduce the knowledge of an *universe*" (*EPEU* 270). In *ERCE*, she is concerned to show that it is reason, in contrast to the "fancy" (the imagination), that enables us to know the Causal Principle (CP) and the CLP (*ERCE* 27, 42, 45). Thus, for Shepherd, understanding (or reason) is the mental power by which we draw conclusions from other sensations in the mind; it is the mental power that makes reasoning possible.

Shepherd also makes it clear that reasoning is a *process* (*ERCE* 139 and *EPEU* 176). Her texts suggest that she thought this process has several components. First, it involves "mixing" or compounding two or more sensations (*ERCE* 45–46). Second, it involves "a comparison of our ideas" or sensations (*EPEU* 143 and 239); more specifically, it involves "*drawing out to observation the relations of things as they are included in their juxtaposition to each other*" (*EPEU* 3). That is, when we compare ideas, we note certain relationships between them. Just as Shepherd thinks that the necessary causal relationships among external objects are independent of us as observers, she also thinks the logical relationships among our ideas are independent of us. She writes that these "relations of ideas" continue when unperceived, "ready to be perceived when called upon by the intellect, and independent of its powers

132　MARY SHEPHERD

for either forming, or perceiving them, although contained in the juxtaposition of the simple ideas themselves, (whether perceived or not, or whether called for or not)" (*EPEU* 82). So the first and second steps in reasoning involve putting two (or more) ideas together and observing the relations that obtain among these ideas.

The comparison and observation of relationships produce a new sensation, which Shepherd characterizes as a "superinduced sensation." As she writes in the context of her reasoning that an external world exists,

> We gain the knowledge that there must needs be some *continuous (independent)* existences, beings that are *not* sensations, by the means of *reasoning*, which *reasoning itself* consists of other and *superinduced sensations*, arising from the comparison of the relations, of simple sensations among themselves, thus testifying the existence of the external objects it represents. (*EPEU* 10)

And, finally, the new sensation produced by reasoning is *judged* to be true (*EPEU* 239 and 50–51).

Strikingly, the language Shepherd uses to describe specific pieces of reasoning echoes the language she uses to describe causation. For example, in her discussion of how we know the CLP, she describes reasoning as a *mixing* of ideas that produces a "compound idea" which then "generates" or "gives birth to" a new idea (*ERCE* 45–46). This language of "mixing," "generating," and "giving birth" is precisely the same as that which she uses when characterizing cause and effect. Indeed, in "Lady Mary Shepherd's Metaphysics," Shepherd makes clear that reasoning is indeed a causal process of mixing ideas: "the combination of ideas in a mind can never give birth to any other effects than the ideas of memory, imagination, and reasoning" (LMSM 705).[19]

---

[19] It should be noted that while Shepherd says that "the ideas and sensations of the sensible qualities of things, *can never be the causes of other sensible qualities of things*" (*EPEU* 125), this does *not* rule out sensations of sensible qualities being combined with other

SENSING AND REASONING   133

So Shepherd takes reasoning to involve compounding two or more ideas, observing some relationship that obtains between those ideas, and thereby producing some further, "superinduced" idea that is judged to be true. Since the relationships we observe when we put ideas together in reasoning are *logical* relationships, we can read Shepherd as saying that reasoning involves combining various *premises*, seeing how they relate to each other, and thereby generating a new idea, a judgment—that is, a *conclusion*. So, for Shepherd, the premises in an argument are not just *reasons* for a conclusion that we judge to be true but are *causes* of the judgment that the conclusion is true; the conclusion is the effect that arises *synchronously* with the mixing of the premises in thought. Moreover, just as Shepherd says that the effect of some causal interaction is already present in the mixture of the causes, there is a sense in which the conclusion of a piece of reasoning is *already included* in the mixture of the premises. So, when we infer some idea from other sensations, Shepherd writes that these ideas are "corollaries included in the impressions of sense" (*EPEU* 224; see also 170). In sum, for Shepherd, to reason is to mix premises in thought, premises that are the causal factors (but perhaps not the only causal factors) leading a reasoner to accept a conclusion that is implicitly present in the combination of the premises.

Shepherd says there is a "variety of intellect, through every gradation, from that of an almost absence of it, to the wisest determinations, resulting from the soundest understandings" (*EPEU* 116). Manuel Fasko has noted that Shepherd refers to three main types of intellect: "minds afflicted with 'idiocy'" (*EPEU* 314–15), "inferior understandings" (*EPEU* 287), and "the soundest understandings" (*EPEU* 116).[20] As Fasko puts it, Shepherd thought that a person born an "idiot" "cannot be consciously aware of the

sensations to give rise to sensations that are *not* sensible qualities (namely, to give rise to ideas).

[20] Fasko, "Mary Shepherd's Threefold 'Variety of Intellect' and Its Role in Improving Education," 186.

134   MARY SHEPHERD

relations that obtain between the sensible qualities we perceive by the organs of sense.[21] This means such a person cannot know the CP and thus cannot infer the existence of an external world, so that a mind affected with idiocy is "trapped in a chaos of unconnected sense impressions."[22] This variety of intellect is rare, however; Shepherd thinks the vast majority of humans do have a faculty of understanding that allows them to engage in reasoning, even if some reasoners—children, non-human animals, and "peasants"— are "inferior" to others insofar as they "consider things to be *like*, or the same kind of object, upon too partial an observation of their qualities or methods of formation" (*EPEU* 287).

Demonstrative and Probable Reasoning

As a careful reader of Hume, Shepherd was certainly aware of his distinction between two kinds of reasoning, what he calls "probability" and "demonstration" in the *Treatise* (1.3.6.5) and "moral reasoning" and "demonstrative reasoning" in the first *Enquiry* (4.18). Indeed, Shepherd uses similar terminology. However, as we will see, she understands those types of reasoning quite differently.

As we saw in chapter 2 of this *Guide*, Hume characterizes demonstrations as involving thought alone and as pertaining to "relations of ideas" (*EHU* 4.1). A relation of ideas is a proposition the contrary of which implies a contradiction; for example, "$2 + 3 = 5$" is a relation of ideas because to deny it (to assert that $2 + 3 \neq 5$) is in essence to assert both that 5 is equal to $2 + 3$ (since 5 is defined as such) and that it is not. Moral reasoning, in contrast, concerns what

---

[21] Fasko, "Mary Shepherd's Threefold 'Variety of Intellect' and Its Role in Improving Education," 189. It should be noted that in Shepherd's day, use of the word 'idiot' to describe a person with profound congenital mental disabilities was not considered offensive. For discussion of how idiocy has been portrayed over time in Western culture, see McDonagh, *Idiocy: A Cultural History*.

[22] Fasko, "Mary Shepherd's Threefold 'Variety of Intellect' and Its Role in Improving Education," 190.

Hume calls "matters of fact"—that is, claims the contrary of which do *not* imply a contradiction (*EHU* 4.2 and 4.18). For example, a proposition such as "the rose in the vase is pink" can be denied; if the rose in the vase is indeed pink, then to deny it is to say something false, but not self-contradictory.

One variety of moral reasoning is causal reasoning, or what Hume sometimes calls "experimental reasoning" since it is based on experience (*EHU* 9.1; see also 4.19 and 8.17). Such reasoning can result in conclusions of varying certainty, either "proofs" or "probabilities," a distinction Hume famously puts to use in his essay on miracles.[23] "Proofs," Hume says in the *Treatise*, are "those arguments, which are deriv'd from the relation of cause and effect, and which are entirely free from doubt and uncertainty" (*T* 1.2.11.2). We can obtain a *proof* that some cause will have a particular effect, or that some observed effect had some particular cause, when our experience of similar causes or effects has been entirely consistent and uniform. To take one of Hume's more notorious examples, we have *proof* that someone who died will not come back from the dead because, in our experience, such an event has never occurred. A "probability," on the other hand, is a conclusion, based on causal reasoning, that is "still attended with uncertainty" (*T* 1.2.11.2; see also *EHU* 10.4) because our past experience has *not* been entirely uniform. For example, dark clouds usually, but do not invariably, result in rain; a prediction that it will soon rain because there are dark clouds in the sky is thus a probability, not a proof.

Shepherd uses the same language of "demonstration," "experimental reasoning," "proof," and "probability," but she deploys these terms in quite different ways. First, "proof" does not seem to have any technical sense in her works, other than to mean a good argument (*EPEU* xvi) or good evidence (*ERCE* 123, 125; *EPEU* 34). Second, and more importantly, while Shepherd contrasts

---

[23] Further discussion of Hume's views on miracles, and Shepherd's objections, can be found in chapter 9 of this *Guide*.

136   MARY SHEPHERD

demonstrative reasoning with reasoning that results only in "probability" (*ERCE* 117, 124, and 187), this distinction does not align, as it does in Hume, with a distinction between reasoning about "relations of ideas" versus reasoning about "matters of fact." For Shepherd, causal reasoning *can* be demonstrative.

But what does Shepherd mean by "demonstration"? She does not define the term in her two books, but in an 1825 letter to Charles Babbage, she says that "demonstration is nothing more than clear perception of an universal relation."[24] This definition raises some questions. First, why characterize a demonstration as a *perception*? Perhaps Shepherd's point is that demonstration is a form of reasoning, and reasoning is a mental process; so, wherever there is demonstration, there must be a thinker perceiving that demonstration. Second, what does Shepherd mean by "universal relation"? At first glance, she might seem to mean a relation that is expressed by a general claim, such as that the interior angles of any triangle add up to 180°. However, as we shall see, Shepherd also thinks that *particular* claims can be demonstrated to be true. Thus, by "universal" relation she seems to mean a necessary relation; if this is right, then to demonstrate something is to establish that the conclusion is a necessary truth. This means the conclusions of demonstrations can be known with complete certainty.

Mathematical reasoning is, for Hume, a form of demonstrative reasoning, and Shepherd agrees. But, as we saw in chapter 3 of this *Guide*, Shepherd also considers mathematical reasoning to be just a special case of causal reasoning. When someone once proves a theorem, that theorem can henceforth be known to hold in all other cases because like causes—diagrams or premises similar to those used before—can be known to have like effects. She writes:

> In the mathematics, diagrams are formed by ourselves, and we may therefore be always *sure* of our future and universal

---

[24] Shepherd, Letter to Charles Babbage of November 18, 1825.

SENSING AND REASONING   137

conclusions; because we frame an *hypothesis*, and examine by one experiment, (i.e. one experience,) the relations which arise; and the same data being given to all future ages, there is nothing supposed which can make any difference amidst these relations; for all particular instances are included in the first experience made. (*EPEU* 288; see also 295; *ERCE* 77; and 1825 letter to Babbage)

Thus, mathematical arguments are not just demonstrations but also *causal* arguments. As Shepherd puts it, "the science of mathematics is truly but one branch of physics" (*EPEU* 278–79). This is a significant departure from Hume, who drew a sharp distinction between demonstrations and causal reasoning and located the mathematical in the realm of the former.

Moreover, Shepherd thinks that, in theory at least, ordinary instances of causal reasoning about physical objects in the world could be demonstrative. In such reasoning, one premise is observational and one premise is a causal principle that has already been demonstrated to be true (*ERCE* 108). Consider learning that heating gold to 1064°C causes it to melt. We can only learn the melting point of gold through experience; but Shepherd thinks one carefully controlled scientific experiment (what she calls an *experimentum crucis* [*ERCE* 53]) is all that is needed. So long as we ensure that the only difference between the gold being solid and the gold melting is the temperature change to 1064°, combining that observation with the CP allows us to conclude that the 1064° temperature (mixed with the gold and other unchanged factors) *necessarily* caused the melting. We are thus entitled to conclude that it is a *necessary truth* that gold melts at 1064°. And this allows us to engage in additional "experimental reasoning" whereby we can make predictions about future similar causes. This reasoning, too, is based on an observation and a demonstratively proven causal principle (*ERCE* 108); in this new piece of reasoning, the observation is that *another* piece of gold is being subjected to exactly similar circumstances as in the previous instance, and the causal

138 MARY SHEPHERD

principle is the CLP. Contrary to Hume's assertion that the prediction that this piece of gold will also melt at 1064° can be known only with probability, Shepherd thinks it can be known with absolute certainty. In sum, on Shepherd's view, truths about physical causes and their effects turn out to be necessary truths that are known a posteriori.

However, for such absolute certainty to be attained—for causal reasoning to be demonstrative—the premises must be known with absolute certainty. In the gold example, this means that the reasoner must be absolutely sure that all conditions are actually held unchanged aside from the temperature of the gold, and that the gold being used has exactly the same qualities as the gold in the previous case. As we saw in chapter 3 of this *Guide*, Shepherd is fairly optimistic about our ability to use what she calls "good sense" (*ERCE* 102) in causal inferences; she thinks we naturally adopt certain strategies, such as considering not just the sensible qualities of two items but also their causal histories, before we judge whether they are the same or not. But Shepherd also concedes that "we frequently make mistakes" in such judgments (*EPEU* 174). And the problem seems more severe than that; we simply *cannot* know the complete causal history of the objects involved in our experiments. In other words, Shepherd's ideal conditions surely obtain very rarely, if ever. And this means that, in practice, causal reasoning only ever reaches the level of probability, not demonstration. As she herself notes, in practice our causal inferences give us not complete certainty but only "*high probability* founded on REASONING" (*ERCE* 124).

But Shepherd is untroubled by this. She writes that

> in cases of high probability the mind is as much *determined* to action, as by demonstration. It cannot stand hesitating, and therefore "takes a step," (in arguing from the sensible qualities to the future effects of things,) governed by a *high probability* founded on REASONING "that *they* ARE" connected with like secret *powers, on which the Effects entirely depend. (ERCE 124)

SENSING AND REASONING 139

Note that Shepherd is not saying that our *justification* in cases of high probability is as good as it is in demonstration. It is not. But she *is* saying that even when some causal inference is of high probability but falls short of demonstration, the mind takes "action" just as it would if the reasoning were demonstrative. The "action" here evidently means *belief* that the effect will occur: a conclusion known with a high degree of probability leads us to *expect* some effect almost as much as would an inference known with demonstrative certainty.

So, even if Shepherd is able to provide a demonstration for the CLP, our application of that principle in practice does not produce demonstrative knowledge. Thus, it seems that Hume turns out to be right: all our experimental reasonings are merely probable. Now, Shepherd might object that she has still done better than Hume. According to Hume's account, all our causal inferences have exactly the same rational justification—that is to say, none. Shepherd at least can distinguish between degrees of probability of different causal inferences. In cases where we know a great deal about the objects in our experience, there is a higher degree of probability that our causal inferences are accurate than in cases where we know less. So that seems to be some advantage to her account. Even if reason cannot provide demonstrations in ordinary and scientific inferences, she may yet be able to claim, against Hume, to have shown that "it is *Reason*, and not *Custom*, which guides our minds in forming the notions of necessary connexion, of belief and of expectation" (*ERCE* 42).

Latent Reasoning

Shepherd maintains that the CP, the CLP, and our belief that there is an external world can be established through explicit reasoning, but she also suggests that they are in some sense known by "infants, peasants, and brutes" through what she terms "latent reasoning."[25]

---

[25] M. Folescu has argued that Shepherd considers the causal principles to be "basic, foundational and, more importantly, self-evident and thus justified in other ways than

140 MARY SHEPHERD

She addresses this in *EPEU*'s short essay 7, "That Children Can Perceive the Relation of Cause and Effect, on Account of Their Being Capable of a Latent Conception of Ideas" (*EPEU* 314).

In her accounts of our beliefs in not only causal principles but also the existence of the external world, Shepherd wants to reject a family of views held by such philosophers as Reid, Stewart, and Brown, who explained these beliefs as in some sense instinctive. Reid epitomizes this view in holding that such beliefs are "first principles" that human nature is set up to believe through "common sense" rather than reason (*IHM* 2.5, 5.7; *EIP* 6.6). Shepherd writes,

> That class of ideas which Dr. Reid terms instinctive, and Mr. D. Stewart considers as composed of simple ideas not *formed* by the senses, but generated upon certain *fit occasions* for their production, I consider to be the conclusions of a latent reasoning; as the mere results and corollaries, included in the relation of those ideas and sensations already existing in the mind and which were previously formed by the senses. (*EPEU* 169–70)

Her objection to explaining our key beliefs as "instinctive" is that instincts are non-rational (*ERCE* 138). To ground beliefs in this way is not to ground them at all, to leave them "wholly without any proof whatever; for, '*that we are incapable of thinking otherwise than we do*,' can itself be no reason we think rightly" (*EPEU* 223; see also 212). Instead, these beliefs are known through "latent reasoning" (*ERCE* 128; *EPEU* 14).

In essay 7, Shepherd maintains that "the child, as well as the peasant, (and even the philosopher when withdrawn from his books" knows that sensible qualities are caused by external objects that persist even when not interacting with the senses (*EPEU* 319),

---

by demonstration," and indeed that Shepherd thought (or should have thought) that they are known by intuition, not reason ("Mary Shepherd on the Role of Proofs in Our Knowledge of First Principles," 2).

SENSING AND REASONING 141

that similar objects will have similar effects in the future (*EPEU* 320), and that every change must have a cause (*EPEU* 322). The process by which they know these things is what she calls "latent reasoning" (*ERCE* 128; *EPEU* 14, 170, 237; see also *EPEU* xii).

Shepherd never explicitly spells out what she means by "latent reasoning." However, the account developed earlier of reasoning *simpliciter* gives us the resources to explain what she might mean. We saw that reasoning involves drawing a conclusion by noticing various logical relationships among ideas we have put together, logical relationships that exist independently of us; certain ideas *really are* such that when mixed with others, another idea is the result. Whether or not we ever *actually do* combine any of the ideas we have, they nonetheless can be said to be such that *if* we combined them, certain results would occur. Thus "latent reasoning" plausibly means *having* ideas that bear various relationships to each other, but have not yet been combined by the thinker in such a way that those relationships have been noted.

In one passage where Shepherd discusses latent reasoning, she writes that the "conclusions of latent reasoning" are "the mere results and corollaries, included in the relation of those ideas and sensations already existing in the mind" (*EPEU* 169–70; see also 224 and 314–15).[26] This suggests that she thinks that in latent reasoning, the ideas and the relations between them that *could* cause a conclusion to be drawn are present in the mind of the thinker, even if the ideas have not yet been actually "mixed" by the thinker. Her discussions of specific instances of latent reasoning bear out this suggestion.

Consider the CP. Recall that she argues for it with a *reductio* argument, in which we imagine a causeless object "START[ING] FORTH into existence, and mak[ing] the first breach on the wide

---

[26] One might think that her reference to "the conclusions of latent reasoning" means that latent reasoning does *in fact* involve drawing conclusions. But the phrase need not imply that; "the conclusions of latent reasoning" can be read as referring to "the conclusions that *could be* drawn by explicit reasoning but have not yet been so drawn."

142   MARY SHEPHERD

nonentity around" (*ERCE* 35); we realize that this assumption results in the contradictory conclusion that the imagined object both has and does not have the quality of coming into existence (*EPEU* 290), leading to the further conclusion that the CP is true. What Shepherd gives us there is explicit reasoning, of course, but she says that this is "the latent reasoning silently generated in the minds of all men, from infancy" (*EPEU* 14). She contrasts a child's "faintest and most indistinct form of latent conception" of the CP with "the relation of cause and effect when fully known and established" (*EPEU* xiii). That is, she suggests that in children there is an earlier stage in which the CP is *latently conceived* and a later stage in which it is *explicitly judged to be true*.

Indeed, Shepherd says that simply to have any new sensation is enough to indicate, in an indistinct way, that the CP is true because the occurrence of *any sensation itself* suggests that there must be a cause for it. In simply having a sensation, an infant already has sufficient ideas to conclude that the CP is true; that is, in infants, *some* of the causes that are necessary to explicitly know the CP are present, although these ideas have not yet been put together or "mixed" and compared. To have these ideas but not yet to put them together is "latent reasoning or "latent conception." This is a kind of "indistinct" belief in a principle. To "fully know and establish" the principle is to judge explicitly that the principle is true.

The second key causal principle for Shepherd is the CLP, that "Like causes necessarily have like effects" (*ERCE* 43–44 and 78; *EPEU* 290). Again, she does provide an explicit argument for the CLP (*ERCE* 45), but she also implies that everyone knows the truth of the CLP as soon as they have had any experiences of change. The experience of closing one's eyes, opening them, and seeing objects again, when the idea of that experience is mixed with the CP, is enough for someone to realize that the same effects will occur in the future, when one's eyes are closed

SENSING AND REASONING 143

and opened again. It is thus part of the constitution of the mind to know the CLP insofar as any experience of change, combined with our knowledge of the CP, will lead us to the conclusion that the CLP is true.

Shepherd says something similar about infants' and brutes' knowledge that an external world exists. She writes that the "knowledge of an external universe" is "the result of perceiving . . . relations amidst our sensations—of a curious and complicated kind indeed—yet always latently worked up with our sensations, and, from having been generated in early infancy, of difficulty in the detection" (LMSM 701; see also *EPEU* 212–13 and 224). Here, too, Shepherd's suggestion seems to be that the reasoning is latent in the sense that the ideas that could allow thinkers to reach the conclusion that the external world exists are present in all conscious beings, even if those ideas have not been put together in the way that would produce the conclusion (and even if, as in "minds afflicted with 'idiocy'" [*EPEU* 314–15], such conclusions will never be drawn). That is, all the premises and principles needed for the conclusion that there is an external world are present in consciousness, and the logical relations among them are already there among our sensations, even when the conclusion is not explicitly drawn. This knowledge is then "gained by reflecting on, or observing the relations of our sensations" (LMSM 700): when we put these sensations together and notice their relationships, the result is the conclusion that the external world exists. Since drawing the conclusion is synchronous with the process of observing these relationships, we can say that the very noticing of the logical relationships among our ideas is the drawing of the conclusion that an external world exists. Our knowledge of an external world is thus an "idea of reason" that is "included in the impressions of sense" (*EPEU* 224); the details of this argument will be examined in the next chapter.

144 MARY SHEPHERD

Suggestions for Further Reading

- On Shepherd's account of degrees of intellect, see Manuel Fasko, "Mary Shepherd's Threefold 'Variety of Intellect' and Its Role in Improving Education."
- There are brief discussions of Shepherd's assimilation of mathematical and physical induction in Cristina Paoletti's "Restoring Necessary Connections: Lady Mary Shepherd on Hume and the Early Nineteenth-Century Debate on Causality" and in Martha Bolton's "Causality and Causal Induction: The Necessitarian Theory of Lady Mary Shepherd."
- For an interpretation of Shepherd as offering non-demonstrative justification of first principles such as the Causal Principle and the Causal Likeness Principle, see M. Folescu's "Mary Shepherd on the Role of Proofs in Our Knowledge of First Principles."

6

The External World

Introduction

Shepherd had originally planned to include an appendix to the *Essay upon the Relation of Cause and Effect* showing how her theory of causation could prove there is an external physical world (*EPEU* xi). However, since her arguments turned out to be too complex for a mere appendix, she published them as a separate book, *Essays on the Perception of an External Universe*. The first long essay of that book, "Essay on the Academical or Sceptical Philosophy," running to nearly two hundred pages, explains and defends her arguments that we can know an external world exists.

As in *ERCE*, Shepherd says she is responding to Hume's *Treatise* and *Enquiry Concerning Human Understanding*; here, however, her focus is on passages expressing Hume's skepticism about belief in the existence of an external world.[1] As she said regarding his theory of causation, she sees Hume's fundamental error as "substituting *'imagination'* and *'vivacity of thought,'* as a ground of belief, instead of *'reason'*" (*EPEU* 3). This time, however, she says Hume's arguments "would be very tedious to examine" (*EPEU* 2), so, instead, she provides her own positive account of knowledge of the external world—thereby answering both Hume's skepticism and Berkeley's idealism, as well as Reid's claim that it is "instinct" that enables us to resist skepticism (*EPEU* 4–5).

---

[1] She quotes or paraphrases *T* 1.4.2.2 and 1.4.2.42 (*EPEU* 1), and *EHU* 12.11, 12.14, and 12.9 (*EPEU* 4).

Mary Shepherd. Deborah Boyle, Oxford University Press. © Oxford University Press 2023.
DOI: 10.1093/oso/9780190090326.003.0006

146   MARY SHEPHERD

Shepherd characterizes the first three chapters of EASP as proceeding in three steps, each establishing the origin and "foundation" of three separate but related beliefs. These are, first, our belief in *continuously existing* objects; second, our belief that those objects must be "outward," or *external* to the mind; finally, our belief that those objects must be *independent* of the mind (*EPEU* 11–12). Her account of the "foundations" of these beliefs involves spelling out the latent reasoning by which we know through reason that objects having these characteristics must exist (*EPEU* xv).

In what follows, each of Shepherd's first three chapters will be examined in turn. Because the final chapter of EASP, the "Recapitulation," expresses many of the same points from the first three chapters in slightly different terms, what follows will also include page references to that chapter rather than treating it separately.

The Argument for Continuously Existing Objects

After explaining her use of the terms 'sensation' and 'perception' (*EPEU* 6–9), Shepherd asks why, since all our sensations are just mental states, we consider *some* of them to be external objects that exist even when we are not sensing them (*EPEU* 9). Her answer appeals to habitual associations—not, as Hume does, to suggest that habit is the only basis for some beliefs, but to claim that our minds habitually *entangle* two very different kinds of sensations: on the one hand, the sensations of *sensible qualities* (sensations of colors, sounds, flavors, and so on), and, on the other hand, the sensation of an *idea* or "notion of some sort of corresponding continuous existence" (*EPEU* 10), an idea we have through "latent" reasoning (*EPEU* 14). Shepherd writes,

THE EXTERNAL WORLD   147

It is owing to the intimate *union* and *association* of the sensible impressions, with the ideas of their *causes*, that these *causes*, (or objects,) can never be contemplated, *excepting under the forms of those unions*; by which it comes to pass, that the *whole union* is considered in a popular way as *existing unperceived*. (*EPEU* 20–21; see also 41)

That is, in ordinary life we do not think of the sensible qualities of objects as being distinct from the external objects that cause them. Detaching these combined ideas from each other "requires a philosophical examination" (*EPEU* 21), as does showing that they "include in *their relations* the necessity, that there should be, and the proof that there are, other existences than the mere sensations themselves" (*EPEU* 10). This is what Shepherd proposes to do in EASP.

For Shepherd, the key to seeing why there must be these "other existences" can be found by considering the "*method*" by which we have particular sensations. There is, she thinks, something about the *way* we experience particular sensations that makes us judge that there is something other than "*the cause of sensation in general*" (that is, the mind itself [*EPEU* 14–15]) that causes particular sensations and that "*may* CONTINUE *to exist* when *unperceived*" (*EPEU* 13). Her point is that our experience of certain kinds of sensations—a sensation of red or of heat, for example—reveals to us that they must be caused by something that exists continuously, externally, and independently of us.

So, how do we experience particular sensations? Shepherd says that we already have a "notion" that it is *possible* that objects exist even when unperceived (*EPEU* 13), but this is not enough to prove that they do.[2] The first step in her argument is to note that in our experience, our particular sensations arise "at the call of the senses"

---

[2] By "notion," Shepherd typically means an idea formed by the understanding (*EPEU* 96–97); see chapter 5 of this *Guide*.

148 MARY SHEPHERD

and are "successively *vanishing*" (*EPEU* 14). What she means is that individual sensory perceptions, including sensations of being in motion (*EPEU* 16), come and go as we use our sense-organs. To take Shepherd's example, suppose I go for a walk. At first, I see a house and a tree, but as I walk past them, my sensations of those things disappear and are replaced by other sensations. When I retrace my steps on my way home, I have sensations resembling the earlier ones; I "can again recover the image of the house, the tree" (*EPEU* 14). And our knowledge of the Causal Principle (CP) tells us that these vanishing and then recurring sensations cannot "BEGIN *their own existences*"; thus, we reason that we can only explain the existence of our vanishing and recurring sensations if they are caused by objects that do *not* vanish, but continue to exist even when we are not having sensory experiences (*EPEU* 14).

Shepherd says this is the "latent reasoning" by which all people, even "the youngest minds," believe in the existence of a world of continuously existing objects that are distinct from and the cause of our sensations (*EPEU* 14). She presents this argument as depending essentially on two premises, the observation of the transitory nature of our sensations, plus the CP (*EPEU* 14; see also 170–71):

1. I experience that certain sensations appear "upon each irregular call of the senses," vanish, and can be recovered by using my senses again (*EPEU* 14; see also 16).
2. Nothing can begin its own existence. [CP]
3. Therefore, there are continuously existing, unperceived beings that cause my sensations. (*EPEU* 14)

Shepherd says that the existence of such unperceived causes is "demonstrably *proved* by these their effects" (*EPEU* 18).

However, the above argument is invalid. In order to reach her desired conclusion, Shepherd needs additional premises that will rule out various other possible causes for these sensations. There seem to be at least four possibilities that a skeptic could raise.

THE EXTERNAL WORLD   149

Perhaps there are no continuously-existing objects out there causing our sensory experiences, and they are really just caused (1) by our own minds, or (2) by our minds and sense-organs. Or perhaps (3) there *are* such objects causing our sensations, but these objects are as transitory as the sensations. This could happen if God creates the causes of our sensations precisely at the moment that we use our sense-organs, and those causes go out of existence when we stop using the relevant sense-organ. Or perhaps (4) God is *directly* causing our sensory perceptions, even though no external objects actually exist. How does Shepherd rule out these possibilities?

Could I Be the Cause of My Sense Perceptions?

Shepherd explicitly considers the first possibility listed above, that the *mind* itself, alone, causes our sensations. She asks,

> do these objects continue to exist in them [i.e., the minds of all people]; and is the eye put in action; and does motion take place in relation only to the mind; or more indefinitely to the object called self (i.e., an individual capacity for sensation in general?) (*EPEU* 14–15)

Her unequivocal answer is "no." Shepherd does think that mind is *among* the causes of sensation; sensations are mental states, and thus the general capacity of mind must be involved in every particular sensation (*EPEU* 71–72). The question is whether all of our sensations could be caused *just* by mind, without the involvement of any other objects. Shepherd's reason for denying this is that we cannot conjure up sensations "by only applying such methods as call upon the inward sentient principle, termed mind" (*EPEU* 15; see also 17). We cannot will to have any sensations whatever; if I want to taste something sweet, I cannot just conjure up the

150 MARY SHEPHERD

sensation without actually eating something sweet. Thus, the causes of such sensations must include something more than just mind.

What about possibility (2) listed above, that is, that the mind *and* the sense-organs together might cause our sensations? Recall that Shepherd thinks the sense-organs include the ability to move, so "sense-organs" for her includes the whole human body, including the brain and nervous system. Is it possible for my mind and body to exist and have sensations even if there are no other continuously existing entities? Shepherd's reason for rejecting this is that "the organs of sense and mind being the same, a *third* set of objects is needed in order to determine those perceptions *in particular* which are neither the organs of sense nor mind *in general*" (*EPEU* 15). Her claim that the mind and sense organs are "the same" does not mean that they are *numerically* the same, that is, the same as each other.[3] Instead, as Margaret Atherton has put it, Shepherd means that mind and sense organs are "on-going unchanging existences"; they are "the same" insofar as they undergo no change in state during sensation.[4] And if they undergo no change, then they cannot be the *sole causes* of a change. Causing an effect means producing a *change*, bringing about a new quality—but where there is no change in the causes, there will be nothing to "make a difference" (*ERCE* 142). Since the general capacities of mind and the sense-organs persist, unchanging, over time, some third factor must interact with them in order to "make a difference" and produce a new quality, a specific sensation.

Shepherd nowhere defends the claim that the mind and sense-organs remain the same in sensory perception. And it might seem they do not: when I use my eyes, for example, the images on the retina change constantly (as Shepherd knew), and this is surely a change in the eye. Perhaps, despite her reference to "organs" of

[3] Elsewhere she treats mind as distinct from the sense-organs, and she accuses "the materialists" of not being able to distinguish between sense-organs and the mind (*EPEU* 376); clearly, she thinks these are not numerically identical.

[4] Atherton, "Lady Mary Shepherd's Case," 351. See *EPEU* 233.

THE EXTERNAL WORLD 151

sense, Shepherd actually means that it is the *capacities* to think, see, hear, and so on that do not change; she may mean that even if sensing results in a physical change in a sense-organ, that does not affect the *capacity* to sense.

Shepherd returns to this point a few pages later when she observes that

> the capacity for sensation in general being given with the use of any particular organ of sense, certain perceptions belonging to that sense do not arise; therefore, when these remain the same, and the perceptions in question do arise, they must be occasioned by *unperceived* causes affecting it. (*EPEU* 17–18)

That is, any time I use any of my sense-organs, I am also using my mind (my "capacity for sensation in general"). Suppose I am using my eyes, looking around my garden, and see no birds; this is a case of "certain perceptions belonging to that sense" *not* arising. Then a bird flies across my field of vision. Nothing has changed in my capacity to sense in general or to see in particular, and yet I am having a new sensation. To explain how this could arise, Shepherd says, we must posit some external cause that interacts with my eyes and mind in order to cause my sensation of the bird.

Could Transitory Objects Be the Cause of My Sense Perceptions?

Shepherd stresses that the reason there must be continuously existing objects, even when we are not sensing them, is because our sensations are transitory and (according to the CP) need a cause to explain their coming into existence. But although the CP tells us that our transitory sensations require causes other than themselves, it is consistent with this that the causes *themselves* are transitory in exactly the way our sense perceptions are. This was the

152   MARY SHEPHERD

third possibility mentioned above: perhaps external objects come into existence just at the right moment—at the "irregular call of the senses" (*EPEU* 14)—to cause the corresponding sensations, and then go out of existence again. This would be a strange scenario, but it seems conceivable.

Shepherd does explicitly mention and reject the possibility that the objects we perceive might be *"created purposely, ready to appear,"* each time we use our senses (*EPEU* 13–14). Oddly, however, she does not actually offer a *reason* for ruling this out. Writing that "the mind perceives that unless they [i.e., the causes of our sensations] are *created purposely, ready to appear,* upon each irregular call of the sense, they must CONTINUE *to exist, ready to appear* to them upon such calls" (*EPEU* 13–14), she suggests that this possibility can be simply dismissed out of hand.

If challenged, Shepherd might note that even if the causes of our sensations came in and out of existence at the very moments we used our sense-organs, those causes would *themselves* require causes, which would themselves require causes, ad infinitum. Without an ultimate cause that does *not* come into and out of existence, there would be an infinite regress of causes. A passing remark in a later essay suggests that Shepherd thinks an infinite regress of causes is as impossible as the existence of an uncaused quality or object: "to imagine the existence of a series of dependent effects without a continuous being of which they are the qualities . . . is equal to the supposition of the possibility of every thing springing up as we see it, from an absolute blank and nonentity of existence" (*EPEU* 391). Thus, there must be *some* ultimate cause of our sensations that does not come into and out of existence. Indeed, it is using precisely this kind of reasoning that Shepherd later argues for the existence of God (*EPEU* 151–52). But could not God simply create transitory objects that, in turn, cause our transitory sensations by coming into existence at just the right moment, but then disappear? Shepherd does not seem to have an argument to rule this out.

Could God Be the Cause of My Sense Perceptions?

Another possibility is that God might be *directly* causing all my sensations, not through creating external objects that cause my sensations but by directly affecting my mind. This possibility (the fourth of the possibilities canvassed above) was endorsed by Nicolas Malebranche (1638–1715) in *The Search after Truth* (1674–75).[5] Shepherd was certainly aware of his proposal, for she later mentions that "*some* philosophers make *God create all the images at the moment they appear in every mind*," and she cites Malebranche in a footnote (*EPEU* 46). Shepherd also discusses Malebranche's view in essay 3 of *EPEU*, as the title of that essay indicates: "That the External Causes Which Determine the Various Perceptions of Sense, Are Not the Immediate Actions of Deity" (*EPEU* 239). But there, too, Shepherd simply notes, without argument, that it is "allowed on all hands" that God does not immediately create our sensations (*EPEU* 239).

When we consider the various options that Shepherd needs to rule out, her argument for continuously existing objects looks much more complicated, and it is clear that she has not adequately defended several of the premises that she needs:

1. I experience that certain sensations appear "upon each irregular call of the senses," vanish, and can be recovered by using my senses again (*EPEU* 14; see also 16).
2. If there were no continuously existing objects to cause these sensations, then either there must be causes that are specially created upon each call of the senses, or these sensations would each in their turn begin their own existence (*EPEU* 13–14, 16).
3. The causes of my sensations are *not* specially created upon each call of the senses (*EPEU* 13–14).

---

[5] According to Malebranche, a "sensation is a modification of our soul, and it is God who causes it in us" (*Search after Truth* 3.2.6).

154   MARY SHEPHERD

4. Nothing can begin its own existence. [CP]
5. So, my sensations cannot each begin their own existence.
6. So, "there must necessarily be some sort of continuously existing beings" that cause my sensations to appear upon the call of my senses (*EPEU* 14).
7. If the continuously existing beings that cause my sensations upon the call of my senses were my sense organs or my own mind, then my sense organs or my own mind would also change when the sensations change.
8. My sense organs and my mind remain the same even when my sensations change (*EPEU* 15).
9. So, the continuously existing beings that cause my sensations upon the call of my senses cannot be my own sense organs or my own mind.
10. God is not the immediate cause of those sensations that arise upon the irregular call of the senses (*EPEU* 239).
11. There are no possible causes for sensations that arise upon the irregular call of the senses than other than continuously existing objects, objects specially created at each call of the senses, my mind, my sense-organs, or God.
12. Therefore, there are continuously existing objects that cause my sensations.

Shepherd maintains that although we only know about these continuously existing objects through reasoning, our evidence for their existence is as good as the evidence we have for the existence of our sensations themselves (*EPEU* 18). She offers a mathematical analogy: the "notion" of the number four includes various "relations" (presumably mathematical relations such as $3 + 1$, $2 + 2$, $5 - 1$, and so on); Shepherd's claim is that we are equally certain of the existence of the notion of four *and* of the existence of the relations it contains (*EPEU* 19). Similarly, since the conclusion of an argument is contained in the combination of the premises, our certainty in the premises (assuming we *are* certain of the premises) should

THE EXTERNAL WORLD 155

carry over to the conclusion, too. Of course, Shepherd concedes, we might *misperceive* the relations contained in any given number, in which case our certainty in those relations would be misplaced (*EPEU* 19); similarly, we might go wrong in our reasoning, perhaps misperceiving a premise or applying inferential rules incorrectly, in which case our certainty in the conclusion would be misplaced (see *EPEU* 143). But, assuming "that the mind . . . observes carefully enough the *relation of its simple sensations*, then the evidence for the existences which depend on them, is *upon the same footing as are the simple* sensations, and must render an equal confidence in it" (*EPEU* 19).

Seven "Corollaries"

In the remainder of EASP chapter 1, Shepherd addresses seven points, which she calls "corollaries" of the conclusion that continuously existing objects exist unperceived. First, she reiterates her earlier point (*EPEU* 10) that we associate those sensations that are the effects of external objects with our ideas of their causes (*EPEU* 20–21). This is not in itself problematic; indeed, as we have seen, the compound of sensible qualities with an idea of their being caused by external objects is just what Shepherd means by 'perceived internal object.' However, people also have a further tendency to think of the "*whole union . . . as existing unperceived*" (*EPEU* 21). In other words, because the sensations and our idea of their cause are difficult to pry apart, people tend to think the sensations, like the causes, exist out there in the world; they think of the cause of, say, a sensation of an apple as *itself* being red, round, and smooth. Even when philosophers attempt to remedy this "popular way" of thinking, they tend to think that some sensations—the "primary qualities"—exist unperceived (*EPEU* 21). This observation leads to Shepherd's second point, which is that Reid mistakenly holds that "primary qualities" give us knowledge of objects "as they exist when unperceived" (*EPEU* 24).

156 MARY SHEPHERD

Locke's framework for understanding the primary/secondary quality distinction prompted critical responses from both Berkeley and Reid. As we have seen, Locke characterized primary qualities as powers of physical bodies to produce ideas of "solidity, extension, figure, and mobility" in perceivers (*ECHU* 2.8.8–9) and secondary qualities as powers, derived from a body's primary qualities, to produce ideas of colors, tastes, sounds, smells, and so on (*ECHU* 2.8.10). While our ideas of primary qualities resemble those qualities in the objects themselves, our ideas of secondary qualities do not (*ECHU* 2.8.15). Indeed, Locke says that the secondary qualities are "in truth nothing in the objects themselves" except powers (*ECHU* 2.8.14).

Berkeley rejects the primary/secondary quality distinction altogether in his *Treatise Concerning the Principles of Human Knowledge* (*PHK* 1.9–10). However, Reid thought Locke got something right about secondary qualities, so instead of rejecting the distinction altogether, he recasts Locke's account of primary qualities. Reid's account invokes a power of the mind that he says has been hitherto overlooked by philosophers, the power of one sensation or thought to "suggest" another (*IHM* 2.7). Sometimes one sensation suggests another because we have experienced them together in the past, as when "a certain kind of sound suggests immediately to the mind, a coach passing in the street" (*IHM* 2.7). Other suggestions are part of our natural constitution (*IHM* 2.7). Recall that Shepherd characterizes sensible qualities as *signs* of external causes (*ERCE* 123; *EPEU* 38), and even as a "language" expressing nature (*EPEU* 261). In this, she echoes both Berkeley and Reid:[6] Reid says sensations are the natural *signs* of qualities of bodies (*IHM* 5.2–3) and that our sensations are a kind of natural language that, through

---

[6] In his *Alciphron: or, the Minute Philosopher* (1732), Berkeley characterizes visual perceptions of color and light as "a language wonderfully adapted to suggest and exhibit to us the distances, figures, situations, dimensions, and various qualities of tangible objects" (dialogue 4, section 10). There is no indication in Shepherd's works that she was familiar with *Alciphron*, however.

THE EXTERNAL WORLD   157

suggestion, reveals features of the world.[7] The thoughts that are suggested to us by sensations are "perceptions" (*IHM* 6.20); they come to us "immediately," that is, without any process of inference or reasoning (*IHM* 6.8).

The details of Reid's account of sensation are complex; just an overview will suffice here.[8] He first examines the senses of smelling, tasting, and hearing, giving similar analyses in all three cases. Each sense modality is affected in some way by external stimuli; in smelling, for example, nerves in the nose meet with "effluvia of vast subtilty," composed of "volatile particles" (*IHM* 2.1). Action in the nervous system produces a sensation in the mind, a sensation that does not resemble anything in the outside world, yet which "suggests" the notion of a cause out there in the world. Thus, Reid writes that

> the smell of a rose signifies two things. *First*, a sensation, which can have no existence but when it is perceived, and can only be in a sentient being or mind. *Secondly*, it signifies some power, quality, or virtue, in the rose, or in effluvia proceeding from it, which hath a permanent existence, independent of the mind, and which, by the constitution of nature, produces the sensation in us. (*IHM* 2.9)

Reid's analysis of touch is more complex. Touch gives us sensations of heat, cold, hardness, softness, smoothness, roughness, pain, pleasure, shape, and motion. Like sensations of smell, those of heat, cold, pleasure and pain are caused by certain physical characteristics of bodies, such as the motion of particles, although

---

[7] Reid characterizes the process of "suggestion" whereby sensations teach us about the world as a non-rational "natural kind of magic" (*IHM* 5.3). We do not need to learn, study, or reason about the language of our sensations; we understand it due to our human nature.

[8] For discussion of Reid's account of visual perception in particular, see chapter 10 of this *Guide*.

158 MARY SHEPHERD

Reid is agnostic about exactly what the physical processes are. When we have sensations of heat, cold, pleasure, or pain, those sensations suggest the existence of those causes, without actually *resembling* those causes (*IHM* 5.1, 5.6). His analysis is a little different for sensations of hardness, softness, smoothness, roughness, shape, and motion. These sensations, too, immediately "suggest" a cause, a "real" quality in external objects; again, the sensations in no way resemble those causal powers in the external world (*IHM* 5.2). However, on Reid's account, the sensations of hardness, softness, smoothness, roughness, shape, and motion differ from sensations of heat, cold, pain, and pleasure in two respects. First, Reid says we have a clear notion of the causes of the former group of sensations; for example, the sensation of hardness suggests the notion of hardness itself, which we clearly understand as "the cohesion of the parts of a body with more or less force" (*IHM* 5.4). In contrast, he holds that we do *not* have clear notions of the causes of heat, cold, pain, and pleasure. Second, sensations in the former group *also* suggest to us notions of extension (taking up space) and motion. That is, "certain sensations of touch, by the constitution of our nature, suggest to us solidity, extension, and motion, which are nowise like to sensation" (*IHM* 2.8); they "suggest primary qualities" (*IHM* 5.5; see also 6.8). In contrast, feelings of heat, cold, pain, and pleasure do not suggest ideas of solidity, extension, or motion.

When Shepherd turns in EASP chapter 1, section 2 to the topic of primary and secondary qualities, she notes her agreement with Reid's diagnosis of ordinary people's error in conflating the so-called secondary sensible qualities of smell, taste, and color with their external causes (*EPEU* 23). But she disagrees with Reid on a number of points: with his claim that we have clear conceptions of the *causes* of our ideas of the so-called primary qualities, with his appeal to the process of "suggestion," and with his insistence that perceptions are not sensations (*EPEU* 24). She also rejects his claim that extension, hardness, figure, and so on, as they exist in the external world, are seen and known "immediately and objectively"

THE EXTERNAL WORLD   159

(*EPEU* 24). Since Reid himself admits that sense-organs are needed for their perception, he is implicitly admitting that these perceptions are mediated by the sense-organs (*EPEU* 24). She ends her criticism of Reid by pointing out a scientific fact that she takes to be incompatible with Reid's claim that we see external objects "immediately": the light of the sun takes more than eight minutes to reach us on earth (*EPEU* 25). Thus, if the sun were destroyed, and no longer existent, we would nonetheless see it for another eight minutes. How could we immediately perceive something that does not in fact exist?

Shepherd's third and fourth "corollaries" pertain to time, and are also related to the early modern primary/secondary quality distinction, for duration was often taken to be a primary quality. In holding that all sensible qualities are *only* in the mind, Berkeley concludes that time, too, is in the mind: it is the succession of ideas in a mind (*PHK* 1.98). As an example of a Berkeleyan interpretation of time, Shepherd mentions a fable in which the passage of time to one man differs from everyone else's, which she says "able men" consider as evidence that time is *only* in the mind, that it is "*nothing*" in itself (*EPEU* 25–26).[9] Shepherd agrees that we have subjective experiences of the passage of time but, in her third corollary, insists that this does not mean there is no such thing as time in itself.

Shepherd's fourth corollary presents her own account of time. Unsurprisingly, she thinks that our sensations of duration require a continuously existing cause as much as do our sensations of colors, flavors, and so on: "The sense and mind being the same, the cause for a long *period of time*, cannot be the same with the cause for a *short period of time*" (*EPEU* 27). Thus, she argues that time must

---

[9] Although Shepherd calls this an "Arabian fable," her reference may be to a Japanese folktale of a man transported under the sea, where he marries a princess but returns home after a few days only to find that three hundred years have passed. This story would have been known in Britain due to its inclusion in Engelbert Kaempfer's *History of Japan* (1727).

160   MARY SHEPHERD

exist independently of us as something that causes our sensations of time passing:

> Thus the existence of *time*, like every other existence in nature, is perceived by some quality it determines to the mind, but has not its whole existence merely in that individual perception. It is the existence of things, and therefore of *time*, which enable them to be perceived, not the perception of them which enables them to exist. (*EPEU* 28)

Or, as she writes later, "*time*, in union with the powers of sensation, may be measured by a succession of ideas in the fancy; but *time* in *nature*, and *unperceived*, measures, and is not measured by, the succession of events, whether sensations or not" (*EPEU* 164).

The last three of Shepherd's corollaries in EASP chapter 1 concern two versions of external world skepticism, plus a more restricted skepticism about the existence of heaven and hell. Descartes had famously suggested that because "all the same thoughts we have when we are awake can also come to us when we are asleep, without any of them being true," it is possible that none of my experiences, even those I have when I believe myself to be awake, are any more true "than the illusions of my dreams."[10] Shepherd acknowledges that the skeptic's worry about distinguishing dream states from waking states poses a challenge for her account. She needs a way to distinguish the sensations that are mere dream states from those that are actually currently caused by external objects. Berkeley's claim in his *Principles* that ordinary daily experience can be explained perfectly well without positing the existence of external material objects also poses a problem to which Shepherd needs to respond.

Shepherd's answers to these worries will be considered in chapter 7 of this *Guide*, but, briefly, Shepherd answers the skeptic's

---

[10] Descartes, *Discourse on Method*, 18. Ultimately, of course, Descartes thinks this skeptical worry can be answered by proving the existence of a benevolent God.

THE EXTERNAL WORLD   161

worry about dreaming by defining what it means to be real and making the case that dreamt-of objects do not meet the criteria for reality (*EPEU* 29–33). She also considers what this account of reality implies about religious ideas such as heaven and hell (*EPEU* 35–37). In reply to Berkeleyan idealism, Shepherd argues that external objects *are* necessary for us to have sensible qualities. Since those who do not accept Berkeley's idealism think that external objects are *not* ideas, and since (according to Berkeley) we perceive only ideas (or, as Shepherd puts it, "notions"), Berkeley thinks it follows that we have no ideas (or notions) of what non-idealists call external objects (*EPEU* 37).[11] But according to Shepherd, we *do* have notions or ideas of external objects, because we infer their existence from our sensations. Of course, we do not *sense* these objects. However, we *can* perceive them insofar as we infer their existence (*EPEU* 168–69; see also 172).

Furthermore, Shepherd says, at the end of chapter 2, that although we cannot directly sense external objects, our sensations indicate certain features of external objects, so we have some knowledge about them. First, we know that the continuously existing objects that we infer to exist are *not* sensations; our idea of something that we merely infer to exist is, like our ideas of sound sleep and death, a "negative" idea (*EPEU* 38).[12] Second, since causes must be qualitatively different from the effects they bring about (for if there is no difference, there has been no change, and thus no causation of anything [*EPEU* 45]), we can know that the causes of our sensations are not *like* our sensations, either (*EPEU* 38). Third, we can know the "proportions" and relationships among external objects, because these can be inferred from the proportions and

---

[11] Strictly speaking, Berkeley does think there are external objects, in the sense that he thinks objects exist that have spatial features such as extension and distance from a perceiver; what he denies is that these external objects are "in an unthinking subject without the mind" (*PHK* 1.15). That is, he denies that there are external *material* objects. But he does sometimes abbreviate his view by saying that he denies that there are "outward objects" (*PHK* 1.15), and this is how Shepherd reads him, too.

[12] She will say more about negative ideas in chapter 2 of EASP.

162 MARY SHEPHERD

relationships among our sensations, their effects (*EPEU* 38; see also 205). As she puts it,

> the soul does truly in a sense *perceive* outward things, *as* they are when existing outwardly, for after *reason* shews that the qualities of things, in a state of *perception,* cannot *be like* them out of a state of perception, yet being conscious that sensation is only a simple act ... *it perceives* by the understanding that the *varieties* of things are in relation to each other *outwardly* in the *same proportion* as are the inward sensations. (*EPEU* 206; see also 165 and 181–82)

That is, as Martha Bolton has explained, Shepherd holds that "there is a structural identity between the sensory effects and the external world which enables us to know relational properties of causes."[13] A little later, Shepherd gives some concrete examples to illustrate this structural isomorphism. If we have distinct sensations of scarlet and blue, this means two distinct external existences must correspond to them; if we have distinct sensations of empty space and extension, such as a sensation of an empty box, the cause of the sensation of emptiness must be something distinct from the cause of the sensation of the box (*EPEU* 48). As Shepherd puts it, the sense-organs and the mind are "always the *same ingredients* thrown into the compound qualities presented to it," and so the fact that our sensations vary means that the *other* causes, the external objects, must be varied (*EPEU* 48). As the external objects vary, so do the internal objects.

But why does Shepherd think this? If the causes of our sensations cannot resemble our sensations themselves, how can she claim that the *proportions* and *relationships* among the causes of our sensations do resemble the proportions and relationships among our sensations? Shepherd takes this up in the "Recapitulation" chapter at the end of EASP. She notes that features pertaining to

---

[13] Bolton, "Causality and Causal Induction," 246.

THE EXTERNAL WORLD   163

how causes relate *to each other*, or how effects relate *to each other*, can in fact be structurally analogous: "For there exists *one* set of exterior qualities, *which we may know of, as resembling such as are inward*" (*EPEU* 182). These include the qualities not just of variety but also independence, existence, duration, identity, cause and effect, and probably others as well (*EPEU* 182–84). These features are common to *both* internal and external objects.

Interestingly, Shepherd here uses a term that she seldom uses elsewhere, 'affection' (*EPEU* 184). This is a more appropriate term than 'quality' because 'quality' suggests either being a causal power (a quality of external objects) or being sensible (a quality of internal objects). But 'affection' is neutral between these: affections are neither the internal effects of external objects nor the external causes of internal effects.[14] For example, an object being "varied" from another is neither a causal power nor something that can be sensed on its own; that my sensation of redness is different (varied) from my sensation of blueness is a fact that I perceive *through having those sensations*, not through some additional sensation of "variety."

Consider another affection, existence. When I have various sensible qualities of, say, redness and roundness, I infer that an external object exists that is comprised of causal powers to produce redness and roundness. That is, I infer simply that the external object *exists*; I do not infer that the bundle of causal powers that cause sensations of redness and roundness includes some *additional causal power* to make me think it exists.[15] Shepherd's idea here might be that treating existence as a further causal power of external objects (or, for internal objects, as a further sensible quality) would lead to a

---

[14] Later, Shepherd says that our idea of existence is an "abstract notion" that can apply to things that are sentient as well as insentient (*EPEU* 83). Since independence, duration, identity, cause and effect, and other "affections" can also apply to more than one kind of object, it seems likely that she would class these, too, as "abstract notions."

[15] There are echoes here of Kant's insistence that existence cannot be part of the concept of a thing (*Critique of Pure Reason*, A 597/B 625). Since Shepherd says that the definition of an external object consists of all (and only) its causal powers, she would agree that the definition of an external object cannot include existence. Likewise, since the

164   MARY SHEPHERD

regress, for saying that *there is* a causal power to make me think an object exists (or that *there is* a sensible quality of existence) would be saying that, in turn, *there is* a causal power to make me think *the causal power* exists; but then this "there is" would need to be cashed out in terms of ascribing yet another causal power to *that* causal power, and so on ad infinitum.

In sum, Shepherd designates as 'affections' those characteristics that are predicable of either internal or external qualities (or bundles of qualities) but that are not themselves qualities (*EPEU* 182). This allows her to say that when I perceive that one of my sensations is different from another, is independent from another, is identical to itself, or has a duration over time, I can infer the same thing about the causes of my sensation. Since the sensible quality of redness is different from the sensible quality of blueness, I can legitimately infer that the cause of redness is different from the cause of blueness. The structure of causes (in the external world) is identical to the structure of effects (in the internal world).

As Shepherd expresses this structural identity, the relationship between our sensations and the external world is analogous to that between algebraic signs and the quantities they stand for, an analogy that appears several times in her work (*EPEU* 38, 47, and 261). In her final published essay, "Lady Mary Shepherd's Metaphysics," Shepherd develops the algebraic analogy further, although she does caution that the analogy should not be taken too strictly (LMSM 704n). There is also an important difference between her employment of the analogy in *EPEU* and in the magazine article. In *EPEU*, algebraic signs are analogous to sensations: the former represent unknown quantities just as the latter represent external objects. In "Lady Mary Shepherd's Metaphysics," algebraic signs are analogous to external objects and sense-organs, and the *square* of a particular sign is analogous to the sensation caused

---

definition of an internal object consists of the bundle of sensible qualities making it up, definitions of internal objects also include no *sensation* of existence.

THE EXTERNAL WORLD 165

by the interaction of the object and sense-organs (LMSM 703–4). Thus, she represents the *causes* of sensory perceptions with letters: c for the cause of a color sensation, s for the cause of a sensation of smell, m for the cause of a sensation of motion, and so on (LMSM 703). Treating the "organ of sense which exists in relation" to each external cause as "equal to" that external cause, Shepherd uses the same symbol to stand for both: c stands for *both* the external object that causes a color sensation *and* for the sense-organ that is required, the eye. A particular sensation results from a mixture of causes, a sense-organ mixed with an external object.[16] As we saw in chapter 2 of this *Guide*, Shepherd sees this mixing as analogous to multiplication; thus, if c represents both a sense-organ and the object perceived by that sense-organ, this can be represented as $c \times c$, or c^2. Since effects are equivalent to the mixture of their causes, this means that c^2 represents the *effect*—in this case, the color sensation. Thus, the algebraic representation allows us to see how the effect correlates to the mixture of the causes. In a much more complicated case of sensing a ship sailing the ocean from Falmouth to Antigua, the relationships (or "proportions") between the external objects— the ship being joined with the sea, the wind moving the ship—are paralleled in the relationships among our sensations of those things (LMSM 703–4): our sensation of the ship is joined with our sensation of the sea, and our sensation presents the ship as having a certain motion away from us. The whole observation of the moving ship leaving Falmouth can be expressed thus: $(s^2 + o^2) - (wm^2) = f^2$ (LMSM 703).[17]

---

[16] Of course, Shepherd thinks that the mind is also a partial cause of sensation; here she simplifies by discussing just two factors, the sense-organ and the external object.

[17] Here, s^2 stands for the perception of the ship (i.e., the effect of the ship itself being mixed with the relevant sense-organ, the eye). That sensation is accompanied by (but not mixed with, hence the sign for addition rather than multiplication) a sensation of the ocean, represented by o^2 (the effect of the ocean itself mixed with the eye). The sensation of the wind in motion (the effect of the wind and whatever motion is in itself) is represented by wm^2; presumably, w and m are represented as multiplied because the

166 MARY SHEPHERD

On Outwardly Existing Objects

Shepherd has now argued that the causes of (some of) our sensations must include things that exist continuously, in contrast to our transitory sensations. Chapter 2 of EASP takes up the second question Shepherd identified in her introductory chapter, the "foundations, for considering such objects EXTERNAL to, instead of a part of, or included in the perceiving mind" (*EPEU* 12). What is the latent reasoning by which we reach this conclusion? Shepherd begins by stating the *conclusion* of this reasoning, which is that the mind (the capacity for sensation in general) possesses inward existence, while the causes of our specific sensations possess outward existence (*EPEU* 40)—that is to say, they are external objects. These differ from internal ("inward") objects in two ways. First, internal objects, being composed of sensible qualities, do not cause sensations in other minds, whereas outward objects can cause sensations in minds other than our own (*EPEU* 42). Second, internal objects do not exist continuously; when not thought of, they are "nought" (*EPEU* 43), whereas outward objects are "continually existing objects" (*EPEU* 43–44). She will elaborate on both these claims later in her chapter.

Shepherd suggests that the reasoning showing that there are outwardly existing objects is not complicated: a conscious mirror that knew only of the images on its surface could infer that the images must be caused by something that exists separately from itself (*EPEU* 44).[18] In fact, as she notes later, it is actually *more*

---

external objects (motion and wind) are interacting with each other. Why Shepherd presents the sensation of wind in motion as being *subtracted* from the sensations of ship and ocean is unclear; perhaps it is because the sensation is of the ship sailing *away* from the city of Falmouth. Presumably, the combination of these perceptions together constitutes the whole observation, f^2.

[18] Shepherd also uses a mirror analogy at LMSM 702, where she describes a conscious mirror that is part of a camera obscura. A camera obscura was a darkened room with a small opening in one wall through which an image of an external object or scene could be projected onto a wall in the room. In thirteenth-century Europe, the camera obscura was used to study eclipses without damaging the eye. Later versions of the camera

THE EXTERNAL WORLD   167

straightforward to infer the existence of objects external to oneself than it is to infer that those objects must exist continuously even when one is not perceiving them (*EPEU* 53). However, she also thinks that while the reasoning for external objects is simple, the conclusion is unnerving. In recognizing that there must be both internal and external objects and that these cannot resemble each other, the mind is "so startled at the discovery as not to know how to settle and arrange its belief on the subject, and is filled with a thousand fears concerning the consequences of it" (*EPEU* 45–46). This reaction has produced a range of philosophical accounts of the relationship between the internal and the external—she cites Malebranche, Leibniz, Reid, Berkeley, and Hume (*EPEU* 46)—all of whom are, according to Shepherd, incorrect.[19] While philosophers might have an advantage over ordinary folks in recognizing the internal/external object distinction, Shepherd thinks that none so far have understood the relationship between them, which is that

> in order to the formation of *all* the effects produced on the mind, through the senses, there must be *efficient causes, not included* in the *general essence* of the mind; and these are "*ever ready to appear*," and that in so *clear, vigorous,* and *uniform* a method, and fashion . . . that whatever they may be, however unknown, they may well be termed *objects, outward objects,* which the organs of sense, and their associations reveal, according to their peculiar bearings upon the mind. (*EPEU* 47)

Shepherd has so far told us the *conclusion* of the argument that external objects exist, and she has insisted that the argument is straightforward, albeit disconcerting. But what is the argument? How do we reach the conclusion that there is a distinction between

obscura were created using portable boxes with mirrors and lenses. For a detailed history, see Hammond, *The Camera Obscura: A Chronicle.*

[19] Another philosopher whom Shepherd thinks has missed the mark is Étienne Bonnot de Condillac (1714–80); her criticisms will be discussed in chapter 8 of this *Guide.*

168 MARY SHEPHERD

the inward and the outward and that the causes of our sensations fall into the latter category?

In the brief second section of this chapter, Shepherd first makes the case that we have an idea of outwardness. She invokes the principle (for which she does not argue) that to have a word implies having an idea that the word signifies (*EPEU* 50; see also 38). Since we have the *word* 'outward,' we must have an idea of outwardness (or, as she sometimes says, "exteriority" [*EPEU* 55, 176] or "distance" [*EPEU* 59]). But the idea of outwardness is a "negative" idea (*EPEU* 50). In chapter 1 Shepherd had characterized our ideas of sound sleep, death, and unperceived objects as both "notions" and "negative ideas" (*EPEU* 37–38). By a "notion" Shepherd evidently means an idea of something that we infer to exist, and by a "negative idea" she seems to mean an idea that we can understand insofar as it is the contrary of something we sense. We can understand what death is not because we have sensible qualities caused by being dead ourselves, but because we can think of the contrary of the sensible qualities caused by being alive. But Shepherd stresses that negative ideas are inferred through reasoning from other ideas, in just the same way that positive ideas are (*EPEU* 52n).

So, in saying our idea of outwardness is a "negative notion," Shepherd seems to mean that we infer that outwardness exists (that is, it is not a sensible quality) and that we can understand what outwardness is insofar as it is the opposite of something we sense directly: inward existence. She offers a mathematical analogy. When we add 5 + 5 and calculate that the answer is 10, the zero in the units place shows that there is nothing there (*EPEU* 50). Nonetheless, we have to calculate that zero as much as we have to calculate the five in the tens place. Similarly, both negative and positive ideas can be reached through the same process of inference.[20]

---

[20] The analogy is a little misleading; the zero in '10' is reached through calculation, but the zero shows that there is nothing there; the zero stands for nothing. The idea of the existence of outward beings, too, is reached through reasoning, but the idea of outwardness

THE EXTERNAL WORLD   169

But Shepherd still has to explain *how* inference enables us to acquire the idea of outwardness. She turns to this project in section 3, describing four *"phenomena which generate the idea of outwardness"* (*EPEU* 51)—that is, four ways by which we come to believe that objects exist at a distance from and externally to us. We come to believe this because (1) our sensations are interrupted, (2) we experience ourselves as moving, (3) we experience objects as being beyond the limit of our skin, and (4) we have a visual sensation of externality. Each of these facts can serve as a premise in a piece of latent reasoning by which we reach the conclusion that there must be outward, *external* objects that cause our sensations of sensible qualities; there are, then, at least four different ways one can reach the conclusion that external objects exist.

First, Shepherd notes that the same interrupted character of our sensations that establishes that objects exist continuously also establishes that these objects are *external* to our own minds (*EPEU* 52). The transitory nature of each particular sensation shows that it needs a cause other than both itself and the general, ongoing capacity of sensation; and to be "other than" the sensations and the mind is precisely what it means for a thing to be outward or "exterior."

Shepherd thinks this reasoning shows us that several *kinds* of uninterrupted things must exist outside our own particular sensations. Our sense-organs are among the causes of sensations, and they, like other external objects, are (typically, anyway) "ready upon the call of the mind to act as such causes" (*EPEU* 54), so our sense-organs too must exist outside our particular sensations even when we are not actually using those sense-organs (when we are asleep, for example). Shepherd uses this as an opportunity to criticize Berkeley for inconsistency: while he wants to say that only minds and ideas exist, he nonetheless appeals to sense-organs as

---

stands for something that *does* exist; there *are* "outward beings," even if we must conceive of these in negative terms as "beings not in the mind" (*EPEU* 50–51).

170   MARY SHEPHERD

among the causes of ideas, assuming their independent existence as *"mechanical instruments"* (*EPEU* 55). She will return to this objection later, in essay 2 of *EPEU*.[21]

Shepherd then switches to a topic that might seem quite different than that of external, outward objects: the mind, that "individual capacity for sensation in general" (*EPEU* 14–15). She argues that the fact that sensations come and go according to the "call of the senses" proves that the *mind itself* can be said to be outward in a sense, at least relative to our particular sensations. There might seem to be a tension in Shepherd's claims here. On the one hand, she says that the mind has internal or inward *existence* that contrasts with the specific externally existing objects that cause particular sensations (*EPEU* 40). On the other hand, now she wants to say there is a sense in which the mind can be said to be *external*: "the mind must be a *continued* and *exterior* capacity fitted to each change" of sensation (*EPEU* 56–57). It is, she says, "exterior to each sensation in particular" (*EPEU* 56). In ascribing both interiority and externality to the mind, Shepherd need not be contradicting herself, so long as she is operating with two different inner/outer distinctions. As a general capacity to sense (*EPEU* 15), the mind is a causal power, which fits Shepherd's characterization of external rather than internal objects—and, like other causal powers, the existence even of one's own mind as a capacity must be *inferred* rather than being directly sensed. So the mind has *interior existence* insofar as it is the capacity for consciousness, but it is an *external object* insofar as it is a causal power, not a sensible quality; the mind is external to the sensible qualities that result from the mind's interaction with external objects. Through reasoning, then, we realize that the mind is a *"continued* and *exterior* capacity"* and that "the pronoun *I* is ever *abstract*: and stands for a BEING *exterior* to, and independent of all the changes of which it is conscious" (*EPEU* 56–57).

---

[21] For discussion, see chapter 7 of this *Guide*.

THE EXTERNAL WORLD 171

Shepherd says that the definition of this 'I'—the mind, the capacity to sense—does not include the capacity that matter possesses "*of exhibiting upon a sentient nature, the sense of solid* EXTENSION in general" (*EPEU* 242). That is, mind does not appear to us as matter does; "*thought, sensation merely*, never suggests the occupation of space as essential to its existence" (*EPEU* 58). Yet the 'I' is joined with a body, which *is* located in space. This fact leads Shepherd to the second of her four ways that we come to believe that there must be outward, external objects.

This second way—the "chief" source of our belief in outward objects—is based on our sensations of being in motion or at rest (*EPEU* 57–58; see also *EPEU* 176).[22] As we saw in chapter 5 of this *Guide*, Shepherd regards motion, the body's capacity to move, as a sixth sense. Since the "intimate sensation of our own mind, separated from the ideas of our bodies . . . has no relation to space, or place" (*EPEU* 58), the (mental) sense of being in motion must mean the body is involved. When we use our bodies, even if only to move a hand to reach some object, we have sensations of being in one place and then in another. This, says Shepherd,

consists in the impression of passing through extended space, and as a corollary with it suggests to the mind, *here,* and *there;* and whilst the *mind* requires *no place*, nor *space*, to *comprehend it*, the sensation of passing through different points of space, suggests the notion, or rather inspires the immediate feeling of the *extension of space*, (or of an unresisting medium,) but never that of the *extension of the sentient principle, the self.* (*EPEU* 58)

---

[22] Shepherd reiterates this argument in the "Recapitulation" chapter, where she says that "it is motion, as first in order, and first in proof, which is impowered to detect the OUTWARDNESS of objects" (*EPEU* 176–77). In a footnote, she distinguishes her view from that of the French Ideologue Destutt de Tracy, who argued that we believe in an external world of objects based merely on the resistance we feel when we try to move among objects. Shepherd stresses that there must also be a "mixture of reasoning" to draw the conclusion that an external world exists (*EPEU* 177–78n).

172　MARY SHEPHERD

So we have an "immediate feeling" of the three-dimensionality of space as we move about. Shepherd does not give this sensation a name, but for convenience we can call it the 'extension-sensation.' This sensation is analogous to our sensations of color, sound, and so on; like them, the extension-sensation comes and goes according to how we move our bodies (*EPEU* 58–59). Thus, there must be some continuously existing cause of the extension-sensation:

> It is hence the immediate consequence of motion also to suggest the corollary that must be included in its essence, that is, the *reality* of distance or outwardness from the *sentient being*, the *self;* which has an equal relation to *rest*, and *motion;* and, therefore, knows of outward existence, as it does of *continued existence*, by a piece of reasoning; viz. that it needs must be in order to justify the possibility of motion when in a state of rest, as well as regularly to respond to its action upon demand. (*EPEU* 59; see also 176)

This, then, is another "piece of reasoning" by which we know about outwardness (*EPEU* 59; see also 174–75). The conclusions of this reasoning are contained implicitly in our very sensations (*EPEU* 169–70). This is Shepherd's meaning when she says that "the soul has the *idea* (or conclusion from reasoning) of distance, mixed with the *sensible impression* of rest; which mixture gives occasion to that just result and consequence, the notion of *outward* and *inward* existence" (*EPEU* 59).[23]

Shepherd's aim here is to show how our own sensations of motion through space give us reason to infer the existence of outwardness. But she adds later that these sensations also give us reason to infer

---

[23] Shepherd first mentions the role of our sensation of *rest*, and then in the next paragraph mentions sensations of *motion*. This can give the impression that she is describing *two* arguments for the idea of outwardness; yet she says that the idea of distance/outward existence results from the impression of rest, so it is unclear what additional role the impression of motion might play. Shepherd may think that the ideas of rest and motion are co-dependent, such that to have an impression of rest is to have an impression of a *contrast* with one's impression of motion.

THE EXTERNAL WORLD   173

the existence of an external object that is *motion itself.* Just as our sensations of colors and sounds give us reason to infer the existence of causal powers interacting with our sense-organs, our sensations of being in motion, or indeed of seeing or feeling something *else* in motion, give us reason to infer the existence of a causal power that is "real" (LMSM 701–2) or "unperceived motion" (OLMS 625). She writes that

> the *cause* of motion, or unperceived motion, is the *essence* of what motion is in nature; and in its unperceived state, we know that it *cannot be like its effect*, a perception; all we know is, that it is in its *unperceived state*, in which it must act as a *cause*, and that the perception of it must be an *effect*, and owe its existence to a prior cause; because it is a *dependent being*, and *begins to be*, even when *un*related to us; for we know our *sensation* of it does not cause it, therefore, something else does. (*EPEU* 60; see also 175)

Because of the principle that there are correlative proportions between our sensations and the causes of those sensations, we actually can know *something* about this unperceived real motion, namely that it is "successive change of place" (LMSM 701–2). However, she stresses, "our perception that this change is going on, is *not* the change itself. We perceive it because it exists; it does not exist because we perceive it" (LMSM 702).

Shepherd's third argument about the source of belief in outward objects is based on her observation that when we touch objects, we experience them as "*beyond the limit of the skin of the body*" (*EPEU* 51; see also 179–80). A contrast with the sense of pain may be instructive: when I sense pain, that sensation seems to be in my body in a way that sensations of trees, houses, apples, and so on are not. While Shepherd identifies the 'I' with the mind alone (*EPEU* 56–57), she acknowledges that we think of ourselves as not just consciousness, but a consciousness that occurs "within a bound, or certain limit . . . and this *limit* we call the skin, within which, is contained *all*

174   MARY SHEPHERD

we call ourselves" (*EPEU* 62).[24] Without using any sense-organs, we could have a "general sensation of life" (*EPEU* 63); that is, we could be aware of our train of thoughts, our heart beating, our muscles flexing, and so on. But "for *particular kinds* of sensation the organs of sense are to be used; which organs are in relation to things that appear *beyond the skin of the body*, and which also require motion, in order to apprehend their tangibility" (*EPEU* 63). In using our sense-organs, our sensations include feelings of interacting with things "beyond the skin," things that we can only reach and handle by using bodily motion (*EPEU* 63). These sensations are sufficiently different from the sensations involved merely in the "general sensation of life" that we consider the two groups to be different "*classes of sensations*," the former coming from "outward existences" and the latter from what exists inwardly (*EPEU* 64).

Finally, Shepherd suggests that just as our sense of motion gives us what we might call an 'extension-sensation,' so too does our sense of *vision*.[25] We have "a power of seeing" the "unresisting medium" through which we move toward objects that are at a distance (*EPEU* 65). That is, we have a kind of *visual* 'extension-sensation' in addition to the sensation we have as we move through space. This sensation, like others, comes and goes; if I close my eyes, I will no longer see objects as being at a distance from me, but when I open my eyes, I will. And just like any other sensation, "it must have its cause" (*EPEU* 65).

Furthermore, Shepherd says that it is not just a general idea of outwardness that we infer from sensation. Through these visual sensations of "*a different degree of distance*," we can infer the

[24] For more on Shepherd's account of the self, see chapter 8 of this *Guide*.

[25] Shepherd thus departs significantly from Berkeley, who had maintained that "the ideas of space, outness, and things placed at a distance are not, strictly speaking, the object of sight" (*NTV* 46). Instead, he held that we learn about the distance, size, and situation of objects originally through touch, whereby we acquire "tangible ideas" (*NTV* 45). We learn through experience that various tangible ideas are coordinated with various visible ideas (which are immediately perceived by vision) so that having a particular visible idea comes to suggest its associated tangible idea (*NTV* 51, 147). For further discussion, see chapter 10 of this *Guide*.

THE EXTERNAL WORLD   175

"relative position of unperceived things" (*EPEU* 66): that is, we can infer that one object is to the left or right, above or below, in front of or behind another object, as well as objects' relations to ourselves. Shepherd suggests that it is because of different color-sensations that we see distance (*EPEU* 65), although her explanation will (as we will see in chapter 10 of this *Guide*) turn out to be more complicated than that. At any rate, these visual sensations of the positions and distances of objects lead us to conclude, through the usual process that Shepherd characterizes as latent reasoning, that there is "an unperceived cause of a certain relation deemed distance," as well as one "*for a different degree of distance*, to what we deem or term our own body" (*EPEU* 66). This unperceived cause is "that common quality called outwardness, which quality CONTINUES *to exist*, EXTERNALLY *to the capacity of sensation in general*" (*EPEU* 67). This is the fourth method by which outwardness is inferred, although Shepherd does note that this reasoning is so "blended together" with the senses that the inference is made "immediately" (*EPEU* 67); the resulting conclusion that outwardness truly exists is just as immediately mixed with the sensations of sensible qualities (*EPEU* 67–68), resulting in the compound entity that is an internal perceived object.

Shepherd closes *EPEU* chapter 2 by showing where she thinks others have gone wrong. Ordinary people have a tendency to conflate internal and external objects, "by a very natural and almost indissoluble association of ideas" (*EPEU* 68; see also 21 and 127–28); we tend to think that the sensible qualities we experience are the very same things as objects out there in the world. Berkeley erred in a different way, by separating sensible qualities from their causes and then "omitting" and ignoring the latter, not seeing that "sensation is but as a thin gauze" that actually enables us to infer that causes must exist (*EPEU* 73)—and that these causes must exist not, as Berkeley thought, as "spirits," but as external material objects with a "proportional relation and variety" that correspond to our sensations (*EPEU* 69). Hume erred in denying that *any* kind of

176 MARY SHEPHERD

external objects could be known by reason to exist, leaving us only with sensible qualities linked by "custom" in the imagination (*EPEU* 69). And even Reid erred in his understanding of the relationship between the internal and the external, despite the fact that he was trying to argue against precisely such errors (*EPEU* 70–71). Reid claimed that primary qualities (the real figure, size, and position of external objects) could be clearly conceived although we have no sensations resembling them; thus, we can know, for example, that real hardness is "a firm cohesion of parts" and real sound is "vibrations of the air" (*EPEU* 70). But, says Shepherd, cohesion, vibrations, and other allegedly "real" features of the external world are *themselves* perceived by sensation, and so they *cannot* be unperceived causal powers out there in the external world (*EPEU* 70; see also 180). Thus, Reid mislocated some sensible qualities as outward rather than in sentient perceivers, leading him to the absurd conclusion that some sensible qualities are the effects of other sensible qualities (see also *EPEU* 127).

On Independently Existing Objects

EPEU chapter 3 takes up the third question from Shepherd's introductory chapter: why do we believe that the objects we infer to exist "are entirely INDEPENDENT of our own existence; although we can only know them by our sensations, which themselves DEPEND upon our existence?" (*EPEU* 12). By one object A being "independent" of another object B, Shepherd sometimes means that A is *considered* without reference to B (*ERCE* 46, 180; *EPEU* 34, 74), but often it expresses an *ontological* independence, where A's existence is not *caused* by B (*ERCE* 32, 72, 148). In chapter 3, Shepherd explores our belief that external objects are independent of our minds in the sense that they are not caused by our minds.

Shepherd offers five reasons for thinking this. First, she says, the argument that establishes that *external* objects exist in order

THE EXTERNAL WORLD   177

to cause our sensations can prove those same objects to be *independent* of our sensations, because whatever objects are "entirely exterior to the cause or capacity for sensation in general, must also be independent of such capacity" (*EPEU* 76–77). She does not offer any further reasoning for this claim, however.

A second reason for thinking external objects are independent of the mind is that they change in ways we do not directly observe or experience (*EPEU* 77). Suppose I see a rosebud, closed in the morning, that has bloomed by evening. I was not there to see it changing, so I can conclude that while the rose bush (or, strictly speaking, the external causal power whereby I have sensations of a rose bush) persisted even when I left the garden, the rose bush also underwent an unobserved change. As Shepherd concludes,

> with respect to those objects which are "ready to appear to the senses," we observe they have gone through *changes of qualities*, the process of which was not observed by us, and which changes therefore, must be independent of any part of ourselves; and not being perceived, cannot be caused by our perception, and must therefore, be wholly independent of it. (*EPEU* 77–78)

If I did *not* have sensations of a change in an object while that change was occurring, then of course my mind cannot have been the cause of the change, and so the object must be independent of my mind (*EPEU* 77).

Shepherd's third argument is very compressed: "Objects are reckoned *independent* of ourselves, because they appear *like ourselves* plus or minus the varieties of qualities; and *we to ourselves* are independent of others, and are minds, beings, capable of sensations" (*EPEU* 78).

Here Shepherd is referring to objects in general, but in a footnote, she alludes to Berkeley's argument for the existence of other minds (*EPEU* 78n), and she goes on to offer her own argument for other

178   MARY SHEPHERD

minds.[26] The argument depends on the CLP, as she emphasizes in the "Recapitulation" chapter: "*Independent* existence . . . is a conclusion of reasoning; an idea in the understanding in relation to the perception of the necessity there should be like cause for like effect, and proportional causes for proportional effects" (*EPEU* 174; see also 187). We each know we have sensations of our own independent existence and of pleasure and pain, and we see other human bodies exhibiting "symptoms" of feeling the same things (*EPEU* 79); for example, I observe a being with a body shaped like mine, exhibiting behavior—crying out, for example—that I know in my own case is caused by feeling pain. Knowing that "*similar sensations are similar objects*, and the *varieties* make the *varieties*" (*EPEU* 78), we can infer from their behavior that other human bodies have sensations like our own, even though we are not conscious of their sensations (see also *EPEU* 172); and, since sensations are the effects of mind, we can infer that those other humans have minds, too. That is, we can infer that there are other minds that are independent of our own.

Shepherd suggests that this argument can be generalized to other objects, so long as they "appear *like ourselves* plus or minus the varieties of qualities" (*EPEU* 78).[27] As Margaret Atherton has noted, this argument seems "initially puzzling" since, according to Shepherd, all we know about other objects is that they are unperceived causal powers whose existence we infer only through their effects.[28] But, as Atherton notes, it is precisely insofar as they are causal powers that external objects resemble us.[29] Tables, houses, and rose bushes are able to cause us to have sensations, just as we ourselves have causal powers. Knowing ourselves to be independent

---

[26] For further discussion of other minds, see chapter 8.

[27] In fact, she thinks that one of Berkeley's mistakes was *not* to have generalized this argument (*EPEU* 208).

[28] Atherton, "Lady Mary Shepherd's Case against George Berkeley," 353.

[29] Atherton, "Lady Mary Shepherd's Case against George Berkeley," 353.

THE EXTERNAL WORLD   179

of others when we operate as causal powers, we can infer that other causal powers, too, are independent of us (*EPEU* 78).

Shepherd next briefly considers an objection to her view that external, continuously existing objects are independent of us. Just as we have sensations of external objects that appear and reappear, sometimes we have a *thought* that we then forget, but can recover through reflection. For example, I might think "I need to buy more bread" but then later, in the store, be temporarily unable to remember what I need. When I give the matter some thought— when I "reflect"—I can remember the forgotten thought. An objector might claim that Shepherd's arguments justify the conclusion that such "lost thoughts" also exist independently of us, but nobody thinks that this is so (*EPEU* 79); my thought "I need to buy more bread" surely did not continue to exist even while I was not thinking of it. Shepherd's response is that reflection is just a process of *retracing* associations of thoughts that cause a *new* thought that is qualitatively (but not numerically) identical to the forgotten one (*EPEU* 79).

Shepherd's fourth point is that in observing that many minds seem to be affected by one object, we infer that the object exists independently of *all* our minds (*EPEU* 80–81). "If five men see a pond, and can only walk round one pond, then there is one pond seen five times over, not five ponds" (*EPEU* 81), she writes. It would be "impossible that there should be as many objects as minds" (*EPEU* 80–81). Shepherd's reasoning here is a *reductio ad absurdum* that depends on her view that a "real" external object meets all that is included in its "whole definition" (*EPEU* 30); a key component of the definition of any external object is whether more than one person can be affected by it (*EPEU* 35).[30] Suppose that the fact that five people sense a pond means that there are, in fact, five ponds. Each pond would meet the chief criterion for being real: if one

---

[30] On real definitions, see chapter 3 of this *Guide*. On her criteria for the reality of objects, see chapter 8.

180   MARY SHEPHERD

person reports that there is a pond, the other four would agree. For each perceiver, the perceived pond would have all the qualities of a real pond. Shepherd's claim is that in this scenario, the many ponds would "merit the definition due to *one pond*"; the definition of one pond would be met by five ponds. Since (according to Shepherd) this is a contradiction (*EPEU* 81), we have reason to reject the initial assumption that five people sensing a pond means that there are five ponds. Thus, "the mind must come to the belief of only *one pond*, seen by five persons; that is, in other words, an independent cause for particular sensations" (*EPEU* 81).[31]

Shepherd's fifth point about the independence of external objects depends on a claim about "relations of abstract ideas" (*EPEU* 81). Her example of an abstract idea is our idea of "existence in general," which can apply to either sentient or insentient beings (*EPEU* 83). Abstraction is "the consideration of any quality apart from others with which it may be usually united, in order to notice what inferences may be drawn from its nature" (*EPEU* 291; see also 85). For example, once we conclude that external objects must exist, we can form an abstract idea of existence by comparing the transitory existence of sensations with the continuous existence of the objects we infer to exist; "by such comparisons of ideas we gain the notion of indefinite unknown existence" (*EPEU* 83–84; see also 162–63 and 182–83). And once we have abstract ideas, we can relate them in various ways (*EPEU* 81), forming "axioms" (*EPEU* 82) or "abstract propositions" (*EPEU* 83). While Shepherd does not mention any specific examples of abstract propositions here, elsewhere she uses the term 'axiom' to characterize the CP and the CLP (*EPEU* 232–33, 285, 290). Indeed, these are plausible

---

[31] Shepherd's only explicit reference to Berkeley's *Three Dialogues between Hylas and Philonous* (1713) occurs here; she says he handles this point "in a very unsatisfactory, hesitating manner in his dialogues" (*EPEU* 81), although she does not say more to identify the basis of her objection.

THE EXTERNAL WORLD   181

candidates to be abstract propositions, insofar as they are about objects considered quite generally; they apply to both internal and external objects.

What do abstract propositions have to do with the independence of objects? Shepherd maintains that for a proposition to be an "*axiom* that is to govern our understanding when not adverted to," its truth must be independent of us (*EPEU* 82). That is, the *relations* among our sensations that enable us to infer (through latent reasoning) the causal principles and the existence of the external world are already there when we have those sensations; we *discover* the truth of such propositions "because the relations exist ready to be perceived" (*EPEU* 83). This fact helps generate the idea of independent existence.

This point also gives Shepherd the basis for an objection to idealists like Berkeley. Berkeley wants to say that the proposition "We know nothing but our perceptions" is an axiom; if this proposition is *not* true, his conclusion that only minds and ideas exist will not follow. But if this proposition *is* true, it must be true independently of being perceived, or else it will be "of no force" when it is not being actually thought of (*EPEU* 82). In other words, Shepherd argues, defending Berkeleyan idealism requires relying on a principle that must be true independently of us; it cannot be true if idealism is true.

The first three chapters of the "Essay on the Academical or Sceptical Philosophy" have laid out Shepherd's argument that there is a world of external objects that are causally independent of us as perceivers and exist continuously even when we do not perceive them. She has mentioned, and sketched responses to, some skeptical challenges to her arguments, such as the worry that our sensations may be mere dreams or illusions (*EPEU* 29–35) and the Berkeleyan charge that we really have no ideas or notions of external objects (*EPEU* 37), but she has much more to say about this in EASP chapter 4 and the first two short essays of *EPEU*. This will be the topic of our next chapter.

182 MARY SHEPHERD

Suggestions for Further Reading

- Shepherd's arguments that we can know there is an external world are discussed in Margaret Atherton, "Lady Mary Shepherd's Case against George Berkeley," 349–53; Antonia LoLordo's introduction to *Mary Shepherd's Essays on the Perception of an External Universe*, 10–17; and Martha Bolton's entry on Shepherd in the *Stanford Encyclopedia of Philosophy*.

7

Skepticism and Idealism

Introduction

Shepherd responds at various points to skeptical challenges posed by phenomena such as dreams and hallucinations: since these states seem indistinguishable from experiences caused by external objects, how can we be sure that life is not merely a "waking dream" or a series of delusions (*EPEU* 33)? Shepherd aims to show that we need not take these skeptical scenarios seriously, although, as we will see, she also concedes that her arguments fall short of being "demonstrations" that establish their conclusions with deductive certainty.

Shepherd is even more concerned to distinguish her view from the idealism and immaterialism advanced by George Berkeley. She lauds Berkeley's aim of trying to provide "the foundation of the most secure belief in Deity" (*EPEU* 5) and agrees with him on several points (*EPEU* 6, 127, 197, 296). However, where Berkeley concludes that there are no grounds for inferring the separate existence of material objects that cause our sensations, and even that "the very notion of what is called 'matter' or 'corporeal substance' involves a contradiction in it" (*PHK* 1.9), Shepherd says this is the result of "fallacious, and inconclusive, and paradoxical reasoning" (*EPEU* 213). Berkeley offers his idealism and immaterialism as a response to skepticism (*PHK* 1.40). In fact, Shepherd thinks, his system is "a source of universal skepticism" (*EPEU* 5).

This chapter considers the various forms of skepticism to which Shepherd responds. The next section discusses Shepherd's stance on dreams and delusions, focusing on her passing remarks in chapter 1

Mary Shepherd. Deborah Boyle, Oxford University Press. © Oxford University Press 2023.
DOI: 10.1093/oso/9780190090326.003.0007

184   MARY SHEPHERD

of EASP and her more detailed discussion in chapter 4. Next, the chapter considers Shepherd's objections to Berkeley's appeal to dreaming and her objections to Reid for his failure to consider dreaming. The final three sections turn to Shepherd's objections to Berkeleyan idealism in *EPEU* essays 1, 2, and 6, respectively.

Dreams, Delusions, and Reality

Descartes' *Discourse on the Method* (1637) and *Meditations on First Philosophy* (1641) both raise skeptical concerns based on the fact that dreams can sometimes be indistinguishable from what we take to be waking life. Might we not, therefore, at any point be mistaken in thinking that we are awake? As Descartes puts it, perhaps *everything* I experience is really "no more true than the illusions of my dreams."[1] Ultimately, of course, Descartes thinks a benevolent God would not allow us to be so systematically deceived. Shepherd, too, thinks she has the resources to respond to such skepticism, although on very different grounds than does Descartes.

Shepherd first brings up dreams in EASP chapter 1, and she devotes all of chapter 4 to the same topic.[2] How can we distinguish sensations that are mere dream states from those that are currently caused by external objects? How can we tell which internal objects come from real external objects? Her answer involves defining what it means to be real and arguing that dreamt-of objects do not meet the criteria for reality (*EPEU* 29–33). "A *real* object," she says, "is that which comprehends all the qualities for which its name stands," one that meets all that is included in its "whole definition" (*EPEU* 30). Or, as she puts it in the "Recapitulation" chapter, "the

---

[1] Descartes, *Discourse on Method*, 18.
[2] Everything Shepherd says about dreams also applies to hallucinations (or, as she more typically writes, "delusions"), but for convenience, this chapter focuses on dreaming.

SKEPTICISM AND IDEALISM 185

being true to expectations formed of their qualities, is the very criterion of reality" (*EPEU* 188).

As we have seen, for Shepherd the real definition of an external object includes all its causal powers; for example, the real definition of gold includes, among many other powers, its power to produce sensations of yellow in human perceivers (under the right conditions).[3] The real definition of food includes a power to satisfy hunger (*EPEU* 88). Of course, our limited experience does not allow us to test and discover every causal power an object might possess, but Shepherd says the "chief" criterion for determining whether a given sensation is caused by something external and continually existing is whether other people agree that it is because they have similar sensations to ours (*EPEU* 35). "When similar objects are perceived at the *same time* by more than one mind, they must necessarily be *external* to each," she writes (*EPEU* 88). Suppose I am in my kitchen and experience the sensible qualities that are part of the definition of gold, but no one else in the room has similar perceptions: I should infer that I am hallucinating and that my gold-like perceptions are *not* caused by real gold.

In the "Recapitulation" chapter of EASP, Shepherd offers an example of an illusion that she might have considered more accessible to her audience, given that hallucination is uncommon: the diorama that had recently been on display in London. Unlike the dioramas showing animals and habitats that began to be employed in natural history museums in the late nineteenth century, dioramas of the early nineteenth century were rotating theaters where viewers could observe paintings of landscapes and building interiors, painted on special transparent canvas and sometimes as large as 22 × 14 meters, illuminated by complicated lighting systems that made the scenes shift realistically in appearance (as if the sun were setting, for example).[4] The first diorama

---

[3] On real definitions, see chapter 3 of this *Guide*.
[4] On the history of the term 'diorama' and the various forms dioramas have taken over time, see Kamcke and Hutterer, "History of Dioramas."

186 MARY SHEPHERD

was opened in Paris in 1822 by Louis Daguerre, with another opening in Regent's Park, London, in 1823. A contemporaneous article in *The Times* of London reported that "even after the spectator is advised that he is looking at a flat surface, the illusion is so strong that it is almost impossible to believe the fact."[5] Shepherd reports having had a similar experience, writing that "this extraordinary fac-simile of nature and art has the power of effecting a complete delusion" (*EPEU* 186). Looking at the scene while not remembering that one is in a theater ("the relation of place being forgotten" [*EPEU* 186]), the mind thinks the scenes are "*real*; i.e. the colouring is symptomatic as a quality of beings, which will fufill the remainder of the qualities belonging to their definitions upon trial, and thus be equal to their whole definitions" (*EPEU* 186–87). For example, the definition of a statue includes the fact that it can be felt—that is, that it has a causal power to produce in a perceiver a sensible quality of a texture. While temporarily deluded, a spectator in the diorama might think it possible to walk into the scene and actually feel a statue depicted there. But upon remembering their actual location, the spectator will realize that attempting to touch the statue is futile; the sensation of the colored scene is not, in fact, a "symptom" that other expectations about statues will be fulfilled.

Shepherd uses her account of reality to consider a rather limited form of skepticism, regarding the reality of religious "notions"[6] that "either alarm or console" (*EPEU* 35)—presumably she means heaven and hell.[7] What if these ideas are just figments

---

[5] "Diorama," *The Times* (London, October 4, 1823), 3.

[6] On Shepherd's rather loose terminology of 'notion,' see chapter 5 of this *Guide*.

[7] Shepherd's analogy of a compass as a sign of the "*real north*" seems to show she is referring to heaven because she says we know there is a real north when "we have so guided our vessel as to find ourselves at last '*at the heaven where we would be*'" (*EPEU* 36). Unfortunately, her apparent reference to "heaven" is a misprint, as the errata page in *EPEU* points out. She is really referring to the Geneva Bible translation of Psalm 107:30, "he bringeth them unto the haven, where they would be," which is also the basis of Isaac Watts' version in his popular book *The Psalms of David* (1719).

of the imagination, resulting merely from "the organization and action of the brain" (*EPEU* 36)? During life, we cannot prove that these ideas are caused by more than the brain (*EPEU* 36); if heaven or hell exist, we could only know for sure after death. Shepherd's reasoning is not especially clear here, but she seems to mean something like the following. Since real objects "fulfill the *whole qualities* for which their names first stood" (*EPEU* 34), a notion of some object will turn out to represent something that really exists if it turns out that there is an object comprised of the causal powers to bring about *all* the qualities we associate with the name of the object. If, after my death, I find out that there really is something that can cause in me the sensible qualities that I previously merely imagined to belong to my notion 'heaven,' I will know then that that notion was real. In the meantime, the notion of heaven makes people *hope* for happiness after death, which inspires them to act virtuously (*EPEU* 37).

Later in *EPEU*, Shepherd makes a similar point about the possible reality of internal objects that are *not* caused by external objects and that are the result of brain activity (interacting with the mind, of course). She considers two cases: instinct in non-human animals and religious prophesies. A bird knows how to build a nest the first time it tries (*EPEU* 160); the bird presumably has a mental representation (or "notions") of the steps needed to do this, but its notions will turn out to be of "*real* beings" if the end result of the bird's actions is, in fact, a nest, an object that has all the qualities involved in being a nest (*EPEU* 160). Likewise, the images in a prophet's minds are *not* (at that time, anyway) caused by using the sense-organs, but these images will turn out to be "real" if, eventually, the events or objects imagined by the prophet "do really happen afterwards, in such fulness, and order, and perfection" that it would be an utterly bizarre coincidence for the prophet to have simply had those images by chance (*EPEU* 161).

Thus, Shepherd allows that we *can* have mental states *not* caused by sensory perception that nonetheless turn out to represent real

188 MARY SHEPHERD

objects. But dreaming, she thinks, is not one of those states. The sensations we have during dreams can be known *not* to be real because we can recognize that they do not "fulfill" the definitions of the objects we take them to be. However, in EASP chapter 1, Shepherd does not clearly explain how we recognize this. She rather cryptically suggests that, once we awaken, we can realize that we were dreaming because "the mind had only been in one place" (*EPEU* 29, 32). To make more sense of this, we need to turn to EASP chapter 4, where it becomes clear that identifying one's location is just *one* of the criteria for judging whether we were dreaming or not.

Chapter 4 begins with Shepherd restating her previous claims that real objects "fulfill their whole definitions" and that, while we are dreaming, our "powers of comparison" are unable to perceive that the objects of our dreams fail to fulfill their definitions (*EPEU* 88–89). Those powers are "restored" when we wake up, when we realize that those objects lacked their usual causal powers. I may have dreamt of eating a huge meal, but when I wake up I will not feel full. Nor will a dreamt-of meal "affect any more minds than one" (*EPEU* 88).

Shepherd notes one "difficulty" with her account of the reality of objects: it presupposes that we can know with certainty that other *people* exist (*EPEU* 88–89). In judging that an object I sense is real because others agree that they sense it too, my knowledge of the object's existence is only as certain as my knowledge that those other people exist. But one can raise exactly the same kinds of skeptical worries about the existence of other people as one can about everything else. Shepherd concedes the difficulty of providing a "demonstration," or absolutely certain proof, that other minds exist, but writes that her arguments come as close to demonstration as possible (*EPEU* 89). The very same reasoning that proves that there must be causes of our sensations of flowers, houses, bread, and so on also proves that there must be causes of our "*complex ideas of other men*" (*EPEU* 90).

SKEPTICISM AND IDEALISM 189

Shepherd's Criticisms of Berkeley's Appeal to Dreams

In section 2 of EASP chapter 4, Shepherd focuses on Berkeley's claims about dreaming, quoting from his *Treatise Concerning the Principles of Human Knowledge* (1710).[8] Among Berkeley's arguments against belief in an external material world is his claim that in "dreams, frenzies, and the like," our ideas are qualitatively indistinguishable from ideas we have when awake, even though the former ideas are not being caused by external objects that resemble them; this shows, he says, that external objects are unnecessary for having *any* ideas (*PHK* 1.18; quoted at *EPEU* 91–92). Shepherd raises a number of objections to Berkeley's reasoning. Although these are not clearly enumerated in the text, she makes, in essence, three points. First, she denies his premise that the collections of sensible qualities in dreams are qualitatively identical to those we have when we are awake (*EPEU* 92–93). Second, although she agrees that there are no external objects directly causing and resembling dream sensations, she thinks that Berkeley has misunderstood the reason for this, and thus has drawn a mistaken conclusion about the causes of dream sensations (*EPEU* 94–95). Third, she thinks Berkeley's argument is invalid because while his premise is about *resembling* external objects, his conclusion is about *all* external objects (*EPEU* 97). Let us consider each of these objections in turn.

Shepherd first denies Berkeley's claim that dream sensations are indistinguishable in all respects from waking sensations. To be sure, the sensations we have in dreams (or in hallucinations or the "frenzies" of insanity) may indeed be "combined in the same forms in which they appear in a waking hour" and may make us think (while we are dreaming) that their causes "will *respond to any future call of the senses*" (*EPEU* 29). That is, when I dream of an apple,

---

[8] Although Shepherd refers once to Berkeley's *Three Dialogues between Hylas and Philonous* (1713), she offers no sustained analysis of it (*EPEU* 81).

190 MARY SHEPHERD

a sensible quality of red may be bundled with a sensible quality of a sphere just as it is in waking life. But Shepherd emphasizes that the *order* of sensations in dreams differs from the order of our sensations when awake (*EPEU* 92 and 107); the "relation of these qualities" is different in dreams and in waking life (*EPEU* 93).

Shepherd's point about the "order" of dream sensations might seem like an acknowledgment of the fact that dream sequences can include sudden nonsensical jumps that we do not experience in waking life. That may be part of what Shepherd means, but there are other ways in which she thinks the order of sensations in dreaming differs from the order of sensations when awake. Specifically, certain sensations are *missing* when we dream, sensations that we *would* have if we were awake. In dreams and frenzies, "those *other ideas such as place, &c. which ought to be compared with them are not in the mind; they are asleep, as it were,* (they are not in being)" (*EPEU* 95–96). The dreaming mind also lacks ideas of the "*methods of formation*" of the dreamt-of objects (*EPEU* 97); recall that Shepherd thinks that we know one object is genuinely similar to another not just when they have similar sensible qualities but when we know that both came from similar causes (*ERCE* 100, 102). In sum, when I dream, I am *lacking* the sensation of being in bed (or wherever I really am) (*EPEU* 30); I do not have experiences of my sensations recurring regularly when I use my senses (*EPEU* 92–93); the objects I dream about do not "fulfill the definitions" of the objects of which they are (allegedly) instances; and I do not know the causal histories of the objects in my dreams, so I cannot tell that they are not really like the objects I have actually sensed in the past. Shepherd characterizes the state of the dreaming mind as "deficient," insofar as it does not include all the sensations that would, were I awake, allow me to reason that there really are external objects causing my sensations: "In that [dreaming] state there is a deficiency of the ideas of the understanding, so that images of sense, appear together confusedly *without order* in the mind, which is not in a state to perceive that they can be but fancies" (*EPEU*

SKEPTICISM AND IDEALISM 191

108). Lacking the complete materials needed for "comparing" my sensations (*EPEU* 87–88), I cannot engage in correct reasoning about the objects, and so I cannot reach the conclusion that I am dreaming.

On the other hand, "in a waking and sane state of mind, the harmony of its ideas, their relations and conclusions, force themselves upon it with a superior and convincing evidence" (*EPEU* 108). Upon waking, I will have the additional sensations that are needed to figure out both that I am now *not* dreaming, and that I previously *was* dreaming. I now realize that I was, in fact, "*in the same place during the time of the dream*" (*EPEU* 30), a clue that my earlier sensations were not caused by objects meeting the criteria of reality. I also realize that the objects I dreamt about do not return when I use my senses; if I dreamt I was counting gold coins in the kitchen and go into the kitchen upon waking, I will not see any gold coins. If I dreamt I ate a huge meal, I will not wake up feeling full. Thus, I can conclude that the "objects which thus appear are not the objects of *sense*, but of the imagination" (*EPEU* 30).

To return to Shepherd's criticism of Berkeley, it is because dreamt-of sensible qualities are "deficient" in these various ways that Shepherd thinks our dream sensations are not, in fact, qualitatively identical to those we have when awake. This is what she means when she writes that "I do *not* consider it as possible for a person to be affected with the *same train of sensations*, and in the *same order* in a dream, or frenzy, as out of them" (*EPEU* 92).[9]

Shepherd's second objection is that although Berkeley is correct that "what happens in dreams, frenzies, and the like" shows that "we might be affected with all the ideas we have now, though no bodies existed without [i.e., externally] resembling them" (*PHK* 1.18, quoted in *EPEU* 91), he has misunderstood *why* this is so: not

---

[9] Thus, Shepherd would also disagree with a key premise of one of Descartes' arguments for doubt, namely that "all the same thoughts we have when we are awake can also come to us when we are asleep" (Descartes, *Discourse on Method*, 18).

192 MARY SHEPHERD

because there are no *resembling* external bodies directly causing our dreams, but because in dreaming there are no such external objects involved *at all*, "either resembling or unresembling the then ideas of sensible qualities" (*EPEU* 94).

However, she stresses, external objects are still needed as the *original* basis for the images we have in dreaming. Consider her analogy with vision (*EPEU* 94–95): a person with congenital blindness, never having seen, would never have color sensations, just as a person who has never experienced some object would never be able to dream of it. On the other hand, a person who becomes blind later in life would, having once had color sensations, be able to *remember* having color sensations, which, since this involves having a fainter version of the sensible quality of color (*EPEU* 137), is still to have a color sensation. Likewise, people can *dream* of objects only of which they have had previous experience (*EPEU* 94–95). Thus, Shepherd thinks that although Berkeley is right that dreaming does not involve causation by external objects at the time of dreaming, he has drawn the wrong conclusion in holding that external objects are *in no way* required for dreaming.

Third, Shepherd notes that "unobserved and apparently slight changes of words and their meanings" in Berkeley's reasoning have produced incorrect conclusions (*EPEU* 93–94). Shepherd thinks that Berkeley illicitly slips from the claim that there need be no external objects *resembling* our dream sensations to the conclusion that there need be no external bodies *at all* for ideas to occur. As he puts it in *Principles*,

> I say it is granted on all hands (and what happens in dreams, phrensies, and the like, puts it beyond dispute) that it is possible we might be affected with all the ideas we have now, though no bodies existed without, resembling them. Hence it is evident the supposition of external bodies is not necessary for the producing our ideas. (*PHK* 1.18, quoted at *EPEU* 91 and 97)

SKEPTICISM AND IDEALISM 193

Berkeley's argument is invalid because he has dropped the word "resembling" in the conclusion, Shepherd says. The fact that the causes of our sensations cannot be external objects *resembling* our sensations does not mean that the causes of our sensations cannot be external objects *at all* (*EPEU* 97–98).

Shepherd wraps up her criticisms of Berkeley's appeal to dreams by insisting again that even dreamt-of and illusory internal objects must be composed of sensible qualities that were caused, originally, by external objects. She alludes to, and rejects, another option that an opponent might suggest. Could dreamt-of and illusory objects result simply from *other* sensations in the mind (*EPEU* 98)? To use a Humean example (although not one that Shepherd invokes), suppose I had never experienced a certain shade of blue. Could my past sensation of some *other* shade of blue cause me to dream of this new shade of blue? No, Shepherd would say: the "*particular* causes for *new* ideas, are not contained in" the sensations already caused in the mind by other objects (*EPEU* 98). Thus, external objects are needed to account for dreams and delusions, even if those external objects are not "continually existent" at the time of the dream or delusion (*EPEU* 98).

The section ends with five numbered considerations that Shepherd says support her "answer" (*EPEU* 100). It is not entirely clear what question she is trying to answer here, but since she has just emphasized the distinction between, on the one hand, real experiences that use the sensory organs and, on the other hand, the "irregular fancies" of dreams and delusions (*EPEU* 99), she may simply be trying to show that we do ordinarily distinguish between the two; if Berkeley were right, she thinks, all experiences would be, in essence, dreams and delusions.

Her first point, that dreaming and delusions require that there be external objects that have acted previously on the senses, is the one she has already made (*EPEU* 98, 100). Her second observation is that no one thinks every "lunatic illusory call of the organs of sense" must be caused by some continually existing external object that

194 MARY SHEPHERD

makes a "regular reply" to perceivers' sense-organs, and her third observation is that sometimes people have "illusive" ideas that other people (assuming there *are* other people) do *not* have under the same circumstances (*EPEU* 100). In other words, we ordinarily take it that sometimes—when in a state of "lunacy" or delusion—people do have sensations that are importantly different from what we take to be real sensory experience.

Shepherd's fourth point rather cryptically appeals to the physical and physiological effects of certain perceptions. Perhaps significantly, she here refers to "perceptions" rather than "sensations"; recall that a perception is, strictly speaking, a "*consciousness of sensation*," a "SENSATION TAKEN NOTICE OF BY THE MIND" (*EPEU* 9). Shepherd says that when we are awake and perceive "lively forcible images," there is "a peculiar action of the circulation" (*EPEU* 101) that does not occur when we have dream sensations. Unfortunately, Shepherd offers no examples of what she means, but she mentions "desires of the mind which seek their objects irregularly" (*EPEU* 101). What she may mean is this: we sense many things that we do not desire, but sometimes ("irregularly") we sense something and *do* form a desire for it. For example, suppose I experience the sensible qualities of a chocolate cake, and these sensations cause in me a mental state of desiring to eat the cake. This would fit Shepherd's claim that sometimes sensations (here, the visual image and aroma of the cake) are the "temporary, but strong excitements" that are the "proximate causes" of a perception (here, a desire) (*EPEU* 101). This desire, in turn, sets the body (specifically the "circulation") in motion to pursue the desired object—the desire causes me to take action to obtain and eat a slice of cake. This process may be what Shepherd means by a "quiet, healthy action of the system" that is "natural and consistent with health" (*EPEU* 101). That is, the body is naturally set up to respond to mental states of desire; although we certainly do not need many of the things (like chocolate cake) that we desire in order to be healthy, health does

SKEPTICISM AND IDEALISM   195

seem to require that the body be able to respond to at least some desires.

How does this bear on the issue of dreaming? Shepherd suggests that it would be peculiar and unhealthy for the body to respond "vividly, forcibly, and regularly" not just to sensed objects but also to dreamt-of objects (*EPEU* 101). It would be unhealthy for the body to have a "capacity for a *constant* ready reply," meaning a tendency to respond to sensible qualities in dreaming as well as in waking life (*EPEU* 101). For if the body *also* responded to dreamt-of objects— if, say, my body were actually set in motion to pursue a slice of chocolate cake of which I am merely dreaming—my body would be in a constant state of pursuit; bodily responses to *every* desire, including those we dream of, would result in "an intranquil, inflamed action" (*EPEU* 101). In other words, our very physiology assumes that we can distinguish between dreamt-of and real experiences.

Shepherd's fifth point is that we distinguish between dreams and delusions, on the one hand, and real experiences, on the other hand, because only in the latter cases are we conscious of using our sense-organs, including our sense of motion through space as "the self [passes] from place to place" (*EPEU* 103). Waking life is not *just* a series of "some irregular sensible qualities, resembling those which may result from the action of the organs of sense and motion" (*EPEU* 102–3); to be awake and living among real external objects is not just to have a "stream of conscious life" (*EPEU* 104). Here, again, Shepherd appeals to a difference in the "order" of our sensations when we are awake (*EPEU* 102): waking life includes the consciousness of actually using our sense-organs and of being in motion through space (*EPEU* 103). This is not to say that we directly sense the use of our sense-organs or movement of our body; since Shepherd holds that we directly sense only sensations, and the sense-organs and the rest of the body are material, the "action or *use* of the organs of sense" is "*unperceived*" (*EPEU* 106).[10]

---

[10] In an errata list, Shepherd added a cross-reference here to *EPEU* 54 and 55, where she had characterized the physical sense-organs as being "justly and reasonably"

196 MARY SHEPHERD

However, one effect of using our sense-organs is a consciousness that we are doing so (*EPEU* 106–7; see also 234), a consciousness that Shepherd thinks is not present when we are dreaming. This is another respect in which the "order" of sensations when we are awake differs from the order of sensations when we are dreaming or deluded (*EPEU* 107).

However, couldn't a skeptic point out that we could *dream* that we are conscious of using our sense-organs? Shepherd concedes this: "'*In the manner of dreams and frenzies*' . . . there exists, indeed, some sensible appearances upon the mind, as if the senses had been in use" (*EPEU* 107–8; see also 235). Here she recurs to her earlier point about the order of sensible images in dreams and the "deficiency" of ideas allowing us to realize when we are dreaming (*EPEU* 108). When we are "in a waking and sane state of mind," we can realize not only that we were previously dreaming but also that we are not now dreaming (*EPEU* 108).

Would a skeptic who worries that we might be dreaming all our experiences be assuaged by Shepherd's arguments? It seems unlikely. Her solution to the problem of dream-skepticism assumes that there are times when I can *know* I am *not* dreaming, times when I know I am awake and can look back at past sensations to judge whether or not they were real. But this solution does not help me ascertain whether I am dreaming *now*, for I could be dreaming that the sensations I am having meet the criteria of reality. I could be dreaming, now, that someone is assuring me that I was just sound asleep in bed and not counting gold in the kitchen, or merely dreaming that I am conscious of using my eyes. Shepherd insists that "in ordinary life," our rational conclusion that we are not dreaming "is not weakened by those sceptical suggestions, which a consideration of the strength of the delusion in dreams, prompts

---

"regarded as continuous existences" that can be proven to exist by the same kind of reasoning as that which proves the existence of other external objects.

SKEPTICISM AND IDEALISM   197

to the more curious enquirer" (*EPEU* 108). Instead, she says, such skepticism is

> only to be corrected by the reflection, that it is not justified by reason, or by that comparison and relation of our ideas, which of whatever difficulty in the performance, can but remain the only method in our power of finding truth, or of forming any proposition whatever. (*EPEU* 108)

It seems, then, that Shepherd concedes that she has no knock-down demonstrative argument against the skeptical scenario that we might be dreaming everything.

Other passages in *EPEU* confirm this. She notes later that "although there may be truth in the world, yet the discovery of an absolute criterion of an understanding capable of detecting it, does not seem to be the lot of human nature" (*EPEU* 236). She also concedes the possibility that in "any other state of being than this," such as in an afterlife, "all our knowledge of outward and independent things could be proved to have arisen only from an action of the brain, and so this life should be shewn to have been but a waking dream" (*EPEU* 33). In other words, she concedes that we *might* be dreaming everything and that this might be revealed to us in an afterlife.

Shepherd also concedes that no one can know with certainty that external objects will continue to exist after one dies and one's perceptions cease altogether. Whether objects will continue to display the same qualities after I die is one effect of external objects that I cannot ascertain (*EPEU* 74, 117, 187). While I can test whether the gold I am thinking of is real by asking others if they see it, there is no way for me to test whether an object will continue after I cease to exist. Shepherd even imagines a scenario in which external objects *would* have to cease to exist when I do: suppose "the causes for *specific sensations in particular, were necessarily mixed up with those* which determined *all sensations in general, in any one individual*";

198 MARY SHEPHERD

in that case, "the universe would be dissolved in the dissolution of such individual" (*EPEU* 117). Or, as she put it earlier in the book, "when *that we call ourselves* shall fail, the *external universe shall also fail*" (*EPEU* 74). What she seems to have in mind is the possibility that external objects, though exterior to some individual mind, are nonetheless *always* mixed with that mind (i.e., with that which "determines all sensations in general"), and are unable to exist entirely separately from the mind. In that case, the cessation of that mind would result in the cessation of the external objects that depend on it.

Shepherd does think we can dispense with this worry through analogical reasoning. She writes,

> All we can do is to refer compound similar and various effects, to compound similar and various causes; which occasions an inference that such causes are like ourselves, plus or minus the varieties, and we finding ourselves independent of them, are led to conclude they will in like manner be independent of us. (*EPEU* 187–88)

We perceive ourselves to continue to exist even when other objects—and other humans—cease to exist; those other objects and humans resemble ourselves in various ways; so we have reason to think that other objects and humans will persist even when we are gone. Again, as with the possibility that we might be dreaming everything, Shepherd allows that while the scenario that everything will cease to exist when we do is "inconceivable," she "hardly dare say we can *perfectly demonstrate* the contrary" (*EPEU* 118).[11] The belief that objects will persist after my death is "an inference

---

[11] In fact, Shepherd says that the destruction of *one part* of the universe would lead to the destruction of the whole because "the frame of nature [is] so completely one whole, and all its changes but such constituent parts of it, that either, on the one hand, it must be wholly impossible for a true annihilation to take place of the essential and permanent existence of any part; or, on the other, that if it were possible, the whole must be destroyed together" (*EPEU* 173). Shepherd seems to mean, then, that no causal power can truly be

SKEPTICISM AND IDEALISM 199

of high probability, yet it is short of strict demonstration" (*EPEU* 187). Regarding dream-skepticism, Shepherd had suggested that the scenario is not one that need bother us, even if it is a metaphysical possibility. Here, she makes a rather different point, stating that we are faced with a *choice* of what to believe: either that "the universe is contained in the existence of a single mind" or that "there are many minds, and many objects which form the universe, and which have means to exhibit their existences on each other" (*EPEU* 118). Everyone, she says, chooses to believe the latter (*EPEU* 199). This is a case in which it is not *reasoning* that leads to the conclusion that the universe will persist after my death—but nor is it instinct, as Reid might have held. On what basis do we make this choice? Shepherd does not say, but perhaps, as with dream-skepticism, she thinks we are simply pragmatic: the possibility that the world will cease to exist after I die is not one that affects my everyday life, and so there is no need to be bothered by it.

All this suggests that Shepherd's argument for an external world of continuously and independently existing objects does *not* have the certainty possessed by the arguments for the two causal principles, despite her claim at the beginning of *EPEU* that the external universe can be "demonstrably *proved* by these their effects" (*EPEU* 18). Indeed, later in the book Shepherd modifies the claim to be able to *demonstrate* that an external world exists: "The reasoning on the point is nearly demonstrative, and practically is entirely so" (*EPEU* 188). Not even God himself could provide us more assurance that the external world exists than the sensations and reasoning skills that allow us to infer its existence (*EPEU* 34). Our evidence that our sensations are caused by real objects that will exist after we die is as good as it could be, and so there is really no point in demanding

eliminated altogether from the world without eliminating the whole causal web in which it is situated. This probably explains why she does not doubt the continued existence of the mind after the death of the body (*EPEU* 377); in some form or other, the capacity to sense must continue even after an individual's body dies—and even the death of the body is not really a destruction, just a sort of recycling of the matter.

200 MARY SHEPHERD

more evidence. So Shepherd is ultimately unconcerned by the skeptic's worries.

Reid's Failure to Appeal to Dreams

After her objections to Berkeley, Shepherd turns in EASP chapter 4, section 3 to Reid. According to Shepherd, Berkeley mistakenly thought dreams provide support for idealism, but Reid mistakenly *failed* to see that the phenomena of dreaming undermine his own rebuttal of Berkeley's idealism.

The brief passage Shepherd quotes is from Reid's discussion of an "*experimentum crucis*" that he thinks can settle whether Berkeleyan idealism should be accepted or not:

> Extension, figure, motion, may, any one, or all of them, be taken for the subject of this experiment. Either they are ideas of sensation, or they are not. If any one of them can be shown to be an idea of sensation, or to have the least resemblance to any sensation, I lay my hand upon my mouth, and give up all pretence to reconcile reason to common sense in this matter, and must suffer the ideal skepticism to triumph. But if, on the other hand, they are not ideas of sensation, nor like to any sensation, then the ideal system is a rope of sand, and all the labored arguments of the skeptical philosophy against a material world, and against the existence of every thing but impressions and ideas, proceed upon a false hypothesis. (*IHM* 5.7)

But, Reid argues, although our sensations of touch *suggest* to us the notions of extension, figure, and motion as qualities existing out there in the world, the sensations are entirely different from the notions and from the primary qualities that the notions represent (*IHM* 5.5). And if extension, figure, and motion are *not* sensations, then there is, in fact, something other than the mere impressions

SKEPTICISM AND IDEALISM   201

and ideas into which Berkeley wants to resolve all real objects. Reid concedes to Berkeley that we cannot establish by *reasoning* that extension, figure, and motion exist as anything other sensations, but, as Reid asks, "are we to admit nothing but what can be proved by reasoning?" (*IHM* 5.7). We have notions of extension, figure, and motion because "the constitution of our nature" is set up so that sensations suggest these notions; belief in extension, figure, and motion are "first principles" to which we cannot help but assent (*IHM* 5.7). Thus, Reid takes it that he has shown that the ideas of extension, figure, and motion are *not* sensations and that idealism is therefore false.

Shepherd, of course, disagrees with Reid's claim that we arrive at notions of extension, figure, and motion through "suggestion" rather than sensation or reasoning; she thinks we use latent reasoning to infer that extension, figure, and motion exist independently of us (albeit in a way we cannot perceive), and so we have knowledge, not mere instinct, that these things exist (*EPEU* 112–13). But here she is primarily concerned with the way Reid seems to slide from talking about *notions* of extension, figure, and motion to talking about extension, figure, and motion *themselves*, as they exist in bodies out there in the world. Shepherd thinks Reid is inconsistent in the way he distinguishes between the mental realm and the external world:

> For although he explains himself in some places as conceiving external objects not to be like sensations;—yet he still keeps the notion by saying, that *perceptions*, or *conceptions* are *not sensations*; *and that he knows the* EXTERNAL NATURE *of a primary quality, as well as its inward sensation.* (*EPEU* 109–10)

Shepherd diagnoses Reid's error as having "associated" or joined together the ideas of *perceptions* caused (via suggestion, according to Reid) by extension, figure, and motion with the ideas of their *causes* (*EPEU* 109). To be sure, this is an entirely natural association that

202 MARY SHEPHERD

is made not just by some philosophers but by all people with "ordinary understandings" (*EPEU* 114); however, "it is the business of an analytical philosophy, which intends to shew the entire method of the generation of our notions, to break up this association" (*EPEU* 114). Because Reid does not clearly distinguish ideas of primary qualities from the external causes of those ideas, he thinks that our ideas indicate to us the true natures of external objects, when in fact "the perceptions of sense, neither immediately, nor mediately as signs of conceived qualities, can ever tell us of their positive nature when unfelt, whether they be primary or secondary" (*EPEU* 110–11).

Shepherd's point is that Reid might not have made this mistake if he had thought more about dreams. "He forgets," she writes, "that in a vivid dream these ideas [of extension, figure, and motion] may take place as perfectly as when the mind is awake" (*EPEU* 109; see also 91). In other words, even if Reid is right that actual sensory experiences suggest these ideas, we *also* have these ideas when we are *not* having actual sensory experiences. This shows, Shepherd thinks, that Reid's characterization of notions of extension, figure, and motion as having been *suggested* by sensory experiences, rather than being sensations themselves, is incorrect, which in turn provides some reason for thinking that ideas of extension, figure, and motion are, indeed, sensations. Reid's *"experimentum crucis"* is aimed at Berkeley's idealism, but since it depends on his argument that ideas of extension, figure, and motion are not sensations, his rebuttal of idealism fails. Of course, this does not mean Shepherd thought idealism was correct; rather, she thought different arguments (that is, her own) are needed to rebut it.

Shepherd ends chapter 4 by listing ten numbered "demonstrative conclusions of the foregoing arguments," by which she means the conclusions not just of chapter 4 but of all four chapters of EASP. EASP chapters 5–8 return to the main theme of arguing for the existence of independent, continually existing, external objects. In this *Guide*, the topics from EASP chapters 5 and 8 have been addressed in chapter 6, the topic of EASP chapter 6 (how Shepherd uses the term 'idea') has been addressed in chapter 5, and the topic of EASP chapter 7 (the mind) will be covered in chapter 8.

Berkeley's Idealism

Berkeley himself insisted on the anti-skeptical import of his idealist system, describing it as "a firm system of sound and real knowledge, which may be proof against the assaults of Scepticism" (*PHK* 1.89). Shepherd is unconvinced, seeing his principles as leading easily to a "universal skepticism" about the existence of the external world (*EPEU* 5). Essays 1, 2, and 6 of part 2 of *EPEU* are devoted to various aspects of Berkeley's idealism.

Essay 1 opens with a series of quotations from Berkeley's *Principles of Human Knowledge*, passages that assert Berkeley's key doctrines: that objects are things we perceive by sense (*PHK* 1.4), that we perceive only our own ideas or sensations (*PHK* 1.4), that an idea can be like nothing but another idea (*PHK* 1.8), that both so-called secondary and so-called primary qualities exist only as ideas in the mind (*PHK* 1.9), and, finally, that we have no reason to think there are any such things as objects existing outside the mind (*PHK* 1.15).

Shepherd then notes her concern that her philosophical system will be identified with Berkeley's, that people will think "that there is no material difference between my doctrine, and his" (*EPEU* 197). Indeed, as she notes, she agrees that nothing can be like a sensation or idea but another sensation or idea (often referred to as the Likeness Principle) and that there is no meaningful distinction between primary and secondary qualities (*EPEU* 197); she holds the latter view because, like Berkeley, she holds that *all* sensible qualities are in the mind. However, unlike Berkeley, she insists that these sensible qualities must be caused by external objects existing independently of the mind. Here, then, she notes four points

204 MARY SHEPHERD

of disagreement, focusing on issues related to the passages she has quoted.

Shepherd's first objection is that Berkeley has misunderstood what a perceived object is. "I do not agree with him, in stating, that *objects are nothing but what we perceive by sense*, or that a complete enumeration is made of *all* the ideas which constitute an apple, a stone, a tree, or a book; in the summing up of their *sensible qualities*" (*EPEU* 197). While Berkeley defines 'object' as a collection of "various sensations or ideas imprinted on the sense" (*PHK* 1.3), Shepherd says this definition is "incomplete" (*EPEU* 198; see also 69). As we have seen in chapter 3 of this *Guide*, Shepherd thinks perceived objects are collections of sensible qualities *plus* the idea of these sensible qualities being caused by externally existing objects:

> For . . . an *object perceived* by the mind is a compound being, consisting of a certain collection of sensible qualities, "mixed with an *idea* the *result of reasoning*" of such qualities being formed by a "continually existing outward and independent set of as various and appropriate causes." (*EPEU* 197–98)

Thus, Berkeley has left out of his definition of 'object perceived by the mind' an absolutely essential component: the "genus" of every perceived object. This component accompanies every collection of sensible qualities making up a perceived object (*EPEU* 198). In providing this "*incomplete definition*" (*EPEU* 198), Shepherd says, Berkeley begs the question in favor of his view that objects cannot be exterior to the mind (*EPEU* 204). An opponent (including "all men," Shepherd says) would argue that 'object' means "a set of qualities exterior to the mind" that can interact with the sense-organs (*EPEU* 204); by ruling this out in advance, Berkeley assumes the very conclusion that he is trying to establish, namely, that there are no such objects.[12]

---

[12] Samuel Rickless observes that in *Three Dialogues between Hylas and Philonous*, Berkeley's spokesperson Philonous provides further argument for the claim that

Shepherd's second and third objections are related; both involve charges that Berkeley equivocates in his terminology. The second point, that Berkeley refers to objects as being "imprinted" on the senses even though he also wants to say that objects are collections of ideas, is one to which Shepherd will return in essay 2, and will be discussed below. She also objects that Berkeley's use of 'perception' is ambiguous (*EPEU* 200). In EASP, she complained that his use of 'idea' was ambiguous, referring sometimes to a collection of sensible qualities in the mind and sometimes to conclusions reached through reasoning (*EPEU* 134); her analogous point now is that he uses 'perception' sometimes to characterize the "mental consciousness" of sensible qualities and sometimes to characterize the "*notice* the mind takes of*" those qualities (*EPEU* 200–1)—a notice that Shepherd thinks indicates to us that the qualities must be caused by something external, even if Berkeley has failed to realize that this is what it indicates.

Indeed, Shepherd thinks Berkeley's equivocation on 'perceive' has misled him in the crux of his argument. Shepherd sees "the sum" of Berkeley's doctrine in *PHK* 1.4, where he asks a series of rhetorical questions:

> For what are the aforementioned objects [i.e., houses, mountains, rivers, and other sensible objects] but the things we perceive by sense, and what do we perceive besides our own ideas or sensations; and is it not plainly repugnant that any one of these or any combination of them should exist unperceived? (*PHK* 1.4, quoted at *EPEU* 201)

Shepherd thinks was made too quickly in the *Principles*, that sensible things are merely collections of sensible qualities, as well as further arguments to show that sensible qualities are ideas (Rickless, "Is Shepherd's Pen Mightier than Berkeley's Word?," 326–27). Had Shepherd paid more attention to this text, Rickless suggests, she would have seen "the numerous and critically important pieces of reasoning Berkeley offers us in *DHP*" for his idealism (326). However, Rickless thinks that Shepherd's third objection, that Berkeley equivocates on what it means to "perceive," poses a potentially much more serious problem for Berkeley (328–29).

206 MARY SHEPHERD

Putting Berkeley's argument in a "regular syllogism" (an argument with two premises and a conclusion) shows that it "contain[s] a middle term of two different and particular significations from which, therefore, nothing can be concluded" (*EPEU* 201). Suppose we recast Berkeley's rhetorical questions as a syllogism with "the things we perceive by sense" serving as the "middle term" in both premises (the first premise being the "major proposition" and the second the "minor" proposition"):

1. Our ideas and sensations are the only things we perceive by sense.
2. The things we perceive by sense are objects.
3. Therefore, objects are only our own ideas and sensations. (*EPEU* 201–2)

Shepherd insists that Berkeley's desired conclusion does not follow because the "middle term" ("the things we perceive by sense") actually refers to a different kind of perception in each premise.[13] 'Perception,' she says, is a general term that has "*two different parts, or kinds*" (*EPEU* 202). In premise 1, Berkeley uses 'perceive' to mean our mental consciousness of sensible qualities; in premise 2, however, he uses it to mean a mental consciousness of sensible qualities that *includes* the conscious use of the *organs* of sense (*EPEU* 202), what she earlier characterized as the "*notice*" the mind takes of qualities where the sense organs have been used (*EPEU* 200). Since the key term in the argument is used in two different ways, the conclusion does not follow.

Shepherd now diagnoses where she thinks Berkeley goes wrong. She notes that we do actually use the *same names* for internal

---

[13] Shepherd refers her reader to a widely used logic book of her time, Isaac Watts' *Logic, or the Right Use of Reason*. She does not here mention a related criticism of Berkeley's argument that she makes in EASP, which is that the proposition used in premise 1, "our ideas and sensations are the only things we perceive by sense," "is, if only a truth when perceived, of no force as an *axiom* that is to govern our understanding when not adverted to; when not a sensation or perception, it would be nought" (*EPEU* 82).

perceived objects (collections of sensible qualities plus the idea of being caused by something external) and their counterpart external objects (the collections of causal powers responsible for those sensible qualities) (*EPEU* 205–6). She had made the same point earlier in the book:

> Now the *names* for the qualities, may indifferently be applied to the *causes*, or *external objects*, or to the *effects* the *inward perceptions*; or to *both together*, as *compound beings*. It is in the latter sense they are *always popularly* applied, and on account of which circumstance there has been so much confusion in the minds of philosophers upon the subject. (*EPEU* 61; see also LMSM 700)

For example, we use the term 'gold' to refer *both* to the sensible qualities of yellowness, hardness, and so on and to the external object that causes those sensible qualities.[14] And this fact, Shepherd says, provides "a full answer to all the puzzling contradictions of Bishop Berkeley's theory" (*EPEU* 206). It is entirely natural for ordinary people to associate the internal and external objects and to use the same term to refer to a combination of both (*EPEU* 10). As she puts it later in essay 1, a word like 'gold' (or 'figure,' the example she uses there) is "*compound*," standing "for *the cause and effect united*, and not *only* for the *effect*" (EPEU 211). It is the job of philosophy to analyze this "compound mixture" of ideas (*EPEU* 169) to show how the two kinds of objects are different; "philosophers," she says, "ought to be capable of perceiving that figure, extension, and motion, &c. are *not only ideas in the mind*, but are capacities, qualities, beings in nature in relation to each other when exterior to mind" (*EPEU* 211–12; see also 299).

---

[14] Shepherd takes herself to be following Locke's distinction between using a term like 'gold' to refer to a "nominal essence" and using it refer to a "real essence" (*ERCE* 158n, referring to *ECHU* 4.6.8–9). For discussion, see chapter 3 of this *Guide*.

208 MARY SHEPHERD

Unfortunately, she thinks, Berkeley has taken this philosophical analysis too far: "Bishop Berkeley does not merely separate what is mixed, but would destroy the whole compound together" (*EPEU* 207). Shepherd does not mince words regarding the outcome of Berkeley's overzealous analysis: "the vicious mixture of philosophical analysis, with some erroneous notions, only gives birth to monstrous opinions" (*EPEU* 22).

Shepherd's fourth objection is that Berkeley is inconsistent. In his argument for the existence of other minds, Shepherd says, he is willing to say that we can know through inference that there are other minds. Berkeley writes:

> I perceive several motions, changes, and combinations of ideas, that inform me there are certain particular agents, like myself, which accompany them and concur in their production. Hence, the knowledge I have of other spirits is not immediate, as is the knowledge of my ideas; but depending on the intervention of ideas, by me referred to agents or spirits distinct from myself, as effects or concomitant signs. (*PHK* 1.145, quoted at *EPEU* 208–9[15])

If Berkeley is willing to say we can *infer* the existence of other minds, why is he unwilling to say we can infer the existence of material objects? As Shepherd expresses her point later, "I divide therefore with Berkeley, by applying the argument he himself uses in behalf of the proof that there are other minds than his own in the universe, to the proof of existences which may be other than mind" (*EPEU* 242).

Shepherd is not done with Berkeley. In section 2 of essay 1, she shifts to a discussion of Berkeley's claims that our ideas require causes, but that these causes are spirits—that is, mind rather than matter. According to Berkeley (as she shows from

---

[15] Shepherd's citation of *PHK* 195 is a misprint.

the passages she quotes at *EPEU* 213–14), the ideas in our minds must have a cause (*PHK* 1.26); a cause is something that "produces and changes" things (*PHK* 1.26); and yet ideas themselves are entirely passive and inactive (*PHK* 1.25). Having shown that there are no external bodies, so that only minds and ideas exist, this leaves only a mind as the possible cause of ideas; but since we are clearly not the causes of all our own ideas, many of which come to us without or even against our will, this means some other mind must cause them (*PHK* 1.29). Berkeley identifies this mind as the "Author of nature" (*PHK* 1.33)—that is, God. Shepherd also quotes Berkeley regarding the role of "laws of nature," the "set rules or established methods" whereby God ensures that our sensory perceptions come to us in regular, predictable ways that we learn from experience (*PHK* 1.30–31, quoted at *EPEU* 214).

Shepherd endeavors to show that Berkeley's reasoning about the causes of our ideas is "fallacious, and inconclusive, and paradoxical" (*EPEU* 213). She points out several respects in which Berkeley's claims are inconsistent with his other commitments. First, she says that Berkeley's claim that spirits are active, indivisible, and simple (*PHK* 1.27) is subject to exactly the same kind of criticism that he himself makes to those who claim that matter is inert, divisible, and varied: if the latter characteristics of matter are merely ideas, existing only in the mind, then the same must be true of the former. Activity, indivisibility, and simplicity *cannot* then apply to something existing outside our own mind, as Berkeley wants to say they do (*EPEU* 215).

Moreover, Shepherd says that Berkeley is not entitled to say that the causes of our ideas must be spirits because causes are "active" but ideas are not (*PHK* 1.25–26); in fact, he is not entitled to say anything at all about causes, because if an idea cannot be a cause, and we can know nothing but our ideas, then we can know nothing about causes (*EPEU* 215–16). To be fair to Berkeley, his claim that we can perceive only ideas is not equivalent to the claim that we

210   MARY SHEPHERD

can know only *about* ideas[16]; Shepherd herself holds that we can perceive only ideas, but nonetheless thinks we can know (through inference) that an external world exists, so it is rather uncharitable of her not to ascribe the same kind of view to Berkeley.

Shepherd raises two further objections. Berkeley appealed to the "rules," "methods," and "laws of nature" whereby God works to produce ideas in our minds. In Berkeley's spare ontology, only minds and ideas exist, but since these rules are themselves not minds or ideas, and cannot be material entities, Shepherd thinks Berkeley has no way to account for them (*EPEU* 216).[17] Finally, she takes issue with a relatively minor point made by Berkeley, that the mind can at will "call upon an idea." To will to do something, the mind must know what it wills; so to will to have an idea, the mind must already have that idea, meaning that the mind must already have thought of it before it can "call upon" it (*EPEU* 216).

After restating her own doctrine of external "causes and capacities" intermixing with the senses and the mind in order to produce sensation (*EPEU* 217), Shepherd has one more barb for Berkeley: the notion that God acts on our senses is "ridiculous" (*EPEU* 218). Shepherd will elaborate on this in essay 6.

Berkeley's "Oversight" Regarding Sense-Organs

In *EPEU* essay 2, Shepherd discusses the role of sense-organs in sensation, and her discussion leads her to formulate more fully an objection she mentioned earlier (*EPEU* 198–99; see *EPEU* 54–55).

---

[16] As Berkeley specified in additions to the second edition of *Principles of Human Knowledge* (1734), he thought that in addition to ideas, minds have "notions" of such things as "soul, spirit, and the operations of the mind" (*PHK* 1.27).

[17] Shepherd herself characterizes the laws of nature as the "capacities of objects" (*EPEU* 289; see also 330–31). Evidently she holds that the laws of nature describe the causal powers of kinds of objects.

SKEPTICISM AND IDEALISM   211

After discussing why knowledge of an external world must derive from reasoning rather than instinct (*EPEU* 221–24), Shepherd claims that Berkeley (among other unnamed writers) begs the question of the existence of the external world when he refers to the sense-organs. He wants to say that "ideas are imprinted on the senses" (*PHK* 1.1, 1.29, 1.33), but Shepherd thinks this means that the sense-organs themselves must therefore *not* be ideas: "Berkeley evidently considers the use of the organs of sense, as a circumstance distinguished and different from 'ideas and sensations,'" as well as different from the "set rules and methods" God uses to introduce sensory ideas into our minds (*EPEU* 225–26). A mere idea or "consciousness" of using a sense-organ cannot cause sensations; only a sense-organ as a continually existing, independent, external object can do so (*EPEU* 227). Of course, Shepherd is careful to note that she is referring to sense-organs as unperceived external objects, whatever they are in themselves (*EPEU* 227).

Reid and Stewart have approached closer to the truth, she thinks, since they characterize sense-organs as "mechanical, extended, figured, solid existences; as means, instruments, and causes, by which we immediately perceive the existence of external objects," but they go wrong in thinking that these sense-organs enable us to know the nature of the extension and figure of the sense-organs in themselves, as they exist unperceived (*EPEU* 228). Suppose a researcher is examining an eyeball by touch. Reid would say the sensation of holding the eye "suggests" its extension and figure, which are "qualities of bodies" inhering in the eye itself (*EPEU* 229–30). As Shepherd has by now made abundantly clear, she thinks the perceived extension and figure of the eyeball are *not* in the external object, the eyeball (whatever that may be in its true nature), but in the mind. What the researcher's sense of touch reveals about the eyeball is merely that it exists as a "continued independent existence" (*EPEU* 230).

We saw in chapter 5 of this *Guide* that Shepherd considers motion to be a sense just like vision, hearing, and so on. The "power

212   MARY SHEPHERD

of motion" is the "sixth organ of sense" (*EPEU* 230). Just as other philosophers must presuppose that eyes, ears, and so on exist unperceived, so too must they presuppose this of the power of motion. According to Shepherd, the true nature of all these sense-organs themselves, considered as unperceived external objects that interact with other external objects, is as mysterious to us as the true nature of any other external object:

> Philosophically, the organs of sense must be considered as *un*known existences in their unperceived state, yet as yielding their own peculiar and appropriate sensations or ideas to the mind; their *continued, independent* existence is found as a result, or perceived by the understanding, as a relation of its simple sensations. (*EPEU* 231)

It is thus that the sense-organs "*form the media of admixture between other objects and mind*"; they are among the causes, along with the external objects and the mind, by which we have sensible perceptions (*EPEU* 234). And another effect of the use of a sense-organ, along with whatever sensations are caused by it mixing with other external objects, is *consciousness* of using the sense-organ: that is, consciousness is itself a sensible quality (*EPEU* 234).

Shepherd opened essay 1 by noting two points of agreement with Berkeley, and she ends essay 2 by defending him against what she apparently takes to be a common misreading: he did not mean that *objects* are created immediately as we perceive them, but just that *sensible qualities* are created every time we have a perception, and she agrees with him on that (*EPEU* 238; see also 72). In bookending her criticisms of Berkeley with positive comments, Shepherd evidently wants to signal that while she thinks some of his claims "from a lapse in the reasoning fail to produce conviction," the "rest of his matter" is "truly consistent, and philosophical, and accordant with experience . . . however much it may vary from commonly received notions" (*EPEU* 167).

SKEPTICISM AND IDEALISM 213

Berkeley's "Notable Dilemma"

Despite her respect for some aspects of Berkeley's system, Shepherd raises further objections to Berkeley in *EPEU* essay 6, "That Sensible Qualities Cannot be Causes." Here she focuses on an "extraordinary paragraph" in Berkeley's *Principles*:

> But, say you, it sounds very harsh to say we eat and drink ideas, and are clothed with ideas. I acknowledge it does so—the word IDEA not being used in common discourse to signify the several combinations of sensible qualities which are called THINGS; and it is certain that any expression which varies from the familiar use of language will seem harsh and ridiculous. But this doth not concern the truth of the proposition, which in other words is no more than to say, we are fed and clothed with those things which we perceive immediately by our senses. (*PHK* 1.38, quoted at *EPEU* 300)

Shepherd identifies the source of this "monstrous thought" (*EPEU* 303) in Berkeley's rejection of abstraction. According to Berkeley, many philosophers have mistakenly endorsed the "doctrine of abstract ideas," the doctrine that it is possible to separate in thought the idea of a sensible object from the ideas of its sensible qualities (*PHK* 1.5).[18] Although Berkeley allows that abstraction in a different sense is possible—we can *concentrate* on just one feature of a thing, without attending to its other features—he denies that we can separate an idea of an object from the ideas of its sensible qualities, or the idea of one sensible quality from the idea of another, thereby creating an abstract idea. Shepherd thinks it is Berkeley who has made a mistake. On the one hand, despite his rejection of abstraction, he has actually over-abstracted: "separating the

---

[18] For further discussion of abstraction, see chapter 1 of this *Guide*.

214   MARY SHEPHERD

notions of external causes from their internal effects" (LMSM 705) and denying the existence of the latter (*EPEU* 207; see also 68). On the other hand, he has *failed* to abstract the causal powers of objects from the sensible qualities they bring about:

> By denying *abstractions*, Berkeley denied analysis—by denying analysis, he truly kept up the *associations* of the vulgar, who *conjoin* the sensible qualities exterior causes create, with those causes themselves;—the very error he wrote to combat. (*EPEU* 304; see also LMSM 705)

When Berkeley's failure to abstract sensible qualities from their causes in the external world is combined with (1) his doctrine that sensible qualities lack causal powers (with which Shepherd agrees [*EPEU* 296]), (2) his doctrine that there are no causes in the external world (with which she emphatically disagrees [*EPEU* 207]), and (3) his desire to explain the fact that there are regular patterns among events in nature, which people take to be causal connections, the upshot is that Berkeley is forced to locate causation in God alone, claiming that God causes these regular patterns by using a "set rule and method" (*EPEU* 297).[19]

As we have seen, Shepherd holds that objects act in predictable ways because of necessary connections between the nature of the object (its causal powers) and its qualities (its effects).[20] These necessary connections, on her view, are synchronous, not successive. But how does Shepherd explain the fact that various *successive series* of events seem invariable? In *ERCE*, her stress on the synchronicity of causes and effects might leave some readers wondering how she can explain what seem very much like causal chains, where one event causes the event that comes after it.

---

[19] Shepherd adds that since Hume eliminated the notion of causation altogether, he was unable even to adopt Berkeley's idea that God causes regularities in nature, leaving open the possibility that there really are no reliable patterns in nature at all (*EPEU* 297).

[20] See chapters 2 and 3 in this *Guide*.

SKEPTICISM AND IDEALISM 215

Suppose I see a flower and then, as I draw closer, I smell it. The connection between the earlier seeing and the later smelling is not, according to Shepherd, a causal one—after all, something might have happened to prevent me from approaching the flower to smell it. Nonetheless, if the flower interacts first with my eyes and then with my nose, Shepherd concedes that the order of my sensations is *necessarily* that the visual precedes the olfactory. But, again, this is not because the visual sensation causes the olfactory one. Rather, it is because *both* sensations are caused by the *same object* that itself has causal powers that necessarily act in a certain order: the power to produce a visual sensation is necessarily activated, as it were, before the power to produce a smell. Thus, the *order* of events might be necessary even if the connections between those events are not causal (*EPEU* 298; see also 130–31 and 306).

Shepherd next diagnoses how Berkeley arrived at his view that we "eat, drink, and are clad, with *those* sensible qualities which can only exist in the mind" (*EPEU* 301). Berkeley faced a "notable dilemma": according to his own principle of not abstracting sensible qualities from external objects, Shepherd thinks he is forced to say *either* (1) that the sensible qualities exist outside the mind yet have the capacity to affect us or (2) that sensible qualities exist in the mind and have causal powers to affect each other (*EPEU* 302). On option 1, he would have to say, for example, not that we eat bread, but that we eat the sensible qualities (the sensations) of the whiteness, chewiness, and flavor of bread. On option 2, he would have to say, again, not that we eat bread, but that certain sensations in our mind swallow other sensations in the mind (*EPEU* 302). The first option was "the very doctrine he combated," while the second is "so confused that nothing can be made of it," and violates Berkeley's own principle that sensible qualities themselves lack causal power (*EPEU* 302–3). Thus, Shepherd thinks Berkeley is forced by the unacceptability of both horns of the dilemma into an even more peculiar doctrine, that God causes

216 MARY SHEPHERD

everything, so that "we eat, and drank, and were clothed with God" (*EPEU* 303).[21]

At this point, Shepherd is done with Berkeley; she does not mention him again in *EPEU*. Rather, she ends essay 6 with some observations on the vexed question of the interaction of mind and body. Shepherd's views on mind and body will be the topic of our next chapter.

Suggestions for Further Reading

- Samuel Rickless' chapter in the *Bloomsbury Companion to Berkeley*, "Berkeley's *Treatise Concerning the Principles of Human Knowledge*," provides a concise introduction to Berkeley's arguments for idealism.
- There are short discussions of Shepherd's account of dreaming in Antonia LoLordo's introduction to *Mary Shepherd's Essays on the Perception of an External Universe* and in Martha Bolton's entry on Shepherd in the *Stanford Encyclopedia of Philosophy*.
- For discussion and critique of Shepherd's objections to Berkeleyan idealism, see Margaret Atherton, "Lady Mary Shepherd's Case against George Berkeley." Samuel Rickless defends Shepherd against Atherton's objections in "Is Shepherd's Pen Mightier than Berkeley's Word?"

---

[21] In her 1832 essay, Shepherd accuses John Fearn of a similarly "monstrous doctrine, fraught with folly and impiety" (LMSM 699).

8
Mind and Body

Introduction

Shepherd argues in *ERCE* that sentience must be due to an immaterial cause, for we cannot adequately explain it by appealing simply to organized bodies (*ERCE* 169). *EPEU* is concerned primarily with establishing that some of our sensations must also be caused by an external world. Thus, there must be a connection between our immaterial mind and the material, external world. Shepherd concedes that this connection is "mysterious" (LMSM 703), but is there anything more to be said about it? And, since the human body is part of the material, external world, how does Shepherd conceive of the relationship between the mind and body in a human being?

This chapter examines these questions by considering what Shepherd says about mind in chapter 7 of *EPEU*'s EASP and in *EPEU* essay 13. Shepherd's terminology requires some clarification; as we will see, she uses the terms 'mind,' 'soul,' and 'self' interchangeably—although for convenience, this chapter will tend to use just 'mind'—and she also seems to work with a narrower and a broader sense of all three terms. The next section lays out the basic features of Shepherd's account of mind, while the two sections following that explore her argument for how each of us knows our own mind exists and her account of our knowledge of other minds. Then, the chapter looks at Shepherd's claims about personal identity over time and explores her distinction between narrower and broader uses of 'soul,' 'self,' and 'mind.' It then considers how Shepherd individuates souls/selves/minds from each other. The final section examines Shepherd's account of the relationship

Mary Shepherd. Deborah Boyle, Oxford University Press. © Oxford University Press 2023.
DOI: 10.1093/oso/9780190090326.003.0008

218 MARY SHEPHERD

between mind and matter and, specifically, the relationship of the mind to the human body.

Soul, Self, and Mind

As we saw in chapter 4 of this *Guide*, Shepherd maintains that sentience—what she more typically calls "sensation"—cannot be explained in purely materialist terms and that we must posit "an immaterial cause, that is, a principle, power, being, an unknown quality denied to exist in matter," which "may be called *soul*, or *spirit*" (*ERCE* 169). The word 'soul' actually appears infrequently in Shepherd's writings; more often she uses the term 'mind.' It is clear that she considers these two terms to be interchangeable, for she refers to "a *principle* of sensation, soul, mind, spirit, or by whatever name may be designated the capacity for sensation in general, and consciousness" (*EPEU* 310; see also *ERCE* 171). And in characterizing the soul as being an "inward sense and consciousness" (*EPEU* 70), as having ideas and notions (*EPEU* 59 and 33), and as perceiving (*EPEU* 206, 260, and 414), she ascribes to soul the same abilities ascribed to mind. 'Soul,' then, does not appear to have any special meaning above and beyond what Shepherd means by 'mind.'

Moreover, in the opening pages of *EPEU*, Shepherd also suggests that the mind/soul is equivalent to the *self*, for she refers to "the mind, or object termed *self*, or simple capacity for general sensation" (*EPEU* 15). Other passages suggest this, too: she refers to the self as "the sentient principle" (*EPEU* 103; see also 59), a phrase she also uses to characterize the mind (*EPEU* 14–15; see also 133). In sum, 'soul,' 'self,' and 'mind' are interchangeable terms for Shepherd. For convenience, however, this chapter will tend to use 'mind.'

What does she mean by 'mind'? Shepherd says that mind is a "simple capacity for general sensation" (*EPEU* 15). This phrase indicates four key features of Shepherd's account of mind, at least in

MIND AND BODY 219

the narrower sense: the mind is a *capacity*; it is specifically a capacity to *sense*; this capacity can be described as *"general* sensation"; and it is *simple*. This section will examine each of these features in turn.

First, Shepherd repeatedly emphasizes that mind is a *capacity*.[1] Strikingly, she does not say it is a substance, as does, for example, Descartes.[2] For Shepherd, a capacity is a power to bring something about—that is, a causal power: "mind is the CAPACITY or CAUSE, for *sensation in general"* (*EPEU* 155). Thinking (or sensing, as Shepherd would prefer to say) is an action, an exercise of the capacity to sense, and it *causes* sensations. In sense perception, mind works with, or "intermixes with," other factors—namely, the sense-organs and external objects—in order to produce particular sensations.

Second, mind is a capacity to *sense*. As we saw in chapter 5 of this *Guide*, 'sensation' for Shepherd is a broad term that includes thoughts that seem to be of external objects as well as those that do not (*EPEU* 7). *Every* conscious mental state is a sensation (*EPEU* 7). Thus, to say mind is a capacity to sense is just to say that mind is a capacity to have conscious mental states. These mental states can be of various types; sensations "should be divided into *the sensations of present sensible qualities, sensations of the ideas of memory, sensations of the ideas of imagination, sensations of the ideas of reason, &c."* (*EPEU* 135–36).

Third, Shepherd calls mind a capacity for "general sensation" or "sensation in general." It is general insofar as it includes capacities to produce sensations of the various types just enumerated, to combine sensations into new ones, to compare sensations, to draw conclusions from sensations, and so on. Moreover, Shepherd's

---

[1] In addition to the passage at *EPEU* 15, Shepherd characterizes mind as a capacity at *EPEU* 56–57, 163, 164, 217, 242, 310, and 375. She also says it is a "power" (*EPEU* 40).

[2] It may seem surprising that, while Shepherd defines the mind as a *"continued* and *exterior* capacity fitted to each change" (*EPEU* 56–57; see also *EPEU* 375), she also describes it as the "subject" or "subject matter" of sensations (*EPEU* 372 and 56). This may seem to indicate something like a Cartesian view, where mind is a *substance* possessing a capacity to sense, in which sensations inhere as accidents or qualities. But she so consistently characterizes mind as a capacity throughout her works that we should not put too much weight on the few cases where she says mind is the "subject" of sensations.

220 MARY SHEPHERD

reference to "general" sensation shows that she means to contrast mind with *particular* sensory perceptions (*EPEU* 15). That is, while mind is a capacity, sensations are *actualizations* of that capacity. Since sensations are, by definition, conscious acts of mind (*EPEU* 6–7; see also 254), mind can be described as a capacity to produce conscious states.[3] Here, too, there is an important difference between Shepherd's account and a Cartesian account of the mind as a substance that thinks. Consciousness does not characterize mind itself; it characterizes the *sensations* that mind causes (either as a partial cause, working together with external objects, the sense-organs, and other causes to bring about sensory perceptions, or on its own, when new sensations are brought about by other sensations in memory, imagination, or reasoning).

A fourth feature of Shepherd's characterization of mind is that it is *simple* (*EPEU* 15 and 239; see also 48). Since, as we saw, particular sensations can be of various types—"*sensations of present sensible qualities, sensations of the ideas of memory, sensations of the ideas of imagination, sensations of the ideas of reasons, &c.*" (*EPEU* 135–36)—sensation understood as a general *capacity* to sense must be similarly expansive, including capacities to produce, combine, compare, and draw conclusions from sensations. But the fact that mind includes multiple capacities does not mean, for Shepherd, that mind is itself complex or compound. Hume's use of the term 'simple' may be helpful here; for Hume, a "simple" perception allows "no distinction nor separation" within it (*T* 1.1.1.2). In saying that mind is "simple," Shepherd may mean that its capacities come as a package; the capacities are not separable from each other.[4] This is further supported by the fact that she also links the

---

[3] This is true of 'mind' in Shepherd's narrow sense. As we will see, she also uses 'mind' in a broader sense to refer to the capacity to sense *plus* the sensations that are the actualizations of that capacity.

[4] However, this is evidently not so for those Shepherd describes as "born idiots": "Idiotcy appears to be little else, than an incapacity for further perception than what resides in the immediate impressions created by the use of the five organs of sense, and the power of motion" (*EPEU* 314–15).

MIND AND BODY 221

mind's simplicity with its unity: "the power of sensation is *one* and *simple*" (*EPEU* 217).

Mind's Continuous Existence

In EASP chapter 2, Shepherd adds a new feature to her account of mind: like external objects, it has a continued existence. Our sensations come and go, and there are periods of time when we have no sensations at all (as in dreamless sleep). Nonetheless, our minds persist through such changes. She offers an argument for this view that I will call the Continuous Mind Argument, and she suggests that it is structurally analogous to her earlier arguments for an external world.[5] She writes,

> if it should be asked, whence the mind knows itself to be exterior to each sensation in particular, and continued in its existence, I answer from the same principle which enables it to judge other things as exterior to itself; namely, from that perception of the understanding which forces upon it the conclusion, that because each sensation in its turn vanishes, and new changes spring up, so there must necessarily be some *continued* existence the subject matter of these changes; otherwise, '*each change would* BEGIN *of itself.*'
>
> Therefore the mind must be a *continued* and *exterior* capacity fitted to each change, upon any present state being interfered with by another object; and thus the pronoun *I* is ever *abstract*, and stands for a BEING *exterior to*, and independent of all the changes of which it is conscious. (*EPEU* 56–57)

In saying that the mind is "exterior," Shepherd means that the mind is distinct from the sensations it causes. The *capacity* to sense and

---

[5] On Shepherd's arguments for an external world, see chapter 6 of this *Guide*.

222　MARY SHEPHERD

think is one thing; the *actual* sensory perceptions and thoughts that result from the exercise of that capacity are something else. Likewise, when she says that the pronoun "I" is "abstract" (*EPEU* 57), she means that it is something separate from its sensations.[6] The mind is an ongoing, uninterrupted capacity for sensation, not the series of sensations that this capacity helps to produce.

Shepherd gives a hint of how she will argue for the continuous existence of the mind in a footnote where she criticizes Étienne Bonnot de Condillac (*EPEU* 43n). In his *Traité des sensations* (1754), Condillac introduced a thought-experiment of a "living statue." Structurally identical to a human and capable of thought, the statue becomes conscious with just the sense of smell, only gradually acquiring the ability to use the other senses.[7] As it smells a succession of odors—rose, carnation, jasmine, and so on—it experiences pleasure or pain, depending on whether the odor is agreeable or not; and as one odor is removed and another presented, the statue grasps the difference between *being in* one state and *remembering* being in a different state.[8] In recognizing that it is no longer in a state that it was previously in, Condillac says, the statue forms the idea of the self, the "personnalité," the "moi."[9] The idea of the self is derived simply from the collection of sensations that the statue is now having and that it remembers having, and the statue takes it that the self is nothing more than that series of sensations.[10]

Shepherd disagrees with Condillac. She claims that if the statue believed that self consists simply in sensations and memories of sensations, then it would have to believe that self could be "annihilated, and again *beginning* of itself" (*EPEU* 43–44n), since

---

[6] Shepherd elsewhere indicates that she uses the verb "to abstract" to mean "to separate" (*EPEU* 85), so to say that the mind is abstract is to say that it is separate from something else—and, as she makes clear, it is separate from its sensations, which are its effects (although, of course, as effects they are necessarily connected with the mind that causes them).

[7] Condillac, *Traité des sensations*, 11.

[8] Condillac, *Traité*, 15 and 17–20.

[9] Condillac, *Traité*, 55.

[10] Condillac, *Traité*, 56.

MIND AND BODY 223

sensations and memories come and go. But the thinking statue, like any child, would grasp that nothing can appear without a cause other than itself, and so the statue would, "whenever it became capable of *reflecting* on its sensations . . . consider self as *continuing* to exist, and not to vanish for one single moment during whatever change might arise, and therefore as an existence independent of each scent in particular" (*EPEU* 44n). In other words, Shepherd is arguing that the idea of self is generated from a series of sensations *in conjunction with* the Causal Principle.

Shepherd does not explicitly set out her argument for the existence of a continually existing mind, but her reasoning can be reconstructed as follows:

1. I experience a series of sensations that appear and then vanish. (*EPEU* 56)
2. If there were no continued existence that is the "subject matter" of these changes, then each change would begin of itself. (*EPEU* 56)
3. Nothing can begin its own existence. (CP)
4. Therefore, there must be a continuously existing subject matter of the series of sensations that is "independent of all the changes of which it is conscious" (*EPEU* 56–57).

Thus, the continued existence of mind is known through reasoning—not direct introspection. We do not, as it were, look inward and *perceive* the mind. Rather, "if it should be asked, whence the mind knows itself to be exterior to each sensation in particular, and continued in its existence, I answer . . . from that perception of the understanding which forces upon it the conclusion, that because each sensation in its turn vanishes, and new changes spring up, so there must necessarily be some *continued* existence the subject matter of these changes" (*EPEU* 56; see also 374–75). The continuous succession of sensations is a *clue* to the continued existence of mind, but we know that the mind persists only through

224 MARY SHEPHERD

reasoning that that succession of sensations requires a continuously existing cause. Drawing on Shepherd's distinction between sensations and ideas, we can say that we have an *idea* of the mind, but not a *sensation* of the mind.

However, just as we can only think of external objects under the "forms" of the sensory perceptions they cause (*EPEU* 49), Shepherd would say we can only imagine the mind under the "forms" of the particular conscious sensations it causes. There is a very strong mental association "between the ideas of the causes and their effects" such that "they cannot be easily disjoined from the fancy" (*EPEU* 41). And just as sensations and our ideas of their causes can only be separated through philosophical analysis, conscious sensations and the idea of the mind can only be separated that way, too.

Other Minds

As we have seen, Shepherd thinks each of us knows the existence of our own mind through a process of reasoning. The same is true about our knowledge of the existence of other minds, although the reasoning is different. In my own case, I perceive that my sensations come and go, and, combined with my knowledge of the Causal Principle, know these sensations must be the effects of something that does *not* come and go. Thus, I infer that there is some ongoing capacity to cause these sensations—my own mind. With other minds, however, our reasoning is analogical, depending on the Causal Likeness Principle.

Shepherd presents two versions of this argument. The first version, in *EPEU* chapter 3, is modeled on an argument in Berkeley's *Principles*, to which Shepherd later explicitly refers. Berkeley says that his knowledge of other minds is "not immediate," but is inferred from the fact that he observes "several motions, changes, and combinations of ideas, that inform me there are certain particular agents, like myself, which accompany them and concur in their production" (*PHK* 1.145; quoted at *EPEU* 208–209). Similarly, Shepherd notes that we each know we have sensations that cause various bodily actions, and we see other human bodies exhibiting "symptoms" of feeling the same things (*EPEU* 79)—that is, we see behavior that we take to be caused by sensations, as they are in our own case. In this case, Shepherd is treating *sensations* as causes, and behavior as effects (*EPEU* 79). Knowing the corollary of the Causal Likeness Principle that "*similar sensations are similar objects*, and the *varieties* make the *varieties*" (*EPEU* 78), we can infer from their behavior that other human bodies have sensations like our own, even though we are *not* conscious of their sensations (see also *EPEU* 172). And, since sensations result from minds, we can infer that other creatures also have minds.

Later, in the "Recapitulation" chapter of *EPEU*, Shepherd offers a variation on this analogical argument for other minds. This one starts with the observation that there are other creatures who, like me, speak or sing (*EPEU* 171). I know that I can speak and sing, but sometimes I hear speech or songs that I know I did not cause. Since similar effects require similar causes, I infer that these sounds were caused by something like me (*EPEU* 172). In this case, unlike in the previous version, I infer not from behavior to a sensation and then to a cause, but from behavior directly to a cause.

Shepherd notes that, observing the various *respects* in which the effects are similar, we conclude "that in as many respects there are *similar* causes" (*EPEU* 172). That is, if I just hear meaningless sounds, I might infer that there is a cause, but not that the cause was a *mind*. If I hear others "speak, or sing," on the other hand, I will infer that the cause was something capable of producing meaning, and so will think a mind is the cause.

226 MARY SHEPHERD

Minds, Selves, and Personal Identity

We saw earlier that there is considerable textual evidence that Shepherd considers 'mind,' 'soul,' and 'self' all to refer to the same capacity to sense. However, in EASP chapter 7, when Shepherd brings up the topic of "our own identity" (*EPEU* 150), she refers to "the compound mass we term SELF" (*EPEU* 152) and "the complicate being *self*" (*EPEU* 154). One natural way to interpret Shepherd is to see her as claiming *not* that the self is equivalent to the mind, but that the self is a compound of mind *and* body. However, there are reasons to think that Shepherd does not take the self to be a mind–body union.

Consider this passage:

> The idea of our own independent existence is generated by observing, that the compound mass we term SELF can exist when we do not observe it; and we have thus the *idea* of our own existence, in that it needs must CONTINUE to exist when *unperceived*, as well as during the *sensation* of it when perceived. (*EPEU* 152–53)

A little later, she continues:

> what we allude to as *self*, is a continued existing capacity in nature, (unknown, unperceived,) fitted to revive when suspended in sleep, or otherwise, and to keep up during the periods of watchfulness the powers of life and consciousness, especially those which determine the union of memory with sense. For as sensation is interrupted, and is an *effect*; the original cause must be uninterrupted; and such an uninterrupted cause as is equal to keep up the life of the body, or mass deemed our own body, and to unite it under that form with the powers of memory and sense. Identity, therefore, has nothing to do with *sameness of particles*,

MIND AND BODY 227

but only has relation to those powers in nature (flowing from that continuous Being the God of Nature) which are capable of giving birth to that constant effect, the *sense of continuous existence*; which sense, when analysed, is the union of the *ideas of memory*, with the *impressions of present sense*. (*EPEU* 153–54)

In explicitly rejecting an account of identity that concerns "sameness of particles," Shepherd may be alluding to a point Locke makes in his discussion of identity in the second edition of the *Essay Concerning Human Understanding*. As we have seen, Shepherd was quite familiar with Locke's writings. Locke argues that different kinds of entities require different accounts of identity, and he observes that living entities are not mere assemblages of "particles of matter any how united" (*ECHU* 2.27.4). Rather, the identity of a living being over time consists in the continuity of changing particles "united" to a body that has a certain "continued organization" of its parts (*ECHU* 2.27.4). Thus, the identity of a human body consists "like that of other animals in one fitly organized body taken in any one instant, and from thence continued under one organization of life in several successively fleeting particles of matter, united to it" (*ECHU* 2.27.6). However, since humans also have consciousness, Locke says that personhood and selfhood are based in this consciousness, and *not* in the continuity of a living body:

For, since consciousness always accompanies thinking, and 'tis that, that makes every one to be, what he calls *self*; and thereby distinguishes himself from all other thinking things, in this alone consists *personal identity*, *i.e.* the sameness of a rational being: and as far as this consciousness can be extended backwards to any past action or thought, so far reaches the identity of that *person*; it is the same *self* now it was then; and 'tis by the same *self* with this present one that now reflects on it, that that action was done. (*ECHU* 2.27.9)

228 MARY SHEPHERD

Shepherd's rejection of an account of the identity of the self in terms of "sameness of particles" and her claim that our "sense of continuous existence" results from the unity of memories with our current perceptions thus echoes Locke's account of the identity of *persons* or *selves*; she agrees with Locke that identity of particles is irrelevant to the identity of selves, and that a "sense of continuous existence" *is* relevant. It is in this sense that Shepherd seems to mean that the self is a "compound mass" (*EPEU* 152) or "complicate being" (*EPEU* 154) and that the idea of self is "compound" (*EPEU* 98). Self is a compound of the capacity to think and the continuous consciousness—the series of conscious sensations—that results from the use of that capacity.

One might object that (as we saw earlier) Shepherd often equates self with mind, but she also says that the mind is "simple." How could a simple mind be identical with a compound self? This is where it is helpful to distinguish broader and narrower senses in Shepherd's use of 'mind,' 'soul,' and 'self.' In the narrower sense, these terms refer strictly to the simple, general capacity to produce sensations—that is, to mind/soul/self as a *cause*. But that capacity produces a wide variety of *effects*, which are sensations, mental states; these conscious sensations can, in a broader sense, be considered part of the mind/soul/self. As Shepherd writes, "let it be remembered, that during any state of continued conscious sensation, the whole is compounded of parts of different kinds: there exists a succession of different sensations, (simple or compound,) each of which in its turn vanishes" (*EPEU* 374). Here, she notes that over time, many particular sensations come and go. We can treat the mind/soul/self—in a broader sense—as the train of sensations *along with* the capacity to have those sensations. That is, in the narrower sense, mind/soul/self is just the cause of sensations; in the broader sense, mind/soul/self is the cause *and* the particular effects (sensations) that it brings about.

It is this broader sense of 'self' that Shepherd seems to intend when she writes that "any particular given state of sensation, mixed

MIND AND BODY 229

with the consciousness of our own continued existence, and the *idea* of its continually existing cause, forms the compound idea called *self* (*EPEU* 98). That is, the idea of the self (in the broader sense) is composed of an idea of mind/soul/self in the narrower sense (the idea of the capacity to sense, the "continually existing cause" of any given sensation) *plus* the "consciousness of our own continued existence." But what is this "consciousness of our own continued existence"? The phrasing is reminiscent of Shepherd's reference to the "sense of continuous life" in another passage: "*Self* is always considered as a *continuity*, and is generated by the sense of continuous life, and the idea of its continued subject which is the subject matter of all the changes" (*EPEU* 138–39n). In yet another passage, Shepherd says that the "sense of continued existence" consists of "the union of the *ideas of memory*, with the *impressions of present sense*" (*EPEU* 154). Evidently, then, the "sense of continuous life" or "consciousness of continued existence" is composed of various memories linked with current sensations.

In sum, the idea of the self (in the broader sense) is a compound idea made up of the idea of the capacity to sense plus various memories and current sensations, and the self itself (in this broader sense) is composed of the capacity to sense (mind in the narrow sense) plus the sensations that it has caused and is causing. We can now see why Shepherd says the self is a "compound mass" (*EPEU* 152) and a "complicate being" (*EPEU* 154): it is, in a broad sense, a being composed of a capacity to sense (a cause) and the sensations that have resulted from that capacity (effects).

One still might be tempted to think that Shepherd uses 'self' to mean a mind–body compound (something like Locke's account of the "man"[11]). As evidence, one might point out that her account of the self also includes the capacity to "keep up the life of

---

[11] Locke writes that "'tis not the *Idea* of a thinking or rational Being alone, that makes the *Idea* of a *Man* in most People's Sense; but of a Body so and so shaped joined to it" (*ECHU* 2.27.8).

230 MARY SHEPHERD

the body." But that is different from saying that the body is *part* of the self. Moreover, in a later passage, Shepherd suggests a thought-experiment in which we are to imagine a "sentient being . . . placed in the midst of various insentient qualities, capable of exciting changes in the sentient being" (*EPEU* 265–66). This being would soon come to have the idea of self, and here Shepherd writes that "self would therefore appear as a general capacity for any sensation, united to a *body*, i.e. a *sphere of certain limited consciousnesses*" (*EPEU* 266). Self, she says, is *united to* a body, but does not *include* the body.

Individuating Selves

We saw in the previous section that Shepherd seems to allude to—and agree with—Locke's account of personal identity when she says that it is not based on "sameness of particles" (*EPEU* 154). As we saw, Locke says that personhood and selfhood are based in consciousness, and that "as far as this consciousness can be extended backwards to any past action or thought, so far reaches the identity of that *person*" (*ECHU* 2.27.9). Likewise, Shepherd suggests that the self (in the broader sense) includes a "sense of continuous existence" resulting from the unity of memories with our current sensations (*EPEU* 154; see also 33). The identity of a person over time thus depends on the continuity of these memories and conscious sensations.

But there is a further, related question to ask about personal identity: what makes one mind/soul/self different from another *at* a given time? In the broad sense of these terms, it is not hard to see Shepherd's answer. Each mind, in the narrow sense of a capacity to produce conscious sensations will, over time, have produced a unique set of sensations, depending on its interactions with external objects and the state of the sense-organs of the body associated it. Since a mind in the broader sense is the capacity to sense

MIND AND BODY   231

plus all the occurrent and remembered sensations it has caused, each mind in the broader sense will, as a matter of fact, differ from the others.

It is less clear, however, that Shepherd has a way to individuate minds in the narrower sense. She characterizes God's creation of a human being as uniting a "finite portion of mental power" with matter (*EPEU* 400; see also 376–77). This suggests that each of us has some allotment of a shared capacity to sense, that our minds are really just "minor portions of mind" (*EPEU* 400). And she clearly thinks that each such portion of the capacity to sense is an individual, distinct from others:

> The capacity of sensation may, as a component part of the whole animal mass, be always generated with it, yet retain its individuality, after having once been formed with each being; . . . analogous to the physical individuality of all the millions of mankind, each of which was formed from the general clay. (*ERCE* 170)

But how, exactly, can Shepherd individuate minds in the narrow sense? If she held a Cartesian-style belief in immaterial substance, then she could argue that each mind differs from others by being associated with (or being identical to) a certain portion of immaterial substance; however, as we have seen, the textual evidence does not support ascribing belief in immaterial substance to Shepherd. She could, however, argue that an individual mind (in the narrow sense) is individuated according to the organized *portion of matter* with which it is united. Some textual evidence supports this interpretation. She writes, "let the capacity to feel exist in its own extraordinary essence; let such be *within the given compass of any individual organization*, and the substance would exist as the capacity of an individual mind" (*EPEU* 388, emphasis added). An "individual organization" is an individual body (*ERCE* 181–82); thus, a mind (in the narrow sense) is apparently individuated by being the portion of the capacity to sense that is "within the compass" of

232 MARY SHEPHERD

one organism. In other words, the individuation of minds (in the narrow sense) depends on the individuation of living organisms.

An analogy that Shepherd provides in another context might help explain this. She notes that the powers of heat, light, and electricity "exist at large in the universe, uncircumscribed by space or duration" (*EPEU* 401). If we want to put one of these powers to some particular use, we can use some "artificial arrangement" in order to direct it to a "circumscribed end" (*EPEU* 401). For example, we can build a battery or electromagnet to harness electricity in a particular portion of matter. Similarly, the power of thought exists infinitely and eternally, but God can, as it were, divide it into smaller portions by joining it with a finite living body.

However, it is not clear that Shepherd has a non-circular way to individuate living organisms. She says very little about this topic, but she does suggest that each of us can individuate our own body from other bodies:

> We consider *that as our own body*, which is within a bound, or certain limit, and is the source of *conscious* pleasure and pain, and this *limit* we call the skin, within which, is contained *all we call ourselves*, and being summed up, is the notion of the conscious sensation of the extension of the body, and of a sufficient cause for life and sensation in general. (*EPEU* 62)

The body here is individuated as that which is within the limit of the skin; the body occupies certain spatial dimensions. If Shepherd individuates portions of mind according to the portions of matter with which they are associated, then my mind is the capacity to sense whatever interacts with the senses of a particular organized quantity of matter within a certain boundary. However, Shepherd suggests that the spatial dimensions marking the boundary of my body are *themselves* determined by what I consciously sense. In other words, I take it that my body ends at the boundary of skin because all my conscious activity appears to occur within that boundary. If the body is defined by the limits of a mind's capacity for consciousness, then the limits of the mind cannot be defined in terms of the body to which it is joined. It seems, then, that Shepherd lacks a non-question-begging way to individuate minds/selves.

If Shepherd cannot individuate particular capacities to sense, then it would seem that there is only one universal mind (in the narrow sense), something like an "eternal ocean of mind" (*EPEU* 378). And if there are no individual minds in the narrow sense, then Shepherd will have a problem individuating minds in the broader sense, too. A set of sensations can be identified as belonging to one mind only insofar as they are all caused by the same mind. But if there is only one universal mind, then all sensations would be caused by that single universal mind interacting with external objects, and so there would really be only one mind. As we will see in chapter 9, this also has possible ramifications for Shepherd's views about an afterlife.

Mind and Body

Shepherd characterizes mind not as a substance but as a capacity, which for her is a causal notion; it is a *power* to produce particular sensations under the right circumstances. What about body? When we perceive external objects, of course, we have various sensations that include extension, shape, and size—the so-called primary qualities, which Shepherd holds are in the mind in exactly the same way secondary qualities (color, sound, temperature, etc.) are in the mind. But *unperceived* body or matter, as it exists in itself, is an "unknown being" (*EPEU* 165). We do not know its "real essence" (*EPEU* 244). All we can know is that it is a causal power: specifically, it is a capacity to produce the sensation of extension in the mind. "Thus," Shepherd writes, "the definition of matter becomes *the capacity of exhibiting upon a sentient nature, the sense of solid* EXTENSION *in general*" (*EPEU* 242; see also 113–14 and 155). That

234 MARY SHEPHERD

is, matter (unperceived) is a capacity to produce a particular *kind* of sensation when it interacts with a mind: a sensation of "solid extension." As we saw in chapter 3 of this *Guide*, perceived matter can be divided into "particles"—yet in themselves, in their unperceived nature, particles too are unknown, except insofar as they are causal powers to make us have various sensations and to make objects appear to us in various ways (*EPEU* 304). The terms 'material' and 'immaterial' are thus simply labels for two kinds of capacities (*EPEU* 113–14).

It seems odd to posit free-floating capacities that are *not* the capacities of an underlying entity. Perhaps Shepherd thinks the capacities that make up mind and body inhere in something else; her reference to "insentient nature" and "sentient nature" (*LMSM* 701) seems to suggest that insentience and sentience are capacities and that "nature" is that in which those capacities inhere. She also says that time, a "capacity of admeasurement," is an "existence in nature" (*EPEU* 28). Possibly, then, Shepherd would say that there is some underlying substratum—"nature"—in which causal powers inhere; but if this "nature" is not a causal power, then we can know nothing about it. Whether the causal power that is mind and the causal power that is matter inhere in a single substance is a question that cannot be answered.

Whether mind and matter can exist separately from each other is another vexed question. Shepherd does not go so far as to say we can never know the answer—perhaps we can learn the answer after death—but she acknowledges its difficulty: "whether these causes or capacities can exist separate from each other, is the question which is always asked, and remains unanswered in philosophy" (*EPEU* 155–56). She observes that in our own experience, sensation always occurs "*in company with that which excites the sensation of extension in particular,*" but that this does not mean it *must* do so; perhaps there are other beings that can sense or remember without being joined with a material body (*EPEU* 156). We will return to this issue in the next chapter of this *Guide*.

MIND AND BODY 235

But even if Shepherd thinks we cannot know whether mind can exist without body, what, if anything, does she say about how mind and body interact? For a substance dualist like Descartes, explaining mind–body interaction is a challenge. For Descartes, mind is essentially just a thinking thing and is non-extended, while body is essentially an extended thing and does not think. How can two entities with nothing in common interact? This was the worry that Princess Elisabeth raised in her correspondence with Descartes.[12] For Shepherd, however, saying that some beings are material and some are immaterial is a claim only that two fundamentally different kinds of *capacities* exist, so her view of mind–body interaction will be quite different. Her view about mind–body interaction is simply that there is a "combination of powers" (*EPEU* 158); what she has to explain is not how two different *substances* interact, but how two *capacities* work together. And, she writes, "it appears perfectly easy that such causes and capacities, such collections of qualities, should intermix" (*EPEU* 217). As an analogy, consider playing music on a piano. A person who knows how to play the piano can be said to have a general capacity to produce music, but for the actual production of music, this capacity needs to be combined with the capacity of a piano to produce sound. The exercise of both capacities together produces, say, the sound of a sonata.

There are two aspects of mind–body interaction that Shepherd needs to explain, corresponding to two kinds of effects. One sort of effect results from the interaction of the human mind and body and is mental: a *sensation*. The other also results from the interaction of the human mind and body but is a physical effect: a *movement* of the body upon a decision to do so. Since the aim of *EPEU* is to explain perception, it is unsurprising that Shepherd says more about the first kind of case, but she does discuss the second kind in *EPEU*'s essay 13, "On the Association of Ideas, and the Interaction

---

[12] See Shapiro, *The Correspondence between Princess Elisabeth of Bohemia and Descartes*, 62.

236 MARY SHEPHERD

of Mind and Body." We will begin with that before turning to her explanation of mind–body interaction in sensation.

In essay 13, Shepherd considers how the mind brings about motion in the body by considering "putting a design in execution" (*EPEU* 404). To take an example from "Lady Mary Shepherd's Metaphysics," suppose I look out a window at a garden and decide to take a walk among the flowers (LMSM 702). This mental state includes at least two sensations that are associated together, "perception and will": I *see* the flowers, and I *choose* to walk among them. Shepherd holds that this mental state is also associated with certain physical states of the sense-organs and brain (*EPEU* 404), but it is the sensations, the "perception and will" that "begin and direct the motions towards the end in question" (*EPEU* 404). How? This, Shepherd concedes, is mysterious:

> Therefore perception and design of *mind* begin, and *direct* motion on matter; the qualities are together; the mind perceives its design, and directs its motion; but the mysterious law, or natural power which is a material property and executes the motion, is hidden from its observation, although it should react upon it, whether by pain or pleasure, in each conceivable variety. (*EPEU* 405–6)

Nonetheless, even if we do not know *how* the physical body exercises its capacity to move when combined with a certain mental state, Shepherd insists that there is "no mystery in this union" (*EPEU* 407). Mind and body, as bundles of capacities, can unite and mix just as any other bundles of capacities can.

The other case of mind–body interaction is human perception. We have already seen Shepherd's account of how sensations of extension, color, sound, and so on result when the sense-organs, brain, and mind interact with external objects. The sense-organs and brain are themselves material, of course, so they have the power that all material things have of producing a sensation of extension when an external observer sees or feels them. Suppose a brain surgeon observes the brain of a patient; the patient's brain exercises a material power in producing a sensation of extension in the brain surgeon's mind. But this is not the power that is relevant when a perceiver is *using* the sense-organs, nervous system, and brain; after all, when I use my ears, nerves, and brain to *hear* something, I am not thereby seeing or feeling the materiality of my own ears, nerves, and brain. Rather, my ears, nerves, and brain are exercising *other* powers, the powers that help produce sensations of sound. Sense-organs are the "mechanical instruments" of the body (*EPEU* 55) that serve as the "causes of introducing these [external] objects" to the mind (*EPEU* 53); the nerves have a power to be "sentient" (*ERCE* 156);[13] and the brain has a capacity for a "distinct and different action" in each case of perception. When these all work together with the general capacity for sensation (mind), the effect is a sensation.

Shepherd hints that other beings might be able to sense or remember without a brain (*EPEU* 156), even though, for us, these mental activities require a brain. Otherwise, though, Shepherd says little in *EPEU* about the role of the brain in thinking. In one of her few references to the brain, she says that "to *perceive* is a mental quality" that "intimately unites in and with the action of the brain" and that such brain action can be "discerned" (*EPEU* 348). More strikingly, Shepherd claims that the brain is related to the mind by being the "exponent" of the latter. She first suggests this in *ERCE*, writing that

a different action of brain is wanted for each *variety of thought and sensation*; and so it must, because there must be a *separate or different* cause, for every separate or diverse Effect in nature, as before discussed. And thus the brain becomes the *exponent of the soul*; or is *in the same proportion in its actions*, as the actions

[13] On nerves and sentience, see chapter 4.

238   MARY SHEPHERD

of mind: and thus what is termed *association of ideas*, must have *corresponding unions*, in the actions of the brain. (*ERCE* 170–71)

There are two similar claims in *EPEU*. In one passage, Shepherd uses the phrase simply in passing, in a discussion of the reality of religious ideas: "The action of the brain is the exponent of the powers of the soul" (*EPEU* 36). In the other, Shepherd says that instincts—a certain kind of mental sensation—can result simply from processes in the brain and mind, without external objects mixing with the brain and mind. She notes that

> as the brain is the exponent of the soul, so any of its actions whatever, being either the effect of an impression from an outward object, or brought about by any other cause adequate to a given action, would equally give rise to the idea of the corresponding object; as in dreams, &c. (*EPEU* 160)

In all three passages, saying that the brain is the "exponent" of the soul seems to indicate that when brain and mind (soul) interact causally, the effects in one correlate with the effects in the other; the mixture of brain and mind results in *both* a change in brain state and a new sensation.

A look at the meaning of the term 'exponent' in Shepherd's day provides further support for this interpretation. While a common meaning of 'exponent' today is that of someone who expounds or sets something forth in words, this meaning was not widespread in Shepherd's day.[14] A different meaning of 'exponent' is more illuminating, however; 'exponent' can mean "he who or that which sets forth as a representative or type, as a symbol or index."[15]

---

[14] The earliest use of this sense of 'exponent' in the *Oxford English Dictionary* is 1812 (see "exponent, adj. and n.," OED Online, June 2022, https://www.oed.com/view/Entry/66688?redirectedFrom=exponent), and it does not appear at all in the 1828 *Webster's Dictionary.*
[15] See "exponent, adj. and n.," OED Online.

MIND AND BODY   239

Interestingly, one example of this meaning cited in the *Oxford English Dictionary* comes from an 1850 book by scientist William Grove (1811–1896), *On the Correlation of Physical Forces*: "The motion of the mass becomes the exponent of the amount of heat of the molecules."[16] What Grove means is that A is an exponent of B when A and B vary in proportion to each other, so that, even if we cannot directly observe or measure B, we can observe or measure A. We can thus infer something about B.[17]

The first edition of Grove's book appeared in 1846, after Shepherd's publications, but a similar usage also appears in David Hartley's *Observations on Man* (1749). There, Hartley presents a theory in which vibrations in the brain correlate with "sensations, ideas, and motions."[18] Comparing the relationship between vibrations and sensations to the relationship between the quantity of matter in a body and the gravity of that matter, he says that if his theory is correct, and "Vibrations can be shewn, by probable Arguments, to attend upon all Sensations . . . and to be proportional to them," then we can say either that vibrations are the exponent of sensations or that sensations are the exponents of vibrations, "as best suits the enquiry."[19]

The presence of this meaning of 'exponent' in texts ranging from 1749 to 1850 shows that this could be Shepherd's meaning in saying that the brain is the exponent of the soul. And, taking a second look at the passage in *EPEU*, we can see an echo of Hartley's claim that vibrations in the brain are "proportional" to sensations: "the brain becomes the *exponent of the soul*; or is *in the same proportion in its actions*, as the actions of mind; and thus what is termed *association*

---

[16] Grove, *On the Correlation of Physical Forces*, 25.

[17] Grove himself makes the interesting observation that "a doubt has recently been thrown upon the prior existence of cause to effect, and their simultaneity argued with much ability" (*On the Correlation of Physical Forces*, 11). He does not name Shepherd, but the possibility remains that he has her in mind. In this case, his use of 'exponent' might actually derive from hers.

[18] Hartley, *Observations on Man, His Frame, His Duty, and His Expectations*, 33.

[19] Hartley, *Observations on Man, His Frame, His Duty, and His Expectations*, 33.

240 MARY SHEPHERD

of ideas, must have *corresponding unions*, in the actions of the brain" (*ERCE* 171).

In sum, in describing the brain as the "exponent" of the soul, Shepherd seems to be suggesting that brain states and sensations in the mind are correlated and that our ability to observe one allows us to make an inference about the other. Suppose we observe a change in someone's brain states; for the brain to be the exponent of the mind seems to mean that a change in brain state is (assuming all else remains the same) an "exponent," or indicator, of a change in the conscious sensation; as the brain state varies, so the *sensation* varies, and vice versa.

If we recall how Shepherd defines 'sensation,' however, the interpretation just offered might face a problem. In glossing sensations as "mental consciousnesses" (*EPEU* 221), Shepherd's suggestion that every event in the brain is correlated with a sensation seems to imply that we are conscious of every event in the brain, which is certainly not the case. How can Shepherd avoid this implication? She could, perhaps, broaden her definition of the mind to include causal powers to produce effects other than sensations, or broaden the concept of 'sensation' so that it includes mental states of which we are not conscious.

There is another potential problem with Shepherd's claim that the brain is the exponent of the soul. Consider Shepherd's argument that there must be continuously existing external objects that change in order for us to have changing sensations, since (so she argues) the mind and the sense-organs do not change. But if changes in our sensations correlate with changes in the brain, it seems that the conclusion should be that *either* the brain *or* external objects have caused the perceptions. Shepherd needs some way to rule out the possibility that our sensations are caused simply by neurological changes rather than by external objects. If she can't rule this out, then the possibility would seem to remain that our sense perceptions are just brain-caused hallucinations or dreams and that her argument for the existence of external objects will turn out to be unsuccessful.

As we saw in chapter 6, however, Shepherd could note that a change in a sense-organ or in the brain *itself* requires a cause. Changes in external objects, then, are needed to explain changes in our sense-organs or brain (*EPEU* 16). Even if a very distant object could cease to exist in the time between setting in motion the causal process that results in my sensation, an external object is nonetheless the necessary cause of what ultimately results, namely, my sensation.

Suggestions for Further Reading

- On Shepherd's account of the self, see Deborah Boyle, "Mary Shepherd on Mind, Soul, and Self," and Martha Bolton's article, "Mary Shepherd," in the *Stanford Encyclopedia of Philosophy*. At the time of publication of this *Guide*, no published research addresses how Shepherd handles the problem of mind–body interaction.

9

Religion

Introduction

In the Preface to *ERCE*, Shepherd expresses concern that Hume's views regarding causation "lead directly to a scepticism of an atheistical tendency" (*ERCE* 4), and she concludes the book by declaring that her own doctrines "are the only true foundations" not just of science and practical knowledge, but of "belief in a creating and presiding Deity" (*ERCE* 194). In *ERCE*, she only briefly mentions how either Hume's or her own account of causation applies to belief in God and in miracles (*ERCE* 93–98), but in essays 8–12 of *EPEU* she takes up several issues in philosophy of religion that this chapter will consider in turn: whether or not we have good reason to believe in reported miracles, the basis of belief in God, the possibility and nature of an afterlife, and divine causation.

Belief in Miracles

Essay 8 is a response to Hume's argument in the *Enquiry Concerning Human Understanding* regarding belief in alleged miracles on the basis of others' testimony. Shepherd had in fact promised in *ERCE* to address his views on miracles in a future work "if these pages should find favour before the public" (*ERCE* 96).

Hume defines a miracle as "a violation of the laws of nature" (*EHU* 10.12). His point in the *Enquiry* is not that violations of the laws of nature cannot occur, but that our evidence that such a violation has *not* occurred will always outweigh any evidence that

Mary Shepherd. Deborah Boyle, Oxford University Press. © Oxford University Press 2023.
DOI: 10.1093/oso/9780190090326.003.0009

it *has* occurred, when that evidence is based on another person's testimony. Having offered the general principle that "A wise man . . . proportions his belief to the evidence," Hume offers his readers two more specific principles for properly proportioning belief: (1) where past experience has shown something *always* to be the case, the wise person considers that experience to be a "proof" that the future will resemble the past in that regard; (2) when experience has been mixed, the wise person "weighs the opposite experiments: He considers which side is supported by the greater number of experiments: To that side he inclines, with doubt and hesitation" (*EHU* 10.4). Hume calls this evidence a "probability" rather than a proof (*EHU* 10.4).[1]

Hume argues that an alleged miracle already has, from the outset, a "proof" against it, namely, all our past experience that such an event has never occurred. When we look at the testimonial evidence *for* the occurrence of the alleged miracle, Hume argues, we will see that such evidence has consisted of supposedly eyewitness reports from a small number of people, not very well educated, typically from "ignorant and barbarous societies" (*EHU* 10.15 and 10.20). Promoters of miracle reports often have something to gain, either to feel the pleasure of exciting wonder and awe in their listeners or to present themselves as inspired prophets (*EHU* 10.16 and 10.29). Moreover, reports of miracles promoted by one religion are contradictory to those of other religions, providing a reason to think that at least one of those reports is untrue (*EHU* 10.24). In sum, this evidence can only constitute a "probability" that the alleged miraculous event has occurred. With a proof on one side and a probability on the other, the wise person concurs with the view supported by proof—in this case, that the alleged event did not occur.

---

[1] Hume also says that if there is experience on both sides of a question, the wise person will weigh them against each other and "deduct the smaller number from the greater, in order to know the exact force of the superior evidence" (*EHU* 10.4). Scholars dispute how exactly to interpret Hume's suggestion, but this debate need not detain us here.

244   MARY SHEPHERD

On some points Shepherd agrees with Hume. For example, Hume notes that, for the most part, we do believe people's testimony, because experience has shown us that people typically do not have motives to lie (*EHU* 10.5). Shepherd agrees that people do tend to tell the truth, especially when "it appears useful and accords with their interest to do so"; even in cases where it might seem useful to lie, people realize that "a superior value is contained in observing a general rule prescribing truth indifferently, whether for or against their interest" (*EPEU* 327–28). Thus, Shepherd follows Hume in holding that we should trust the testimony of others "in all cases where we cannot distinctly perceive any motive to falsehood" and that we should look carefully for self-interested motives when people report "*marvellous events*" (*EPEU* 328).

However, Shepherd maintains that Hume incorrectly defines miracles as "violations of the laws of nature" (*EPEU* 329). Her criticism is based on her theory of causation: since similar causes *necessarily* result in similar effects, the laws of nature (which concern what kinds of causes follow from what kinds of effects) *cannot* be violated (*EPEU* 334–35; see *ERCE* 79–80). Not even God can bring it about that objects identical to those that existed in the past (and acting in circumstances identical to those of the past) now have different effects. Since a given object of a certain type just *is* a certain bundle of causal powers, changing one of the causal powers of that object changes what type of object it is. Suppose God were to change snow so that instead of having the causal power of making a perceiver feel cold, it causes the perceiver to feel hot. But then "it" would not be snow, but some other, new kind of object. In such a case, God's action has *created a new kind of object*, rather than changing the laws of nature regarding how snow behaves. God has acted as an "additional cause" (*EPEU* 329; see also 145) in the apparently miraculous situation of what appears to be snow feeling hot. In other words, God's intercession into the normal course of nature does not involve God making like causes have different effects; God's intercession involves God *adding his own action* to

RELIGION 245

a set of causes that are otherwise like those of the past. Thus, the apparently miraculous situation does *not* consist of causes exactly like those in the past; it consists of those causes *plus* God's action. And since the causes are now different, the effects will necessarily be different.

Having objected to Hume's definition, Shepherd goes on to raise three more objections. First, she takes issue with Hume's claim that "experience has established the laws of nature" (*EHU* 10.12). By "laws of nature," she takes Hume to mean "the original inherent qualities of the 'secret powers' and capacities of bodies and minds," that is, "the mysterious influences of distinct masses of things, antecedent to their operation upon our senses" (*EPEU* 330–31). In fact, she says, our experience only *reveals* these laws, which exist externally to and independently of us.

Second, Shepherd notes that "in all classes of things" there are "exceptions to hitherto universal experience" (*EPEU* 331). Here she appeals to Hume's own example of the Indian prince, who, having always lived in warm climates where frost did not occur, did not initially believe that frost could exist; Hume says the prince was reasonable to require "very strong testimony" before believing the report (*EHU* 10.10). Shepherd says that we are *all* often like the Indian prince, forming expectations based on limited experience and then being surprised by some exception to that experience. But just because we see exceptions does not mean that there has been a violation of the laws of nature; they are merely exceptions to the "*apparent* course of nature" (*EPEU* 331–32). As she put it earlier in the book, "a regularity with respect to certain events in one country, does not *prove* there must be the same regularity in another. Nor does that which is a regular appearance in one age of the world *prove* the same must exist in all ages of the world" (*EPEU* 147).

Shepherd's third argument is *ad hominem*:[2] she notes that while Hume had argued that there is no contradiction in nature changing

---

[2] On the role of *ad hominem* arguments in early modern philosophy, see Moriarty, "The Ad Hominem Argument of Berkeley's *Analyst*," 436–39.

246   MARY SHEPHERD

its course, he then "suddenly turns the tables" and argues that if some past uniformity in nature suddenly no longer holds, that would be a violation of the laws of nature (*EPEU* 333–34; see also *ERCE* 95).[3] Hume, suggests Shepherd, cannot have it both ways.

With her objections in place, Shepherd identifies three distinct questions that she thinks are often conflated: (1) Can the apparent course of nature in fact change? (2) Do we ever have credible evidence to believe that it has changed? (3) Assuming we do have credible evidence, can this be used as the basis of religious doctrine (*EPEU* 335–36)?

To the first question, Shepherd answers "yes," referring her reader to *ERCE*, where she had stressed that not even God can make a cause that is truly exactly identical to another cause result in different effects:

> For nature otherwise to change, and to vary either her "*Effects*," or "*Secret powers*," without varying the causes or prevening circumstances whose junction formed the objects, whence these result;—is so obviously impossible, that we cannot even suppose the will and power of the Deity to be able to work the *contradiction*. (*ERCE* 72)

Nonetheless, as we have just seen, she thinks God *can* act as "an additional *cause*, equal to the alleged variety of effects" (*EPEU* 329). That is, rather than God making exactly identical causes bring about different effects (which is impossible), God adds his own power to the action of some cause, so that a *new* cause brings about the new effect.

To the second question, as we have also seen, Shepherd thinks we *may* sometimes have credible evidence to believe a report of a

---

[3] This criticism anticipates one by C. S. Lewis, namely, that Hume's argument against belief in miracles in *EHU* 10 "is quite inconsistent with the more radical, and honourable, scepticism of his main work" (*Miracles: A Preliminary Study*, 124).

RELIGION   247

"marvelous" exception to the normal course of nature. Shepherd agrees with Hume that believable reports require that "no sufficient motive can be imagined to tempt the witnesses to falsehood" (*EPEU* 337). But she actually goes a step further, maintaining that the credibility of a report increases if the person relating it actually might *suffer* from the telling of it (*EPEU* 337; see also 339–40).

Finally, may credible reports of marvelous events be used as evidence for the truth of a religious doctrine? Shepherd suggests that this depends on the nature of the religious doctrine. She first asserts that nature uses "necessary means towards every event that is brought about" (*EPEU* 338–39), and then suggests that marvelous events are the necessary means by which a deity of superior power would bring people to believe in the deity's existence (see also *EPEU* 147).[4] Such a use of power should not be surprising, she says; thus, "however marvellous they may be, as exceptions to nature's course in fact, they are nevertheless *probable events*" (*EPEU* 338). On the other hand, Shepherd says, "When a doctrine is either a wicked or foolish doctrine, such events are so *improbable* to occur as connected with it, that the same evidence will not answer, and I will venture to add, has never been offered" (*EPEU* 339). Claiming that it is *unlikely* that nature would use the means necessary to bring about belief in a wicked or foolish doctrine, Shepherd thinks that if we hear of alleged miracles being used to support some "trifling dispute" (*EPEU* 339), we should give such a report little credence. Perhaps her idea here is that if a marvelous, apparently miraculous event brought about belief in something silly or evil, this would be a case of the means being *disproportionate* to the end achieved; it would be like using a sledge-hammer where much less force is needed. If this is her argument, though, it depends upon a contentious assumption about means and ends in nature.

---

[4] Berkeley expressed a similar view about the purpose of miracles: "It may indeed on some occasions be necessary that the Author of nature display His overruling power in producing some appearance out of the ordinary series of things" (*PHK* 1.63).

248   MARY SHEPHERD

At any rate, Shepherd thinks that when a marvelous event is presented as evidence for belief in a beneficial and serious religious doctrine, we should not dismiss it out of hand. We should consider whether the witnesses reporting the case might have been tricked; the case needs to be such that "the senses cannot be mistaken" (*EPEU* 340). We should also consider whether the witnesses making the report have anything to gain or lose by doing so; for the report to be believable, "there should be some notable overt acts of the witnesses, of sufficient self-denial in their sacrifices, in order to prove they believe in their own assertions" (*EPEU* 340). Although Shepherd thinks that many alleged miracles turn out to fail these two tests, she allows that in principle there might be reports that do not, and thus that we might have reason to believe a religious doctrine on the basis of a reportedly marvelous event.

Shepherd next notes two objections to the above reasoning. The first objection is "*That to say, the doctrine proves the miracles, and that the miracles prove the doctrine, is to argue in* A CIRCLE" (*EPEU* 341). While Shepherd agrees that it would be circular to maintain both that (1) a legitimate report of a miracle can support the truth of some religious doctrine and (2) a report of a miracle can be established as legitimate because that true religious doctrine shows it to be so, she denies that that is how she is arguing. Rather, she says, her view is that (1) a religious doctrine might be the sort of doctrine—that is, something momentous and good rather than trivial or harmful—that would be worth it for a deity to show to be true by interfering with the apparent laws of nature, and (2) when such a doctrine exists, and is known to be momentous and good independently of whether or not any alleged miracles support it, there could be *further* evidence for it in the form of a marvelous event (*EPEU* 342). As she puts it, "the excellence of a doctrine therefore, merely proves, that it might be of God, but miracles are wanted to prove that it *is* of God" (*EPEU* 343).

The second objection to Shepherd's reasoning regarding miracles is that "as martyrs have believed false religion, therefore

RELIGION   249

the sufferings of other martyrs cannot afford the proof of a true revelation" (*EPEU* 343). As Shepherd points out, however, dying for one's religious beliefs only shows that a person was not a hypocrite or imposter, not that the doctrine professed was true or that the person was not deluded (*EPEU* 344). But there is value in knowing that someone was committed enough to a belief to die for it, Shepherd says, and so such a report at least "obliges every honest mind to open his books and examine it with impartiality" (*EPEU* 344).

Belief in the Existence of God

In chapter 7 of EASP, Shepherd offers a hint of how she will argue for the existence of God later in the book:

> For after some contemplation upon the phenomena of nature, we conclude, that in order to account for the facts we perceive, "there must needs be" one continuous existence, one uninterrupted essentially existing cause, one intelligent being, "ever ready to appear" as the renovating power for all the dependent effects, all the secondary causes beneath our view. (*EPEU* 151–52)

This passage actually hints at two lines of argument. First, she suggests a cosmological argument, in which it is necessary to posit God as a first cause (itself uncaused) for all the phenomena we observe. But Shepherd's suggestion that this cause must be *intelligent* goes beyond what a cosmological argument is usually taken to establish and suggests that she will also offer a teleological argument, one that infers intelligence in the cause of the universe from the apparent presence of design in the universe's orderly phenomena. M. A. Stewart has argued that "half consciously, the first-cause and design argument are often presented together, as if mutually supportive, in textbooks and lectures" in eighteenth-century

250 MARY SHEPHERD

Scotland.[5] The first-cause argument was taken to establish God's necessary existence and attributes such as eternity, infinity, and unity; the design argument was thought necessary for establishing God's wisdom and benevolence.[6] Shepherd seems to be working within this tradition, for she does not always clearly distinguish the two arguments. Nonetheless, for the purposes of exposition, this chapter will consider them separately.

Shepherd's Teleological Argument

Shepherd presents her teleological argument first, in *EPEU*'s essay 9, "On the Objection Made to Final Causes as Ends, on Account of the Existence of Physical Efficient Means." She does not name names here, but is addressing materialists who think that because all phenomena in the universe can be explained by efficient causes, there are no grounds for asserting that the universe has a final cause (*EPEU* 346). By 'efficient causes,' she means whatever physical causes are needed to produce some effect; by 'final cause,' she means a cause with purposes and intentions. Her objection to the materialists is that they cannot explain the "*appearance* of contrivance in the universe" (*EPEU* 346). When we look around us, we see that nature appears to have goals and purposes; for example, it seems that the purpose of the eye is to see. This appearance of design and purpose is a *quality* that we perceive when we look at natural phenomena, and as such it needs a cause, for no quality comes into existence without a cause.

Humans act as final causes all the time, Shepherd thinks. For example, in knitting a sweater, the knitter is producing the sweater to achieve a specific purpose, although of course knitters must also use materials such as yarn, knitting needles, and their own hands as

[5] Stewart, "Religion and Rational Theology," 39.
[6] Stewart, "Religion and Rational Theology," 39.

RELIGION 251

efficient causes to bring about the intended goal. Shepherd analyzes the concept of a final cause based on what we know from our own experience, observing that for a human to act as a final cause that works toward a goal or purpose, two mental states must be present: (1) some "perception of future qualities" that do not yet exist but could be brought into existence and (2) "that intention to create them." As she puts it,

> A final cause properly signifies the mental perception of an attainable end; the contemplation of a certain number of qualities, the determination of whose existence is known to be in the power of the efficient agent, by his voluntary direction of the motion of those already present with him. (*EPEU* 359–60)

Final causes must thus be *perceptive* causes (*EPEU* 347), which means that only entities with minds can operate as final causes. The idea of the goal to be attained then becomes "the efficient cause that determines the will," and the act of will sets matter in motion in the right way to bring about the intended result (*EPEU* 360). Thus, the final cause (the agent's volition) *becomes* an efficient cause (*EPEU* 359), another factor whereby some new quality is produced. Indeed, Shepherd says, we can think of all the components needed for an entity to operate as a final cause as one "compound set of PHYSICAL EFFICIENT CAUSES" (*EPEU* 361).

However, the ability to think and the presence of will are "not to be descried by any sense of instrument, chemical, or mechanical, in our power" (*EPEU* 348). And if mental capacities cannot be observed using physical means, then a purely materialist explanation of some natural phenomenon would by its very nature preclude our detecting whether or not *intention* was among its causes (*EPEU* 348). Consider the action of a bird building a nest: even if we identify "every *material* motion, which could be detected by the senses, or by the nicest experiments, and all the general laws as they are called of physical attributes, whether mechanical or chemical,"

252   MARY SHEPHERD

we would not be able to explain why the bird "first exerts itself," why it flies in the direction it flies, why it puts its nest in this tree rather than that (*EPEU* 360). A full understanding of nature, as of human artifacts, requires knowing the intentions at play; even Francis Bacon recognized this, Shepherd says, despite his emphasis on identifying and describing physical processes (*EPEU* 357–58 and 364).

As an example of a failed attempt to avoid invoking intentions, Shepherd considers the Newtonian concept of attraction (*EPEU* 362–64)—that is, of gravity. Acknowledging that it is "bold to venture any objection to the Newtonian theory" (*EPEU* 364), Shepherd nonetheless criticizes Newtonians who say that motions of bodies toward each other are *caused* by gravitational attraction, that attraction is "*an attribute of all matter as matter,* by which it *begins* and *directs* the motions of bodies according to their densities, at a distance from each other" (*EPEU* 364–65). She has no objection to using the word 'attraction' to characterize "the *effect,* the direction of the motion of *bodies towards each other,* according to those laws of velocity which given densities observe" (*EPEU* 362), but to say that a body has a causal power "which makes it endeavour to *draw* other *matter* at a distance towards it" (*EPEU* 362) is to ascribe to matter a power of endeavor and intention that properly pertains only to *conscious* entities. Such a power cannot be detected empirically; Shepherd even describes an experiment that could (she thinks) show that such a power does *not* exist. Suppose two balls at rest are located some distance apart in an empty container (one without even air); they will never start moving toward each other unless some *additional* causal factor is added (*EPEU* 363; see also 368–69). Shepherd takes this to show that there is no inherent force in matter that causes one body to draw other entities toward it. If inanimate bodies (bodies that we take to be made only of matter and not to be conscious) move toward each other, there must, in fact, be some other cause of that motion, some "extraneous" cause (*EPEU* 370) that is not empirically detectable—an intention (*EPEU*

RELIGION   253

365). God must have acted on matter to set it in motion: to appeal to Newtonian attraction to explain physical phenomena is to try to "keep the Deity forever out of view" (*EPEU* 368) and has "afforded atheism its most powerful refuge" (*EPEU* 368).

But if empirical tests and experiments cannot reveal the presence of intentions, then what can? With objects we produce ourselves, we know that intentions are present "by experience of what passes within ourselves"; with objects not produced by ourselves, we may know it through analogical reasoning (*EPEU* 350). This requires comparing the object in question to our own creations—"with such things as we know to be governed, arranged, and adopted by mental qualities"—and then to "judge with discretion and impartiality, whether they be of *a like kind*" (*EPEU* 350; see also 365–66). And, of course, if they are of a like kind, then the Causal Likeness Principle tells us that they must have similar causes, including mind.

Shepherd thinks it is not easy to judge whether an object resembles another in being the effect of intention; thus, Shepherd says, an "Esquimaux Indian" might be astonished at a clock or steam engine, yet nonetheless think that such wonders might have been brought about purely by the actions of natural laws (*EPEU* 351–52).[7] But she does not think there is much difficulty in judging that there is an "*appearance* of contrivance in the universe" (*EPEU* 346); such phenomena as "the eye, and the heart, and the brain in animals; the sun, the earth, and the moon, amidst what is termed inanimate existence, and all things of a like kind must all have been matters of contrivance" (*EPEU* 354). Thus, mind—the divine mind—must be among the causes of these things (*EPEU* 370–71).

Shepherd returns to her teleological argument in essay 11, on the immateriality of mind. Every sensation must be a quality of *something*; space is required for anything—even immaterial things—to

---

[7] Shepherd paraphrases, in French, a passage from the materialist philosopher Pierre J. G. Cabanis (*Rapports du physique et du moral de l'homme*, 1:358), although Cabanis was actually making a point about the wonders of animal bodies.

254   MARY SHEPHERD

exist; thus, each sensation must be an "unextended quality of some kind of extension, whether considered as empty space, or as solid matter; or as some form of extended being not detectable by any organ of sense" (*EPEU* 386). She rules out sensations being qualities of empty space on the grounds that "*nothing . . . could never be rendered a something*" (*EPEU* 386). Assuming that sensation "does not occupy space as solid extension" (*EPEU* 385), this leaves the third option: sensations are qualities of "some form of extended being not detectable by any organ of sense," by which she presumably means they are qualities of immaterial mind (*EPEU* 387).[8] After asserting that individual human minds are constituted by mind existing "within the given compass of any individual organization [i.e., body]" (*EPEU* 388), she then turns to God's mind:

> Since we perceive instruments in existence which are means to ends, there must be the director of motion, the *perceiver of ends*, the former of instruments in the universe;—perception of ends and direction of means, are mental qualities; are the properties of the continued existence, called mind; mind therefore must have been at the fountain head of these contrivances; but not a mind whose existence is more invisible than that of our own minds to each other; although experience informs us, that the great, the universal mind which must have executed these works is not united to any small defined body with which we can become acquainted by our senses; therefore it is a hidden mind, although we know of its existence, by means of REASON. (*EPEU* 389–90)

Even if we grant that there is order, and thus apparent contrivance, in the universe, we might wonder whether Shepherd's argument establishes that the mind responsible for that order must be

---

[8] Elsewhere, Shepherd denies that mind is extended (LMSM 697–99), so by "some form of extended being not detectable by any organ of sense," she may not mean what she usually means by 'extension.'

RELIGION 255

infinite, eternal, and "universal." Shepherd clearly thinks it does, for she says this argument leads her to think of "such an adequate and efficient cause as . . . suggests a conception commensurate with the Deity it demonstrates, and compels an unlimited worship of his unbounded essence" (*EPEU* 371). In Hume's *Dialogues Concerning Natural Religion* (1779), the skeptical character Philo challenges Cleanthes, who had defended a teleological argument for the existence of God. Philo insists,

> By this method of reasoning, you renounce all claim to infinity in any of the attributes of the Deity. For, as the cause ought only to be proportioned to the effect, and the effect, so far as it falls under our cognisance, is not infinite; what pretensions have we, upon your suppositions, to ascribe that attribute to the Divine Being?[9]

Like Philo, we might wonder how Shepherd can infer that the cause of the universe is infinite and eternal, given that our own perspectives are limited and finite. Shepherd claims to know that the universe itself is infinite and eternal (*EPEU* 371), but of course we do not perceive this directly, and it is unclear how she thinks we can infer it. It seems that Shepherd needs a different argument—the cosmological argument, perhaps—to establish that the intelligent designer of the universe has an "unbounded essence." The fact that Shepherd suggests that the teleological argument does so indicates that she herself does not sharply distinguish the two arguments.

Shepherd's Cosmological Argument

Shepherd's other argument for belief in God is structurally similar to the argument she used previously to establish that there is an

---

[9] Hume, *Dialogues Concerning Natural Religion*, part 5, paragraph 7.

256 MARY SHEPHERD

external world of continuously and independently existing objects. It runs like this:

> After some contemplation upon the phenomena of nature, we conclude, that in order to account for the facts we perceive, "there must needs be" one continuous existence, one uninterrupted essentially existing cause, one intelligent being, "ever ready to appear" as the renovating power for all the dependent effects, all the secondary causes beneath our view. (*EPEU* 151–52; see also *ERCE* 95)

And she makes a similar claim a little later:

> With respect to the nature of God, (in which all men are so much and justly interested) his essential existence, his continued existence is demonstrated, by the abstract argument used in this treatise. Whatever variety and changes of beings there are, all changes must finally be pushed back to that essence who *began not,* and in whom all dependent beings originally resided, and were put forth as out goings of himself in all those varieties of attitudes which his wisdom and benevolence thought fit. (*EPEU* 189; see also 219)

Finally, she alludes to this cosmological argument in her discussion of the teleological argument, writing,

> let it not be retorted, that it is easier to conceive of all the little changing beings we know of, as existing without a creator than of such a being; for I answer, it is *not* easier so to think; the one side of the dilemma involves a contradiction, the other does not; the one is to imagine the existence of a series of dependent effects without a continuous being of which they are the qualities, and is equal to the supposition of the possibility of every thing springing up as we see it, from an absolute blank and nonentity

RELIGION 257

of existence; the other is the result of referring like effects to like causes. (*EPEU* 391)

Recall that Shepherd's argument for belief in external objects had posited the changing nature of our sensations; to account for the fact that our sensations come and go, there must be causes that exist continually and externally to us.[10] Her argument for the existence of God assumes the existence of those causes, what she refers to as "secondary causes" (*EPEU* 152), but now depends on the additional observation that those causes, too, come and go. For example, the rose bush that causes a perceiver's sensations continues to exist even when the perceiver is not in the garden looking at it— but the rose bush is not eternal. The bundle of causal powers that comprises the rose bush came into existence at some point, and will go out of existence when the rose bush dies. Since whatever object comes into existence requires a cause, Shepherd's point now is that *these* causes themselves must be effects, dependent on some other cause. She explicitly rules out the possibility of an infinite regress of causes, suggesting that this is "equal to the supposition of the possibility of every thing springing up as we see it, from an absolute blank and nonentity of existence" (*EPEU* 391). There must, then, be some uncaused cause of all these changes—that is, God.

Belief in an Afterlife

In essay 10 of *EPEU*, Shepherd raises questions about the existence of the mind after the death of the body. She does *not* doubt that, in some form or other, the mind *will* continue to exist in an afterlife. Mind is the "mysterious eternal power of feeling, which has been conveyed to each animal as its inheritance from the commencement of its species" (*EPEU* 376–77). And, again, "the invisible, but

---

[10] See chapter 6 in this *Guide*.

258   MARY SHEPHERD

demonstrated existence, must live for ever; it may be interfered with more or less,—it may be modified more or less, by all kinds of organs and their powers;—but its essence is one, and for ever" (*EPEU* 377–78).

What she says is uncertain is the *form* in which the mind continues its existence, and she offers two different possibilities for an afterlife: (1) the mind will "be lost in the eternal ocean of mind" or (2) the mind will "retain its individual consciousness of personality (*EPEU* 377–78). These possibilities can be seen in the following passage, using the added annotations of [1] and [2] to indicate which of the two Shepherd means:

Memory of sensations in the rounds of time may be [1] obliterated or [2] retained, according to the mysterious and occult laws which govern the interferences;—but the capacity, the being, which can respond to joy or sorrow; can be lofty or degraded; can be wise or foolish; can be "*the first-born of all things*," or the crawling insect; can "understand" *the imaginary motions* of "fluxions,"—or being fastened to the rock, possess no powers of motion, even of the simplest kind, whereby to resist or escape the influence of the surrounding wave;—this subject matter for each variety of sentient perception, or action, must for ever exist: it may, for aught *we can demonstrate*, [2] retain its individual consciousness of personality, communicated to it by particular interferences as in man, or [1] be lost in the eternal ocean of mind: it may, [2] under such modification, be improved and go on in a state of moral amelioration from the smallest touches of instinctive affection towards the first of its own kind which it acknowledged, to the perception of all the charities of friendship, and kindred, as preliminary to the consummation of angelic love hereafter; or be absorbed amidst the properties only subservient to animal existences . . .

. . . But the inquiry should be, whether when the organs which are in relation to any individual capacity, undergo the change called DEATH, if the *continuing mental* capacity [1] become

RELIGION 259

simple in its aptitudes again, or, [2] whether it remain so far in an altered state by what it has gone through in the present life, that it continues as the result of that modification? [2] Whether from any other interfering powers than those of the visible body, memory and sense shall be elicited; or [1] whether a total variety from any memory shall be the result and consequence of its former state,—analogous to the powers of knowledge which fetal consciousness yields to infancy, and infancy to manhood, without conscious *memory occurring* as an intervening cause?— [1] Whether as a dormant capacity it remain unexcited and unconscious of existence during eternity, or, whether [2] amidst the infinite changes of duration it shall start into life, under the modification of appropriate interfering qualities? (*EPEU* 377–80)

To see the difference between options 1 and 2 more clearly, it may be helpful to recall the distinction drawn in chapter 8 of this *Guide* between broader and narrower conceptions of the mind/soul/self. Narrowly understood, mind/soul/self is just the capacity to sense; more broadly understood, mind/soul/self is composed of that capacity to sense *plus* the various memories and current sensations that it has caused and is causing.

Consider option 2, in which the mind persists and retains "its individual consciousness of personality, communicated to it by particular interferences as in man" (*EPEU* 378). This would be the mind in the broader sense continuing to exist: the mind would continue as an individual capacity to sense; its past sensations—the "memory of sensations in the rounds of time" (*ERCE* 377)—would be *retained*, not obliterated; and it would presumably be able to form new sensations that would be integrated into that "*sense of continuous existence*; which sense, when analysed, is the union of the *ideas of memory*, with the *impressions of present sense*" (*EPEU* 153–54).

If this is possible, then a further question opens up: how could the mind recall its memories and form new ones if it is no longer

260 MARY SHEPHERD

joined to a body? Must the mind in the afterlife be associated with some different, new body? Shepherd's answer is that although we, as humans, *do* require sense-organs and a brain as partial causes in order to have sensations, this does not prove that mind *must* exist in conjunction with body (*EPEU* 155–56). "Abstractedly there seems no hindrance for such separate existence," she says, suggesting that perhaps in other kinds of beings, "sensations may . . . go on without brain" (*EPEU* 156). Our experience shows us that nerves are necessary for *us* to sense, but, in principle, things besides nerves might "elicit sentiency" (*EPEU* 157) or serve as "interfering powers" in order to bring about sensations (*EPEU* 379). Moreover, if the individual capacity to sense continues to have sensations, both remembered and new, even without the body it had during life, then "moral amelioration" or improvement in the afterlife would be possible. What this means, Shepherd does not say; without a body, one could not act, so perhaps she just means that one would improve in one's thinking.

In option 1, the mind's memories of its previous sensations *would* be obliterated. Stripped of its memories and not forming new ones, the mind would simply return to being "a dormant capacity," "unexcited and unconscious of existence during eternity" (*EPEU* 379–80). It would go from being a mind in the broad sense of a capacity to sense plus all the sensations that capacity has helped cause, back simply to being a mind in the narrower sense, a mere capacity to sense. In fact, not only would the mind in the broader sense disappear altogether, losing its remembered and present sensations, but the mind in the narrow sense would no longer be an individual, numerically distinct capacity to sense. Insofar as no particular sensations and no particular body would be associated with it, it would become just like every other capacity to sense; this is what Shepherd means when she suggests that the individual mind would become "lost in the eternal ocean of mind."

Which of these two options does Shepherd think is likelier? Although we cannot prove or "demonstrate" either possibility

(*EPEU* 378), Shepherd considers whether "the analogy of nature" can help settle the question (*EPEU* 380). She offers two considerations that support part of option 2, that in the afterlife the mind continues to sense. First, we should not expect "that a total obliteration of feeling should take place when there is a capacity for it" (*EPEU* 380). She seems to be suggesting that ordinarily, where a capacity is present and has once been actualized, it usually continues to be actualized. Second, Shepherd says, "by the laws of the same analogy every thing is progressive," which she glosses as meaning that everything is "a means to an end" (*EPEU* 379). If all our moral and intellectual achievements disappear when we die, what would have been the point of it? It is more likely, Shepherd suggests, that there is a connection between the state of the mind during a human's lifetime and the state of the mind in the afterlife (*EPEU* 381); presumably her thought is that those who had "superior benevolent feelings" and "virtuous habits" (*EPEU* 381) will be rewarded in the afterlife, while those who did not will be punished.[11]

This, Shepherd says, is as far as reason can take us. We cannot prove with certainty that the individual ability to sense continues after death, but this kind of analogical reasoning provides "a very strong presumption in favour of the testimonies of tradition," or "revealed religion," that say there is an afterlife that is connected in *some* way with one's actions during one's human lifetime (*EPEU* 381).

Another part of option 2 is that the mind in the afterlife remembers sensations formed during life, but Shepherd thinks not even analogical reasoning can settle whether this is likely. There is an "analogy of nature" showing that "extinction of memory" is possible (*EPEU* 381), for as the body grows through the stages of being a fetus, infant, and adult, the mind continues to improve even as it *forgets* its previous sensations (*EPEU* 381–82; see also 379). Our

---

[11] In this passage, Shepherd seems to use "cause and effect" in a more traditional sense, not as synchronous but as successive.

262 MARY SHEPHERD

current knowledge is based on earlier experiences, many of which we have since forgotten; for example, none of us remembers how we first learned our native languages, even though we are now fluent (*EPEU* 383). This suggests that in a new stage, the afterlife, the mind might not remember what it experienced during human life. Shepherd even speculates that after the resurrection of the dead on Judgment Day, those resurrected may have no memories of their previous lives:

> so may there in succeeding ages arise from the ashes of this, another universe connected with it as its natural effect and consequence:—Then every sentient power it may elicit, every single thought each various being may possess; every capacity which shall then be demonstrated, may be the results of the present universe of thought, will, passion, suffering, or joy; ignorance or knowledge, virtue or vice, faith or profaneness; and that perhaps without any acquaintance being imparted to it of the former state on which its then destination shall hang. (*EPEU* 383–84)

On the other hand, there are also analogies in nature "in favour of conscious memory hereafter," such as the fact that adults *do* remember many of their experiences from earlier stages of life (*EPEU* 384). Analogical reasoning thus results in a "balance." The upshot, then, is that what happens in the afterlife cannot be answered by either demonstration or reasoning probabilistically from nature.

Shepherd notes that there is no "philosophical difficulty" with holding that souls in an afterlife retain their memories, but that she herself would be "content" even if it turns out that individual minds existing in an afterlife have no memories of their human lives (*EPEU* 384–85). But it seems that there *is* a philosophical difficulty—for her, anyway—with the latter view. As we saw in chapter 8 of this *Guide*, Shepherd faces a problem of how to individuate minds in the narrow sense, as a bare capacity to sense and not as united with memories of sensations they have caused. So, if she thinks minds can continue to exist in an afterlife without those memories, she may not be entitled to say that they exist as individuals with a "personal consciousness," able to feel happiness and love and to practice virtue (*EPEU* 385).

It is interesting that in her discussion of the afterlife Shepherd suggests that there is a third source of knowledge, what she calls "the testimony of scripture" (*EPEU* 384). Since probabilistic reasoning by analogy leads to a "balance" of arguments, she concludes that "the testimony of scripture in favour of the renewal of conscious memory is as a casting die, which to any man who reasons as a philosopher, must affect his judgment" (*EPEU* 384). Shepherd does not cite any particular biblical passages, nor does she explain what she means by "the renewal of conscious memory," but she seems to be suggesting that the Bible supports the claim that the mind in the broader sense does continue to exist in the afterlife, even if this cannot be established by philosophical methods.

This is the only passage in which Shepherd mentions using scripture as a basis for drawing philosophical conclusions, so there is not much to go on, but she evidently thinks it can reasonably be used when there are no demonstrative arguments available and when probabilistic reasoning results in a "balance." We might think that in such cases, philosophy has failed, but Shepherd does not see it like that; she says that "the testimony of scripture" should, "to any man who reasons as a philosopher . . . affect his judgment" (*EPEU* 384). And thus she thinks we *can* have knowledge of what happens to the mind after the death of the body.

Divine Creation

Essay 12 takes up another question in philosophy of religion: whether or not God has a body (or "organization"). In human life, a living body with sensory organs is necessary for sensation (*EPEU* 395), although, as we saw in Shepherd's discussion of

264 MARY SHEPHERD

William Lawrence's account of life,[12] she also maintains that it is not sufficient, since a capacity for mind is also necessary (*ERCE* 169). But even if a body with sensory organs is necessary for human sentience, that does not mean it is necessary for God. Indeed, as we have seen, Shepherd also leaves open the possibility that in an afterlife, the human mind might be able to sense without a body, even if we cannot conceive how that would be possible.

Shepherd offers an intriguing explanation of *why* sentience must be joined with sensory organs in humans (at least while we are alive) but not in God. An individual human being is a body joined to some "portion" of mind in general (*EPEU* 381; see also 400). Shepherd now adds that the purpose of the body is to individuate a new person from their "parent stock" (*EPEU* 395): "The organs . . . are necessary to circumscribe individual capacities to sensation" (*EPEU* 399). Her picture seems to be this: when humans reproduce, they produce a new living organism. The bodily organs and the "power of inward motion" by which the body is *alive* come from the parents. But why should we view a newly born living human baby as a distinct person, rather than, say, as a part of the human mother that just happened to become physically separated from her? What makes this portion of matter and life a distinct person, according to Shepherd, is that God has united a "finite portion of mental power" with that particular finite body (*EPEU* 400); the "junction" of the organs and a "minor" part of mind makes possible the "finite perception" characteristic of human minds (*EPEU* 400–1). That is, particular bodies are needed to individuate particular minds, although, as we have seen, this view poses some problems for Shepherd. Shepherd suggests that God's action of joining the general power of mind to a specific physical body resembles human actions when we use light, heat, and electricity. The general powers of heat, light, and electricity "exist at large in the universe, *uncircumscribed* by space or duration," but

[12] See chapter 4 in this *Guide*.

RELIGION   265

can be joined with a specific physical "artificial arrangement" to put them to use (*EPEU* 401); for example, a battery can be used to harness electricity.[13] Shepherd's thought seems to be that just as heat, light, and electricity can exist without being joined with physical entities, so God can exist without a body. Being infinite and eternal, God's powers are entirely *uncircumscribed*, and "stand in need of no organs in order to their determination" (*EPEU* 401).

There is one further issue to which essay 12 alludes, and that is the nature of divine causation. This issue was also mentioned briefly in *ERCE*. As we have seen, Shepherd's account of causation involves the interaction of two or more objects so that a new quality is produced; since objects are bundles of qualities, this means that a new object is produced. This new object is distinct from each of the causes considered separately, but is numerically identical to the combination of the causes. But how could God be the creator of the universe if God is just one entity and causation requires two or more entities mixing?

In *ERCE*, Shepherd addresses this question and makes clear that she thinks her account of causation can answer it. She writes:

> Should an objection arise to my doctrine, that on account of supposing causes to act as the junctions of different qualities, and yet by pushing back all causes to the ONE UNCAUSED ESSENCE; I thereby prevent the idea of him being reposed in as a Cause; as he forms ONE object only: I answer, that the uncaused essence, however mysterious in his nature, and however awful and distant to our speculations, must nevertheless have attributes; or in

---

[13] Although Shepherd does not cite batteries as an example, Alessandro Volta had developed the galvanic pile, the first electric battery, in 1800. Shepherd would almost certainly have been familiar with this and other experiments in electricity, which were widely known and discussed in Britain in her day. For example, she might have read about these in "The History of Galvanism," a series of articles published in *The Scots Magazine* in 1803.

266 MARY SHEPHERD

other words, its own peculiar qualities, which required no former beings, to *give birth to them*. (*ERCE* 96)

Here in essay 12, Shepherd says more about how her theory applies in God's case:

> Now, in the Eternal Essence *which began not*, and in whom must have resided the original capacities for all qualities, there must have essentially existed, not only mind or a capacity to feel, but that coalescence of qualities which must have formed his magnificent and innumerable perceptions ... [U]nderived, by eternal self-existence, there must be the *necessary* union of similar qualities in a *like nature* of existence in as far as it is *perception*; but *unlike* in every other respect, by all the difference between God and man—between essential, and dependent being. (*EPEU* 398–99)

Note Shepherd's claim that God is a mind that contains a "coalescence" or "union" of qualities. In essay 11 she had referred to "the amalgamation of all possible qualities in nature in One Being necessarily existing" and "the eternal, necessary, and essential union" of qualities in God (*EPEU* 390). This talk of "union" and "coalescence" is exactly the same language she uses to describe how objects interact in causation (*ERCE* 141–42). Objects are bundles of qualities; to be more specific, external objects are bundles of causal powers. Just as the causal powers comprising two distinct objects can interact, Shepherd seems to be suggesting that the powers *within* one object can interact. If so, then although God is just one being, his powers can combine and thereby produce effects. Thus Shepherd refers to God "holding in unison by the mysterious nature of his essence ... such qualities as are fitted to give forth those changes which form the creatures" (*EPEU* 399–400). Similarly, in *ERCE* she suggests that among God's qualities are wisdom, benevolence, and other powers unknown to us, and that in the union of those qualities God produces "inferior beings," that is, the universe. Indeed, she even says there that God "gives birth" to finite things (*ERCE* 96–97).

Interestingly, Shepherd refers to the "eternal, necessary, and essential union" of qualities in God (*EPEU* 390–1) and remarks that "the *operation* of that essence must ever have been the same from all eternity" (*ERCE* 96–97). To say that the qualities that cause the universe are always combined in God—and thus continually causing the universe—implies that the universe is eternal, since God is an eternal being. Christian doctrine holds that the universe had a beginning in time and is *not* eternal; indeed, Shepherd herself quotes from Genesis when writing about God's creation: " 'Let there be light,' said God, 'and there was light' " (*ERCE* 97). We might, therefore, expect Shepherd to try to avoid the conclusion that the universe is eternal. However, she certainly does not reject this possibility, writing that God's

> original intention, with its effect, the immediate direction of motion, may have commenced in the eternal mind at the beginning of this universe, or it may have existed through eternity, coeval with and essential to the Deity: As to which of these, we have no possibility of preferable conjecture. (*EPEU* 353–54)

Later she actually embraces the idea that the created universe itself is eternal, writing that to think of "all the little changing beings we know of" as having a cause is "to believe in the infinite universe of mind, matter, space, and motion, eternally and necessarily existing" (*EPEU* 391–92; see also *ERCE* 98). Here she suggests that mind and matter are *themselves* eternal, the constant creations resulting from the eternal combination of qualities in God's essence.

Some philosophers who have maintained that the universe is eternal have combined this with an interpretation of God's creation in terms of emanation, whereby the universe "flows" continuously from God. For example, Plotinus considered the relationship between higher and lower beings to be like that of the sun and

268   MARY SHEPHERD

the light that emanates from it: so long as the sun exists, the light flowing forth from it exists too.[14] Shepherd's language sometimes hints at an emanationist view of God's creation, for she writes of properties that are "out goings" of God (*EPEU* 189; see also 191). She writes of the powers in nature "flowing from that continuous being the God of Nature" (*EPEU* 154) and of a "perpetual series of changes flowing from the only origin of all things" (*EPEU* 245). She also writes that each created object "must be regarded as containing in its degree, some portion of its celestial origin, though incapable of diminishing the plenitude of his infinity, or subtracting from the splendor of his incommunicable mystery" (*EPEU* 402), language that has echoes of Plotinus' conception of emanation as the transmission of qualities to a lower being from a higher being that does not lose those qualities.

There is a further surprising implication of Shepherd's causal theory as she applies it to God. Consider her claim that an effect is numerically identical to the combination of the causes: "the union" of the factors needed to produce something "is the proximate Cause of, and is *one* with the Effect" (*ERCE* 187). If this is so, then the universe is actually the *same* as the combination of those of God's qualities that are responsible for its existence.[15] This identification of God and the material universe also flies in the face of Christian doctrine, and has echoes of Spinoza, whose views at this time in Britain were still viewed with suspicion.[16] Whether Shepherd realized that her theories had this implication is unclear.

---

[14] Plotinus uses the example of the sun at *Ennead* I.7.1. There is considerable scholarly debate, which need not detain us here, about how to understand Plotinus' conception of emanation.

[15] Antonia LoLordo has also noted this implication, as well as Shepherd's apparent emanationism ("Introduction," 20).

[16] It was only in the 1830s that British attitudes toward Spinozism started to become more positive. See van Bunge, "Wayne I. Boucher (ed.), *Spinoza: Eighteenth and Nineteenth-century Discussions*: A Review-Essay," 66.

RELIGION 269

Suggestions for Further Reading

- At the time of publication of this *Guide*, almost nothing has been published on Shepherd's philosophy of religion, although it receives brief discussion in Antonia LoLordo's introduction to *Mary Shepherd's Essays on the Perception of an External Universe* (20–23) and in LoLordo's overview of Shepherd's philosophy in *Mary Shepherd*.

10

Vision

Introduction

Shepherd mentions vision throughout her writings. The example she uses to explain the Causal Likeness Principle is of closing and opening one's eyes (*ERCE* 44–45); she compares the mind to a camera obscura (LMSM 702); in her criticisms of Reid's views on primary and secondary qualities, she zeroes in on his account of "visible figure" (*EPEU* 23–25); and essay 4 in *Essays on the Perception of an External Universe* is devoted to the relationship between perceptions of extension and of color. Essay 14, the final essay in that book, lays out Shepherd's solutions to two puzzles about vision. First, given that we have two eyes, and thus images of every seen object on two retinas, why do we not see two of everything (*EPEU* 408)? Second, why, since the retinal images are inverted, do we not likewise *see* objects as inverted (*EPEU* 412)? Shepherd was sufficiently interested in these two questions to return to them in another essay, "On the Causes of Single and Erect Vision," published in the scientific journal *The Philosophical Magazine and Annals of Philosophy* in 1828. This essay was reprinted the following month in two consecutive issues of the popular English weekly magazine *The Kaleidoscope; or, Literary and Scientific Mirror*.

Since Shepherd was responding to theories of vision propounded by Berkeley and Reid, this chapter offers overviews of their accounts as well as of Shepherd's criticisms of specific aspects of their accounts. The chapter starts by surveying the geometrical accounts of vision to which Berkeley and Reid were both opposed, and then

Mary Shepherd. Deborah Boyle, Oxford University Press. © Oxford University Press 2023.
DOI: 10.1093/oso/9780190090326.003.0010

sketches Berkeley's alternative account of distance perception. It then considers Shepherd's brief criticisms of Berkeley's account in EASP chapter 3 and outlines some main features of Reid's account of vision, also setting out Shepherd's criticisms (in essay 4 of *EPEU*) of Reid and his follower Dugald Stewart on why color perceptions are associated with visual perceptions of shape. The chapter then turns to Shepherd's own account of visual perception, and specifically to her account of how we perceive distance. The puzzles Shepherd addresses in *EPEU* essay 14 are the topics of the final sections of the chapter.

Berkeley's Account of Visual Perception

Two of the philosophers with whose work Shepherd was most engaged, Berkeley and Reid, had a great deal to say about vision. Indeed, one of Berkeley's earliest published works was his *Essay Towards a New Theory of Vision* (1709); he returned to the topic in *The Theory of Vision, or Visual Language . . . Vindicated and Explained* (1733). This section will present, in broad terms, sketches of the geometrical theory of vision that Berkeley rejected and of the alternative theory he proposed instead.

Geometrical Theories of Vision

Berkeley was responding to theories of visual perception to be found in Descartes' *Optics* (1637) and Malebranche's *The Search after Truth* (1674), "geometrical" theories that Berkeley characterized as "very unsatisfying" (*NTV* 14 and 8). Such theories explained our perceptions of the distance, size, and position of objects as inferences made on the basis of implicit geometrical reasoning; yet, as Berkeley put it, "those lines and angles, by means whereof some men pretend to explain the perception of distance, are themselves

272 MARY SHEPHERD

not at all perceived, nor are they in truth ever thought of by those unskillful in optics" (*NTV* 12).

Geometrical explanations of vision go back to Euclid's *Optics* (c. 300 BCE), were developed by medieval writers such as Alhazen (965–1039) and Witelo (1250–75), and were the basis of Kepler's work on optics in the early seventeenth century, with which Descartes was familiar.[1] So Descartes' geometrical approach was not new; what was new was the mechanistic framework in which he deployed that approach.[2] In his *Optics*, Descartes offered a mechanistic account of vision that explained sensations of light and color in terms of matter in motion—specifically, the motion of particles of light as they hit the eye and are refracted by the lens of the eye, causing retinal images that in turn cause movements of the pineal gland that, in those perceivers who have a mind (i.e., human beings), result in mental sensations of color and light.[3] As part of his broader project to identify the laws of motion and thereby explain a wide range of natural phenomena, Descartes discussed the laws of reflection and refraction of light as well as the physiology of the eye, nerves, and brain, providing geometrical explanations of how rays of light are refracted during vision.

In addition to explaining color and light sensations in geometrical terms, both the *Optics* and the Sixth Set of Replies to the *Meditations* contain geometrical explanations of our perception of *distance*. In the former text, Descartes suggests that we perceive objects as being at various distances on the basis of changes in the angles of our lines of vision;[4] in the latter text, he maintains that our beliefs about the distance, size, and shape of external objects

[1] Osler, "Descartes's Optics," 124–25. For discussion of the texts on optics available to Descartes, see Smith, "Descartes's Theory of Light and Refraction: A Discourse on Method," 7–12.

[2] A. Mark Smith has argued, however, that Descartes' mechanistic optics had precedents in medieval theories ("Descartes' Theory of Light and Refraction," 45–46 and 64–65).

[3] On Descartes' account of vision, see Osler, "Descartes's Optics."

[4] Atherton, *Berkeley's Revolution in Vision*, 26–27.

VISION 273

are judgments that the intellect makes on the basis of sensory perceptions of color.[5]

Malebranche, too, appealed to geometrical considerations in explaining our visual perceptions of distance and size, as well as of shape and motion. Light and color are registered on our retinas, but in perceiving distance, size, shape, and motion, what we *see* often outstrips what these retinal images depict. As Margaret Atherton explains, Malebranche accounts for perceptions that outstrip the information contained in retinal images by appealing to "natural judgments" that depend on an implicit knowledge of laws of optics and geometry:

> When someone walks towards you, what is registered on the retina gets bigger, but what is seen is a person remaining the same size but getting closer. . . . These phenomena are like judgments because we account for the fact that what we see looks other than the way it is registered by referring to additional information in our possession, or, rather, in the possession of the visual system.[6]

Thus, Malebranche maintains that the human visual system includes not just what we directly and immediately see (patches of color and light), but also what we unconsciously infer (distance, shape, size, motion) using "a kind of natural geometry."[7] There is

---

[5] Atherton, *Berkeley's Revolution in Vision*, 20–21. Atherton identifies important different in Descartes' two accounts, even if both appeal to geometrical considerations (*Berkeley's Revolution in Vision*, 19–33). As she puts it, "Descartes has an account, on the one hand, of how we come to attribute spatial properties to external bodies, to be found in the Sixth Set of Replies, and an account, on the other, of how we come to have visual experiences of a spatial world, to be found in the *Dioptrics*" (32). These differences need not detain us here.

[6] Atherton, *Berkeley's Revolution in Vision*, 37. Strictly speaking, Malebranche holds that the possession of the relevant knowledge of optics and geometry is not in us but in God, who makes these natural judgments for us and gives us the sensations that appropriately follow from them (*Search after Truth*, "Elucidation on Optics," sections 25 and 43).

[7] Malebranche, *Search after Truth* 1.9.3, quoted in Atherton, *Berkeley's Revolution in Vision*, 38.

274 MARY SHEPHERD

a way, then, in which Malebranche says we do see distance, shape, size, and motion: we see them indirectly and mediately, via our direct perceptions of color and light and the laws of geometry and optics built into our visual system.

Berkeley on Perceiving Distance, Size, and Situation

Although Berkeley rejects geometrical explanations of vision, he nonetheless also employs a distinction between what we see immediately and what we see mediately.[8] The immediate objects of vision—what Berkeley calls "visible ideas"—are simply patches of light and color that vary in size, clarity, and faintness (*NTV* 50). Like Descartes and Malebranche, Berkeley holds that the distance, size, and situation[9] of objects are *not* among the original deliverances of vision. However, while Descartes and Malebranche thought that we make implicit judgments about spatial features of objects using geometrical calculations, Berkeley explains our visual perception of distance, size, and situation as the result of learning how visual perceptions and perceptions of touch given in experience are coordinated.[10]

According to Berkeley, the *primary and original* source of sensory information about distance, size, and situation is touch. We learn about the distance of objects by experiencing how far through space we must go to be able to touch them; similarly, we learn about objects' sizes and positions relative to each other through reaching

---

[8] For an argument that Berkeley also availed himself of geometrical explanations despite his avowed opposition to them, see Hatfield, "Geometry and Visual Space from Antiquity to the Early Moderns," 217–21.

[9] An object's situation is its position relative to the eye of the perceiver.

[10] Whether or not Berkeley thinks these associations have to be learned or are known naturally is the subject of some debate in the secondary literature; see Copenhaver, "Berkeley on the Language of Nature and the Objects of Vision," for the second kind of interpretation. Reid himself has the first kind of interpretation of Berkeley; as he puts it, Berkeley holds that "we can learn only by experience how one sense will be affected, by what, in a certain manner, affects the other" (*IHM* 6.11).

VISION 275

for and handling those objects. Thus, we learn about the distance, size, and situation of objects originally through *touch*, not vision. Berkeley calls our perceptions of these features "tangible ideas" (*NTV* 45). But, Berkeley says, we also learn through experience that various tangible ideas are coordinated with various visible ideas (which are immediately perceived by vision). For example, as children, we learn that a faint, confused color patch that appears small (that is, a certain kind of visible idea) is typically correlated with a long distance (a certain kind of tangible idea) (*NTV* 21).[11] The mind thereby develops a habit: when a very small, faint, confused color patch is seen, this "suggests" the tangible idea that has been experienced to be coordinated with it (*NTV* 147). When we learn a language, we come to associate certain audible words with certain ideas, so that hearing a particular word is enough to suggest its associated idea; similarly, after we have experienced certain visible ideas as regularly coordinated with certain tangible ideas, having a particular visible idea is enough to suggest its associated tangible idea (*NTV* 51, 147). Visible ideas serve as a "universal language," set up by God, whereby we experience the distance, size, and situation of objects by sight.

In a sense, then, we can be said to "see" distance, size, and situation: we see these things *mediately*, by way of the tangible ideas that are suggested by the visible ideas with which they are coordinated and have come to be associated. As Atherton sums up Berkeley's view,

A problem that arises because we seem to be able to learn more through seeing than we are equipped to learn by our visual system is solved by showing that the initial visual data are not

---

[11] Berkeley's view is actually somewhat more complex than this; many of the associations he identifies are not between a tangible idea and a visible idea but between a tangible idea and the *physiological sensations* that accompany a visible idea. For example, a tangible idea of a certain distance might be correlated with a sensation of eye strain (Atherton, *Berkeley's Revolution*, 83–84).

276 MARY SHEPHERD

supplemented by calculations relating the retinal stimulus to other extended objects but are instead supplemented by cues that suggest data from another sensory modality, that of touch.[12]

Shepherd's Criticisms of Berkeley on Distance Perception

Shepherd takes issue with Berkeley's account of distance perception, saying that he developed it "in order to prove it to be a sensation of *mind only*" (*EPEU* 68). Atherton has argued convincingly that Berkeley's *New Theory* has frequently been *misread* as intended to buttress Berkeley's idealist belief that visual objects exist only in the mind.[13] As Atherton notes, this reading of Berkeley's theory of vision does draw some support from a passage in his *Principles*, where he says the following:

> For, that we should in truth see external space, and bodies actually existing in it, some nearer, others farther off, seems to carry with it some opposition to what has been said of their existing no where without the mind. The consideration of this difficulty it was, that gave birth to my *Essay Towards a New Theory of Vision*, which was published not long since. (*PHK* 43)

Here, Berkeley seems to be saying that his *New Theory* was designed to show that space and objects exist only in the mind, and even that we do not really see objects at a distance. However, Atherton points out that in the *New Theory* itself, Berkeley makes it clear that he thinks we *do* see objects at a distance—since how we do so is precisely what he says he will be explaining.[14] Atherton gives an

[12] Atherton, *Berkeley's Revolution in Vision*, 122.
[13] Atherton, *Berkeley's Revolution in Vision*, 9–15.
[14] Atherton, *Berkeley's Revolution in Vision*, 10–11.

alternative interpretation of the *Principles* passage, on which the "consideration" that led Berkeley to write the *New Theory* was not the question of whether ordinary objects exist in the mind (the question addressed by the *Principles*) but, rather, the correctness of geometrical theories of vision; Atherton concludes that Berkeley developed his theory of vision to better explain visual perception, not to support immaterialism or idealism.[15]

In linking Berkeley's account of vision with his idealism and suggesting that the former was part of the basis for the latter, Shepherd seems to be guilty of precisely the misreading that Atherton describes. According to Shepherd, Berkeley "wrote his theory of vision to obviate an objection that might be made on the score of '*visible distance*,' in order to prove it to be a sensation of *mind only*, suggested by tangibility, &c" (*EPEU* 68–69). Here she is clearly alluding to his characterization of the *New Theory* in the *Principles*, rather than to the *New Theory* itself. Shepherd then criticizes Berkeley on the grounds that proving visible distance to be a mental sensation does not succeed in "explain[ing] away that *condition* of *being*, which, when unperceived, must be a proportional relation and variety amongst unperceived objects, and capable of affecting the touch, sight, and other senses in its own way" (*EPEU* 69). That is, she objects that Berkeley's account of distance perception does not—as she takes him to think it does—support idealism. She is right, but this is no criticism of Berkeley if his account of distance perception was not intended to support idealism in the first place. Moreover, as we will see below ("Shepherd's Account of Visual Perception"), Shepherd does ultimately offer an account of distance perception very much like Berkeley's, in which sensations of motion (and hence of distance) are associated with visual sensations of color and shape, so that the latter can indicate to us what sensations we might have if we were to use our senses of touch and motion.

---

[15] Atherton, *Berkeley's Revolution in Vision*, 14.

278 MARY SHEPHERD

Reid's Account of Perceiving Distance, Size, and Situation

Thomas Reid devoted the longest chapter of his *Inquiry into the Human Mind* (1764) to vision and took the issue up again in *Essays on the Intellectual Powers of Man* (1785). Reid agrees with Berkeley both that the distance, size, and situation of objects are not the immediate deliverances of visual experience[16] and that the Cartesian–Malebranchian "geometrical" explanations of how we mediately perceive distance, size, and situation should be rejected.[17] Reid also draws on Berkeley's terminology of "suggestion," writing approvingly of Berkeley's characterization of vision as employing a kind of "natural language" (*IHM* 6.2).[18] However, Reid's account differs from Berkeley's in important respects.[19]

The details of Reid's account are rather baroque, but a general sketch suffices for the purpose of understanding Shepherd's arguments in essays 4 and 14 of *EPEU*.[20] Reid holds that rays of light make "material impressions" on the eye's retina that have two kinds of effects, one related to color perception and one related to our perceptions of the "figure" of an object, that is, its

---

[16] While Berkeley's *New Theory of Vision* focuses systematically on how we perceive distance (sections 11–51), size or magnitude (sections 52–87), and situation (sections 88–120), Reid tends to lump together our perceptions of the distance, magnitude, figure, extension, situation/position, and motion of objects, all of which he distinguishes from our perceptions of color.

[17] Reid briefly discusses such geometrical explanations in his account of why we see objects as upright even though they are inverted on the retina. Descartes' solution—that we deduce the correct position through reason—is unacceptable because it assumes that we know that the retinal images are inverted and that we know the laws of optics, things which "are absolutely unknown to the far greatest part of mankind" (*IHM* 6.11).

[18] Reid also praises Berkeley's account of vision for its "very important discoveries, and marks of great genius" (*EIP* 2.10).

[19] For a helpful overview of points of agreement and disagreement between Berkeley and Reid on vision, see Copenhaver, "Berkeley and Reid."

[20] In the interest of brevity, the following account is merely a sketch, and omits discussion of Reid's important distinctions among sensation, perception, and conception. For discussion, see Copenhaver, "Thomas Reid on Acquired Perception," and van Cleve, *Problems from Reid*, 9–21.

VISION 279

shape, size, and situation (*IHM* 6.8).[21] Regarding color, Reid says that, due to the "will of our maker," our natural constitution is such that impressions on the retina "suggest" certain visual sensations of color (*IHM* 6.8). Reid calls these color sensations "visible appearances" or "apparent" color (*IHM* 6.3); although we are conscious of them, they are so fleeting that we pay no attention to them at all.[22] In themselves, color sensations do not indicate anything to us about the nature of external objects (*IHM* 6.3). However, they do *suggest* something further to the mind, something that *does* give us information about the external world. What visible or "apparent" colors suggest are the "qualities" or "modifications" of bodies out there in the world that we think of as being "fixed and permanent" despite the changing appearances they present to our senses (*IHM* 6.4). While these qualities of external objects *cause* our color sensations, they do not *resemble* those sensations (*IHP* 6.6).

The second effect of light rays hitting the retina, according to Reid, is that the retinal impressions "suggest" to the perceiver the "apparent" or "visible" figure of a physical object (*IHM* 6.8). That is, in normal vision, a color sensation caused by light rays from an object hitting the retina is also accompanied by a suggestion of that object's *visible figure*. The visible figure of an object is how it appears to a perceiver—for example, a round coin seen from an angle actually appears like an ellipse.[23] Unlike apparent colors, which are sensations, visible figures are not sensations (*IHM* 6.8). That is, the visible figure of an object is not in the mind; it is a real quality of

---

[21] Reid acknowledges that there are other physical components to the visual system, such as the optic nerve, the choroid membrane, and the brain; but "while we know so little of the nature and office of these more immediate instruments of vision, it seems to be impossible to trace its laws beyond the pictures upon the retina" (*IHM* 6.12).

[22] Artists are exceptions to this, Reid says, for "perspective, shading, giving relief, and colouring, are nothing else but copying the appearance which things make to the eye" (*IHM* 6.3).

[23] For this example and the following account of what Reidian 'visible figure' is, see van Cleve, *Problems from Reid*, 226 and 184–91. Briefly put, van Cleve argues that Reidian visible shape, size, and position are properties an object possesses "relative to our point of view" (191).

280 MARY SHEPHERD

body, consisting, says Reid, "in the position of [a body's] several parts with regard to the eye" (*IHM* 6.7). For most people, a visible figure is "presented to the mind" along with a color sensation, but Reid acknowledges that sometimes, as in people with cataracts, color sensations might be so diffused that the perceivers "perceive the color, but nothing of the figure or magnitude of objects" (*IHM* 6.8).

Just as Reid thinks the material impressions of light rays on the eye suggest the visible figure of an object (*IHM* 6.8), its visible figure in turn suggests the real "qualities" or "modifications" of the body out there in the world that are the causes of its visible figure (*IHM* 6.7). And unlike in his account of color (where Reid insists that color sensations do *not* provide us with clear ideas about the qualities in external objects that cause them), Reid says that visible figures *do* provide us with clear ideas ("distinct conceptions") of the actual figures of the external objects that cause them (*IHM* 6.7).

Nonetheless, if we only perceived objects by sight, Reid thinks we would get only a "very partial notion" of the *three-dimensionality* of external objects (*EIP* 2.19), that is, their distance from us (and each other) in space and their three-dimensional shape. A visible figure might be able to suggest that an object is *circular* (a two-dimensional feature), but it does not, Reid thinks, suggest whether an object is *spherical* (a three-dimensional feature). Like Berkeley, Reid thinks the three-dimensional features of objects are originally given to us by touch, not vision.[24] As we saw, Berkeley thought we learn through experience that certain *tangible* ideas (of the three-dimensional features of objects) are coordinated with certain *visible* ideas (of colors varying in size, clarity, and faintness), such that the latter can serve as signs of the former. Reid maintains that on Berkeley's account, the "correspondence" between the tangible

---

[24] As van Cleve points out, human binocular vision does, in fact, allow us to perceive the (relative) distances of objects from ourselves; however, this was only discovered in 1838, by Charles Wheatstone (*Problems from Reid*, 483–84).

VISION 281

figure and the visible figure of some object is "merely arbitrary"; Reid insists, in contrast, that they are related by geometrical laws (*EIP* 2.19).[25] Moreover, he holds that it is simply part of human nature to grasp that visible figure is a sign of the tangible qualities of external objects. We understand "through a kind of instinct" that they are related; our thought "by natural impulse" moves from the sign (the visible figure) to what it signifies (the tangible figure) (*IHM* 6.8). Nonetheless, Reid does think experience is required for us to learn what visible figure signifies what tangible quality (*IHM* 6.4). The relationship between visible figure and the tangible—like that between color sensations and the real colors of objects and between visible figure and real figure—is a kind of natural language, and we naturally know that this is so; nonetheless, we must learn its vocabulary.

Shepherd's Criticisms of Reid (and Stewart) on Perceiving Color and Extension

EPEU essay 4 is devoted to Reid's account of how perceptions of color and extension are related to each other. Shepherd opens by criticizing Dugald Stewart's claim that while there is an "intimate association" in the mind between the two "notions" of extension and color, there is no necessary connection between the two (*EPEU* 246).[26] Stewart is, in effect, reiterating Reid's claim that color appearances are, in normal vision, accompanied by perceptions of the visible shape and size of objects but that this is a contingent feature of human visual perception. This constant association between a sensation of color and a perception of extension means, says Stewart, that we cannot think of the *notion* of color without also

---

[25] For further discussion, see Copenhaver, "Berkeley and Reid," 623–26.
[26] Shepherd quotes Stewart's *Elements of the Philosophy of the Human Mind*, vol. 1, chapter 5, part 2, section 1.

282 MARY SHEPHERD

thinking of the *notion* of extension. Now, Shepherd is interested in Stewart's comment primarily because Stewart was an "avowed admirer and supporter of Dr. Reid's philosophy" (*EPEU* 247–48); Reid's account of vision is her real target. Thus, she criticizes Reid's account of how visible figure "suggests" through "instinct" the nature or "essence" of the real distance and figure of external objects (*EPEU* 248), and she objects to Reid's characterization of visible figure (which she glosses simply as "vision"). ·

In Shepherd's initial criticism of Stewart, she (perhaps unfairly) reads his claim that the "notion" of color is associated with the "notion" of extension as a claim that color sensations are associated with perceptions of extension. For Shepherd, this means that Stewart and Reid should hold that both are in the mind, since perceptions and sensations are both mental entities; perceptions, like sensations, "must necessarily be *conscious*" (*EPEU* 254). As Shepherd puts it later in this essay, "colour or extension must stand, or fall together" (*EPEU* 262): either both color and extension are in the mind (as sensations or perceptions), or both are out of the mind (as qualities of external objects). Shepherd herself has no objection to saying that *sensations* of color are associated with *sensations* of distance, shape, size, and so on, in which case the whole compound is in the mind (*EPEU* 251). However, Reid denies that we have *sensations* of distance, shape, size, and so on, saying instead that we have "perceptions" of these things, and (as Shepherd puts it) Reid has fought "many battles" to argue that the *perception* of extension is not in the mind (*EPEU* 251–52). Presumably here Shepherd takes Reid's "perceptions of distance, (etc.)" to mean "visible figure," which he does indeed maintain is not in the mind. As she sees it, in denying that visible figure is a sensation, impression, or idea, yet insisting that it is "presented to the mind along with the colour" (*IHM* 6.8), Reid (and Stewart in following him) is positing an impossible entity, a combination of what can only be external (the extension, shape, figure, and size that the material impression "suggests") with what is clearly internal, the color sensation (*EPEU* 250; see also CSEV 411–12).

Shepherd concludes her criticism by considering a specific problem case for Reid and Stewart: our perception of the sun. She notes that it is a "notorious fact, according to the laws of light, that were the sun blotted from the heavens, it would still continue to be seen eight minutes after such an event" (*EPEU* 255).[27] Given their view that visible figure is associated with a sensation of the sun's brilliance, Shepherd infers that Reid and Stewart must hold that the visible figure of the sun is both colored and extended (*EPEU* 255). But, again, since they want to hold that visible figure is not in the mind, she sees them as forced into the untenable position that the sun's brilliance—which they consider to be a sensation, and thus in the mind—must in fact be outside the mind (*EPEU* 255). Again, Shepherd insists, either both color and extension are in the mind (as sensations), or both are out of the mind (as qualities of external objects); there can be no "colored extension" such that the extension is out of the mind while the color is in the mind (see *EPEU* 260).

Toward the end of this chapter, Shepherd offers her own account of what 'visible figure' can mean. She agrees with Reid and Stewart that visible figure accompanies color sensations; but for Shepherd, since it is visible, it must be a sensation, not a feature of external objects. Visible figure is simply "a conscious line of demarcation between two colors, and so must itself be color" (*EPEU* 261). Both visible figure and color are sensations, and both are in the mind, so there is no problem for Shepherd with holding that they can accompany each other.

---

[27] Shepherd mentions the same fact at the beginning of *EPEU*. Since light from the sun takes eight minutes to reach us, "*the sun being blotted from the universe, would still be seen eight minutes after its destruction*" (*EPEU* 25). Shepherd finds this fact hard to square with Reid's claim that we "immediately" perceive external objects.

284 MARY SHEPHERD

Shepherd's Account of Visual Perception

As we have seen, Shepherd maintains that our sensations are signs of external objects and their qualities; like Berkeley and Reid, she uses an analogy with language (*EPEU* 261). However, Shepherd prefers to compare the relationship between our mental contents and the external world to that of algebraic symbols and the quantities they stand for (*EPEU* 38, 47, 261; LMSM 703). As we saw in chapter 6 of this *Guide*, Shepherd thinks our sensations necessarily have the same relationships and "proportions" to each other as the external objects that cause them (*EPEU* 27); since an algebraic equation expresses such relationships and proportions among quantities, this provides a better analogy than language to express the way sensations are signs of the external world.

For Shepherd, a sense perception is a conscious mental state that is the effect of the interaction of an external object, a sense-organ, the nervous system and brain, and the capacity for sensation that is the mind. This general account is meant to apply to all sense modalities—seeing, hearing, taste, smell, touch, and motion.[28] Shepherd's chapter and essay on vision are the only texts where she offers more details about a *particular* sense modality, although she ends her later essay on vision with the hope that her account "may throw some light upon those [phenomena] which belong to every analogous operation of the human senses and intellect" (CSEV 416).

"Vision," Shepherd says, is "a consciousness in the mind" that results from an external object interacting with the eyes and brain (CSEV 406). Like her contemporaries, Shepherd describes the production of an image on a retina as "painting" (*EPEU* 409).[29] The retinal image itself serves as a "physical impulse" that contributes

---

[28] For Shepherd's account of "the power of motion" as a "sixth organ of sense" (*EPEU* 230), see chapter 5 of this *Guide*.

[29] For example, see Robert Smith's 1738 book, *A Compleat System of Opticks*; Smith refers to images being "painted upon the retina" (29).

to the production of the visual sensation (CSEV 406). It, not the external object, is the "proximate cause" of vision, for, as Shepherd notes, a very distant object like the sun might send out its rays, but then be obliterated before the rays reach our eyes; we will still have a visual sensation despite the non-existence of the object (CSEV 413). Shepherd does not actually discuss the role of the optic nerve or brain. She may hold that the retinal image interacts with the optic nerve, resulting in some kind of neural action in the brain; the brain state mixes with the general capacity for thought, resulting (synchronously) in a mental sensation.

As we have seen, Shepherd criticizes Reid and Stewart for their accounts of how sensations of color and perceptions of visible shape are coordinated; she herself holds that visual sensations of shape are possible *because of* our sensations of color. As she puts it in her 1828 essay "On the Causes of Simple and Erect Vision," "vision of *one colour only* can never yield the vision of figure, because the proximate cause of the vision of figure is a line of demarcation formed by the sensation of the junction of *two colours*" (CSEV 406).[30] Sensations of shapes occur in the mind along with sensations of colors because it is simply "in the nature of things" that this is how visual perception works (*EPEU* 409).

But this is an explanation only of two-dimensional visual perception. Color and two-dimensional shape sensations alone are not very informative about the *three-dimensionality* of objects. We would be able to tell the relative distances of two objects from each other if they were both located at the same distance from us, but, without more information, we would be unable to perceive the three-dimensional features of the objects, including their distance from ourselves. As we have seen, Descartes, Malebranche, Berkeley, and Reid all offered explanations of how we are able to perceive

---

[30] The examples Shepherd gives are contrasts of hue (for example, red, blue, orange), but presumably she would not deny that figure could also be perceived by contrasts in the brightnesses or saturations of a single hue.

286 MARY SHEPHERD

distance even though what is registered on the retina is simply a two-dimensional image. How does Shepherd think this is possible?

This issue comes up in Shepherd's discussion of the "outwardness" of external objects in *EPEU*. As we saw in chapter 6 of this *Guide*, Shepherd thinks there are four methods by which we know there are objects existing at a distance from us. The fourth of these methods is that *vision* allows us to sense both the extension of space and "the relative position of unperceived things" (*EPEU* 65–66). Shepherd says we can see the "unresisting medium" of extended space that is around and outside us, through which we move and in which objects are located, because we can see "the difference of its colouring in comparison of those objects" (*EPEU* 65). In other words, she seems to be suggesting that visual sensations alone can give us sensations of three-dimensionality, without any coordination with tangible sensations. This would be a significant departure from Berkeley and Reid, for whom the distance, shapes, and sizes of objects are not the primary deliverances of vision but come to be knowable through vision through their coordination with tangible sensations.

But Shepherd also says that the "chief" method by which we get sensations of the outwardness of objects is that we feel our bodies moving through space as we interact with objects; this sensation of motion "suggests the notion, or rather inspires the immediate feeling of the *extension of space* (or of an unresisting medium)" (*EPEU* 58). In other words, even if she thinks we can get some information about three-dimensionality from the sense of vision, she thinks we get more information from the sense of *motion*. And in her later essay "Lady Mary Shepherd's Metaphysics," Shepherd suggests—along the lines of the accounts offered by Berkeley and Reid—that these motion sensations do come to be associated with certain visual sensations:

> I conceive ideas of colour to be from habit immediately associated with those of touch and motion. Contrasting colours yielding us,

therefore, by means of their associations, the ideas of distance and of tangible figure, we set ourselves in motion accordingly. . . .

Our sensations, therefore, of coloured surfaces of different magnitudes, are to be apprehended as such in relation to touch and motion; otherwise they would be varieties of feeling, having no more to do with the occupancy of place, than the contrasting passions of joy and sorrow, tranquility and anger, under the modification of their different intensities; in other words, their different degrees or magnitudes. (LMSM 701)

It is striking that Shepherd suggests that we come to associate certain motion sensations with certain visual sensations "from habit." As we have seen, while Shepherd rejects Hume's explanation of causation in terms of habitual associations, she does recognize the role of association in memory (*ERCE* 110), and she says that it is part of God's design that the mind is capable of "powerful" associations (*EPEU* 127). She may think, then, that it is divinely ordained that human perceivers come to associate certain motion sensations with certain sensations of color and size.

Two Puzzles about Vision

In *EPEU* essay 14, Shepherd takes up two puzzles that had been raised by Reid in his *Inquiry into the Human Mind*. Why, since the images of objects are upside-down on the retina, do we not perceive objects as upside-down? And why, since we have two eyes, do we not perceive two of every object?[31]

After having devoted four hundred pages in *EPEU* to lofty metaphysical questions, Shepherd's preoccupation with these two very

---

[31] Reid raises the puzzles of inverted retinal images at *IHM* 6.11–12 and of why we see single images at *IHM* 6.13. He also discusses a third puzzle that Shepherd does not take up: why the eyes move in parallel although they are controlled by different sets of muscles (*IHM* 6.10).

288 MARY SHEPHERD

specific empirical questions in the final chapter of the book may seem surprising. How, if at all, is this chapter related to the rest of her philosophical project? Since the theme throughout *EPEU* is how our sensations represent objects in the external world, one might think that she sees her account of sensory perception as uniquely able to solve these two puzzles about vision. But that cannot be right; according to her account, in vision, an external object mixes with *two* eyes, resulting in images on two retinas, so it would seem that the effect would be two brain states and thus *two* sensations. In other words, her account of sensation has as much difficulty explaining single vision as any other account. Nor is there anything in her account of sensation that would explain why we see objects as upright, given the inversion of our retinal images.

A second possibility is that Shepherd discusses single and upright vision in order to address potential *problems* with, or objections to, her account of the relationship between sensations and external objects. However, the puzzles about single and upright vision are not actually about how our *sensations* represent objects in the *external world*. After all, our visual *sensations* represent external things in the same way that our sensations of touch represent them (i.e., as single and upright). The problems posed by the puzzles of single and upright vision are about why the images on our *retinas* (not our sensations) represent external objects as double and inverted. So even if Shepherd's account of sensory perception does no better than other theories to explain these two visual puzzles, it also does no worse.

The puzzles about single and upright vision concern the *causal chain* when we sense external objects using vision. How do we explain these apparent anomalies in the steps involving our visual system, such that the way our retinas register information is different from the way the external objects exist *and* the way our sensations represent them? This suggests that Shepherd was primarily interested in how her *causal theory*—not her theory of the sensation of external objects—can help explain these puzzles. In a

VISION 289

sense, the final essay of *EPEU* is a return to the issues of Shepherd's first book, the *Essay upon the Relation of Cause and Effect*.

Puzzle #1: Seeing Single with Two Eyes

The first puzzle Shepherd raises is about the phenomenon now known as binocular single vision: how do we manage to see just *one* object despite seeing it with *two* eyes? Shepherd specifically criticizes Reid's explanation, although the topic interested vision theorists as far back as Ptolemy and Aristotle.[32] In his *Inquiry*, Reid considers an explanation of binocular vision offered by Robert Smith in his *A Compleat System of Opticks* (1738). Smith had suggested that a retina can be considered as made up of points,[33] with the exact center of the retina in one eye being a "corresponding point" with the exact center of the retina in the other eye; accordingly, all points on one retina situated at the same distances from the center of the other retina are also corresponding points.[34] When a person directs both eyes in parallel at a single object, the two retinas will have identical images located at identical corresponding points. Smith maintains that our natural condition is *not* to use our eyes in parallel; that is, our natural condition is to see double. However, since the sense of touch tells us that there is just one object when we see two, we quickly learn to keep our eyes parallel so our visual experiences are consistent with our experiences by touch.[35] Smith does not, however, offer an explanation of *why* corresponding points on the retina would produce single vision.

---

[32] In his discussion of binocular vision, Reid mentions theories of Galen, Gassendi, Baptista Porta, and Rohault surveyed in William Porterfield's 1759 two-volume work, *A Treatise of the Eye, the Manner and Phaenomena of Vision* (*IHM* 6.13). For a survey of the history of research on binocular single vision, see Wade, *A Natural History of Vision*, 256–73.

[33] Smith, *Compleat System*, book 1, chapter 3, sections 82 and 84.

[34] Smith, *Compleat System*, book 1, chapter 5, section 137.

[35] Smith, *Compleat System*, book 1, chapter 5, section 137.

Rather, he treats it as a brute fact that when our eyes are in parallel, "the predominant sense of feeling has originally and constantly informed us that the object is single."[36]

Reid argues against Smith's claim that we learn to see objects singly, maintaining instead that our normal and natural condition is for the images depicted on a perceiver's two retinas to coincide perfectly.[37] As Reid puts it, "in perfect human eyes, the centres of the two retinae correspond and harmonize with each other and . . . every other point in one retina, doth correspond and harmonize with the point which is similarly situate in the other" (*IHM* 6.14). There are cases, of course, where the eyes are *not* perfect, and people see double; it is also possible to induce double vision by, for example, focusing on an object across the room while stretching out a hand and holding up a finger. In such cases, Reid says, "the pictures of the objects which are seen double [i.e., the images of the finger], do not fall upon points of the retinae which are similarly situate, but . . . the pictures of the objects seen single do fall upon points similarly situate" (*IHM* 6.13).

But *why* do perfectly coinciding images on two retinas result in a visual sensation of one object? Like Smith, Reid treats this as a brute fact; it is, he says, simply one of the "laws of vision in the human constitution" (*IHM* 6.14), "an original property of human eyes" (*IHM* 6.17). Reid suggests that animals whose eyes are on the sides of their heads, such as chickens and cows, are able to see objects as single because the points of their retinas correspond in different ways than they do in human eyes; the eyes of such animals "may very probably be subjected to different laws of vision, adapted to the peculiarities of their organs of vision" (*IHM* 6.14).

[36] Smith, *Compleat System*, book 1, chapter 5, section 137.
[37] In his explanation of seeing single with two eyes, Reid emphasizes frequently that the explanation applies only to "sound and perfect" eyes (*IHM* 6.13); that is, the eyes must be properly formed so that the points of the retinas correspond correctly, and a person must be able to direct both eyes to a single object.

VISION 291

Shepherd accepts the part of Reid's explanation that appeals to the images on the two retinas having "corresponding points": we see objects singly when their images are "painted upon corresponding points,—that is, a similar point of colouring taken as a centre in each retina" (*EPEU* 411). What she *rejects* is Reid's claim that it is a law of our "constitution" that coinciding images in our retinas result in a single image. Reid's account seems to allow that, had God designed our nature differently, we might see two objects even when there is only one out there in the world and we have identical retinal images. Shepherd thinks, instead, that our seeing just one object when there are coinciding images in our retinas is "in the very nature of things" (*EPEU* 411).

What does she mean by this? Although Shepherd does not explicitly appeal to the Causal Likeness Principle, it seems to play a role here. This principle holds that different effects must have different causes; we infer that there is a variety of causes out in the world because our sensations themselves are varied. In the case of visual sensations coming from two retinas, the causes are alike; indeed, there is just *one* external object, and while there are two eyes, the eyes are so alike that, when each mixes with the same external object, the effects in the mind are *qualitatively indistinguishable* from each other. As Shepherd puts it in her longer essay on vision, there will be a "*coalescence of points*" (CSEV 408), and so the sensation resulting from the external object interacting with *one* eye will be identical in all respects to the sensation resulting from the object's interaction with the *other* eye. With nothing to distinguish between them, the mind experiences simply *one* sensation, one "simultaneous single sensibility" (CSEV 40).

In essay 14, Shepherd offers a brief sketch of how a *difference* between two retinal images could occur.[38] Normally, assuming we are not in darkness, our visual field contains a vast array of colors in

---

[38] Shepherd's essay "On the Causes of Single and Erect Vision" (1828) gives a more thorough account of her explanation, with examples.

292   MARY SHEPHERD

various patterns and shapes. We distinguish one object from another when there is a change in color that forms "a line of demarcation around its edges" (*EPEU* 408–9). In other words, what makes a color-patch a "visual figure of an object" is that there is "a line of demarcation between it and some surrounding object of another color" (*EPEU* 409). When the eyes are properly aligned, these lines of demarcation are exactly the same on the two retinas. However, if the eyes are misaligned, the image on one retina will be shifted slightly to one side compared to the image on the other retina. In this case, if we were to superimpose one image on the other, there would be an additional "line of demarcation" and "*there will necessarily appear to the mind some extra coloring between the edges of the figures*" (*EPEU* 411). Because differences in the causes produce different effects, this difference between the two retinal images will *necessarily* result in a different effect, a different kind of sensation—not of one object, but of *two*. Although Shepherd does not specify the conditions under which the retinas might have different images, she would presumably allow that this could happen if an eye is damaged.

Shepherd also diagnoses why previous writers found it difficult to explain why we don't see single items as double: this is because (she says) we tend to think that the space between our eyes *also* causes there to be a space between the two images on the retinas (*EPEU* 410). If there were a space between the two images, there would be what she calls a "line of demarcation," and we would perceive the single object as two. However, there is in fact no image on the retina of the space between our eyes; we do not see the space between our eyes. The images from the two retinas are exactly superimposed, one on the other, with no line of demarcation between them, and so we perceive only one object (*EPEU* 410).

Shepherd's account does raise some questions. She appears to be conceding that we do have two visual sensations every time we see one object; they are, as it were, superimposed upon each other, so we experience only one. But if sensations are necessarily conscious

VISION 293

(*EPEU* 7), it seems we should somehow be conscious of both; yet clearly we are not. One might think Shepherd could answer this challenge by noting that she distinguishes between perceptions and sensations; perceptions are sensations that have been taken notice of by the mind (*EPEU* 9). Perhaps, then, there are two sensations in every instance of vision, but just one perception. But this would mean that every visual experience counts as a perception, undermining the very distinction Shepherd wants to draw between perception and sensation.

Puzzle #2: Perceiving Objects the Right Way Up

The other puzzle that Shepherd addresses in essay 14 is that of the inverted retinal image. The images of objects we see appear on the retina upside down and inverted from right to left. There is no puzzle about why the retinal images are inverted: as Kepler first observed, light rays coming from the upper part of an external object will, even after refraction, hit the bottom part of the retina, and vice versa.[39] Rather, the "mystery," as Shepherd puts it, is why "objects [are] being painted inverted on the retina and yet seen as erect" (*EPEU* 412). If the retinal image is inverted, why do we not perceive objects in the world as upside-down?

As with the explanations of distance perception, there were both geometrical and empiricist accounts of how we perceive the orientation of objects. For theorists like Descartes and Malebranche, who believed (roughly) that perceivers perform unconscious geometrical calculations to perceive the distance of objects, there is no

---

[39] Leonardo da Vinci, in the early sixteenth century, appears to have been the first to compare the human eye to a camera obscura; as da Vinci realized, the image projected in a camera obscura would appear upside down (*Notebooks*, 110–111). The phenomenon was noted by Kepler in 1604 and by Christoph Scheiner in 1630, and it was experimentally verified in the seventeenth century by experiments with the eyes of oxen. See Wade, "Vision and Visualization," 280–281, and *A Natural History of Vision*, 322–25.

294   MARY SHEPHERD

reason why they could not also posit that it is built into the visual system to unconsciously flip the retinal image, as it were, so that our visual experience matches our tangible experiences.[40] Berkeley attempted to dispel the problem altogether by arguing that since the images on a perceiver's retina are not known through vision (for we do not *see* the back of our own retinas [*NTV* 50]), their orientation is irrelevant. It is true that if a researcher could somehow observe what is going on in *another* perceiver's eye and in *that* perceiver's mind, the two images would have opposite orientations; but the fact that the images would appear inverted to someone *else* is irrelevant to the perceiver (*NTV* 116).[41] The orientation of images on our retinas makes no difference to how we see the orientation of objects. Rather, Berkeley emphasizes, we perceive orientation because we come to associate information about the situations of objects learned through touch and bodily cues (such as how we must move our eyes) with various visible ideas (*NTV* 94, 98). That is, Berkeley's account of how we perceive objects as erect is analogous to his account of how we see distance.

But it is Reid's approach that interests Shepherd. Reid, like Berkeley, rejects the geometrical explanation of erect vision on the grounds that we do not *reason* that what we see has a certain orientation; it seems, rather, to be an "immediate perception" (*IHM* 6.11). Moreover, Reid thinks we *couldn't* reason in this way, since "we have no feeling or perception of the pictures upon the retina, and as little surely of the position of them" (*IHM* 6.11). But Reid also rejects Berkeley's solution to the puzzle of erect vision.[42] It is not, Reid thinks, that we come to perceive objects as upright

[40] For Malebranche's account, see *The Search after Truth*, "Elucidation on Optics," section 43.

[41] Berkeley's arguments are more complex than this, and their interpretation is debated in the secondary literature, but these details need not concern us here. For discussion, see Atherton, *Berkeley's Revolution in Vision*, 163–69; and van Cleve, *Problems from Reid*, 199–203, and "Reid Versus Berkeley on the Inverted Retinal Image."

[42] For discussion of the grounds on which Reid rejects Berkeley's solution, see van Cleve, *Problems from Reid*, 203–5.

because of associations that we form through experience. Rather, Reid holds that it is a "law of nature, or a law of our constitution, of which law our seeing objects erect by inverted images, is a necessary consequence" (*IHM* 6.12). Reid concedes that we do not know why certain laws of nature obtain: "we must often be satisfied with knowing, that certain things are connected, and invariably follow one another, without being able to discover the chain that goes between them" (*IHM* 6.12). It is simply a fact about how light rays enter our eyes that the retinal images are inverted, and a fact about human nature that that causes us to perceive objects as upright, even if we can offer no further explanations of those facts.

Shepherd's objection in essay 14 to Reid's explanation is not especially satisfying, for she focuses on a trivial problem in Reid's explanation of erect vision. Reid gives an example of both seeing and feeling his walking cane, saying that in both cases "I conceive the horizon as a fixed object both of sight and touch, with relation to which, objects are said to be high or low, erect or inverted" (*IHM* 6.11). Thus, when he sees the point of his cane below the horizon, he also *feels* it as being below the horizon; human nature is such that we see things as we feel them. Shepherd objects that it is simply false that "*the (visible) horizon is taken as a fixed point in relation to which objects are erect or inverted*" (*EPEU* 415), for the image of the horizon would be as much inverted on the retina as the other objects perceived by sight (*EPEU* 415). Instead, she emphasizes that *everything* in the visual field is inverted, as a "whole piece" (*EPEU* 415).

But this alleged error by Reid does not bear on his broader point that our *constitution* is such that we see things the way we feel them. Indeed, Shepherd's other brief comments in this chapter seem to suggest that she actually agrees with Reid on that broader point. She writes that "the sense of the soul must be to perceive the whole relative position of objects, precisely in that relation of parts they appear to have to touch and motion" (*EPEU* 414) and that "the soul can only have the sense of one piece (or canvass), of relative colouring, which upon motion, or touch being applied to the

296   MARY SHEPHERD

corresponding external varieties, will reply to those actions in the same relative proportions" (*EPEU* 415–16). But Shepherd does not explain *why* we must visually perceive things as having the same proportions that we feel them to have. Does she, like Reid, think that this is just a fact of human nature?

Shepherd's 1828 essay on vision can help elucidate her views. In that essay she emphasizes two points. First, she stresses that we cannot compare our retinal images with other visual perceptions of objects that do not involve our retinal images, for *all* visual perceptions of objects involve retinal images; that is, retinal images are all we have to go on. Philosophers who worry about how we see objects as erect

> really suppose . . . that mental vision arises from, and is occupied about, *two* sets of objects at the same time; viz. the *external object in nature*, and the *inverted images of them on the retina*: whereas the external object becomes virtually null and void immediately upon the rays of light being emitted from it. (CSEV 414)

To worry about how objects seen via retinal images (that is, inverted) would appear in comparison with how they would appear without retinal images is pointless, for we simply do not see in the latter way. Shepherd thinks that the fact of retinal inversion is simply *irrelevant*. A perception of inversion is only possible when one can compare two images; but in the case under consideration, there is no comparison to be made between the retinal images and some other set of images, because we only have access to the former.

Second, Shepherd stresses that sensed objects (internal perceived objects) have the same "relative proportion" to each other whether we sense them by vision or by touch and motion (CSEV 414). She says the same thing in essay 14: "the sense of the soul must be to perceive [by vision] the whole relative position of objects, *precisely in that relation of parts they appear to have to touch and motion*" (*EPEU* 414, emphasis added). If I see an apple on a table and I reach

VISION 297

out to touch it, I will also *feel* a sphere on a plane (under normal conditions, anyway). Moreover, Shepherd holds that this similarity between the proportions and relationships among seen objects and proportions and relationships among the same objects perceived by touch is *necessarily* the case (CSEV 414). That is, under normal conditions, if I *see* one object as resting on another, then reach out to feel them by touch, I will necessarily also *feel* the first as resting on the second.[43] If I see one object as smaller than another, then when I approach them so that I can touch them, I will also necessarily feel the first as smaller than the second. This claim sets Shepherd apart from both Berkeley (who thought any connections between tangible ideas and visible ideas are merely contingent and learned by experience) and from Reid (who thought such connections are due to a law of human nature set up by God, but thus—according to Shepherd—also merely contingent).

Shepherd's belief that the proportions and relationships among *seen* objects must necessarily be similar to the relationships among the same *felt* objects derives from two theses: (1) her bundle theory of objects, such that sensations of different sensory modalities can be caused by a single object that is itself a bundle of causal powers to produce those varied sensations, and (2) her view that the proportions between and relationships among *external objects* out there in the world must be similar to the proportions and relationships of our *sensations* of them.

Consider thesis 1, Shepherd's bundle theory of objects. Suppose I am simultaneously seeing and touching the apple. Because of the way my color sensation of red occurs together with the tangible sensation of a sphere, I can infer that there is a single object out there in the world that has the causal powers to produce both visible and

---

[43] Of course, this might not be the case under abnormal conditions—say, if someone is trying to deceive us.

298 MARY SHEPHERD

tangible sensations.[44] The same is true when I see and touch the table: I can infer that there is one object causing both sensations.

Having inferred that there are two separate objects out there in the world, the apple and the table, I can now consider the relationships and proportions among the sensations they cause. Suppose I sense the apple as being on top of the table. According to thesis 2, the proportions between and relationships among *external objects* out there in the world must be similar to the proportions and relationships of our *sensations* of them: "When unperceived, the proportions and relations of things, must have their own position to each other; and these, when meeting with a sentient nature, must inspire the sensation of proportional positions" (*EPEU* 65–66; see also 27 and 181–82). This is because of the Causal Likeness Principle; two different sensations must have different causes. The cause of a sensation of an apple *on* a table must be different from the cause of a sensation of an apple *under* a table. Since (under normal conditions) there are no changes in our sense-organs that would explain this difference in the sensations, the difference must be due to the objects out there in the world (*EPEU* 27). That is, there is something about the *relationship* between the external objects that causes a sensation of apple-on-table that differs from the relationship of the external objects when I have a sensation of apple-under-table. Shepherd herself uses an example of a sensation of something round and the external object that causes that sensation:

For let us consider a round figure, for instance, apart from our perception of it; the *line* which bounds this solid substance *outwardly*, (whatever *line* and *solid* may be,) and parts it from the

[44] As we saw in chapter 3 of this *Guide*, Shepherd says nothing about how to individuate external objects from each other. Presumably we infer that the causal power to give me a sensation of red is associated in the external world with a causal power to give me a sensation of a sphere because those sensations are associated together; that is, the individuation of external objects derives from how we individuate internal objects. This presupposes, of course, that Shepherd has a way to individuate internal objects, another issue she does not address.

VISION 299

surrounding atmosphere, (whatever *parting* or *atmosphere* may be,) must still be a *variety*, or *change*, or *difference*, among these outward things. (*EPEU* 211)

I cannot know the true nature of the cause of my sensations of the apple and the table, and indeed I cannot know the true nature of the *relationship* between them, either. The external object causing my sensation of the apple may not actually be *on* the external object causing my sensation of the table. Nonetheless, whatever that relationship is among external objects that causes me to sense one object as on another will be the same whenever I have such sensations.

In sum, whatever proportions obtain among my visual sensations must be due to analogous proportions among the external objects causing them. The same is true of tangible sensations. And when my visual and tangible sensations are of the *same* two objects, I can be sure that how I feel objects will resemble how I see them. Thus, the fact that *all* the objects are inverted in retinal images makes no difference at all. What matters are the relationships and proportions *among* my sensations.

If this reconstruction of Shepherd's reasoning is accurate, then her criticism of Reid goes deeper than just objecting to his assumption that the horizon is not inverted in our visual images. In fact, her criticism of Reid's account of erect vision is similar to her earlier criticism of his account of binocular single vision. In both cases, Reid has mistaken a *real necessity* for a contingent fact about our nature. If Reid were correct, Shepherd thinks, it would be possible for God to have designed us so that we see two objects even when we have identical retinal images, or that we see all things upside-down from how we feel them. But if the optical facts about single and erect vision are *necessary* truths deriving from the necessary causal principles, then not even God could change this.

Shepherd ends her *Essay upon the Relation of Cause and Effect* with the pronouncement that the Causal Principle and the Causal Likeness Principle are "the only true foundations of scientific

300 MARY SHEPHERD

research, of practical knowledge, and of belief in a creating and presiding Deity" (*ERCE* 194). Her *Essays on the Perception of an External Universe* address all three: practical knowledge of external objects and how they affect us; religious belief in an omnipotent God; and, with the final chapter, scientific research on how to understand two puzzles about human vision.

Suggestions for Further Reading

- Shepherd's "On the Causes of Single and Erect Vision" is reprinted in full in Deborah Boyle, ed., *Lady Mary Shepherd: Selected Writings*.
- There is currently (at the time of publication of this book) no published research on Shepherd's views on vision. For excellent general overviews of the philosophical context in which Shepherd was writing, see the two essays by Lorne Falkenstein in the *Routledge Companion to Eighteenth Century Philosophy*: "Theories of Perception I: Berkeley and His Recent Predecessors" and "Theories of Perception II: After Berkeley." On Berkeley's account of vision in particular, see Margaret Atherton, *Berkeley's Revolution in Vision*, and Rebecca Copenhaver's "Berkeley on the Language of Nature and the Objects of Vision." James van Cleve's *Problems from Reid* has a helpful chapter on Berkeley and Reid on the puzzle of inverted vision.

Glossary of Terms

abstraction The mental process of considering some quality of a thing in isolation from the other qualities with which it usually occurs. See *EPEU* 85 and 291.

affection A characteristic that can be predicated of both external objects and internal objects. Shepherd's examples include variety, independence, existence, duration, identity, and cause and effect. See *EPEU* 182–85.

axiom A fundamental principle or maxim established through reason. Shepherd's key axioms are "nothing can come into existence without a cause other than itself" (the Causal Principle) and "like causes must have like effects" (the Causal Likeness Principle).

camera obscura Originally a darkened room or a box with a small opening through which an image of an external object or scene could be projected on a wall; after the thirteenth century there were smaller, portable versions, sometimes used by artists.

Causal Likeness Principle The maxim that "a like Cause must produce a like Effect" (*ERCE* 45, 78, 144); that is, objects that are similar in kind to each other must necessarily have effects that are similar in kind. Corollaries to this principle are that different kinds of causes produce different kinds of effects (*ERCE* 73), that similar effects must come from similar causes (*EPEU* 99), and that different effects must come from different causes (*EPEU* 169).

Causal Principle The maxim that "there is no object which begins to exist, but must owe its existence to some cause" (*ERCE* 36), where the cause must be something other than the object itself. Sometimes Shepherd says that no *quality* can begin to exist without a cause other than itself (*ERCE* 43–45), but this comes to the same thing since objects are bundles of qualities.

causation The mixture or interaction of two or more objects to produce, synchronously (simultaneously), a new object with a new quality. The conjunction of the causes *is* the effect.

cause A factor that, when conjoined with one or more other factors, contributes to the production of a new quality in an object. See *ERCE* 63.

302 GLOSSARY OF TERMS

Shepherd contrasts this with Hume's definitions of 'cause' as an object that is experienced always to precede another or that leads a perceiver to think of another object because of habit based on such experience.

demonstration An argument that establishes its conclusion with complete certainty, in contrast to an argument that establishes its conclusion merely with some degree of probability. See *ERCE* 117, 124, and 187.

discerptibility The causal power to divide something into parts. Shepherd says that fire has this quality; when fire interacts with a piece of wood, the synchronous effect of the mixture is that the wood disintegrates. See *ERCE* 48–49.

effect A new quality or object that results necessarily from, and consists in, the joining of certain causes. See *ERCE* 57 and 63.

efficient cause The productive cause, which may be either a physical object or a mental state, of some effect. For Shepherd, all causes are efficient causes.

end A goal, purpose.

essence The true nature of a thing.

experimentum crucis Deriving from Francis Bacon, Robert Boyle, and Robert Hooke, this phrase for Shepherd means a scientific experiment in which all factors but one are controlled, in order to identify the key factor in bringing about an effect. See *ERCE* 43.

exponent An object whose effects correlate with the effects of another object. See *ERCE* 170–71.

extension Three-dimensionality.

external object A bundle of qualities, where the qualities are causal powers. These are never sensed by perceivers; we know them only through their effects on us. External objects may also include causal powers to bring about changes in other external objects.

fancy Imagination.

final cause For Shepherd, to be a final cause is to have a mental perception of a future state of affairs and an intention to bring about that state of affairs (*EPEU* 347, 359). A final cause becomes an efficient cause when the intention determines the will to put matter into motion in order to bring about the desired state of affairs (*EPEU* 360–61).

idea (1) In its strict sense, a particular type of sensation, namely one that results from reasoning that shows that there must be a cause of sense perceptions. See *EPEU* 133–34. (2) Used in a popular, broader sense, 'idea' is just another word for 'sensation'; see *EPEU* 134.

idealism The philosophical doctrine that holds that all the objects we sense are composed of ideas. George Berkeley is the primary idealist against whom Shepherd argues.

immaterialism The philosophical doctrine, held by George Berkeley, that matter does not exist.

instinct A belief or idea that is not based on reason or on experience but arises simply from action of the brain (and mind). See *EPEU* 161.

internal object A bundle of sensible qualities (see *EPEU* 71–72). One type of internal object is *perceived* objects, which are bundles of sensible qualities mixed with the idea of an external cause of those qualities (see *EPEU* 197–98). Images produced by the imagination or dreaming are bundles of sensible qualities that either lack the idea of an external cause or are incorrectly bundled with it (see *EPEU* 11n, 237). Memories are internal objects that are bundles of faint sensible qualities mixed with an idea of having been caused by external objects in the past (*EPEU* 137).

intuitive belief A proposition that is true by definition. Shepherd also calls this an 'intuitive proposition.' See *ERCE* 138 and 145.

latent reasoning The possession of ideas and sensations that bear various relationships to each other such that if they were combined, they would give rise to further ideas. See *EPEU* 170. Shepherd thinks all humans, no matter their stage of life, as well as non-human animals, engage in latent reasoning.

life For Shepherd, either (1) the quality of an organism having the qualities of assimilating new particles, separating old particles, and not succumbing to the environment or (2) the cause of an organism having those qualities; see *ERCE* 163.

materialism The philosophical doctrine that holds that only matter exists and that all phenomena can be explained in terms of matter, without appeal to immaterial entities. Shepherd takes William Lawrence to be an example of a materialist; see *ERCE* 171.

matter Existing unperceived in itself, matter is a causal power or capacity to give a perceiver a sensation of solid extension. See *EPEU* 113–14, 155, and 242.

mind In its narrower meaning, a general, ongoing causal power or capacity to have sensations (conscious mental states), whether of sensible qualities,

304 GLOSSARY OF TERMS

of ideas, of memories, etc. See *EPEU* 15 and 155. In its broader meaning, mind is the ongoing capacity plus whatever sensations have resulted from mind (in the narrower sense) over time. In no sense is mind a substance for Shepherd.

miracle An effect in which God intervenes in the natural order, acting as a cause to bring about an unusual effect. See *ERCE* 79.

motion (1) "Real" motion exists unperceived in an external object; it is a capacity to give a perceiver a sensation of that object as passing successively through extended space. (2) Motion as a sensible quality is in the mind of a perceiver; it is a sensation of oneself or another object passing through space, being first in one place and then in another. (3) Motion is also a sixth sense in humans (and other organisms); it is a capacity to sense oneself as passing successively through extended space.

necessary connection (1) Shepherd typically uses this to mean the relationship between an external object and its qualities. Since an external object is also a cause, and its qualities are its effects, necessary connection also obtains between a cause and its effects. See *ERCE* 63 and 154. (2) In another usage, this means the definitional relationship between an arbitrarily chosen name and the qualities we associate with it. See *ERCE* 154. (3) Rarely, Shepherd uses this to mean the invariable successive order of certain sensible qualities that results from the successive actions of a perceiver's different sense-organs with the same external object. See *EPEU* 131 and 298.

negative idea A notion that we understand because it is the contrary of something we know by sense. See *EPEU* 50.

nominal definition In contrast to a real definition, this kind of definition identifies the qualities (whether sensible qualities or causal powers) that we associate with a particular term. See *ERCE* 153, 157–58.

notion An idea that is inferred through reason, in contrast to sensible qualities. Shepherd's examples include notions of existence (*EPEU* 162–63), extension (*EPEU* 165), "*unperceived* exteriority" (*EPEU* 175), external objects (*EPEU* 207), time (*EPEU* 288), and the causal principles themselves (*EPEU* 169, 373).

object A bundle or collection of qualities. Shepherd distinguishes between internal objects (collections of sensible qualities) and external objects (collections of causal powers, including the powers to produce the sensible qualities).

organization An organic body.

GLOSSARY OF TERMS   305

outwardness The causal power to give perceivers the visual and tangible sensations of objects being external and at a distance from them.

particle A very small portion of extended matter.

perception (1) In its strict sense, a perception is a sensation that has been consciously noted by the mind (*EPEU* 9). (2) In a broader sense, 'perception' is interchangeable with 'sensation' (*EPEU* 203; see also 39). Shepherd specifically notes that 'perception' does not mean sensory perception (*EPEU* 7–8).

power Another word for 'cause.' See *ERCE* 63–64.

primary qualities Traditionally contrasted with secondary qualities, these were either the sensations of solidity, extension, figure, and motion or the powers in a physical body to cause these sensations; physical bodies were thought to have these powers because they actually *are* solid, extended, shaped, and in motion. For Shepherd, both primary and secondary qualities are types of sensible qualities.

proof Any kind of good argument (*EPEU* xvi) or good evidence (*ERCE* 123, 125; *EPEU* 34).

proximate cause A cause that is immediately responsible for the production of an effect, in contrast to a remote cause. Proximate causes are synchronous with their effects. See *EPEU* 71.

quality A characteristic or property that, with other qualities, makes up an object. The qualities of internal objects are sensible qualities (*EPEU* 71–72); the qualities of external objects are causal powers (*EPEU* 127). A third kind of quality (affections) applies to both internal and external objects (*EPEU* 182).

real A characteristic of an object that has all the qualities we would expect it to have due to its definition; it fulfills all the criteria that are part of its real definition. See *EPEU* 30, 188.

real definition A definition specifying all the causal powers of an external object; a real definition tells us what qualities (effects) the object will have under various conditions. See *ERCE* 157–58. Shepherd herself does not use this phrase, but it seems to be what she means by the 'whole definition' of an object.

reasoning A causal process whereby the mind observes the relationships among its sensations and draws a conclusion. See *EPEU* 10, 19.

reasoning upon experiment A case of reasoning where the premises are a causal principle (known a priori) and an "*experimentum crucis*," or "crucial

306 GLOSSARY OF TERMS

experiment" (*ERCE* 43), an experiment that decisively settles some scientific question.

remote cause A causal factor that occurs earlier in a chain of causal conjunctions (which occurs over time; see *ERCE* 50–51).

secondary qualities Traditionally, in contrast with primary qualities, these were either sensations of colors, tastes, sounds, smells, and so on or (for Locke) the powers of a physical body to produce these ideas; secondary qualities were traditionally thought not to resemble anything in physical objects themselves. For Shepherd, both primary and secondary qualities are types of sensible qualities.

secret powers The causal powers of external objects; although we can never sense the causal powers themselves, we learn of them through their effects. See *ERCE* 60. Shepherd's source for this phrase is Hume.

self Used interchangeably with 'mind' and 'soul.' See *EPEU* 15, 103. Like those terms, 'self' can mean, narrowly, just the causal power or capacity to sense. Used more broadly, it refers to a compound entity, the capacity to sense plus the successive sensations that result over time from exercising that capacity. See *EPEU* 152, 154.

sensation (1) Occasionally Shepherd uses this to refer to a general capacity to have sensations; in this usage, it is equivalent to mind, self, soul, and sentience. See *EPEU* 15, 155, 217, and 310. (2) More often, Shepherd uses 'sensation' to refer to a particular conscious act (effect) of the mind. See *EPEU* 6–7. Shepherd divides the class of sensations into subtypes: sensations of present sensible qualities, sensations of the ideas of memory, sensations of the ideas of imagination, and sensations of the ideas of reason. See *EPEU* 6–7 and 135–36.

sense-organs The "mechanical instruments" or means that a living body uses, along with the mind and external objects, thereby producing conscious sensations. See *EPEU* 53, 55. Shepherd discusses the usual five senses of vision, hearing, touch, smell, and taste; but she also characterizes motion as a sense.

sensibility A term used by William Lawrence and other physiologists to mean (roughly) the capacity of nerves in a living body to transmit sensations to the brain when a sensory organ is stimulated; see *ERCE* 152–53.

sensible quality A feeling in the mind, arising originally from the use of the sense-organs interacting with external objects; examples include "blue or red, sweet or sour, hard or soft, beautiful or ugly, warm or cold, loud or low"

GLOSSARY OF TERMS 307

(*EPEU* 135). Dreams, memories, and images produced by imagination are composed of fainter sensible qualities.

sentience The power of sensing; equivalent to mind, soul, self in their narrower senses. Sometimes Shepherd calls this the 'sentient principle' (*EPEU* 103).

soul Used interchangeably with 'mind' and 'self'. See *EPEU* 310 and *ERCE* 171.

time (1) As an unperceived causal power in nature, it is a capacity of measurement of some object's existence. (2) As a perceived object, time is a sensation of the succession of thoughts. See *EPEU* 26 and 28.

understanding The mental capacity that produces ideas; an ability to draw conclusions from other sensations. See *EPEU* 67–68, 108.

visible figure The appearance of the shape of a thing.

Bibliography

Primary Sources

Abernethy, John. *An Inquiry into the Probability and Rationality of Mr. Hunter's Theory of Life*. London: Printed for Longman, Hurst, Rees, Orme, and Brown, 1814.

Bennett, Betty, ed. *The Letters of Mary Wollstonecraft Shelley*. Vol. 2. Baltimore: Johns Hopkins University Press, 1980.

Berkeley, George. *Alciphron: or, the Minute Philosopher*. 1732. In *George Berkeley: Philosophical Writings*, edited by Desmond M. Clarke, 269–313. Cambridge: Cambridge University Press, 2008.

Berkeley, George. *An Essay Towards a New Theory of Vision*. 1709. In *George Berkeley: Philosophical Writings*, edited by Desmond M. Clarke, 1–66. Cambridge: Cambridge University Press, 2008.

Berkeley, George. *The Theory of Vision, or Visual Language . . . Vindicated and Explained*. 1733. In *Works on Vision*, edited by Colin Murray Turbayne, 121–52. Indianapolis: Bobbs-Merrill, 1963.

Berkeley, George. *Three Dialogues between Hylas and Philonous*. 1713. In *George Berkeley: Philosophical Writings*, edited by Desmond M. Clarke, 151–242. Cambridge: Cambridge University Press, 2008.

Berkeley, George. *A Treatise Concerning the Principles of Human Knowledge*. 1710. In *George Berkeley: Philosophical Writings*, edited by Desmond M. Clarke, 67–149. Cambridge: Cambridge University Press, 2008.

Blakey, Robert. *History of the Philosophy of the Mind*. Vol. 4. London: Saunders, 1848.

Boyle Deborah, ed. *Lady Mary Shepherd: Selected Writings*. Exeter: Imprint Academic, 2018.

Brandreth, Mary Elizabeth Shepherd. *Some Family and Friendly Recollections of Seventy Years*. Westerham, England: C. Hooker, 1886.

Brightwell, Cecelia Lucy. *Memorials of the Life of Amelia Opie*. Norwich: Fletcher and Alexander, 1854.

Brown, Thomas. *Lectures on the Philosophy of the Human Mind*. 4 vols. Edinburgh: Printed by James Ballantyne and Co., 1820.

Brown, Thomas. *Observations on the Nature and Tendency of the Doctrine of Mr. Hume, Concerning the Relation of Cause and Effect*. Edinburgh: Mundell and Son, 1805.

310   BIBLIOGRAPHY

Brown, Thomas. *Observations on the Nature and Tendency of the Doctrine of Mr. Hume, Concerning the Relation of Cause and Effect.* 2nd ed. Edinburgh: Mundell and Son, 1806.

Brown, Thomas. *Observations on the Zoonomia of Erasmus Darwin, M.D.* Edinburgh: Mundell and Son, 1798.

Brown, Thomas. *Inquiry into the Relation of Cause and Effect.* Edinburgh: Archibald Constable, 1818.

Brown, Thomas. "Viller's Philosophy of Kant." *Edinburgh Review* 1, no. 2 (1803): 253–80.

Cabanis, Pierre J. G. *Rapports du physique et du moral de l'homme.* Vol. 1. Paris: Crapart, Caille, et Ravier, 1802.

Clarke, Samuel. *A Demonstration of the Being and Attributes of God and Other Writings.* 1705. Edited by Ezio Vailati. Cambridge: Cambridge University Press, 1998.

Cogan, Thomas. *Ethical Questions; Or Speculations on the Principal Subjects of Controversy in Moral Philosophy.* London: Printed for T. Cadell and W. Davies, 1817.

Coleridge, Samuel Taylor. *The Notebooks of Samuel Taylor Coleridge, Vol. 5: 1827–1834, Part 2.* Edited by Kathleen Coburn and Anthony John Harding. Princeton: Princeton University Press, 2002.

Condillac, Étienne Bonnot de. *Traité des sensations.* 1754. Paris: Librairie Arthème Fayard, 1984.

Descartes, René. *Discourse on Method and Meditations on First Philosophy.* 4th ed. Translated by Donald A. Cress. Indianapolis: Hackett Publishing Co., 1998.

Descartes, René. *Optics.* 1637. In *Discourse on Method, Optics, Geometry, and Meteorology.* Translated by Paul J. Olscamp. Indianapolis: Hackett Publishing Co., 2001.

Fearn, John. "A Reply to Lady Mary Shepherd on Impiety, and Professor Stewart." *Metropolitan Magazine* 4, no. 16 (August 1832): 349–52.

Fraser, Alexander Campbell. "The Edinburgh Ladies' Educational Association." *The Scotsman* (November 24, 1868): 5.

Gleig, George, and John Robison. "Philosophy." In *Encyclopaedia Britannica: or, A Dictionary of Arts, Sciences, and Miscellaneous Literature*, edited by Colin Macfarquhar and George Gleig, 14:573–600. 3rd ed. Edinburgh: Printed for A. Bell and C. Macfarquhar, 1797.

Grove, William. *On the Correlation of Physical Forces.* 2nd ed. London: Samuel Highley, 1850.

Hartley, David. *Observations on Man, His Frame, His Duty, and His Expectations.* London: Printed by S. Richardson for James Leake and Wm. Frederick, 1749.

"The History of Galvanism." *The Scots Magazine* (August 1803): 514–20; (September 1803): 608–10; (October 1803): 701–2.

BIBLIOGRAPHY 311

Hobbes, Thomas. *Elements of Philosophy, the First Section, Concerning Body.* London: Printed by R. & W. Leybourn for R. Crooke, 1656.

Hume, David. *Dialogues Concerning Natural Religion.* 1779. 2nd ed. Edited by Richard H. Popkin. Indianapolis: Hackett Publishing Co., 1998.

Hume, David. *An Enquiry Concerning Human Understanding: A Critical Edition.* 1748. Edited by Tom L. Beauchamp. Oxford: Oxford University Press, 1999.

Hume, David. *A Treatise of Human Nature.* 1739–40. Edited by David Fate Norton and Mary J. Norton. Oxford: Oxford University Press, 2000.

"An Inquiry into the Probability and Rationality of Mr. Hunter's Theory of Life." *Edinburgh Review* 26, no. 46 (1814): 384–98.

Kaempfer, Engelbert. *A History of Japan.* Translated by Johann Caspar Scheuchzer. London, 1727.

Kant, Immanuel. *Critique of Pure Reason.* 1787. Translated and edited by Paul Guyer and Allen W. Wood. Cambridge: Cambridge University Press, 1998.

Lawrence, William. *Lectures on Physiology, Zoology, and the Natural History of Man.* London: Printed for J. Callow, 1819.

Lawrence, William. *Lectures on Physiology, Zoology, and the Natural History of Man.* 3rd ed. London: Printed for James Smith, 1823.

Leonardo da Vinci. *Notebooks.* Selected by Irma J. Richter and edited by Thereza Wells. Oxford: Oxford University Press, 1982.

Leslie, John. *An Experimental Inquiry in the Nature and Propagation of Heat.* Edinburgh: J. Mawman, 1804.

Locke, John. *An Essay Concerning Human Understanding.* 1700. Edited by Peter H. Nidditch. Oxford: Clarendon Press, 1979.

LoLordo, Antonia, ed. *Mary Shepherd's* Essays on the Perception of an External Universe. New York: Oxford University Press, 2020.

Malebranche, Nicolas. *The Search after Truth.* 1674–75. Translated and edited by Thomas M. Lennon and Paul J. Olscamp. Cambridge: Cambridge University Press, 1997.

McRobert, Jennifer, ed. *The Philosophical Works of Mary Shepherd.* 2 vols. Bristol: Thoemmes Press, 2000.

Mill, John Stuart. *A System of Logic, Ratiocinative and Inductive.* 2 vols. London: John W. Parker, 1843.

Milne, James. *Enquiry Respecting the Relation of Cause and Effect.* Edinburgh: James Ballantyne, 1819.

Molière. *The Imaginary Invalid: Le Malade Imaginaire.* 1673. Translated by Charles Heron Wall. Auckland, New Zealand: Floating Press, 2009.

Newton, Isaac. "A Letter of Mr. Isaac Newton . . . Containing his New Theory about Light and Colours." *Philosophical Transactions* 80 (1672): 3075–87.

Nitsch, Friedrich. *A General and Introductory View of Professor Kant Concerning Man, the World, and the Deity.* London: J. Downes, 1796.

312 BIBLIOGRAPHY

Plotinus. *Ennead 1*. With English translation by A. H. Armstrong. Loeb Classical Library. Cambridge, MA: Harvard University Press, 1966.

Reid, Thomas. *Essays on the Active Powers of Man*. 1788. In *Thomas Reid: Inquiry and Essays*, edited by Ronald E. Beanblossom and Keith Lehrer, 127–296. Indianapolis: Hackett Publishing Co., 1983.

Reid, Thomas. *Essays on the Intellectual Powers of Man*. 1785. In *Thomas Reid: Inquiry and Essays*, edited by Ronald E. Beanblossom and Keith Lehrer, 297–368. Indianapolis: Hackett Publishing Co., 1983.

Reid, Thomas. *An Inquiry into the Human Mind on the Principles of Common Sense*. 1764. Edited by Derek R. Brookes. University Park: The Pennsylvania State University Press, 1997.

Richardson, John. *Metaphysical Works of the Celebrated Immanuel Kant*. London: Printed for W. Simpkin and R. Marshall, 1836.

Shelley, Mary. *Frankenstein*. 1818. 3rd ed. Edited by D. L. MacDonald and Kathleen Scherf. Peterborough, Ontario, Canada: Broadview Press, 2012.

Shepherd, Lady Mary. *An Essay upon the Relation of Cause and Effect*. London: Printed for T. Hookham, 1824.

Shepherd, Lady Mary. *Essays on the Perception of an External Universe, and Other Subjects Connected with the Doctrine of Causation*. London: John Hatchard and Son, 1827.

Shepherd, Lady Mary. "Lady Mary Shepherd's Metaphysics." *Fraser's Magazine* 5, no. 30 (July 1832): 697–708.

Shepherd, Lady Mary. Letter to Charles Babbage of November 18, 1825. Western Manuscripts Add. MS 37183, f. 204. British Library.

Shepherd, Lady Mary. "Observations by Lady Mary Shepherd on the 'First Lines of the Human Mind.'" In *Parriana: or, Notices of the Rev. Samuel Parr, L. L. D*. Vol. 1. London: Henry Colburn, 1828.

Shepherd, Lady Mary. "On the Causes of Single and Erect Vision." *The Philosophical Magazine and Annals of Philosophy* New Series, no. 18 (June 1828): 406–16.

Shepherd, Lady Mary. "On the Causes of Single and Erect Vision." *The Kaleidoscope; or, Literary and Scientific Mirror* 9, nos. 420–21 (1828): 13 and 22–3.

Smith, Robert. *Compleat System of Opticks*. Cambridge: Printed by Cornelius Crownfield, 1738.

Stewart, Dugald. *Elements of the Philosophy of the Human Mind*. Vol. 1, 5th ed. London: Printed for T. Cadell and W. Davies, 1814.

Stewart, Dugald. *Elements of the Philosophy of the Human Mind*. Vol. 2, 2nd ed. Edinburgh: Printed by George Ramsay and Company, 1816.

Stewart, Dugald. *Philosophical Essays*. Edinburgh: Printed by George Ramsay and Company, 1810.

BIBLIOGRAPHY 313

Stewart, Dugald. *A Short Statement of Some Important Facts, relative to the late election of a mathematical professor in the University of Edinburgh.* Edinburgh: Printed by Murray and Cochrane, 1805.

Virgil. *Eclogues. Georgics. Aeneid: Books I–VI.* Translated by H. Rushton Fairclough and revised by G. P. Goold. Loeb Classical Library. Cambridge, MA: Harvard University Press, 1999.

Watts, Isaac. *Logic, or the Right Use of Reason,* new ed. London: Printed for C. and J. Rivington, 1824.

Watts, Isaac. *The Psalms of David Imitated in the Language of the New Testament.* London: Printed for J. Clark, 1719.

Willich, Anthony F. M. *Elements of the Critical Philosophy.* London: Printed for T. N. Longman, 1798.

Wirgman, Thomas. "Kant." In *The Encyclopaedia Londinensis,* 11:603–29. London: Printed by J. Adlard, 1812.

Secondary Sources

Atherton, Margaret. *Berkeley's Revolution in Vision.* Ithaca, NY: Cornell University Press, 1990.

Atherton, Margaret. "Lady Mary Shepherd's Case Against George Berkeley." *British Journal for the History of Philosophy* 4, no. 2 (1996): 347–66.

Atherton, Margaret. "Reading Lady Mary Shepherd." *The Harvard Review of Philosophy* 8, no. 2 (2005): 73–85.

Bird, Alexander, and Emma Tobin. "Natural Kinds." In *Stanford Encyclopedia of Philosophy,* 2017. Article published September 17, 2008; last modified January 28, 2022. https://plato.stanford.edu/entries/natural-kinds/

Bolton, Martha. "Causality and Causal Induction: The Necessitarian Theory of Lady Mary Shepherd." In *Causation and Modern Philosophy,* edited by Keith Allen and Tom Stoneham, 242–61. New York: Routledge, 2011.

Bolton, Martha. "Lady Mary Shepherd and David Hume on Cause and Effect." In *Feminist History of Philosophy: The Recovery and Evaluation of Women's Philosophical Thought,* edited by Eileen O'Neill and Marcy P. Lascano, 129–152. Cham: Springer, 2019.

Bolton, Martha. "Mary Shepherd." In *Stanford Encyclopedia of Philosophy,* 2017. Article published May 28, 2017; last modified November 13, 2017. https://plato.stanford.edu/entries/mary-shepherd/

Bow, Charles Bradford. "In Defence of the Scottish Enlightenment: Dugald Stewart's Role in the 1805 John Leslie Affair." *The Scottish Historical Review* 92, no. 233 (2013): 123–46.

Boyle, Deborah. "Expanding the Canon of Scottish Philosophy: The Case for Adding Mary Shepherd." *The Journal of Scottish Philosophy* 15, no. 3 (2017): 275–93.

314 BIBLIOGRAPHY

Boyle, Deborah. "Mary Shepherd on the Meaning of 'Life.'" *British Journal for the History of Philosophy* 21, no. 2 (March 2021): 208–25.

Boyle, Deborah. "Mary Shepherd on Mind, Soul, and Self." *Journal of the History of Philosophy* 58, no. 1 (2020): 93–112.

Boyle, Deborah. "A Mistaken Attribution to Mary Shepherd." *Journal of Modern Philosophy* 2, no. 1 (2020). http://doi.org/10.32881/jomp.100

Campbell, W. A. "Oxalic Acid, Epsom Salt and the Poison Bottle." *Human Toxicology* (March 1982): 187–93. https://www.ncbi.nlm.nih.gov/pubmed/6757103

Cheyne, Peter. "Coleridge the Philosopher." *Aeon* (April 2021). https://aeon.co/essays/the-spectacular-originality-of-coleridges-theory-of-ideas

Class, Monika. *Coleridge and Kantian Ideas, 1796–1817*. London: Bloomsbury, 2012.

Copenhaver, Rebecca. "Berkeley and Reid." In *The Oxford Handbook of Berkeley*, edited by Samuel Rickless, 615–36. New York: Oxford University Press, 2022.

Copenhaver, Rebecca. "Berkeley on the Language of Nature and the Objects of Vision." *Res Philosophica* 91, no. 1 (2014): 29–46.

Copenhaver, Rebecca. "Thomas Reid on Acquired Perception." *Pacific Philosophical Quarterly* 91 (2010): 285–312.

Dixon, Thomas. "Introduction." In *Thomas Brown: Selected Philosophical Writings*, edited by Thomas Dixon, 1–30. Exeter: Imprint Publishing, 2010.

Dumitru, Claudia. "Crucial Instances and Crucial Experiments in Bacon, Boyle, and Hooke." *Societate si Politica* 7, no. 1 (2013): 45–61.

Falkenstein, Lorne. "Theories of Perception I: Berkeley and His Recent Predecessors." In *The Routledge Companion to Eighteenth Century Philosophy*, edited by Aaron Garrett, 338–59. Abingdon, England: Routledge, 2014.

Falkenstein, Lorne. "Theories of Perception II: After Berkeley." In *The Routledge Companion to Eighteenth Century Philosophy*, edited by Aaron Garrett, 360–80. Abingdon, England: Routledge, 2014.

Fantl, Jeremy. "Mary Shepherd on Causal Necessity." *Metaphysica* 17 (2016): 87–108.

Fasko, Manuel. "Mary Shepherd's Threefold 'Variety of Intellect' and Its Role in Improving Education." *Journal of Scottish Philosophy* 19, no. 3 (2021): 185–201.

Fieser, James, ed. *Early Responses to Hume's Metaphysical and Epistemological Writings*. 2 vols. 2nd ed., revised. Bristol, England: Thoemmes Continuum, 2005.

Folescu, M. "Mary Shepherd on the Role of Proofs in Our Knowledge of First Principles." *Noûs* 56, no. 2 (2022): 473–93. https://onlinelibrary.wiley.com/doi/10.1111/nous.12365

Gambarotto, Andrea. *Vital Forces, Teleology and Organization: Philosophy of Nature and the Rise of Biology in Germany*. Cham: Springer, 2018.

BIBLIOGRAPHY 315

Glover, Katharine. *Elite Women and Polite Society in Eighteenth-Century Scotland*. Woodbridge, England: Boydell Press, 2011.

Grandi, Giovanni B. "Providential Naturalism and Miracles: John Fearn's Critique of Scottish Philosophy." *Journal of Scottish Philosophy* 13, no. 1 (2015): 75–94.

Hacking, Ian. "A Tradition of Natural Kinds." *Philosophical Studies* 61, no. 1 (1991): 109–26.

Hammond, John H. *The Camera Obscura: A Chronicle*. Bristol, England: Adam Hilger, 1981.

Hatfield, Gary. "Geometry and Visual Space from Antiquity to the Early Moderns." In *Space: A History*, edited by Andrew Janiak, 184–222. Oxford: Oxford University Press, 2020.

Jacyna, L. S. "Immanence or Transcendence: Theories of Life and Organization in Britain, 1790–1825." *Isis* 74 (1983): 311–29.

Jessop, T. E. *A Bibliography of David Hume and of Scottish Philosophy*. London: Brown and Sons, 1938; reprinted, New York: Garland Publishing, 1983.

Jones, Jan-Erik. "Locke on Real Essence." In *Stanford Encyclopedia of Philosophy*, 2017. Article published December 19, 2012; last modified September 2, 2022. https://plato.stanford.edu/entries/real-essence/

Kamcke, Claudia, and Rainer Hutterer. "History of Dioramas." In *Natural History Dioramas: History, Construction and Educational Role*, edited by Sue Dale Tunnicliffe and Annette Scheersoi, 7–21. Dordrecht: Springer, 2015.

Kennedy, Emmet. "'Ideology' from Destutt de Tracy to Marx." *Journal of the History of Ideas* 40, no. 3 (1979): 353–68.

Kripke, Saul. *Naming and Necessity*. Cambridge, MA: Harvard University Press, 1980.

Landy, David. "A Defense of Mary Shepherd's Account of Cause and Effect as Synchronous." *Journal of Modern Philosophy* 2, no. 1 (2020): 1–15. http://doi.org/10.32881/jomp.46

Landy, David. "Shepherd on Hume's Argument for the Possibility of Uncaused Existence." *Journal of Modern Philosophy* 2, no. 13 (2020): 1–14. https://jmp hil.org/articles/10.32881/jomp.128/

Lefranc, Jean. *La philosophie en France au XIXe siècle*. Paris: L'Harmattan, 2011.

Lewis, C. S. *Miracles: A Preliminary Study*. New York: The MacMillan Co., 1947.

LoLordo, Antonia. "Introduction." In *Mary Shepherd's Essays on the Perception of an External Universe*, edited by Antonia LoLordo, 1–24. New York: Oxford University Press, 2020.

LoLordo, Antonia. *Mary Shepherd*. Cambridge Elements on Women in the History of Philosophy. Cambridge: Cambridge University Press, 2022.

LoLordo, Antonia. "Mary Shepherd on Causation, Induction, and Natural Kinds." *Philosophers' Imprint* 19, no. 52 (2019): 1–14. https://quod.lib. umich.edu/p/phimp/3521354.0019.052/1

316 BIBLIOGRAPHY

Macpherson, Fiona. "Introduction: Individuating the Senses." In *The Senses: Classical and Contemporary Philosophical Perspectives*, edited by Fiona Macpherson, 3–43. Oxford: Oxford University Press, 2011.

McCosh, James. *The Scottish Philosophy: Biographical, Expository, Critical, from Hutcheson to Hamilton*. New York: Robert Carter and Brothers, 1875.

McDonagh, Patrick. *Idiocy: A Cultural History*. Liverpool: Liverpool University Press, 2008.

McRobert, Jennifer. "Introduction." In *The Philosophical Works of Mary Shepherd*. 2 vols. Bristol: Thoemmes Press, 2000.

McRobert, Jennifer. "Mary Shepherd and the Causal Relation." 2002; revised 2014. http://philpapers.org/rec/MCRMSA

Mogi, Akira, and Hiroyuki Kuwano. "TP53 Mutations in Nonsmall Cell Lung Cancer." *Journal of Biomedicine and Biotechnology* 2011 (2011), article ID 583829. https://doi.org/10.1155/2011/583929

Moriarty, Clare Marie. "The Ad Hominem Argument of Berkeley's *Analyst*." *British Journal for the History of Philosophy* 26, no. 3 (2018): 429–51.

Naragon, Steve. "Kant in Translation." Last modified June 3, 2015. https://users.manchester.edu/facstaff/ssnaragon/kant/Helps/KantsWritingsTranslations.htm#Richardson1836

Nolan, Lawrence, ed. *Primary and Secondary Qualities: The Historical and Ongoing Debate*. Oxford: Oxford University Press, 2011.

Osler, Margaret. "Descartes's Optics: Light, the Eye, and Visual Perception." In *A Companion to Descartes*, edited by Janet Broughton and John Carriero, 124–41. Malden, MA: Wiley-Blackwell, 2007.

Paoletti, Cristina. "Restoring Necessary Connections: Lady Mary Shepherd on Hume and the Early Nineteenth-Century Debate on Causality." In *Hume, Nuovi Saggi=Hume, New Essays*, 47–59. Padova: Il Poligrafo, 2011.

Perkins, Mary Anne. "Shepherd (née Primrose), Lady Mary (1777–1847), Philosopher." *Oxford Dictionary of National Biography*. 2004. https://doi.org/10.1093/ref:odnb/58699

Rickless, Samuel C. *Berkeley's Argument for Idealism*. Oxford: Oxford University Press, 2013.

Rickless, Samuel C. "Berkeley's *Treatise Concerning the Principles of Human Knowledge*." In *The Bloomsbury Companion to Berkeley*, edited by Bertil Belfrage and Richard Brook, 99–120. London: Bloomsbury Academic, 2017.

Rickless, Samuel C. "Is Shepherd's Pen Mightier than Berkeley's Word?" *British Journal for the History of Philosophy* 26, no. 2 (2018): 317–30.

Rosebery, Lady Deirdre. *Dalmeny House Guide*. Broxburn, Scotland: Alna Press, n.d..

Sabra, A. I. *Theories of Light from Descartes to Newton*. Cambridge: Cambridge University Press, 1981.

Shapiro, Lisa, ed. and trans. *The Correspondence between Princess Elisabeth of Bohemia and René Descartes*. Chicago: University of Chicago Press, 2007.

BIBLIOGRAPHY 317

Smith, A. Mark. "Descartes's Theory of Light and Refraction: A Discourse on Method." *Transactions of the American Philosophical Society* 77, no. 3 (1987): i–viii, 1–92.

Smith, C. U. M. "Brain and Mind in the 'Long' Eighteenth Century." In *Brain, Mind and Medicine: Essays in Eighteenth-Century Medicine*, edited by Harry Whitaker, C. U. M. Smith, and Stanley Finger, 15–28. New York: Springer, 2007.

Stewart, M. A. "Religion and Rational Theology." In *The Cambridge Companion to the Scottish Enlightenment*, 2nd ed., edited by Alexander Broadie and Craig Smith, 33–59. Cambridge: Cambridge University Press, 2019.

Tanner, Travis. "How Good Was Shepherd's Response to Hume's Epistemological Challenge?" *British Journal for the History of Philosophy* 30, no. 1 (2022): 71–89.

Temkin, Owsei. "Basic Science, Medicine, and the Romantic Era." *Bulletin of the History of Medicine* 37, no. 2 (1963): 97–129.

Thorne, R. G. "Shepherd, Henry John (?1784–1855), of 1 Pump Court, Temple, London." *The History of Parliament: The House of Commons 1790–1820*. 1986. http://www.histparl.ac.uk/volume/1790-1820/member/shepherd-henry-john-1784-1855

Van Bunge, Wiep. "Wayne I. Boucher (ed.), *Spinoza: Eighteenth and Nineteenth-Century Discussions*: A Review-Essay." *Intellectual News* 6, no. 1 (2000): 65–70.

Van Cleve, James. *Problems from Reid*. Oxford: Oxford University Press, 2015.

Van Cleve, James. "Reid Versus Berkeley on the Inverted Retinal Image." *Philosophical Topics* 31, no. 1–2 (2003): 425–55.

Wade, Nicholas J. *A Natural History of Vision*. Cambridge, MA: MIT Press, 1998.

Wade, Nicholas J. "Vision and Visualization." *Journal of the History of the Neurosciences* 17, no. 3 (2008): 274–94.

Welch, Cheryl B. *Liberty and Utility: The French Idéologues and the Transformation of Liberalism*. New York: Columbia University Press, 1984.

Wiest, Gerald. "The Origins of Vestibular Science." *Annals of the New York Academy of Sciences* 1343, no. 1 (2015): 1–9.

Wilson, Jessica. "On Mary Shepherd's *Essay upon the Relation of Cause and Effect*." In *Neglected Classics of Philosophy*, Vol. 2, edited by Eric Schliesser, 141–71. New York: Oxford University Press, 2022.

Wilson, Robert A. "Primary and Secondary Qualities." In *A Companion to Locke*, edited by Matthew Stuart, 193–211. Malden, MA: Wiley-Blackwell, 2016.

Index

For the benefit of digital users, indexed terms that span two pages (e.g., 52–53) may, on occasion, appear on only one of those pages.

Abernethy, John, 90, 111–12
abstract ideas. *See* ideas: abstract
abstraction, 15–18, 180–81, 213–14
affection, 56n.3, 163–64
afterlife, 105–6, 197–98, 233, 257–63
algebra, 164–65, 284
analogies
  biological, 44
  with language, 284
  mathematical, 42–43, 154–55, 164–65, 168
  with powers of heat, light, electricity, 232, 264–65
  See also reasoning: analogical
analysis, philosophical, 207–8, 214, 224
animals, non-human
  consciousness and, 94–95, 251–52, 257–58
  instincts and, 85–86, 187
  latent reasoning in, 86n.38, 139–40, 143
  understanding in, 133–34
Aristotle, 119, 289–90
association
  among ideas, 19, 51, 77–78, 236, 237–38, 281–83
  in causal inference, 9–10, 76
  in memory, 76, 124–25
  of qualities (sensations) with words, 62–63, 96, 97–98

in reflection, 179
of sensible ideas with ideas of their cause, 17–18, 146–47, 155, 175–76, 201–2, 207–8, 214, 224
of visible ideas with tangible ideas, 174n.25, 274–75, 286–87, 293–94
atheism, 75, 82–83, 84, 242, 252–53
Atherton, Margaret, 150, 178–79, 273, 275–77
attraction, gravitational, 252–53
autonomy. *See* freedom; will
axiom, 180–81

Babbage, Charles, 75n.23, 136
Bacon, Francis, 251–52
beliefs
  as actions, 139
  of common sense, 10–11, 12–13, 140
  intuitive, 65, 83–84, 85–86, 140
Berkeley, George
  abstraction, 15–18, 213–14
  distance perception, 174n.25, 274–77
  dreams, 189–90, 191–93
  idealism, 14–18, 115, 160–61, 169–70, 181, 183, 203–10, 276–77
  meaning of 'idea,' 118–19
  mind (spirit), 127–28, 175–76, 208–10, 224–25

320 INDEX

Berkeley, George (*cont.*)
  primary versus secondary
    qualities, 156–57
  sense-organs, 210–11
  sensible qualities, 14–18, 56,
    212, 215–16
  time, 159
  vision, 156n.6, 271–72, 274–76,
    278, 280–81, 293–94
Blakey, Robert, 21–22
body
  death of, 101–2, 198–
    99n.11, 257–58
  individuation of, 232–33, 264–65
  physiology, 91–95, 105–6, 123,
    128–29, 194–95
  See also matter; mind–body
    interaction; sense-organs
Bolton, Martha, 40–41, 162
brain
  disorders, 105–6
  as exponent of soul or mind, 104–
    5, 237–41
  imagination and, 186–87
  instinct and, 187
  sensation and, 91, 93–94n.7,
    104–5, 112–13, 236–37, 240–41,
    259–60, 284
  as sense-organ, 150
  skepticism and, 186–87, 197
  vision and, 284–85, 287–88
  See also nerves; sense-organs
Brandreth, Mary Elizabeth
  Shepherd, 1, 3
Brown, Thomas
  causation, 4, 82–87
  common sense philosophy, 13, 140
  Leslie affair, 24–25, 82–83, 84
brutes. *See* animals, non-human

Cabanis, Pierre J. G., 20, 253n.7
camera obscura, 166–67n.18, 270,
  293n.39

capacities. *See* powers, causal
causal chains, 40–41, 45–46, 111–12,
  152, 214–15, 288–89
causal inference
  Hume on, 27–29, 34, 38–39, 72–
    74, 77, 135, 139
  Shepherd on, 34–39, 43n.18, 73–
    74, 75, 76–80, 138–39
Causal Likeness Principle (CLP),
  34–39, 78–79, 131, 137–38,
  299–300
  corollaries of, 39, 122, 153, 224–25
  known by latent reasoning,
    32, 142–43
  Shepherd's proof for, 34–36
  in vision, 291, 298, 299
causal power. *See* powers, causal
Causal Principle (CP), 30–33, 70,
  73–74, 78–79, 131, 137–38,
  147–48, 222–23, 224, 298,
  299–300
  known by latent reasoning,
    32, 141–42
  Shepherd's proof for, 31–32
causation
  among objects, 41–43
  divine, 265–68
  efficient, 130, 250, 251
  final, 130, 250–51
  as mixture, 39–40, 42–44, 85, 104–
    5, 107, 132–33, 164–65, 235
  modelled on chemical
    synthesis, 44
  as necessary connection, 34–36,
    39–41, 50–51
  as synchronous, 39–41, 42–43,
    46, 214–15
  'cause,' definition of, 29, 30–31, 49–
    52, 64n.12
children
  latent reasoning in,
    86n.38, 139–42
  understanding in, 133–34

INDEX 321

Christianity. *See* religion
Clarke, Samuel, 32–33
Cogan, Thomas, 40n.14
Coleridge, Samuel Taylor, 8–9
color
distance and, 174–75, 273–75, 280–81
extension and, 281–83, 285–86
sensation of, 164–65, 192, 272, 278–80, 282–83
shape and, 285–86, 291–92
common sense, Scottish philosophy of, 8–13, 140
compatibilism. *See* freedom
conceivability, 26–27, 33, 48, 71–72, 263–64. *See also* separability
Condillac, Étienne Bonnot de, 4, 8–9, 18–20, 222–23
consciousness
brain and, 240
limits of, 173–74, 177–78, 231–33
mind as power of, 112–13, 218, 219–20
personal identity and, 227–29, 257–63
sensations and, 116–18, 219–20, 284–85, 292–93
sense-organs and, 195–97, 210–11, 212
will and, 130
creation, divine. *See* causation: divine
custom. *See* habit

Daguerre, Louis, 185–86
death. *See* afterlife; body: death of
definitions
absolute, 65
of arbitrary names versus of objects, 61–62, 63
Locke's views on, 61–63
nominal versus real, 46–47, 63–67
See also 'cause,' definition of; 'effect': definition of

de Gérando, Joseph Marie, 4, 20
Deity. *See* God
delusions, 58–59, 184–88, 193–94, 195–97, 240–41
demonstration. *See* reasoning: demonstrative
Descartes, René
metaphysical and mathematical proofs, 74–75
mind as substance, 219, 235
primary and secondary qualities, 16
skepticism, 160, 184, 191n.9
vision, 271–73, 278n.17, 293–94
design argument. *See* God: teleological argument for existence of
Destutt de Tracy, Antoine, 4, 19–20, 20n.47, 171n.22
Diorama, 185–86
disorders, 89n.1, 105–6, 123
distance
as cause of sensation of motion, 124
idea of, 118–19, 168, 172, 173–75
visual perception of, 272–77, 280–83, 285–86
See also extension; outwardness; space
dreams
objects in, 58–59, 126–27, 188, 190–91, 193, 194–95
Reid's rebuttal of idealism and, 202
skepticism and, 160–61, 184–85, 187–88, 189–97, 240–41
duration. *See* time

'effect'
definition of, 30–31, 49–50
equivalent to 'quality,' 41, 46–47, 56, 107
emanationism, 267–68
empiricism, 18–19, 293–94

322 INDEX

eternity
  of mind, 232, 233, 257–59, 260
  of universe, 255, 267–68
Euclid, 272
examples of Shepherd's
  balls at rest, 252–53
  bilious man, 102–3
  bird building nest, 187, 251–52
  bread, 66–67, 66n.15
  camera obscura, 166–67n.18, 270
  closing and opening eyes, 34–35
  Diorama, 185–86
  eggs, 77
  Epsom salts, 37, 66, 77
  fire, 38
  flint and steel, 30–31
  gold, arbitrary name of, 64–
    65, 98–99
  Indian prince, 245
  light from sun, 158–59, 283
  living statue (see Condillac,
    Étienne Bonnot de)
  mirror, 166–67, 166–67n.18
  natural kinds, 66
  Newtonian attraction, 252–53
  nourishment, 46
  oxalic acid, 37, 66
  perceiving round figure, 298–99
  schoolboy recalling Virgil, 77–78
  ship sailing from Falmouth to
    Antigua, 164–65
  snow, arbitrary name of, 61
  uncaused object coming
    into existence, 31–32, 54–
    55, 141–42
  uncolored space, 68–69
  walking in garden, 130, 236
existence
  abstract idea of, 17–18, 163n.14
  as affection, 163–64
experimentum crucis, 34–35, 35n.10,
    36–37, 75, 137–38, 200, 202
exponent, 104–5, 237–41

extension
  color and, 281–83
  sensation of, 171–72, 174, 211,
    233–34, 236–37, 286
  See also distance;
    outwardness; space
external world
  arguments for existence of, 146–
    54, 166–75, 176–81, 199–200
  as cause of sensations, 17–18,
    56–57, 58–60, 121–22, 123–24,
    128–29, 192–94, 210–11, 240–
    41, 284–85
  latent reasoning about, 143, 148
  skepticism about, 79, 145, 184–85,
    189, 197–200, 203
  structurally isomorphic to
    sensations, 161–63, 164–65,
    284, 286, 297
  See also objects

fancy. See imagination
Fasko, Manuel, 133–34
Fearn, John, 6–7, 8–9, 14n.33, 216n.21
Fraser, Alexander Campbell, 21–22
freedom, 127, 129–31. See also will

Gérando, Joseph Marie de, 20
God
  body and, 263–65
  changing the course of nature, 71,
    244–45, 246
  cosmological argument for
    existence of, 32–33, 249–
    50, 254–57
  as creator, 87, 112–13, 231, 232,
    252–53, 265–67
  divine creation by, 265–68
  knowledge of external world and,
    148–49, 152–53, 154, 199–200
  mind of, 253–55
  qualities of, 105–6, 254–55, 266–
    67, 268

sensory perceptions and, 148–49,
152–53, 154, 199–200, 208–9,
210, 214, 215–16
as source of life, 109–10
teleological argument for
existence of, 249–55
good sense, 37, 76, 138
gravity. *See* attraction, gravitational
Grove, William, 238–39

habit
Hume on, 9–10, 13, 28, 51, 72–73
Ideologues on, 18–19
memory and, 76, 77–78, 124–25
sensations and, 146
vision and, 274–75, 286–87
Haller, Albrecht von, 91
hallucinations. *See* delusions
Hartley, David, 82n.30, 239–40
Hobbes, Thomas, 40n.14
Hume, David
causal inference, 27–29, 34, 38–39,
72–74, 77, 135, 139
causation, 9–10, 29–31, 32–33,
50–52, 87
demonstrative versus moral
reasoning, 27–28, 134–35
knowledge of external world,
145, 175–76
Leslie affair, 24–25, 84
memory, 125
miracles, 135, 242–46
relations of ideas versus matters of
fact, 26–27, 134–35
religion, 84, 254–55
secret powers, 47–49, 81
simple perceptions, 220–21
uniformity of nature, 28n.6, 35–
36, 69–72, 80

idealism
Berkeley on, 14–18, 115, 160–61,
169–70, 181, 183, 203–10, 276–77

in Britain, 8–9
Reid's rebuttal of, 200–2
ideas
abstract, 15–16, 17–18, 62–63,
163n.14, 180–81, 213–14
association of (*see* association:
among ideas)
as conclusions of reasoning, 118–
19, 122
copied from impressions, 72–73
Ideologues' science of, 19
of imagination, 58, 125–27, 186–
87, 191
instinctive, 140
of memory (*see* memory:
objects of)
negative, 161–62, 168
as objects of thought, 118–19
relations of, 26–27, 131–32, 134–
35, 180–81
tangible, 174n.25, 274–75, 280–
81, 296–97
visible, 174n.25, 274–75, 293–
94, 296–97
See also notions; perception;
sensation
identity. *See* external world:
structurally isomorphic to
sensations; personal identity
Ideologues, 18–20
illness. *See* disorders
illusions. *See* delusions
imagination, 30–31, 58–59, 125–
27, 186–87, 191. *See also*
conceivability
immanentism. *See* life: immanentism
versus transcendentalism
immaterialism, 14–15, 183, 276–77
individuation
in the afterlife, 258–63
of human bodies, 232–33
of objects, 60n.8
of selves, 230–33

324 INDEX

induction
mathematical, 74–75
physical, 43n.18, 68–72
problem of, 28n.6
See also causal inference
inference, causal. *See* causal
inference
instinct, 80, 83–84, 85–86, 140, 187,
201, 238, 280–82
intellect. *See* understanding
intention, 250–53
intuitive proposition, 65, 86
irritability, 91, 92–94, 95, 97–98,
101–2, 103

Kant, Immanuel, 4, 7–8, 8n.19,
8n.20, 163–64n.15
Kripke, Saul, 35n.11, 67

latent reasoning. *See*
reasoning: latent
Lawrence, William
debate on nature of life, 89–
91, 106
definition of 'life,' 94–95, 107–10
Humean causation, 4, 89, 92–94,
100–1, 103
materialism, 103–4, 105–6, 109
necessary connection, 95–
100, 101–3
sensibility (sensitivity, sentience),
91, 93–94, 97–98, 102–3
vital processes, 91–95, 108–9
laws
of belief, 12–13
of nature (*see* nature: laws of)
of optics, 272, 273–74, 278n.17,
283, 290
Leslie affair, the, 24–25
Leslie, Sir John, 24–25, 82–83, 84
life
as causal power, 101–2, 111–14

definition of, 109–10
distinguished from
sentience, 94–95
immanentism versus
transcendentalism, 89–90, 91–
92, 108–9, 111–12
nature of, 89–92, 106–14
Locke, John
causation, 32–33
general terms, 62, 98–99
identity, 227, 229–30, 229n.11
meaning of 'idea,' 118–19
primary and secondary qualities,
16n.36, 119–21, 156
real versus nominal definitions, 63
real versus nominal essence, 61–
63, 80–81
LoLordo, Antonia, 44, 80–81
Lyell, Charles, 2–3

Malebranche, Nicolas
God as cause of sensations, 153
vision, 271–72, 273–74, 293–94
Malthus, Thomas, 2–3
marvelous events
belief in, 246–47
distinguished from
miracles, 246–48
as evidence for religious doctrine,
246, 247–48
See also miracles
materialism, 103–4, 105–6,
109, 150n.3
mathematics. *See* analogies:
mathematical;
reasoning: mathematical;
science: mathematical
matter
Berkeley on, 14–16, 183, 208–9
as eternal, 267
of living organisms, 89–90, 91,
103–4, 108–9, 111–12

particles and, 60, 227, 233–34
real essence of, 233–34
See also body; mind–body
interaction
matters of fact, 26–27, 134–35
McCosh, James, 13n.32
McRobert, Jennifer, 20–21
memory
in afterlife, 258–60, 261–63
faculty of, 76, 78, 124–25
objects of, 57–58, 125–26
Mill, James, 4
Mill, John Stuart, 76
Milne, James, 3
mind(s)
afflicted with idiocy, 133–
34, 220n.4
afterlife of, 198–99n.11, 257–63
broad versus narrow senses of,
228–29, 259–60, 262–63
as capacity to sense, 93–94, 112–
13, 116, 121–22, 218–20
as causal power, 147, 149–50, 165–
66n.17, 170, 219, 228, 233–34
continuous existence of, 221–24
as created, 104
as eternal, 257–58, 267
as external to particular
sensations, 170, 221–22
of God, 253–55, 266–67
as immaterial, 171, 218, 233–
34, 253–54
individuation of, 230–33, 262–63
inward existence of, 166, 170
knowledge of, 11–12, 13
latent reasoning and, 141–43, 148
other, 166, 177–78, 179–80, 188,
198–99, 208–9, 224–25
as self, 173–74, 177, 218, 226–30
sensible qualities and, 56, 57,
57n.6, 58–59, 118n.6, 121–22,
159, 215–16, 283

as simple, 220–21, 228
as soul, 218
as unchanging in sensation, 122,
150–51, 154, 159–60, 162
as unhesitating, 79, 138
as uniform power in nature,
128n.17
See also brain; mind–body
interaction; mind(s): other
mind–body interaction, 173–74,
233–37, 264–65
miracles
distinguished from marvelous
events, 246–48
Hume on belief in, 242–46
impossibility of, 244–45, 246
laws of nature and, 242–43, 244–
46, 248
See also marvelous events
mixture. *See* causation: as mixture
Molière, 113–14
motion
life and, 94–95, 109–10, 113–14
real, 123–24, 172–73
sensation of, 123–24, 171, 172–
73, 286–87
as a sense, 123–24, 171
See also attraction,
gravitational; space
muscles. *See* irritability

names, 61–62, 63, 64–65, 96–97
natural kinds, 62, 66, 98
nature
changes in apparent course
of, 245–46
laws of, 92, 129–30, 208–9, 210,
210n.17, 242–43, 244–46, 248,
251–52, 294–95
as underlying substratum, 60
uniformity of, 68–72, 78–80
See also natural kinds

326 INDEX

necessary connection
   between cause and effect, 34–36,
      40–41, 50–51, 63–64, 65–66,
      137–38, 244–45
   as constant conjunction, 9–10, 13,
      50–51, 72–73, 92, 93, 95
   between name and definition,
      61–62, 64–65, 67, 96–97, 98–
      99, 102
   between object and qualities, 61–
      62, 66n.14, 67, 96–98, 99–100
   of successive events,
      96n.11, 214–15
nerves, 91, 92–94, 97–98, 101–3, 108,
      236–37, 259–60, 284–85. See
      also brain; sense-organs
Newton, Isaac, 35n.10, 252–53
notions, 119, 160–61, 163n.14, 168,
      186–87, 281–83

objects
   causal histories of, 77
   external versus internal, 54–60,
      121–22, 155, 161–65, 166–68,
      175–76, 193, 207–8
   of imagination, 58–59, 125–27
   individuation of, 60n.8, 298n.44
   as masses (bundles) of qualities,
      31–32, 41–42, 54–60, 266–
      67, 297–98
   of memory, 57–58, 125–26
   real, 184–85, 186–91, 199–200
   See also definitions
O'Neill, Eileen, 21–22
Opie, Amelia, 82n.30
organization. See body
other minds. See mind(s): other
outwardness
   as extended space, 124
   idea of, 168–69, 173–75
   sensation of, 171–72, 286
   See also distance;
      extension; space

particles
   life and, 94–95, 109–10, 111–12
   light and, 272
   matter and, 46, 60, 233–34
   personal identity and, 226–
      27, 228
perception, 117–18, 136. See also
      sensation
personal identity, 226–30. See also
      mind(s): as self; individuation:
      of selves
plants, 94–95, 103–4, 109–10
Plotinus, 267–68
power, idea of, 84, 86–87
powers, causal, 39, 49–50, 59–60,
      63–67, 96–100, 163–64, 178–79,
      198–99n.11, 210n.17, 214–15.
      See also life: as causal power;
      powers, secret
powers, secret, 47–49, 59, 70, 81
Prévost, Pierre, 4
Priestley, Joseph, 3, 3n.12, 4
primary qualities. See qualities:
      primary versus secondary
probability, 38–39, 78–79, 135–36,
      138–39, 198–99, 242–43
probable reasoning. See reasoning:
      probable
proof, 135–36, 242–43. See also
      reasoning
prophecy. See religion: prophecy
proportions
   of belief and evidence, 177–
      78, 242–43
   of causes and effects, 177–78, 255
   of internal and external objects,
      161–63, 164–65, 173, 277, 286,
      297, 298–99
   of mind and brain, 237–40
   represented algebraically, 164–
      65, 284
   of visual and tangible perceptions,
      295–97, 298–99

INDEX 327

qualities
as causal powers, 42, 59–60
as effects, 46–47
of God, 265–67
objects as bundles of, 31–32,
41–42, 54–60, 125–27, 266–
67, 297–98
primary versus secondary, 16,
119–21, 155–57, 158–59, 203–4
sensible, 15–18, 42, 48–49, 56–59,
77, 81, 117, 121, 146–47, 175–
76, 206–8, 215–16
TP53 mutation, 44–46
See also definitions; necessary
connection; objects

reality. See objects: real
reason. See understanding
reasoning
analogical, 198–99, 224–25, 253,
260–62, 263
causal (see causal inference)
as causal process, 131–33
demonstrative, 27–28, 73–75,
134–39, 188, 199–200
upon experiment, 34–37
experimental, 135–36, 137–38
latent, 32, 86n.38, 139–43, 146,
148, 166, 169, 174–75
mathematical, 73–75,
75n.23, 136–37
mistakes in, 36–38, 78, 138
moral, 27–28, 134–35
probable, 38–39, 134–35, 138–39
Reid, Thomas
common sense philosophy, 8–13,
140, 145, 198–99
Humean causation, 51
primary and secondary qualities,
155–57, 158–59, 175–76, 201–
2, 270
rejection of idealism, 200–2
sensory perception, 157–59

suggestion, 156–59, 200–2, 211,
278, 282–83
vision, 278–81, 289–91, 294–
96, 299
relations
causal, 39–40, 41, 42–43, 64n.12,
85, 267–68
of ideas (see ideas: relations of)
logical, 133, 141, 143
mathematical, 75, 154–55
among objects (see proportions: of
internal and external objects)
among sensations, 117, 131–32,
133, 141, 143, 181
universal, 136
religion, 66, 105–6
belief in afterlife, 257–63
belief in existence of God, 249
belief in miracles, 242–49
Christian doctrine, 1–2, 267, 268
divine creation, 263–68
martyrs, 248–49
prophecy, 187
prophets, 187, 243
See also afterlife; God; marvelous
events; miracles
rest, 171, 172, 172n.23,
See also attraction,
gravitational; motion
retinal images, 272, 273, 278–
80, 284–86
differences between, 291–92
double, 287–91, 292
inverted, 278n.17, 287–89, 293–
95, 296, 299
Ricardo, David, 2–3
Rosebery, 3rd Earl of (Neil
Primrose), 1

science
of human nature, 11–12
of ideas, 19
mathematical, 75, 137

328   INDEX

science (*cont.*)
  physical, 66, 74, 75, 81, 89, 93,
    114, 242
Scottish philosophy. *See* common
    sense, Scottish philosophy of
Scripture, 186n.7, 263
secondary qualities. *See* qualities:
    primary versus secondary
secret powers. *See* powers, secret
self. *See* mind(s); personal identity
sensation
  as capacity to sense, 104, 116,
    128n.17, 218–20, 228
  as conscious mental state, 116–17,
    219–20, 228, 240
  of duration, 159–60
  of extension, 171–72, 174, 211,
    233–34, 236–37, 286
  general (*see* sensation: as capacity
    to sense)
  of motion, 123–24, 171, 172–73
  Reid's account of, 157–58, 200–1,
    202, 278–80
  superinduced, 132
  as transitory, 147–48, 151–52,
    153–54, 169, 170, 177, 221–
    22, 223–24
  types of, 104–5, 117, 118–
    19, 220–21
  See also brain; sense-organs
sense-organs
  as causes of sensation, 121–22,
    150–51, 162, 164–65, 173–74,
    236–37, 240–41, 284
  conscious use of, 195–96
  external existence of, 169–70,
    195–96n.10, 210–12
  See also brain; motion;
    nerves; vision
sensibility, 91, 93–94, 94n.8, 97–
    98, 101–3
sensitivity. *See* consciousness; nerves;
    sensibility

sentience. *See* consciousness
sentient principle. *See* mind(s)
separability, 15–16, 17–18, 26–27,
    30–31, 213–14, 234. *See also*
    abstraction; conceivability
Shelley, Mary, 2–3, 106
Shepherd, Henry John, 2–3
Shepherd, Lady Mary
  biography, 1–3, 6–7
  reception, 21–22
  writings, 4–7
sight. *See* vision
skepticism
  Berkeley and, 183, 203
  dreaming and, 184–85, 196–97
  about external world, 145, 148–
    49, 160–61
  Hume and, 8–10, 14, 35–36, 81,
    86–87, 145, 254–55
  Locke and, 81
  ordinary people and, 38, 79–80,
    198–200
  about other minds, 188, 198–99
  Reid and, 145
  about religion, 86–87, 186–87
  about uniformity of nature, 65–80
Smith, Robert, 284n.29, 289–90
Smith, Sydney, 2–3
social reforms, 20–21
Somerville, Mary, 2–3
soul. *See* mind(s)
space
  between eyes, 292
  eternity of, 267
  Kant on, 7–8
  mind and, 171–72, 253–54
  motion through, 124, 172–73, 174,
    195–96, 274–75, 286
  sensation of, 162, 171–72, 174
  vision and, 274–75, 276–77, 280–
    81, 286
  See also distance; extension;
    outwardness

Spinozism, 268, 268n.16
Stewart, Dugald
  common sense philosophy and, 4,
    8–9, 12–13, 140
  and Humean causation,
    12n.31, 74
  on Kant, 7–8
  on the Leslie affair, 24–25, 82–83
  on perceiving color and
    extension, 281–83
  on sense-organs, 211
Stewart, M. A., 249–50
successive causation. *See* time:
  causation and
synchronous causation. *See* time:
  causation and

tangible figure, 280–81
tangible ideas. *See* ideas: tangible
testimony
  regarding miracles and marvelous
    events, 242–44, 245
  of Scripture, 263
time
  abstraction and, 62
  causation and, 29, 39–41,
    42–43, 45–46, 45n.22, 51,
    96n.11, 214–15
  dreams and, 191, 192,
    193, 196–97
  duration of objects through, 60n.8,
    150, 227
  idea of, in imagination, 126, 127
  idea of, in memory, 57–58,
    126, 127
  identity of persons
    through, 230–31

independent existence of, 159–
  60, 234
Kant on, 7
of mind–body union, 104
notion of, 119
as succession of ideas, 159
See also eternity
transcendentalism. *See* life:
  immanentism versus
  transcendentalism

understanding
  as mental power, 119, 131
  varieties of, 38, 79, 133–34
uniformity of nature. *See* nature:
  uniformity of

vibrations, 239–40
Virgil, 77–78
visible figure, 279–83
visible ideas. *See* ideas: visible
vision
  erect (upright), 287–300
  geometrical explanations
    of, 271–74
  sensation of extension, 174
  single, 289–93
  See also Berkeley, George; brain;
    outwardness; Reid, Thomas
volition. *See* will

Watts, Isaac, 49n.24, 70n.18, 186n.7,
  206n.13
Whewell, William, 2–3, 21–22
will, 127–31, 208–9, 210, 236,
  246, 251–52

world, external. *See* external world